Recall
and
Recognition

Recall
and
Recognition

Edited by
John Brown
Department of Psychology,
University of Bristol

A Wiley–Interscience Publication

JOHN WILEY & SONS
London · New York · Sydney · Toronto

Library of Congress Cataloging in Publication Data:

Main entry under title:

Recall and recognition.

  'A Wiley–Interscience publication.'
  Includes indexes.
  1.   Recollection (Psychology) 2. Recognition
(Psychology) I. Brown, John, 1925– [DNLM:
1. Memory. BF371 R294]
BF371.R33   153.1'23
ISBN 0 471 11229 1

Photosetting by Thomson Press (India) Ltd.,
New Delhi and printed in Great Britain by The Pitman Press Ltd.,
Bath, Avon.

Contributors

JOHN BROWN — *Department of Psychology, University of Bristol, England*

ALDWYN J. R. COOPER — *Department of Psychology, University of Bristol, England*

FERGUS I. M. CRAIK — *Department of Psychology, University of Toronto, Canada*

DAVID GAFFAN — *Department of Anatomy and Embryology, University College London, England*

VERNON GREGG — *Department of Psychology, Birkbeck College, University of London, England*

LARRY JACOBY — *Department of Psychology, University of Toronto, Canada*

ROBERT S. LOCKHART — *Department of Psychology, University of Toronto, Canada*

ANDREW MONK — *Department of Psychology, University of Bristol, England*

ALLAN PAIVIO — *Department of Psychology, University of Western Ontario, Canada*

LEO POSTMAN — *Department of Psychology, University of California, Berkeley, USA*

ENDEL TULVING — *Department of Psychology, University of Toronto, Canada*

ELIZABETH WARRINGTON — *The National Hospital, London, England*

Preface

A dramatic but familiar experience is a frustrating failure to put a name to a face in the certain knowledge that recognition of the name would be both immediate and certain. This dissociation of recall and recognition highlights the fact that they are non-equivalent measures of memory. Until the early 1960s, studies of recognition memory were comparatively rare. It was tacitly assumed that whatever was true of recall would also be true of recognition. This can now be seen to have been a gross error. Moreover, important insight into the nature of any memory phenomenon can be gained by studying whether it holds both for recognition and recall. For example, a variable which affects recall but not recognition can, at a simple level of analysis, be assumed to control 'retrieval' rather than 'discrimination'.

This book consists of eight invited chapters and one uninvited chapter (my own). The first three chapters are mainly concerned with general issues, and offer alternative clarifications of the differences between recall and recognition. In addition, I attempt to cover some methodological problems in my own chapter (Chapter 1). Chapter 2 is a typically provocative and stimulating contribution from Endel Tulving; the reader will note that he must now add the word 'ecphoric' to his vocabulary. In Chapter 3, Lockhart, Craik and Jacoby elaborate their interesting ideas about depth of processing and its effects on memory. Each of the remaining chapters is concerned with a more specific topic, and several include extensive reviews of relevant experimental work. Predictably, perhaps, the chapters by Allan Paivio and Leo Postman concern imagery and interference theory respectively but, equally predictably, they have very illuminating points to make about the work they describe (Chapters 4 and 6). Anyone who has not kept in touch with developments in interference theory may be startled by how much it has changed during the last 10 years. Chapter 5 by Aldwyn Cooper and Andrew Monk provides the first comprehensive review of the differential effects of study and test trials. It also includes descriptions of new experiments which yield especially interesting data on latencies. Vernon Gregg in Chapter 7 provides a comprehensive review of another topic, the differing effects of word frequency on recognition and recall, and likewise describes important new experiments. The two final chapters are concerned with the pathology of memory. In Chapter 8, Elizabeth Warrington describes studies of recall and recognition in amnesic patients and discusses the theoretical implications of the results obtained. Finally, in Chapter 9, David Gaffan describes experiments on the effects of fornix lesions in monkeys; these lesions affect analogues of recall and recognition in strikingly different ways.

The attention of the reader should be drawn to the combined references/ author index on page 243. All authors, including second and third authors, are listed alphabetically. The page numbers where an author is cited will be found at the end of each of his listed papers.

My warm thanks are due to all those who have assisted me, in one way or another, in editing this book: in particular to Stella Mathias, Aldwyn Cooper, Andrew Monk and to my wife.

JOHN BROWN
January 1975

Contents

1 *An analysis of recognition and recall and of problems in their comparison*

JOHN BROWN

Recognition and recall can be studied in an almost infinite variety of situations. This chapter will be mainly concerned with the recognition or recall of a single word from a previously presented list. However, the theoretical and methodological issues discussed have, I believe, a much wider relevance.

Underlying processes

Test situations and their consequences

The terms 'recall' and 'recognition' are used to refer both to test situations and to memory processes. This is a potent source of confusion. We can identify the formal difference between test situations fairly easily. The processes which occur in these test situations are a matter for research and theory. Moreover, there is no necessary correlation between the formal characteristics of a test situation and the processes it evokes in the subject. At the same time, the formal difference between recall and recognition makes possible process differences which may, on occasion, be highly important. I find it worth *recalling* and I hope the reader will find it worth *recognizing* that a similar confusion between process and experimental paradigm has bedevilled the use of the terms 'short-term memory' and 'long-term memory'.

• The essence of a recall test is that the subject has to generate the target or targets meeting the definition of the target in the recall instruction. The target may or may not be a member of a well-defined set and the set may be either large or small. If the target is a word, he may have to speak or write it: if it is a picture or an idea he will have to describe or draw it.

• The essence of a recognition test is that one or more potential targets are presented to the subject. Accordingly there is no requirement for overt generation of the target. The recognition response may consist in accepting or rejecting a given choice, rating it, assigning a subjective probability to it, ranking it in relation to other choices present, or, in the case of a multiple-choice test, choosing the most plausible item.

These definitions correspond roughly but not exactly with everyday usage. Some vigilance is therefore necessary when classifying tasks as recall or recognition tasks. For example, suppose part of a target is presented and the task is to identify it. There is a tendency to classify this as a recognition task, in line with an everyday usage of the term 'recognition'. In terms of the definitions given above, however, it is a recall task unless one or more possibilities are provided for the missing part.

As already implied, recognition may sometimes be mediated by processes characteristic of recall, i.e. processes which do not depend on the presence of potential targets (choices) in the recognition test. Features of recognition tests likely to encourage the use of recall to mediate recognition include:

(a) The need for recoding. The correct choice may be a recoded version of the original fact or event. Indeed, to some extent this is always the case. If decoding a choice is difficult, it may be easier for the subject to recall the fact or event first and then attempt to match it to the choice or choices provided in the recognition test. For example, suppose the subject is required to assign a word from a previously presented list to the box on a response sheet which corresponds to its input position in the list. The boxes on the response sheet formally constitute a multiple-choice recognition test. The correct box, however, is a coded version of the fact to be recognized and recognition is likely to be mediated by recall.

(b) Embeddedness of the target. If the target has been learned as part of a coherent structure, recall of some or all of this structure may be required before a recognition decision is possible. The recognition of position in the situation just cited constitutes one example. As another example, the question 'Does the letter "g" occur in the Lord's Prayer?' can only be answered by overt or covert recitation of the prayer.

(c) The need for inference. Memory is often reconstructive rather than direct (Bartlett, 1932). Where this is the case, recognition presupposes recall. For example, if a man is asked 'Did you go to the seaside on Sunday?', this is a recognition test requiring a yes/no decision. However, he may only be able to answer the question by working out how he spent his weekend. Inference can play a role even in free recall of unrelated words. For example, if the test word is 'horse', the subject may infer that it is incorrect because he can recall 'pony', and he thinks that he would have noticed the presence of two such closely related words as 'horse' and 'pony' in the input list. (See discussion of memorability judgments later.)

(d) Many choices. If the recognition test requires the subject to search for a single target amongst many-choice items, his best strategy may be to recall target first and then to search for it. One reason is that this may take considerably less time, especially if the choices are systematically arranged in the test, and a second reason is that examination of many incorrect alternatives may cause confusion. The failure of Davis, Sutherland and Judd (1961) to find a difference between recall and recognition when the subject had to search through 90 items for the targets is explicable on this basis. (Their experiment is discussed more fully in a later section.)

(e) Recognition tests of short-term memory. In a short-term memory experiment, the subject may still be rehearsing the material at the time the test is administered. Since rehearsal involves repeated recall, recall inevitably mediates recognition in the test.

The Generation–discrimination Theory

This is currently the most popular and influential account of the processes underlying recognition and recall: although primarily a theory of recall, it also involves a simplistic theory of recognition. Recent versions of the theory have been stated by Estes and DaPolito (1967), Peterson (1967), Kintsch (1970a) and Anderson and Bower (1972). Early versions are to be found in William James (1890) and Müller (1913).

According to the theory, there are two basic underlying processes, only one of which is involved in recognition. The theory is most readily stated in relation to the recall or recognition of words from a recently presented list. In recall, possible words must first be generated, searched for or retrieved. Each retrieved word is then subjected to a recognition test. The recognition test involves discriminating whether the word was or was not included in the list and the discrimination is usually said to be based on a familiarity judgment. Without further assumptions, the theory readily explains why recognition tends to be better than recall, since a word which the subject is capable of recognizing will fail to be recalled if it is not generated. It also helps to explain why high-frequency words are easier to recall than low-frequency words, if we make the plausible assumption that common words are easier to generate. Finally, it explains why high-frequency words are *harder* to recognize than low-frequency words: if recognition is based on familiarity, the occurrence of a high-frequency word in a list would have only a marginal effect on the word's already high familiarity.

However, in its simple form, the generation–discrimination theory is unable to account for the success of the generation process. The number of words is extremely large. Consequently, unless the number of words generated is also extremely large, the probability of retrieving target words is very small. The generation process needs to be guided if it is to have a reasonable chance of success, unless both generation and discrimination of each word are extremely fast. It is usually assumed that guidance is provided by associations formed between the words of the list. Kintsch (1970a), who gives a persuasive account of the generation–discrimination theory, emphasizes the 'utilization of existing inter relations among items' (p. 362). Roughly, he views these inter relations as common properties ('markers') which are tagged at input (given a familiarity

4

boost), thus building up a system of cross references between the words of the list. These tagged properties then guide memory search. So modified, the generation–discrimination theory explains why organization is important for successful recall. It also explains why organization is *not* so important for successful recognition. Indeed, Kintsch 1970a took the position that organization should not affect recognition at all. This was a logical position given his assumption that recognition depends merely on a familiarity judgment for the item concerned. It should be noted, however, that even this position is consistent with organization affecting recognition indirectly via an effect on initial learning: when a list is presented, the familiarity boosts given to the words may be greater if it is an organized list. Both the following findings are interpretable on the assumption that organization affects recall much more than it affects recognition. Firstly, intention to learn facilitates recall but appears to have little effect on recognition (e.g. Estes and DaPolito, 1967). It is plausible to suppose that the effect of intention is to make the subject organize the list. Secondly, test trials and study trials have differential effects on subsequent recall and recognition (see Chapter 5). Test trials are relatively more important for subsequent recall, whereas study trials are relatively more important for subsequent recognition. It can be hypothesized that test trials force the subject to organize the list, thus facilitating recall; whereas study trials allow the subject to learn more but without organizing much of what is learned for effective recall (cf. Rosner, 1970).

The modified generation–discrimination theory is much less distinctive than the theory in its simple form. Moreover, Kintsch (1970a, p.362) allows for the formation of new associations to connect several of the list words to 'some kind of starting symbol, like LIST ONE'. (These words correspond to ENTRYSET words in Anderson's FRAN (Anderson, 1971).) Their learning thus depends on contextual associations. With new or strengthened associations between the words of the list to guide the generation process as well as contextually linked words to get the generation process started, the generation–discrimination theory comes close to conventional associationism. One strange feature of the theory is that the new or strengthened associations which guide the generation process are given no role in the recognition decision, which is said to be based on familiarity or trace newness (Kintsch, 1970a, p.361). In my view, their existence provides evidence in favour of the item generated and this helps to produce a correlation between retrievability and discriminability. However, a total rejection of the whole notion of generation–discrimination seems unwarranted, both on theoretical and on introspective grounds. Indeed, the tip-of-the-tongue phenomenon is a familiar everyday example of generation–discrimination: attributes of the target word are recalled and generation takes place on the basis of these attributes (cf. Brown and McNeill, 1966).

Evidential Basis of Recognition

The account provided of recognition in the generation–discrimination theory described above is simplistic. Recognition of whether a word belongs to a list (list recognition) must depend on stored information of its occurrence in the list. Neither familiarity, trace strength or trace newness can possibly provide adequate evidence, except in limiting cases. (For an extended discussion of this point see Anderson and Bower, 1972.)

Familiarity seems to have crept into the analysis of recognition for want of a better term. However, unless the word is used in a special sense, it has no real relevance to recognition of whether a word was included in a specified list. To say that a word is familiar can have one of two meanings. The first is that the word has been encountered previously. The second is that it has been encountered repeatedly. Neither familiarity in the first sense nor familiarity in the second sense can enable a subject to decide whether a given word belongs to the list. Familiarity is directly relevant only to recognition of familiarity. It might be argued that what counts is not familiarity in itself, but familiarity in a context. This position can be accepted. The question is what conclusion can be drawn from it. The familiarity of an item in a particular context is a matter of the evidence linking the item with that context. The difficult problem is to give an account of this evidence and of how it is assessed.

Trace newness is a fairly plausible basis for deciding whether a word was included in a list presented immediately previously. It cannot be the basis for recognition in general. For example, if two separate lists are learned one week and tested the next, impossibly fine discriminations of trace newness would be needed to differentiate the words of the two lists. Yet, given high degrees of initial learning, the necessary discriminations can certainly be made.

Trace strength is an equivocal and rather abstract concept. If it means some weighted combination of the frequency and the recency with which an item has been encountered, then like trace newness it may contribute evidence of list membership in some situations but it cannot be the primary basis on which such membership is assessed. If it means the strength of evidence for list membership, then it is merely a synonym for such evidence and it becomes vacuous to say that list membership is assessed on the basis of trace strength.

Some versions of the generation–discrimination theory incorporate a list-tag theory of recognition instead of a familiarity theory. In its standard form, this theory is equally simplistic. Learning a list of words is held to involve attaching a specific list tag to the internal representations of the words. Subsequent recognition of whether a given word belongs to the list depends on the presence or absence of the list tag. If the tag is still present, access to it from the internal representation of the word is presumed to be immediate and automatic. This theory is a marginal improvement over the familiarity theory: it acknowledges that something specific to each list must be stored along with the representations of the words, if lists are to be discriminated from one another. However, it involves three simplistic assumptions all of which have to be abandoned in any realistic theory of recognition. These are:

Assumption 1. The theory assumes that the internal code for a word is simple and unitary or that, if other codes exist, they are irrelevant to recognition.

This assumption is incompatible with the observation that attributes of a target word can sometimes be recalled when the word itself cannot be recalled. This implies that the attributes can be tagged separately from the unitary word code. Such tagged attributes could hardly be irrelevant to recognition. Evidence that they do influence recognition is provided by the fact that, if the first attempt in a multiple-choice recognition test is incorrect, then the second attempt has an above-chance probability of success (e.g. Brown, 1964). This suggests that second choices are sometimes guided by tagged attributes.

Assumption 2. The list tag is also assumed to be simple and unitary. If this were so, it is difficult to see how the recognition instruction could enable the appropriate list tag to be selected and identified. The specification of the list in the instruction may take one of many forms. Some examples: 'The list you learned last week', 'The list you learned with Dr Smith', 'The list you learned in this room'. None of these specifications can directly correspond to the list tag. Instead they provide information on the basis of which list-identifying information can be recalled. This applies even when the subject has managed to link the words to a list label, such as LIST TWO, since the list labels must be selected and authenticated on the basis of the recognition instruction.

Assumption 3. The third assumption is that access to the list tag from the word code is immediate and automatic. This assumption becomes improbable as soon as the list tag is no longer regarded as simple and unitary. Another argument against this assumption is that, if it were true, then there ought to be immediate and automatic access to *all* the occurrence tags attached to a given word code. This suggests that both recognition and recall should be cluttered with an awareness of irrelevant occurrences–a state of affairs which we are fortunately spared.

A list-tag theory which explicitly abandons the second of these assumptions has been put forward by Anderson and Bower (1972). They proposed that recognizing a word from a list depends on retrieving contextual information stored along with the word when the list was learned. The context information is not single and unitary. On the contrary, they postulate a pool of context elements. When a word is presented during learning, a sample of elements from the pool becomes attached to its internal representation via a list tag. Each word acquires its own list tag and each tag is linked to an independent sample of contextual elements. If a word is repeated within the same list, two separate tags will become attached to it. If a word occurs in two different lists, again two tags will become attached to it but the samples of contextual elements linked to them will now come from two different, although presumably overlapping, pools of contextual elements. The function of list tags in this theory is to enable the subject to keep track of separate occurrences of the same item. Anderson and Bower argue that direct linking of contextual elements to the representations of words would not achieve this. This list-tag theory is quite different from the traditional theory. In their version, the list tag carries information about list membership only by virtue of being linked to a sample of contextual elements. Indeed, the evidential basis for recognition is said to depend on the number of contextual elements from the list pool linked to the list-tag. They do not explain how the subject classifies elements as belonging to one list pool rather than to another nor how the appropriate list tag is selected.

A realistic account of list recognition must take account of complex word coding as well as of complex tagging. Various codes contribute to the word code; an attempt to classify such codes is made later. Two important classes of codes are unit codes for a word and attribute codes. A unit code for a word uniquely specifies that word and is accessed in an all-or-none manner. (Although many attribute codes may also be accessed in an all-or-none manner, in this chapter 'unit code' always refers to 'unit word code'.) A necessary condition for reliable recognition is that the tagged code for the word fully specifies the word. If a unit code for the word is tagged, this condition is automatically met. It is probable that at least two unit codes exist for every word, corresponding to the visual and auditory forms of the word. Either or both codes may be tagged at the time of learning. In addition, one or more attribute codes of the word may be tagged: the attributes concerned may be number of syllables, rarity, semantic category, and so forth. These can also be regarded as part of the word code. Attribute codes normally provide only a partial specification of the word. Thus if the only tagged codes accessed at the time recognition is tested are attribute codes, recognition will probably be unreliable but will nevertheless be better than chance. On occasion, tagged attribute codes may suffice for recognition. For example, if all the distractor words in a multiple-choice recognition test are incompatible with the tagged attribute codes, this leaves the correct word as the only rational choice. The principle which emerges is that recognition is limited by the adequacy of the tagged word code for the actual recognition task the subject is asked to perform.

Another factor likely to contribute to the evidential basis for recognition is the judged memorability of the word to the subject. Everyday experience has given each of us intuitive knowledge of when we are likely to have a clear memory of an event and of when we are likely to have only a hazy memory. The judged memorability of a word at the time recognition is tested will depend not only on the word itself but also on the way it relates to other words recognized as belonging to the list. It will also depend on the conditions of the experiment, especially the length of the retention interval. If the judged memorability is high, the subject will expect to have a tagged unit code for the word if it was included in the list. Consequently the *absence* of a tagged unit code is stronger evidence *against* the word when the judged memorability is high than when it is low. To take an extreme example, supposing recognition of a list of Christian names is tested and the name 'Christine' is included in the list. A subject in love with a girl of this name will probably feel quite sure that he would have remembered the name clearly if it had been included in the list. Consequently, in the absence of a tagged unit code, he will reject the name with high confidence even if it is compatible with tagged attributes such as 'two-syllable', 'begins with C', 'rhymes with Maureen'. Given these same tagged attributes, another subject might well *accept* 'Christine' with low to medium confidence.

It could be argued that a memorability judgment affects the recognition criterion rather than the amount of evidence for a particular recognition decision. This view is superficially attractive because a more adequate tagged code is demanded for acceptance of a word of high memorability. However, it is *because* a word has high memorability that the absence of a tagged unit code makes it unlikely that the word was included in the list. If something (the judged memorability) affects the probability that a certain event occurred (inclusion of the word in the list), then that something is evidence for or against the occurrence of that event. Memorability judgments are useful primarily for words of high memorability. Consequently, they further increase the reliability with which words of high, as compared with words of low, memorability are recognized.

A memorability judgment may affect recognition when an attribute code is tagged as well as when the unit code is untagged. This is partly because an attribute code is more likely to be tagged for a word of high memorability. A more important reason is that a memorability judgment may lead to *specific* expectations regarding tagged codes. For example, if the words 'Eskimo' and 'reindeer' both appear in a recognition test, then the subject may expect the attribute 'a strong relationship to another word in the list' to be tagged when he decides to accept or reject 'reindeer'. Tulving and Thomson (1971) found that words presented singly were less likely to be recognized if tested as members of pairs, in an experiment in which some words *were* presented as pairs. This is explicable if the absence of a tagged attribute relating the words of a pair predisposes the subject to reject both words.

So far it has been implicitly assumed that the evidential basis of recognition depends only on the adequacy with which the tagged word code specifies the word. This assumption holds when the tagging code is adequate, but not otherwise. If the tagging code only partly identifies the correct list, recognition will be unreliable even when the tagged word code is adequate for specifying the word. The tagging code must represent features of the context in which the list is learned. An alternative name for the tagging code is therefore 'context code'. The context code must enable the correct context to be differentiated from alternative possible contexts. To the extent that it achieves this, the context code is adequate. The overall adequacy of the tagged word code is a joint function of the adequacy of the tagged word code for specifying the word and of the adequacy of the context code for identifying the context. (The function concerned should be multiplicative. If p is the probability of choosing the correct context, when the context code is inadequate, and q is the probability of choosing the correct word, when the word code is inadequate, then the overall probability of correct choice is pq.) The adequacy of the context code is partly dependent on the task. For example, a context code adequate for deciding whether a word was included in either of two lists may be inadequate for deciding whether a word was included in a particular list. In addition, the context code may be richer and therefore more adequate for some words of a list than for others. For example, it may be richer for the first word or two of a list, when awareness of contextual features is presumably higher, although it should not be assumed that a feature is only incorporated into the context code if the subject is aware of it. This would help to explain the primacy effect in list recognition.

The context code may represent features either of the external or of the internal context present during learning. The latter may include feelings and thoughts and also the states of various biological clocks. It may also include a label for the list kept in mind by the subject throughout learning. The nature of a recognition test guarantees access to the unit code for a word (although there are complications if the word has two meanings, as the experiment of Light and Carter-Sobell (1970) shows). In addition, access to the unit code obviously increases the probability of access to attribute codes. Access to the context code is less certain. As pointed out previously, the subject must *recall* some of the context in order to access the context code on the basis of a specification such as 'the list you learned last week'. Access to the context code is not necessarily immediate (so that a warm-up task might be found to improve *recognition*) and is not necessarily all-or-none.

A possible method of exploring the contents of the context code would be to try using different recognition instructions. For example, if an instruction specifying the time of learning is effective, this is *prima facie* evidence that the code includes a temporal component. However, since alternative ways of interrogating memory may map on to one another, the method is not straight-forward.

The evidential basis for recognition depends on the adequacy of the word code (the tagged part of it) and on the adequacy of the context code. However, memory does not consist of target codes and context codes. Strictly, the target code only becomes the target code and the context code only becomes the context code when the recognition task is specified.

The foregoing account of the evidential basis of recognition has concerned recognition of whether a word belongs to a previously presented list. In principle, the account seems generalizable to many other forms of recognition. Consider, for example, the problem of recognizing whether a particular method of solving a mathematical equation can be applied in a given instance. This appears to be a quite different sort of recognition task, and in many ways it is. However, the task requires the subject to recall the criteria for deciding whether a method is applicable, i.e. it requires the subject to recall the context for the method.

Two sorts of recognition test are commonly employed. The first is the multiple-choice test. In this test the rational subject chooses the item for which the evidence is strongest. The second is the yes/no recognition test. Here the decision will depend on the recognition criterion as well as on the evidence for the item concerned. Traditional signal-detection theory defines the criterion in terms of a likelihood ratio. With appropriately behaved distributions, this likelihood ratio corresponds to a single point on the signal strength/plausibility dimension, above which words are accepted and below which they are rejected. ('Plausibility' here means 'the evidence favouring acceptance' and formally corresponds to 'signal strength' in the original formulation of signal-detection theory.) Among the objections to this definition is the very basic one that, since the subject typically has no opportunity to learn what the underlying distributions of plausibility are, he cannot possibly compute a likelihood ratio. Parks (1966) and Thomas and Legge (1970) have therefore suggested that, in recognition tests, subjects tend to select a criterion which will give approximately the correct proportion of targets, or what the subject thinks is the correct proportion of targets. Instructions may also influence the criterion adopted: an instruction to be quite sure that a word was in the list before recognizing it will lead to the adoption of a more stringent criterion than instruction to guess freely.

Evidential Basis of Recall

In both recognition and recall, the context code must be retrieved on the basis of the instructions. Whether a word can be identified as belonging to a previously presented list depends on whether it is linked to the appropriate context code. The primary difference between recall and recognition is that in recall access to the unit word code must be from the context code, but in recognition access is guaranteed by the physical presence of the word itself. Access from the context code to the word code is unreliable even when a link between them is extant. Evidence for this statement is the fact that confident and reliable recall sometimes occurs only after a delay. However, once a particular word code has been accessed, the evidence in its favour should be as strong as in recognition: the overall adequacy of the target word code should not be diminished by the fact that the subject has generated the word himself. An interesting question is whether it can be *higher* in recall. Three factors can be identified which might favour recall.

The first factor is the following. Each time a distractor is encountered in a recognition test this may produce interference with memory, so that decisions about subsequent items are less reliable. More than one mechanism for such interference can be envisaged. A possible mechanism for false alarms is as follows. There is evidence that involuntary learning of distractors occurs. This implies that the corresponding word codes will become linked to a code representing the test context. Under some circumstances, this test context code may be close to the original context code—for example, if both learning and testing take place in the same room. Accordingly, if an attribute of a distractor is tagged during testing, this may lead to erroneous acceptance of another distractor with this attribute. An additional assumption enables this mechanism to account for misses as well as false alarms. In order to avoid false alarms, the word code for a distractor may be voluntarily tagged 'non-list' as well as being involuntarily tagged by the test context code. If a distractor attribute is so tagged, then a list word having this attribute may be erroneously rejected. In practice, distractor interference is probably a minor effect in most experiments, although its incidence awaits systematic exploration. Evidence suggesting that distractor interference can affect a recognition decision comes from an experiment of Carlson and Duncan (1955) on memory for form. In the recognition test, the alternatives were presented in booklet form. They found a statistically significant tendency for subjects to select an alternative similar to the one first encountered. However, there is also evidence that recognition performance, when assessed by a bias-free technique, is little influenced by the number of distractors included in the recognition test (Brown and Routh, 1968; 1970). This is contrary to what we would expect if distractor interference seriously impairs recognition. Unless otherwise stated, it will be assumed elsewhere in this chapter that distractor interference is negligible. (One effect of brain lesions may be to make this assumption false: see Chapter 8.)

A second factor potentially favouring recall is the following. The existence of a link between a word code and the appropriate context code constitutes the basic evidence that the word was included in the list. In recognition, the context code is accessed by the instruction and the word code is accessed by the physical presence of the word. Consequently, detection of the link cannot readily be formulated in stimulus–response terms. If two codes have already been accessed, it is difficult to see how the power of one code to evoke the other can be evaluated by the memory system. (This may explain why so many theorists have attributed recognition to a familiarity judgment.) However, in *recall*, the context code does in some sense evoke the word code. It could be argued that this increases the evidence for a link between the two, thus making the evidential basis for recall stronger than the evidential basis for recognition. A difficulty for this view is that words can be retrieved in many accidental ways. For example, a word may be retrieved because it has a strong pre-experimental link with another word. It is far from clear that retrieval *per se* has any evidential value. A possible method of investigating the role, if any, of this factor experimentally is as follows. For one group of subjects, retention of a list is tested first by free recall. Next, non-recalled items are tested by recognition. From the recall data and the recognition data a composite index of retention is obtained. For a second group, retention is tested by recognition only. If the factor is operative, the composite index for the first group should be higher than the recognition index for the second group. A way of obtaining a composite index for recall and recognition would be to require rating of items into one of four categories both in recall and recognition: the ratings could then be combined into a single table before devising an index of retention. A promising index would be the *R*-measure, described later.

(Mandler (1972) has suggested that a 'retrieval check' may be used as an aid to recognition. I find this notion especially puzzling because, since the word code has already been retrieved in recognition, a retrieval check is likely to be strongly biased in favour of success.)

The third factor which may favour recall concerns the ordering of decisions. In free recall, words are recalled in an order determined by the subject. This implies that the order of decisions about words is subject-determined. In contrast, the order of decisions in a recognition test is usually experimenter-determined, either completely or to a large extent. If list and non-list words are presented one by one and in random order, the order of decisions is necessarily random. Even if they are presented in random order on a sheet, the order of decisions remains biased by the chance positions and juxtapositions of the words. To the extent that words are coded independently, the ordering of decisions will not affect access to relevant codes. However, if the coding of several words is interconnected, the evidential basis for any one word of the cluster may be influenced by whether decisions are taken concurrently about other words in the cluster. Consequently, an organized list might be easier to recall than to recognize in random order. This point can be made with even greater force in the case of serial learning. For example, if the words of a familiar poem are presented in random order mixed with distractors, it will be difficult to recognize reliably which words belong to the poem unless recall is used to mediate recognition and the poem is recited over and over again.

Codes and Their Accessibility

The evidential basis for accepting a word as a list word is primarily the extent to which tagged codes specify the word. Many discussions of recall and recognition proceed as though the only possible tagged code is a single tagged code for the word. So far tagged codes of two types have been distinguished, tagged unit codes and tagged attribute codes. This twofold classification of codes, although a step forward, is inadequate as a basis for understanding recall and recognition. Codes which fall outside this classification will now be identified and attribute codes will be divided into two types. The proposed classification is provisional and is far from exhaustive. However, the nature of codes established during learning is, in my view, of central importance to the analysis of recognition and recall and of the relation between them, so that an attempt at classification is worthwhile. Codes potentially contributing to retention of a word include:

(a) Unit word codes, A^*. As already noted, there are probably at least two unit codes for every word, corresponding to the visual and auditory form of the word. Further unit codes may exist. Thus there is probably a unit code representing the word independently of modality. In addition, there may be a unit code which is activated when the word is spoken and another unit code which is activated when the word is to be written down. If a unit code for a word is tagged, then the word is fully identified. A unit code for word A will be denoted A^*. The tagging of a code will be indicated by adding the letter k, where k denotes the context code. Thus Ak* denotes that A* is tagged. As a conceptual simplification, Ak* will sometimes be referred to as *the* tagged unit code, despite the possibility that there may be more than one such code. Although a tagged unit code fully identifies the word, it reliably identifies the word as belonging to the target list only if the context code is adequate.

(b) Chunked codes, AB*. Two or more words may be familiar as a unit. For example, the two words MOTHER DAUGHTER form a familiar pair for which there is probably a unit code AB*, where A and B denote the two words involved. This code, if tagged, identifies both words as list words. Novel chunked word codes are probably formed and tagged during the presentation of a list: if chunked codes exist, it must be possible to establish new ones. The establishment of a durable chunked code may depend on many repetitions of the words involved in a fixed order. If so, novel chunked codes following a single list presentation will tend to be very transient. However, some sets of list words may already correspond to partially established chunked codes. If there is a pre-experimental association between two list words, this may constitute a partially established chunked code. In these cases, a sufficiently durable chunked code for at least short-term retention may be formed during a single presentation of the list. For example, two words may be close associates. Even if they do not occur adjacently in the list, rehearsal may produce functional adjacency and enable a chunked code to be formed.

(c) Mono attribute codes, a*. If PEACH is a list word, then an attribute such as 'fruit' or 'soft' may be tagged. Unlike tagged unit codes and tagged chunked codes, a tagged attribute code does not uniquely specify a word. In recognition, a tagged attribute code will assist guessing, in the absence of a tagged unit code for the word. In recall, it will also facilitate retrieval of unit codes for the word, which may or may not turn out to be tagged. Thus, potentially, the tagged attribute code has an evidential role and also has a retrieval role. This is also true of the three remaining types of code.

(d) Relational attribute codes, ab*. A relational attribute relates two or more list words. For example, if MARE and FOAL are list words, then 'parent–offspring' may be a tagged relational attribute. The code for the attribute relating two words A and B will be denoted ab*. Category names or concepts are often tagged as relational attributes. If several list words are the names of fruit, then 'fruit' can be tagged as a relational attribute. 'Fruit' is tagged as a property of a number of words of the list, i.e. as a property relating these words. This is not the same as tagging 'fruit' as an attribute of each word individually.

(e) Image codes, I*. Constructing an image can aid both recognition and recall (see Chapter 4). In contrast to a chunked code, a durable image representing several words can apparently be formed quite readily, at least by some subjects under some conditions. Perhaps this is because several concepts can be related together *simultaneously* in the image. An interesting question is how the relevant part of the image can be differentiated from the irrelevant parts. For example, if HORSE and BANANA are list words, the subject might generate an image of a horse with a hat on its head sitting in a chair and eating a banana. How can the subject tell that HORSE and BANANA are list words whereas HAT and CHAIR are not? One possible answer is that the image is not an adequate code in itself and must be supplemented by tagged additional codes to which it helps to give access. If this hypothesis is accepted, then an appropriate notation for the image as a tagged code is I.k*, where the dot indicates that the tagging is qualified. Thus I.k* only implies that *some* of the contents of the image correspond to list words. On this hypothesis, the role of an image code in recognition is to assist guessing when tagged unit codes for the words are not available. In recall it will also have a retrieval role: its efficiency is typically much higher than the efficiency of an attribute code in producing retrieval of list words.

(f) Association codes. If the list includes the word CAR, then the word may evoke the word ACCIDENT as an association. ACCIDENT may then function as an association code for CAR. An association code has affinities to both attribute codes and image codes. In a broad sense, the tendency of a word to evoke a particular associate is an attribute of that word. The association code is like the image code in that, if the list word and the associate are included in it, it consists of both relevant and irrelevant parts: there is a danger that the associate will be accepted as a list word. Sometimes the associate can be excluded because it lacks a property common to list words, as, for example, when the list words are nouns and the associate is an adjective. Sometimes the basis of exclusion seems to depend on an explicit memory of the list word evoking the associate at the time of learning: this presupposes that both the associate and the list word are retrieved. If the associate is to aid retrieval it must itself be retrieved first. This implies that it must be tagged at the time of learning. As in the case of an image code, the tagging may differ in some way from the tagging of a list word: if so and this difference in tagging is reliable, it will constitute another possible basis for differentiating an associate from a list word.

Access to these codes in recognition will be considered first. The view that the physical presence of a word in a recognition test guarantees access to all relevant stored information is at best a rough approximation to the truth. The physical presence of the word does indeed guarantee access to some, although not necessarily all, unit codes for the word. Moreover, a high proportion of hits in recognition may be based on tagged unit word codes, i.e. represent direct recognition. Nevertheless, recognition is sometimes influenced by other codes to which access is less certain. Access to a chunked code is made likely by retrieval of one of the words of which it is composed, but access does not automatically follow such retrieval. Some attribute codes may be accessed as a necessary part of the process of identifying the word.

For example, if unit word codes are nodes in a classification network in which other nodes are attribute codes, then identification of a word will necessarily involve access to lower-level attribute codes. Access to higher-level attribute codes will be optional. (Compare Lockhart, Craik and Jacoby's suggestion in Chapter 3 that the durability of a memory depends on the depth of encoding and that retrieval can involve a reconstruction of the encoding operations.) The probability of retrieving relational attribute codes is likely to depend partly on the juxtaposition of words in the recognition test: if two related words are next to one another in the test, the probability of a relational attribute concerning these words must be increased. Successful image codes are accessed rather easily—hence their usefulness in recall—but this statement is close to a tautology: some image codes may be unsuccessful simply because they are not easily accessed, even in recognition. Finally, association codes, even when based on strong pre-existing associations, will only be accessed if the associates are themselves accessed.

Thus, a recognition test does *not* guarantee access to codes other than the unit word code. This is clearly demonstrated experimentally in an experiment reported by Tulving and Thomson (1973): recall aided by cue words which had been present at input was better than unaided recognition. A recognition test eliminates 'retrieval failure' only in the restricted sense that it eliminates failure to access the word. Moreover, recognition presupposes access to the context code on the basis of the recognition instruction, and such access involves a large element of implicit recall. What a typical recognition test does achieve is a high probability of access to stored information, since the unit code for a word can be used as a focus in the search for other codes.

In recall, access to the unit code for the target word is a prerequisite for success, whether or not this code is tagged. Accordingly, tagged partial codes have a retrieval function in relation to the unit code in addition to a specifying function. There appear to be two distinct ways in which such codes can facilitate retrieval, one indirect and the other direct. A tagged partial code can facilitate retrieval indirectly by guiding search. Introspective evidence suggests that it can also directly facilitate access to the unit code when the unit code is tagged: sometimes when an attribute is recalled, the word itself is then recalled immediately and confidently. The search value of a partial code will tend to be related to its evidential value. Thus a tagged attribute code consistent with very few words will provide stronger evidence for a particular word and a better basis for retrieving the word than a tagged attribute code consistent with many words. However, sometimes a tagged partial code, such as an association code, may have high retrieval value but low evidential value, or vice versa.

Word Retrievability and Discriminability

The analysis given above implies a tendency for targets to be retrieved in recall rather than distractors. Moreover, the higher the probability that a particular target is retrieved, the higher the evidence in favour of that target is likely to be. Consquently, a fairly strong relation between word retrievability and discriminability is expected. This expectation is at variance with Underwood's view (Underwood, 1969a; 1972) that discriminative and retrieval attributes are distinct and have little overlap. He holds that the attribute primarily responsible for discrimination is situational frequency, although attributes such as spatial and temporal attributes also play some role. In contrast, the attributes responsible for retrieval are attributes linking words with the context or words with one another.

In support of this view, Underwood (1972) cites the rather low correlation between recognition and recall found in studies in his own laboratory. Paivio in Chapter 4 also reports low correlations between the two measures, especially for pictorial as opposed to verbal material. Tulving in Chapter 2 cites published work in which low correlations were again found. This apparently low correlation between recognition and recall is surprising on almost any theory of memory, unless recognition and recall depend on distinct memorial systems. Even if Underwood is correct in supposing that discriminative and retrieval attributes have little overlap, discriminative attributes are relevant to both recognition and recall and this should produce an appreciable correlation. The low correlation so far found is especially embarrassing for the analysis of recognition and recall presented in this chapter. A substantial correlation is predicted, not only because recall and recognition are held to share the same evidential basis for accepting or rejecting a word (see earlier), but also because of the fairly strong relationship expected between word retrievability and discriminability. It remains possible that the low correlations so far obtained are due to noise variables, such as variations in the learning material; further research is needed.

The relation between discriminability and retrievability is not fixed but variable. Andrew Monk and I have unpublished data showing that within a given experimental task it can vary from one subject to another: the evidence is that there are statistically significant individual differences in the discrepancy between recall and recognition. The relation between discriminability and retrievability is also a function of various manipulable features of the experimental task. These include:

(a) Word frequency. Words of high frequency tend to be easier to recall but more difficult to recognize than words of low frequency (see Gregg, Chapter 7). Another way of expressing this is to say that the discrepancy between recall and recognition is lower for high than for low-frequency words. The relative ease of recalling high-frequency words is usually attributed to their higher retrievability. Within the context of the present theoretical analysis, this explanation requires amplification. The retrievability of high-frequency words in random search is irrelevant, since there are too many high-frequency words for random search to have an appreciable probability of success. However, if a tagged partial code is recalled, then the high retrievability of such words becomes significant. For example, if 'fruit' is a tagged code, it is easier to think of the word BANANA than the word LYCHEES. The relative difficulty of recognizing a high-frequency word is commonly and plausibly attributed to its lower distinctiveness. Since the tagging of a unit word code for a high-frequency word should constitute as much evidence in its favour as the tagging of the unit code for a low-frequency word, the greater distinctiveness of the latter must involve codes such as attribute codes. An attribute code is distinctive if the number of words with which it is compatible is small.

(b) Interference. If two lists are learned in succession, the learning of the second list makes the first list difficult to recall but not to recognize (see Postman, Chapter 6). Postman attributes the interference in recall to response set interference (RSI). According to this theory, original list responses are suppressed *as a set* during the learning of the second list. If we ignore the complication that he is mainly concerned with paired-associate learning, a possible interpretation of RSI is in terms of the potency of the context code, i.e. its capacity to give access to word codes with which it is linked. The context codes for the first and second lists, when they are learned in immediate succession, are likely to overlap substantially. If the potency of the context code to elicit a particular code is inversely related to the number of codes attached to it, then its potency will fall in relation to all first-list responses as the second-list responses are learned. In addition, apart from the sheer number of responses attached to the context code, it is plausible to suppose that as its potency rises in relation to one set of responses it will fall in relation to a second set. Experimental evidence for reciprocal facilitation and interference of *sets* of responses includes Brown (1968) and Tulving and Hastie (1972).

(c) Conditions of learning. One example is the differential effect of study and test on subsequent recognition and recall (see Cooper and Monk, Chapter 5). Within limits, time during learning devoted to study favours subsequent recognition, whereas time devoted to testing what has already been learned favours recall. A rough explanation of this finding is that low levels of learning suffice for recognition but high levels of learning are necessary for recall. Time devoted to study presumably allows tagged codes to be established for many items, whereas time devoted to testing enables the accessibility of codes to be increased. A second example is the differential effect of intentional versus incidental learning on recognition and recall. Intentional and incidental learning tend to be equally efficient for recognition but not for recall. This implies that the discrepancy between recall and recognition is greater for incidental than for intentional learning. Presumably under intentional learning subjects tend to establish codes which will be especially effective in mediating retrieval.

One important factor affecting the retrievability of a word is the extent to which it has been 'primed', because either it or a related word has recently occurred. It is not clear whether priming is a process, like habituation, to be distinguished from learning proper. If a word has occurred recently, then there is likely to be reciprocal overlap between the context of its occurrence and the current context of the test. Consequently, it could be argued that the test context has a tendency to elicit the word and that it is this tendency which is the basis of priming. On this theory, priming would be a consequence of the attaching of codes to contexts which appears to be the basis of all learning. A list word could then be retrieved either from the context code established during learning of the list or from the test context, if the word has recently occurred in this or a similar context. An alternative theory is that when a code is accessed, this lowers the threshold for its activation. One attraction of this view is that the physiological basis for such an effect can readily be envisaged. On both views, priming by a related word would be explained by priming of attribute codes common to the two words. Both views will explain priming by words presented shortly before a test or recall. However, on the second theory but not the first, priming can be a distinct process contributing to the accessibility of all codes tagged during learning. If the second view is correct, this entails modifications to the theoretical analysis presented in this chapter, *when short retention intervals are involved.* For example, generation–discrimination becomes a more plausible account of recall if generation is biased by the priming of words during learning.

Paths to Recognition and Recall

The foregoing accounts of recognition and recall are schematic but complex. The complexity is a consequence of the attempt at realism. The accounts imply that there are many possible paths to both recognition and recall. Some of these paths are illustrated in Tables 1 and 2. An examination of these paths will serve to summarize and hopefully to clarify much of what has been said. The paths shown either lead to successful recall or recognition of word A from a previously presented list (a 'hit'); or to erroneous rejection of word A (a 'miss'); or to erroneous acceptance of distractor word D (a 'false alarm'); or to correct rejection of word D.

Each path starts with the input to the subject and then shows the sequence in which codes are accessed. If the *tagged* codes accessed do not uniquely specify a single word, the subject is likely to make memorability judgments. These concern what tagged code or codes he would expect to find at the time of the retention test if the word was included in the list. (Literally, of course, the subject does not find tagged codes. Instead he remembers or fails to remember information related to the word retrieved and does so because of the existence or non-existence of tagged codes.) The primary evidence provided by tagged codes as well as the secondary evidence provided by memorability judgments combine to produce a resultant degree of evidence for accepting the word. If this is sufficiently high and exceeds the subject's criterion for acceptance of the word, then a hit or a miss results, according to whether the word is a list or a non-list word. The amount of confidence the subject has in his decision will tend to be low if the degree of evidence is close to his criterion and high if it is

Table 1. Recognition paths

Path	Input	Codes accessed		Memorability	Outcome	Confidence
1	Instruction	→ k*	→ Ak*	—	Hit	High
	Word A	→ A*				
2	Instruction	→ k*	→ ak*	Average	Hit	Low
	Word A	→ A*				
3	Instruction	→ k*	→ ak*	High	Miss	Medium
	Word A	→ A*				
4	Instruction	→ k*	→ abk*	Average	Miss	Low
	Word A	→ A*				
5	Instruction	→ k*		Low	Hit	Low
	Word A	→ A*				
6	Instruction	→ k*	→ ak*	Average	False alarm	Low
	Word D	→ D*				
7	Instruction	→ k*	→ ak*	High	Correct rejection	Medium
	Word D	→ D*				
8	Instruction	→ k*		Average	Correct rejection	Medium
	Word D	→ D*				

well above or below it. The final confidence level shown in the tables is tentative. In practice, the confidence level will depend on the actual evidential value of the codes accessed rather than on their abstract classification. For example, a tagged attribute code may have either high or low evidential value. All the confidence levels shown presuppose that the context code is adequate, i.e. that it uniquely specifies the list designated in the recognition or recall instruction. If the context code is only partially adequate, decisions will be made with less confidence.

Table 1 shows paths to yes/no recognition. In all these paths, the input is the recognition instruction together with word A. The recognition instruction give access to the context code k* and the word gives access to code A*. Access to these two codes does not necessarily constitute two independent events. Access to code k* from the instruction may be facilitated by access to code A*

Table 2. Recall paths

Path	Input	Codes accessed	Memorability	Outcome	Confidence
9	Instruction	$\rightarrow$ k* $\rightarrow$ Ak*	—	Hit	High
10	Instruction	$\rightarrow$ k* $\rightarrow$ ak* .. $\rightarrow$ Ak*	—	Hit	High
11	Instruction	$\rightarrow$ k* $\rightarrow$ ak* .. $\rightarrow$ A*	Average	Hit	Low
12	Instruction	$\rightarrow$ k* $\rightarrow$ abk* .. $\rightarrow$ A*	Average	Miss	Low
13	Instruction	$\rightarrow$ k* $\rightarrow$ Bk* $\rightarrow$ abk* .. $\rightarrow$ Ak*	—	Hit	High
14	Instruction	$\rightarrow$ k* $\rightarrow$ I.k* .. $\rightarrow$ Ak*	—	Hit	High
15	Instruction	$\rightarrow$ k* $\rightarrow$ ak* .. $\rightarrow$ D*	Average	False alarm	Low
16	Instruction	$\rightarrow$ k* $\rightarrow$ abk* .. $\rightarrow$ D*	High	Correct rejection	Low

However, access to code A* does *not* give automatic access to the context code in the absence of the instruction, even when the two codes are linked.

In path 1, simultaneous access to these codes leads to detection of a link between them, this constituting access to Ak*, where Ak* denotes that code A* is tagged. This is simple direct recognition and leads to high-confidence acceptance of word A, since it is uniquely specified by code A*.

In paths 2 and 3, the only tagged code accessed is an attribute code. If an attribute of word A is tagged, this is evidence in favour of accepting it but not decisive evidence. Accordingly, the subject is likely to make a memorability judgment. If the judged memorability is only average (path 2), the absence of any clear recollection that the word was included in the list, due to the absence of adequate tagged codes, is likely to be only weak evidence against the word: it will be strong evidence against only if the conditions of the experiment are such that the subject expects to remember *all* words clearly, as will be the case when the degree of learning is high and the retention interval is short. Low-confidence acceptance of word A is therefore likely. In path 3, the judged memorability is high, so that the absence of an adequate tagged code constitutes moderately strong grounds for rejection; this leads to a medium-confidence miss.

In path 4, a tagged relational attribute is accessed instead of a tagged attribute involving word A alone. Membership of a category to which a number of list items belong is one example of a relational attribute. Accordingly, its evidential value can be low and a miss with low confidence is shown as the outcome of this path. With a different relational attribute, the evidential value could be higher and a hit result. In path 5, no tagged code is accessed so that there is no positive evidence for accepting the word. Nevertheless, because the word has low judged memorability, it is quite possible that the subject will guess that it is a list word, although with low confidence.

The remaining paths involve a distractor, word D. Path 6 is similar to path 2 except that the word listed is now a distractor so that acceptance leads to a false alarm. Path 7 is similar to path 3 but rejection is now correct. Finally, path 8 is similar to path 5 except that the judged memorability is average instead of low. This, combined with the total absence of tagged codes, leads to rejection of word D with medium confidence.

Table 2 shows some recall paths. In each, the input is the recall instruction. On the basis of this instruction, the context code must be accessed. Naturally, it is easy to envisage other paths in which the input for the recall of a given word consists of the instruction plus previously recalled words plus cues provided by the experimenter. However, both in principle and in practice recall *is* possible simply on the basis of a recall instruction without previous recall of other words and in the absence of explicitly provided cues. At the same time, it should be noted that the interpretation of the recall instruction is likely to be influenced by the fact that it is given by a particular person in a particular context.

In path 9, the instruction gives access to the context code which in turn gives access to the unit word code. It is assumed that there is immediate detection of the link between the two codes when one code leads to retrieval of the other. In effect, therefore, it is the tagged unit word code which is accessed. Path 9 represents simple direct recall.

In path 10, access to the tagged unit word code is mediated by access to a tagged attribute code. Such a path is possible because, even when the link between the context code and the unit word code is extant, it does not necessarily function to produce retrieval of the word. A dotted arrow is shown from the attribute code to the unit word code to indicate that possible words are generated on the basis of the attribute and then discriminated. When the combination of the context code and the attribute code gives direct access to the unit word code, this constitutes another path to recall, in the representation of which the dotted arrow would be replaced by a solid arrow.

Path 11 is similar to path 10 but the unit word code is no longer tagged. It is also similar to path 2 in Table 1 and has the same outcome: the difference is that, as a recognition path, path 2 does not involve generation of possible words. Path 12 is similar to path 4. Again, the evidential value of code abk* is
 lower than the evidential value of code ak* so that, in contrast
miss. If the relational attribute ab concerns member-
al list items, then this path depicts one way in which
asier to recall: once code abk* is accessed, it may be
nber of list items from it.
code leads to direct recall of another list word, word B.

This word gives access to a tagged relational attribute which in turn gives access to the tagged unit word code. Thus the path illustrates how recall of one list word can aid recall of a second list word. In path 14, an image code is accessed. The image is presumed to include a representation of word A but, because not all features of the image represent list items (this is indicated by the dot between the 'I' and the 'k'), recall here depends on the image code giving access to the tagged unit word code.

Paths 15 and 16 concern word D, a distractor. In path 15, the distractor is generated on the basis of a tagged attribute and, in path 16, on the basis of a tagged relational attribute. Path 15 for recall corresponds to path 6 for recognition. Path 16 partially corresponds to path 7. However, code abk* is assumed (for the purpose of illustration) to provide less evidence in favour of word D than code ak*, so that rejection is made with lower confidence.

The paths shown in Tables 1 and 2 are highly schematic and fail to represent the richness of the processes which may sometimes underlie recognition or recall. Both recognition and recall can be a reconstructive inferential process based on general knowledge as well as on specific context-linked codes. Moreover, the context codes may become adequate only after the subject has recalled similar contexts and has found ways of differentiating between them.

Comparing Efficiencies

Rationale and Assumptions

Recall appears to be a less sensitive measure of retention than recognition. Indeed, at one level of analysis, this is merely a statement of fact: recognition is often appreciable when recall is almost totally absent. However, as Davis, Sutherland and Judd (1961) pointed out, the amount of information required for a correct response is typically lower in a recognition test than in a recall test. One important theoretical question is whether the apparently lower efficiency of recall reflects a difference in the underlying processes or whether it is merely an artefact of biased comparisons. We should not expect a simple answer to this question. If there is a genuine difference between the efficiencies of recognition and recall, this difference is likely to vary with the experimental conditions. Indeed, if this were not the case, variables such as word frequency could not affect recognition and recall differentially.

A second important question is how any difference between the effects of recognition and recall can be interpreted. An obvious interpretation is that the difference reflects failure to retrieve targets in recall for which recognition would have been above chance. There seems little doubt that this is part of the story. After three unsuccessful attempts to recall a word, recognition can be well above chance (Brown, 1965b). However, whereas failure to retrieve targets will tend to reduce the recall score, failure to retrieve distractors favour recall by reducing false alarms. At best, therefore, the difference the net effect of item retrieval failure (IRF). There is a further com

Recall may differ from recognition, not only because of IRF, but also because of factors affecting the evidential basis for accepting a word. Earlier, three factors were discussed which may increase the evidential basis in recall as compared with recognition. They were: (i) the examination of distractors in recognition may produce some sort of interference, (ii) in recall, retrieval of the unit word code from the context code may provide additional evidence for a link between them, and (iii) in recognition, the order of decision-taking imposed by the order of the items may reduce retrieval of relevant tagged codes. In general, therefore, the only safe conclusion is that any difference between the efficiencies of recognition and recall represents the net effect of all the factors favouring recall and of all the factors favouring recognition. Despite this, it is plausible to suppose that the main factor is IRF and that the main component in IRF is failure to retrieve targets which would have been accepted.

The traditional method of comparing recognition and recall is based on the assumption of all-or-none discrimination so that the recognition score can be corrected for guessing. (The recall score can also be corrected for guessing, if the number of alternatives is sufficiently small for a correction to make any difference.) The all-or-none assumption implies that list words are adequately tagged or are not tagged at all. The corrected recognition score gives an estimate of the number of tagged words. The recall score gives a second estimate, biased by IRF. Consequently, the difference between the two estimates is a direct estimate of failure to generate tagged words in recall.

A general method of comparing recognition and recall, of which the traditional method is one example, is to assess recall as though it were implicit recognition. This can make it possible to compare recognition and recall in terms of the same measure. In the case of recall, the measure is biased by IRF. This should not be seen as a weakness of the method. On the contrary, it is the discrepancy between the unbiased assessment of discrimination in recognition and the biased assessment in recall which provides an index of the effect of IRF on recall. It is difficult to find a satisfactory basis for comparing recognition and recall except under highly restrictive conditions. Potentially this limits the value of any results obtained. However, if a valid method of comparing recognition and recall is devised, then manipulation of variables can reveal what controls the size of the discrepancy. This is likely to give us important insights into the relation between recognition and recall even outside the restrictive conditions.

The following restrictive assumptions will be made. First, it is assumed that recognition and recall are relative to a known pool of possible items such as 'the digits 0 to 9', 'the months of the year', 'the counties of England'. Second, it is assumed that both the original list and the distractors in the recognition test represent random selections from the pool. This second assumption is necessary for the following reason. On the all-or-none model, no importance attaches to the selection of distractors. On all other models, partial retention can occur so that a distractor similar to a target will tend to be a more potent distractor. Thus the discrepancy between recognition and recall will be a function of the distractors used. Random selection of distractors from the pool has the advantage that it is a readily specifiable method of selecting distractors, and, unless there is a special reason for adopting some different method, represents the least arbitrary choice.

Measures

Measures available for assessing recognition, and therefore measures potentially available for assessing recall treated as implicit recognition, include:

(a) Corrected per cent recognition. Because of its simplicity, this traditional measure is apt to seem attractive. Unfortunately, the all-or-none assumption which the measure requires is known to be false. Moreover, it is widely recognized that, given the assumptions underlying the use of the d' measure of signal-detection theory, the use of the traditional guessing correction will lead to an apparent fall in recognition efficiency as the number of choices in a multiple-choice test rises. More generally, it can be shown that this bias as a function of the number of choices is inevitable, given only that the all-or-none assumption is false (Brown, 1965a). Empirical evidence shows that the bias can be far from trivial (Brown, 1965b; Brown and Routh, 1970).

(b) The d' measure. This well-known measure assumes that the strength of the evidence in favour of a target is normally distributed, that the strength of the evidence in favour of a distractor is also normally distributed, and finally that the variance of the two distributions is equal. The separation of the means of the two distributions in standard deviation units is d'. (See, for example, Banks (1970) for details.) The use of this measure in psychology generally and in memory in particular tends to lead to more appealing results than traditional alternatives. However, unless the distributional assumptions on which it is based are correct, its use may be misleading.

The standard method for checking the distributional assumptions involves plotting the data points of the ROC curve on double probability paper. If there is no evidence of departure from linearity, this is taken to imply that the underlying distributions are normal. If the slope of the best fitting line is unity, this is taken to imply that the variances are equal. In practice, use of this method usually depends on the availability of rating data, so that several data points can be obtained by collapsing on either side of successive category boundaries. It will be a sensitive method only if each data point depends on a fairly large number of homogeneous observations. Homogeneity presupposes that there is no pooling across subjects and that the relevant characteristics of the individual subject's behaviour stay constant throughout the data collection period. Finally, Lockhart and Murdock (1970) claim that normal distributions are not the only ones that give a straight-line plot on double probability paper, so that the conclusiveness of the method is in doubt. An adequate check on the assumptions is not readily achieved.

On theoretical grounds we can expect the distribution for list words to be strongly skewed towards maximum plausibility shortly after learning a list, since tagged unit codes will be extant for most of the words. This implies an extreme departure from normality for the target distribution. A corollary is that the shapes of the target and distractor distributions will differ. Moreover, it is likely that the shape of the target distribution changes as the retention interval lengthens, with the degree of skewness gradually lessening. Alternatives to d', based on different distributional assumptions, are equally hazardous. This includes the alpha parameter of Luce's choice theory (Luce, 1959; 1963), which covertly assumes logistic distributions of equal variance. In the study of memory, this measure has been used by Ingleby (1969; 1973).

The use of any measure based on distributional assumptions is especially hazardous if multiple-choice recognition is compared with recall. This is because the number of choices (N) open to the subject in recognition and recall often differs greatly. Consequently, deviations from the assumptions which may be of no consequence for comparisons involving equal N may produce a substantial bias when N is unequal. Brown and Routh (1970) studied the recognition of words presented through headphones masked by noise. Recognition was assessed both by d' and a distribution-free alternative (the R-measure —see below). The number of choices varied from three to sixteen. Apart from a slight fall from three to five choices, recognition remained invariant with the number of choices on both measures. In this instance, the use of the d' measure did not distort the results, although certain details (relating the probability of a first-choice success to the probability of success on subsequent attempts, if the first choice was incorrect) were inconsistent in terms of d'.

(c) The R-measure (area measure). This is identical to the area measure of signal-detection theory. It was originally defined (Brown, 1965a) as the average probability of rejecting a distractor. In two-choice tests, consisting of a single target and a single distractor, the average probability of rejecting a distractor is the same as the probability of choosing correctly. This probability has been used as a recognition index since the early days of psychology. As an index of recognition, it is very simple and has intuitive appeal. The crucial question is whether it can be estimated from recognition tests other than two-choice tests. It turns out that it can be estimated satisfactorily both from ranking tests (Brown, 1965a) and from rating tests (Brown, 1974).

Consider a multiple-choice test consisting of a single target and three distractors. If the subject puts the items in rank order of plausibility, four outcomes are possible. The target may be put first, second, third or fourth. If it is put first, this implies that all three targets are rejected (using an operational definition of 'rejection'). If it is put second, this implies that two distractors are rejected. If it is put third, it implies that only one distractor is rejected. Finally, if it is put fourth, this implies that none of the distractors are rejected. Accordingly, the number of distractors rejected in the test can readily be determined. Over a series of tests, the total number of distractors rejected divided by the total number of distractors presented is an estimate of the average probability of rejecting a distractor. This is illustrated in the following hypothetical example.

Test	1	2	3	4	5	6	
Target rank	2	1	1	4	3	2	
Distractors rejected	2	3	3	0	1	2	$\sum = 11$

Estimate of $R = 11 \div (6 \times 3) = 0.61$

In fact, each test can be regarded as the equivalent of the three two-choice tests which can be formed by combining the target with each of the distractors in turn. This ranking method of estimating the R-measure can be shortened in two ways. First, in individual testing, the subject can be asked to continue making attempts until he chooses correctly. The number of attempts taken indicates the rank of the target. Second, a limit can be placed on the number of items the subject is asked to place in rank order. For example, with up to about 20 items in the test, a good estimate of R can be obtained when only the three most plausible items are put in rank order. The estimate then involves some extrapolation but, within wide limits, the exact method of extrapolation adopted makes little difference (Brown, 1965a; 1965b).

The advantage of the R-measure estimated from ranking is that it is intrinsically independent of the number (N) of items in the multiple-choice test. Formally, it makes no difference whether an N-choice ranking test is used or the $(N-1)$ two choice tests which can be formed from it. Unlike the d' measure, it is free from distributional assumptions. This freedom is bought at the cost of a more complex experimental procedure.

The R-measure can also be estimated from rating. It is then usually known as the area measure of signal-detection theory. A proof that the area under the ROC curve equals the probability of choosing correctly in a two-choice test can be found in Green and Swets (1966). Reference to the ROC curve is not essential in deriving R from a table of ratings. Like ranked items, rated items can be decomposed into equivalent two-choice tests. Indeed, ratings can be regarded as ranking with lots of ties. Suppose 10 list words (targets) and 10 non-list words (distractors) are rated for list membership into the categories high, medium and low. The results might be as follows.

	High	Medium	Low
Targets	7	2	1
Distractors	0	4	6

From 10 targets and 10 distractors, 100 two-choice tests can be formed by pairing each target with each distractor in turn. The results just given enable us to predict the outcomes of these 100 tests. The probability of a successful outcome should be unity when a target is paired with a distractor from a lower category. When a target and a distractor from the same category are paired, we can provisionally assume the probability of a successful outcome to be one-half. Now the seven targets in the high category can be paired in 7×10 ways with the 10 distractors in lower categories. Similarly, the two targets in the medium category can be paired in 2×6 ways with the six distractors in the low category. For all these $7 \times 10 + 2 \times 6 = 82$ tests, the probability of a successful outcome is unity. Of the remaining 28 tests, $2 \times 4 + 1 \times 6 = 14$ are formed by pairing a target and a distractor from the same category. With these tests, the probability of a successful outcome will be one-half, if the subject guesses at random. Consequently the predicted number of successful outcomes in all 100 tests is $82 + \frac{1}{2} \times 14 = 89$. Dividing by 100, we obtain 0.89 as the estimate of R. The calculation proceeds in exactly the same way if the number of targets and distractors is unequal.

In the example just considered, there were only three categories. However, an appreciable bias towards underestimation of R is likely if less than four categories are used. The bias arises from treating targets and distractors within a category as equally plausible. With four categories or more the bias is likely to be very small, unless one of the categories is virtually ignored (Brown, 1974).

An advantage of the R-measure is that, unlike some other measures of discrimination, it is not subject to a bias as a function of sample size. In addition, estimates can be averaged, again without bias. A minor disadvantage of the measure is that it has an expected value of one-half when discrimination is absent and choices are made at random. A related measure is the A-index, which can be defined as the observed minus the chance values of R divided by the maximum minus the chance values. This implies $A = 2R\text{-}1$. The A-index has a value of zero when discrimination is absent and of unity when it is perfect. If discrimination is all-or-none, but not otherwise, the expected value of the A-index is the probability of recognition corrected for guessing. The A-index is probably the most suitable recognition index to compare directly with the probability of recall.

Using computer simulation, Pollack and Hsieh (1969) have investigated the sampling variability of the area under the ROC curve, i.e. of the R-measure. Sampling was from normal, uniform and negative exponential distributions. For all distributions, the standard deviation was lower than the standard deviation for the corresponding binomial proportion. The standard deviation depended on the value of R itself rather than on the nature of the underlying distributions. A curiosity is that the results are presented as though they related to the estimation of R by the rating method. In fact, their simulation procedure involved rankings, not ratings. In practice, a knowledge of the theoretical sampling variability of R is not often needed. If an independent estimate of R is obtained for each subject in each experimental condition, then the resultant table of estimates can be subject to analysis by standard methods such as analysis of variance.

Methods of Comparison

Recognition tests are of two types, for which appropriate names are 'forced recognition' and 'unforced recognition'. The first is typified by the multiple-choice test. Recognition is forced in that the subject is required to pick out the most plausible from the presented set of items, independently of whether he recognizes it in an absolute sense. Such a test is usually called a forced-choice test, but this is misleading since the subject is forced to choose even in yes/no recognition. Yes/no recognition typifies unforced recognition. Unforced recognition concerns the degree of plausibility of a given item relative to a criterion for placing it in a certain category, such as the 'yes' category in yes/no recognition. Recall tests can also be divided into forced and unforced. Moreover, corresponding to each specific recognition test, a corresponding recall test can often be found: this is illustrated in each of the methods of comparison listed below. It should be noted that, although it is natural to compare recall and recognition tests which correspond, this is not absolutely necessary, since different recognition tests can yield identical estimates of recognition efficiency.

Various test situations in which recognition and recall might be compared will now be discussed. They will be illustrated, where possible, by published experiments. Because of the technical difficulties of achieving a satisfactory basis for comparison, there are relatively few such experiments. It is hoped to show that the difficulties are not insuperable.

(a) Multiple choice. If the number of choices in recall and recognition are equal, then the probability of correct recognition can be compared directly with the probability of correct recall. Norman and Wickelgren (1969) studied the relations between two-choice recognition, four-choice recognition and four-choice recall (primarily for comparisons using the d' measure). On each trial, a brief interference task preceded and followed the presentation of four digit pairs. Retention of the right-hand digit of a pair, given the left-hand digit, would then be tested. For recall, the left-hand digit was presented alone. Recall was four-choice since only 6, 7, 8 and 9 were used as right-hand digits. Omissions were not permitted. Recall was therefore formally equivalent to four-choice recognition. Not surprisingly, no difference between the four-choice recognition and the recall probabilities was found. The direct comparison of these probabilities is valid because the recognition test consists of all items from the pool.

Brown and Routh (1968) conducted a considerably more complex experiment, based on Brown (1965a). First, a list of CVC words, all having a different initial letter, was presented once. Next, successive words were tested by recognition and recall in alternation. The recognition test for a word consisted of the target word and all CVC words with the same initial letter, apart from a few excluded words. The excluded words kept the number of choices to either 12 or 18 in order to facilitate pooling of the results. In recall, the initial letter was provided. If the subject produced an excluded word as a recall attempt, he was asked to try again. Up to three attempts at recognition or recall were made, but only the first-attempt data are of immediate interest. For 12- and 18-choice recognition, the probabilities of a correct first attempt were 0.64 and

0.60: the corresponding probabilities for recall were 0.37 and 0.45. This yields an average discrepancy of 0.21, so that retrieval failure reduced recall by about 33 per cent relative to recognition. Thus recognition was considerably more efficient than recall when first-choice probabilities were used as the basis for comparison. (Recall was only about 12 per cent below recognition when they were assessed, not in terms of first-attempt probabilities, but in terms of the R-measure by making use of the further-attempts data. This emphasizes that the numerical value of a discrepancy is relative to the measure and data used.)

In order to equalize the number of choices in recognition and recall comparatively small sets of possible items have to be used. In the experiment just described, the size of the set was kept small by using only CVC words and cueing with the initial letter in recall. Another possibility would be to use a list in which each of the words to be tested was selected from a different category of small size. Category cueing could then be used instead of initial-letter cueing.

When the number of choices (N) is unequal, the comparison of recognition and recall requires the use of a measure intrinsically independent of N. If the all-or-none assumption is made, then the score corrected for guessing is an N-free measure. Alternatively, if the standard assumptions of signal-detection theory are adopted, the probability of recognizing in a multiple-choice test with N_1 choices can be converted to a value of d'. Similarly, the probability of recall when there are N_2 choices can also be converted to a value of d'. The latter estimate will be biased by IRF, so that the difference between the two estimates is a measure of the effect of IRF on recall.

If ranking or further-attempts data are obtained in both recognition and recall, then estimates of R can be derived. This permits a comparison without strong assumptions since, as shown earlier, the R-measure is independent of the number of choices in the test and can be derived from such data. Brown (1965a) compared three-choice recognition with 12- or 18-choice recall of CVC words in an experiment similar to the one described above. Testing was individual and up to three attempts at recognition or recall were made, the experimenter providing feedback to tell the subject whether an attempt was correct or incorrect. To estimate R, extrapolation from the observed data was necessary, but different methods of extrapolation produced very similar outcomes. Using the intuitively most satisfactory method, the estimates of R were 0.94 and 0.96 for 12-and 18-choice recognition as compared with 0.83 and 0.82 for recall. This yields an average discrepancy of 0.12, so that the efficiency of recall was about 11 per cent below the efficiency of recognition (as compared with 12 per cent in the Brown and Routh study described earlier). An incidental finding is of interest. If more than one attempt at recall was needed, a correct attempt was made with significantly higher confidence than the previous attempt. This suggests that retrieval of the correct word occurred on this attempt for the first time. This was confirmed by spontaneous utterances by subjects such as 'Oh, of course'. This draws attention to a criticism of the ranking method. With this method, it is difficult to impose a time limit on attempts, if sufficient data are to be obtained. Yet the probability of retrieving the target word depends on how long the subject is prepared to spend in searching for possible words before he makes an attempt. Indeed, if he was asked to write down five words and then rank them, somewhat different results would presumably be obtained.

(b) Forced list. A recognition list consists of targets and distractors in random order. If the instruction is to select a specified number, this is one form of forced-list recognition. For example, the subject might be asked to select the 10 most plausible items out of a list of 20. An experiment might run as follows. A list of 20 States of the Union is presented once to two groups of subjects familiar with the names of all the States. One group is tested by recognition with the instruction to select the 20 most likely states from a sheet containing all 52 states. A second group is tested by recall with the instruction to write 20 most likely states. Here recognition and recall can be directly compared in terms of the number of hits. One requirement of this method is that *all* subjects comply with the instruction to produce the specified number of items in recall. One way of ensuring that it is met is to use a highly familiar pool. This solution is not available if it is desired to use pools both of high and low familiarity in order to study the effect of familiarity on the recognition–recall discrepancy. Another solution is to use a relatively small number of items from the pool for the list and to add filler items to produce a to-be-remembered list of adequate length.

If the number of choices in recognition and recall is unequal, a comparison is possible in terms of the R-measure if ranking data are obtained. In recognition, the subject can be asked to rank the whole list. (With a long list, it can be troublesome for a subject if he is asked to write the rank beside each word. It is preferable to have the words on cards which the subject can move around.) In recall, the subject is unlikely to produce a complete ranking, since this requires retrieval of all items from the pool. Thus, with recall, an assumption needs to be made about the ranks of items he fails to produce. A simple assumption is that the unused ranks are to be assigned at random to the remaining items.

(c) Yes/no and unforced list. In recognition, if list and non-list items are presented one by one and the subject makes a yes/no response to each item, the resultant data can be classified into hits, false alarms, misses and correct rejections. From such data a value of d' can be estimated, given the appropriate distributional assumptions. In the corresponding recall test, the subject is instructed to recall as many items as he can. When recall is regarded as implicit recognition, he is in effect saying 'no' to all items from the pool which he fails to produce as recall attempts. Here again the data can be classified into hits, false alarms, misses and correct rejections. In principle, therefore, an estimate of d' for recall can also be obtained, although the number of false alarms are likely to be too small for a satisfactory estimate. The estimate of d' for recall will be biased towards underestimation because of IRF: of the items which the subject fails to retrieve and which are placed in the 'no' category in the analysis, most of those sufficiently plausible to belong to the 'yes' category will be targets.

Unforced-list comparison is similar to yes/no comparison: the only difference is that all the items are presented simultaneously. Accordingly, one method of analysing the data is to estimate d' for recognition and for recall. In what appears to be the only published experiment using unforced-list comparison, (Davis, Sutherland and Judd, 1961), an attempt was made to estimate information transmission in recognition and recall. On each trial, a list of 15 items selected from a clearly defined pool of 90 items was presented once. The items were either digit pairs or letter pairs. Retention was then tested by recognition or recall. In recognition the subject was instructed to check the items he recognized on a sheet containing the 15 list items together with 15, 45 or 75 distractors. In recall he was instructed to call out all items he could remember. In order to compute information transmitted, it was assumed that errors were random. Their overall conclusion was that at least as much information was transmitted in recall as in recognition. However, information transmitted cannot be recommended as a basis for comparison. Unless the number of choices is equal in recognition and recall, the opportunity to transmit information is less in recognition than in recall. Thus even perfect recognition may not transmit as much information as imperfect recall. For example, in their recognition test in which the 15 list items were presented with 15 distractors, perfect performance would transmit 27.2 bits of information, whereas perfect performance in the recall test would transmit 55.3 bits. A possible solution would be to express information transmitted as a proportion of the opportunity to transmit information but it is not clear what assumptions this solution would involve. Another disadvantage of the information measure is that it is impossible to use unless simplifying assumptions are made. The assumption made by Davis *et al.* that errors were random amounts to assuming that discrimination was all-or-none. Given this assumption, the straightforward way to compare recognition and recall is simply to correct scores for guessing.

(d) Rating. One disadvantage of yes/no data is that the R-measure, with its freedom from distributional assumptions, cannot be used. For a good estimate of R at least four rating categories are required, whereas 'yes' and 'no' provide only two (Brown, 1974). However, provided there are at least four categories, the way they are used (i.e. the placements of the category boundaries) can vary within quite wide limits without affecting the resultant estimate. Thus recognition and recall can be compared via the R-measure, estimated in each case from rating with at least four categories. In the analysis of the recall data, all the items from the pool which the subject fails to retrieve are put in the lowest category. This leads to a biased estimate of R from recall which can be compared with the unbiased estimate from recognition to obtain an index of IRF. With this procedure, it is important to urge the subject to produce and rate any item from the pool he can think of. Unless this is done, a proper estimate of retrieval failure will not be obtained.

An alternative analysis, if the appropriate distributional assumptions are made, is to estimate d'. One method is to combine the categories on either side of a category boundary to produce the equivalent of yes/no data. By choosing an appropriate category boundary it should be possible to obtain a sufficient number of false alarms to permit a satisfactory estimate of d' for recall as well as for recognition. The rating method is therefore preferable to the yes/no method.

The method of estimating d' used by Murdock (1966), based on the response-conditional paradigm of Clarke, Birdsall and Tanner (1959), is not the one advocated here. Murdock ignored pool items which were not produced as recall attempts. However, the sample of items the subject produces cannot safely be taken as representative of items in the pool. There is almost certainly a strong correlation between discriminability and retrievability (see earlier). This correlation will produce a biased sample. Even if the sample were representative, it would be inappropriate to estimate d' in this way *given that the aim is to obtain a measure of the effect of item-retrieval failure*.

Rating data are of especial interest for what they can tell us about the relation between discriminability and retrievability. Assume that the category boundaries are the same in recognition and recall (for example, that the degree of plausibility required for placing an item in the highest category is constant). In addition, assume that the plausibility of an item once retrieved is the same in recall as in recognition: the case for adopting this assumption was considered in the section on the evidential basis of recall. Finally, assume that the subject complies with the instruction to rate every item from the pool he is able to retrieve. Given these assumptions, an equal number of targets ought to be placed in a given category in both recognition and recall, apart from retrieval failure in recall. This also applies to distractors. Thus comparison of the distributions of targets over categories in recognition and recall, and similarly for distractors, reveals fairly directly the relation between discriminability and retrievability. One interesting question is how the ratio of targets to distractors for a given category changes from recognition to recall. If, for example, the ratio is lower in recognition for the highest category, this would suggest that recall is facilitated by failure to retrieve high-plausibility distractors. Such facilitation is, of course, compatible with an *overall* impairment of recall due to retrieval failure.

Assessing Differential Effects

Problems and Possible Solutions

A change in a variable such as word frequency may affect recognition and recall differently. Such differential effects are the major concern of other chapters in this book rather than the relative efficiency of recognition and recall. It is therefore appropriate to conclude this chapter with a brief discussion of some of the problems which arise in detecting differential effects. A simple classification of differential effects is as follows. If a change in a given variable facilitates recall but impairs recognition, or vice versa, this can be called a plus–minus interaction or differential effect. If the change affects recall but not recognition, or vice versa, this can be called a plus–equal interaction. Finally, if the change affects recognition and recall in the same direction, but unequally, this can be called a plus–plus interaction. (In this notation, 'plus' is used to indicate an effect, whether the effect is facilitation or impairment, and 'minus' is used to indicate a contrary effect.) Apparent interactions, even when they are statistically significant, cannot necessarily be accepted at their face value because of criterion, level and scaling effects.

(a) The criterion problem. An apparent interaction may reflect a change in the criterion for accepting a word in recognition or in the criterion for accepting a word in recall rather than a differential change in efficiency. One solution is to use forced recognition and recall so that the criteria for acceptance become irrelevant. Another is to use indices, such as d' or the area/R-measure, which are not criterion-dependent. This second solution may allow a criterion change to be detected if this is of interest. However, a criterion change is easy to detect and easy to interpret only when efficiency stays constant.

(b) The scaling problem. This is a serious problem when trying to decide whether a plus–plus interaction is genuine. The nature of the problem can be illustrated by considering two-choice recognition and assuming that discrimination is all-or-none. If p is the probability of recognition, then $(2p-1)$ is the probability corrected for guessing. Now $(2p-1)$ changes twice as quickly as p. Accordingly, if manipulating a variable appears to have a greater effect on recall, if recognition is assessed by p, the interaction may disappear if it is assessed by $(2p-1)$. Since the pool of items is usually sufficiently large for a guessing correction to have a negligible effect on recall, the $(2p-1)$ measure of recognition is the correct one here, given the all-or-none assumption. Indeed, irrespective of this assumption, it is likely to be more sensible to compare the corrected probability of recognition with the probability of recall, unless more sophisticated measures are used. The scaling problem is not directly relevant to detecting plus–minus or plus–equal interactions, although it is of course relevant to assessing their magnitudes. An obvious step towards the solution of the scaling problem is to assess recognition and recall on a common basis in such a way that their efficiencies can be compared. This is not necessarily a complete solution because of level effects.

(c) The level problem. If the same amount of learning precedes the test of recognition and the test of recall, floor or ceiling effects are liable to occur. If recognition is moderate, recall may be very low. If recall is moderate, recognition may be very high. A floor or ceiling effect will tend to produce a spurious plus–equal interaction. However, the level problem is not just a matter of floor and ceiling effects since differences in level will intensify the scaling problem. For example, if recognition and recall are assessed using the R-measure, a change in R for recall from 0.6 to 0.7 is not necessarily comparable to a change in recognition from 0.8 to 0.9. One method of attempting to avoid the level problem is to equalize the level of either recognition or recall: it does not matter which. For example, if the variable is word frequency, the level of recognition for high-frequency and low-frequency words could be equalized in a number of ways, such as by varying list length or learning time. If the difference between recognition and recall is then found to be greater for, say, high-frequency words, it is safe to assume that there is an interaction. Unfortunately, however, the interaction may be complex and involve the manipulation used to equalize the level of recognition. The alternative is to tolerate level differences, provided floor and ceiling effects are avoided, but to analyse the data for an effect of level on the interaction, perhaps by using multivariate methods.

Recall Followed by Recognition

One perennial question in experimental psychology is whether to use between-subject or within-subject designs. In assessing differential effects, an extremely tempting within-subject design is available. Retention can be tested first by recall and then by recognition. This greatly increases the precision of the experiment since recall and recognition are then tested on the same subjects, on the same material and on the same occasions. One practical difficulty is that the statistical analysis of the results can be tricky. A simple solution if recognition and recall are assessed using the same measure may be to analyse in terms of the difference score (recognition minus recall) for each subject: the statistical analysis is then conducted on a table of independent difference scores. The fundamental question is whether results obtained with this sequential design are generalizable to designs in which recognition is not preceded by recall. It is certainly the case that recall can sometimes affect subsequent recognition (e.g. Brown and Packham, 1967). It does not follow that either the nature or the magnitude of any interaction effect is contingent on whether recognition and recall are tested separately. The issue can only be settled by comparative experiments. Given the power of the design, it has much to commend it, especially for exploratory experiments.

Summary

Recall or recognition of list membership is discussed and the following conclusions are reached (1) Once a word is retrieved, the evidential basis for accepting it is the same in recognition and recall, although three factors are identified which might favour recall. (2) Recognition is easier because, under comparable conditions, the presence of a target word facilitates access to stored information but without guaranteeing that all stored information will be accessed. (3) There is no place for a 'retrieval check' in recognition. (4) Confidence is influenced by the judged memorability of a word. (5) Various codes partially or wholly specifying a word may be tagged at input. (6) Tagging a code consists in linking it to a code representing the input context. (7) Both recall and recognition presuppose access to the context code from the instructions. (8) Any tagged code, partial or complete, is potentially relevant to recall or recognition. (9) Recall can be achieved directly from the context code or after search guided by tagged partial codes. (10) There are many possible paths to both recognition and recall.

, In principle, the efficiency of recall relative to recognition can be assessed by treating recall as implicit recognition. The resultant discrepancy in efficiency represents the effect of IRF (item-retrieval failure) on recall. In practice, efficiencies can only be compared under restrictive conditions, unless strong assumptions are made. Despite this, interesting comparisons are possible. Various situations are examined in which recognition and recall have been or could be compared. The use of the non-parametric R-measure (Brown, 1965a; 1974) as the basis for comparison is advocated and methods of estimation are described; the R-measure is the same as the area measure of signal-detection theory. A method of investigating the relationship between word retrievability and word discriminability is briefly suggested. The chapter concludes with a short discussion of possible artefacts and their avoidance when assessing whether manipulation of a given variable has differential effects on recall and recognition.

2 Ecphoric processes in recall and recognition

ENDEL TULVING

Recall and recognition, like many other concepts in psychology, have a number of different but related meanings. Among other things these two terms refer to (a) experimental tasks given to subjects in a memory experiment, (b) methods of measuring retention, (c) different experiences, or kinds of responses, of a rememberer, and (d) hypothesized processes of utilizing stored information. When we talk about recall and recognition as tasks, methods, experiences or behaviours, they are obviously different in several ways, and the question as to the nature of the relation between them in these respects can be answered relatively simply. When, on the other hand, we wonder about the processes involved in remembering that are not directly observable, the relation between recall and recognition becomes less obvious and a more searching analysis is necessary. The purpose of this chapter is to provide one such analysis of recall and recognition processes.

This analysis will focus on two different theoretical positions that have been advanced to describe the relation between recall and recognition. One, the two-stage theory, assumes that recall and recognition are basically different processes, either because recognition is included as a subprocess in recall, or because recall is assumed to contain certain retrieval processes not present in recognition. The two-stage theory has appeared in several different versions and has recently undergone major revisions.

The second type of theory holds that recall and recognition represent basically similar processes of utilization of stored information and that the differences between them are minor. The basic assumption here is that remembering of an event both in recall and recognition comes about as a consequence of interaction between *trace information*, aftereffects of the initial encoding of the event, and appropriate *retrieval information* from other sources. Recognition and recall differ only with respect to the exact nature of the retrieval information available to the rememberer. In recognition, retrieval information is carried by a literal copy of the event or item to be remembered; in recall, the retrieval information is contained in cues other than copy cues. In other respects the process of utilization of trace information in the act of retrieval is thought to be essentially the same for recall and recognition. This type of theory will be referred to as the episodic ecphory theory, for reasons given later in the chapter.

The question of whether recall and recognition are basically similar or essentially different is not necessarily the most fruitful one to ask about their relation, but since a good deal of theorizing has been focused on this issue, it can serve as a starting point of our discussion. A more appropriate question might be one that initially assumes that the two processes share some commonalities and reveal certain differences, and then asks about the nature of the relation: in what sense are the two different and in what sense are they similar?

The chapter is organized into five main sections. We begin with an overview of the staged nature of the memory process together with a brief discussion of certain terminological problems. The second major section reviews the two-stage theory and experimental evidence on which it has been based. This is followed by a consideration of some difficulties of the two-stage theory. In the fourth section certain additional experimental evidence is described that appears to be relevant to the evaluation of the two-stage theory. In the fifth part of the chapter the episodic ecphory theory is presented as an alternative to the two-stage theory. A final very brief section will present the general conclusions of the analysis of the relation between recall and recognition.

Memory Process and its Description

To place the issue of the relation between recall and recognition into a suitable perspective and to facilitate communication, we begin by presenting a schematic overview of the staged nature of the memory process and by briefly mentioning some terminological problems.

Stages of Memory

The memory process comprises a number of more or less clearly identifiable successive stages. Theorists may disagree on the exact number and nature of these stages, but the general idea of stages is accepted by all. One schematic summary of the staged nature of the memory process is contained in Table 1. The first column of Table 1 lists the three major observables of a complete memory episode: (a) the stimulus event perceived by the rememberer, (b) the instructions and cues given to him for the retrieval of the trace of the event, and (c) the overt response he makes. The second column lists nine directly unobservable process stages, in the order in which they are realized in the system. The stages are numbered in the third column.

The perception of the stimulus event (E_1) is followed by its encoding, translation of the percept into a memory trace (T_E). The trace may undergo changes as a consequence of additional inputs (E_2) into the memory system—we designate these changes as recoding. The recoded trace (T_R) is contacted, activated, matched or complemented by the information provided by the retrieval query, together with one or more specific cues (Q), resulting in the retrieval of stored information (stage 6 in Table 1).

It is at this point that the two-stage theory and the episodic ecphory theory

Table 1. A schema of the stages in the memory process

Observable	Process	Stage
Stimulus event E_1 ⟶	Perception	1
	↓	
	Encoding	2
	↓	
	Trace (T_E)	3
	↓	
(Stimulus event E_2) ⟶	(Recoding)	4
	↓	
	Trace (T_R)	5
	↓	
Query and cue (Q) ⟶	Retrieval	6
	↓	
	(Decision)	7
	↓	
	Conscious memory	8
	↓	
Overt response (R) ⟵	Output decision	9

introduce different assumptions. According to the former, retrieval (the first stage in the theory) consists in the implicit generation of possible response candidates which are then subjected to a recognition decision (second stage). Depending upon the acceptance or rejection of an implicitly retrieved item by the decision mechanism, it is produced or not produced as an overt response. The episodic ecphory theory, on the other hand, postulates no separate decision process following retrieval (stage 6 in Table 1) and prior to the conscious awareness of the remembered event (stage 8). Whenever the trace information is combined with appropriate retrieval information, retrieval is successful and its product is entered into conscious awareness of the rememberer (stage 8). Since the existence, or heuristic usefulness, of the preconscious decision stage (stage 7) is accepted by one theory but not by the other, it is placed in parentheses in Table 1.

Two-stage theories have usually made no reference to the conscious memory stage, and hence its position in the overall sequence in Table 1 may be questioned. It must be shown somewhere in the overall schema, however, because it is at this stage that the memory processes end and other, non-memory processes take over. These other processes, collectively referred to as 'output decision' (stage 9), translate, if conditions warrant it, the conscious contents of memory into an overt response.

Stage 9 in our schema, output decision, serves as a reminder of the fact that not everything the person is consciously aware of and remembers need be reflected in his overt behaviour. In memory experiments, for instance, instructions may be given that the subject recall only the names of the items in the list he studied, although he may know many other things about the retrieved items as well. Similarly, in experimental tasks such as free recall, the person may retrieve and become consciously aware of an item and yet decide not to produce it overtly, because he has already made the same response on the same trial. A third example of the control by the output decision mechanism over overt recall comes from experiments (e.g. Roediger, 1973; Rundus, 1973; Slamecka, 1968) in which the subject is provided with list items as retrieval cues for recall of other items. In these situations, too, the subject may retrieve an item but refrain from overtly producing it, because it is one of the 'cue' items.

As already noted, the exact behaviour of recall or recognition is of little interest in memory experiments. (This is one feature that distinguishes between experiments concerned with memory and those concerned with learning in the sense of modification of behaviour.) The learner can write the recalled word, speak it out aloud, record it in some other language that he knows, and so forth. The experimenter is usually willing to give him equal credit for each of these performances, since they constitute observable manifestations of the same underlying memory state. The same holds for recognition. Again, it does not matter whether the learner checks a test word as 'old', circles its printed form, says 'yes' to an appropriate query, or pushes a button. What does matter is the underlying state in the system, the conscious memory for the event in question. To the extent that the learner's recognition response provides reliable evidence about such a state of the system—and, of course, we know of situations in which it does not—the format of the overt response itself is totally uninteresting to the memory theorist. Theories of memory are concerned with remembering, not with the rememberer's behaviour.

Ecphory and Retrieval

The term 'ecphoric process' is used in this chapter in the sense of 'the process by which information stored in a specific memory trace is utilized by the system to produce conscious memory of certain aspects of the original event'. It comprises stages 5 to 8 in the schema in Table 1. The term 'ecphory' is adopted from Semon (1909), who used it in the sense of 'activation of a latent engram', a sense that is basically the same as the somewhat more elaborate definition given above. Semon also was the first person to use the term 'engram' to designate the aftereffects of stimulation that endured over time, but since there is little danger in confusing 'engram' with its more widely used synonym 'trace', the latter term will be used throughout this chapter.

The adoption of the term 'ecphory', together with its derivatives, was necessary in the present instance because the alternative term 'retrieval' that has usually served to carry the meaning assigned to ecphory (Melton, 1963) had to be reserved for a more specific purpose, namely, to designate the first of the two hypothesized stages in the two-stage theory of recall. The term 'retrieval' in what follows refers to implicit production of response candidates, or covert access to the stored representation of an item in permanent (semantic) memory (Anderson and Bower, 1972; Bahrick, 1970; Kintsch, 1970b).

Like encoding and storage of the trace, ecphory is a process of which the person is not and cannot be consciously aware. Claims of such awareness are more reasonably interpreted to mean that the person is aware of the *product* of ecphory rather than the process. The subjective experience corresponding to the hypothesized stage 8 in our schema is called *remembering*. Thus, remembering refers to the cognitive awareness that results from the successful completion of the ecphoric process. The term 'recollection' is sometimes used as a synonym for remembering.

Recall and Recognition

Our primary interest in recall and recognition in this chapter has to do with them as partly similar and partly different modes of ecphory, that is, as memory processes underlying the conversion of trace information into conscious awareness of certain features of the original stimulus event.

What we have to say about recall and recognition in this chapter is limited to simple episodic memory (Tulving, 1972) experiments in which to-be-remembered materials are familiar words presented for study in unfamiliar collections or lists, and in which the learners' memory for these word events is tested by measuring the relative frequency with which they can reproduce or correctly identify the names of the words. Learners store a good deal more information about the list words than just their names, but tests of these other features are excluded from the present analysis. It is not quite clear what it would mean to say that the subject *recalls* the sensory modality (vision *versus* audition) in which the word occurred, or *recalls* the number of times that one and the same lexical unit appeared in a list, since it seems to be equally meaningful to say that he *recognizes* the presentation modality or occurrence frequency. Hence a contrast between recall and recognition in memory tasks of this sort makes less sense than in the classical situation involving names of word episodes. The issue of the relation between recall and recognition can be raised only if the two processes are at least initially regarded as distinctive.

In this chapter we also ignore experiments in which to-be-remembered units are letters or digits or numbers. Memory processes for these units may not be drastically different from those entailed in remembering word events, but when to-be-remembered items come from such easily numerable sets it again is not clear whether the person recalls or recognizes a learned item when he is tested for it. Murdock, for instance, has suggested that the 'basic difference between recall and recognition is probably whether or not the (subject) can readily generate all possible alternatives. If he can, or if they are physically present, the method would be recognition. If he cannot, and they are not physically present, then the method would be recall' (Murdock, 1970, p. 70). If we accept Murdock's definition of the difference, then, as D'Amato (1973) has pointed out, tasks in which the subject is required to recall digits and letters must be regarded as recognition tasks, and it is not possible for the subject to recall these kinds of materials. If we do not accept Murdock's reasoning, then we may commit the error of confusing subjects' behaviour with underlying processes.

Two-Stage Theory of Recall

The two stages of the initial versions of the two-stage theory applied only to recall. Recognition was assumed to entail only the second stage. More recent versions of the two-stage theory envisage the possibility that at least certain recognition performances are based on both stages, retrieval and decision. In this section we are concerned primarily with the earlier forms of the theory.

Nature of the Theory

Hollingworth, writing more than 60 years ago, summarized the difference between recall and recognition in the following words.

'Schematically, at any rate, the difference between recall and recognition seems to be a rather simple matter. Recall is that aspect of memory process in which a *setting*, a background or association-cluster, is present in clear consciousness, but the desired *focal element* is missing. . . Recognition is, schematically, just the reverse of this process. In recognition the focal element is present, in the form of sensation, image, or feeling, and the question is whether or not this element will recall a more or less definite setting or background' (Hollingworth, 1913, pp. 532–3).

In this statement, Hollingworth does not just describe the differences between recall and recognition as methods of measuring retention, but rather points to differences in the underlying processes. Contemporary theorists describe the distinction in rather similar terms. Here, for instance, is what Norman says.

'Recall and recognition represent two different forms of queries to the storage system. In a recall task, the initial query consists of the context surrounding the sought for item; the task is to generate the item given its context . . . . In recognition, the required task is just the reverse. Here the item itself is given; the question is whether the context surrounding the item is appropriate . . . . The recognition task does not require the same type of search used in recall; the recursive query–output–decision–query chain is not needed. All that is required in recognition is an assessment of the appropriateness of the various associations surrounding a stored item to the association demanded by the query' (Norman, 1968, p. 533).

Thus Norman, like Hollingworth, is impressed by the reversal of the process as one goes from recall to recognition. In both cases it is a matter of association between item and context, but while in recognition the task is to proceed from the item to the context, in recall the task is the reverse, to 'generate the item given its context'. Norman, like many other two-stage theorists, also believes that recognition in some sense represents a simpler process than recall '*All* that is required in recognition ... '.

Kintsch (1970b) has formalized the distinction between a simpler process of recognition and a more complex one of recall by bringing up to date an old theory described, among others, by G.E. Müller (1913). The basic assumption of this two-stage theory is that recall involves two successive ecphoric stages, retrieval and decision, while recognition involves only the last of the two. Since recognition is a subprocess of recall, and recall involves a stage of information processing that is absent in recognition, the two modes of ecphory are regarded as qualitatively different.

Kintsch summarizes the two-stage theory as follows.

'The basic difference between recall and recognition appears to be that recall involves a search process and recognition does not. In recognition, the problem of retrieval is simple: the item is sensorily present and it is a simple matter to retrieve its corresponding representation in memory (although how this is done is by no means obvious); the subject then has some means of judging the newness of the trace (response strength, familiarity); if the newness satisfies some criterion, the subject says he recognizes the item; otherwise he calls it new; irrelevant alternatives are not considered in this judgement .... The problem in recall is very different. Items are not sensorily present to be judged for the newness, but they must be retrieved from memory. Retrieval involves getting from one memory trace to the next. What is important therefore are inter-item relationships. An item in a free-recall experiment is not retrieved *in vacuo*, but only as a member of a larger structure' (Kintsch, 1970b, p. 337. Reproduced by permission of Academic Press, Inc.)

Here we have the basic ingredients of the two-stage theory succinctly summarized. (a) Recall entails a process that is absent in recognition, namely, search, or retrieval. (b) Recognition thus represents a simpler process than recall. (c) Retrieval of an item's representation in memory through the copy cue is always guaranteed. (d) Recognition requires only a decision about the 'newness' or familiarity of the trace.

A somewhat different version of the two-stage theory of recall was proposed by Anderson and Bower (1972). These authors conceptualize human memory as a huge network of nodes interconnected by associations. The nodes represent concepts, plus corresponding words, while inter-node associations refer to existing relations between word concepts. Learning a list of words results in (a) a probabilistic marking of pathways in the network between nodes corresponding to list words, and (b) an independent process of associating words to the context in which they are presented, the context being conceptualized as 'list markers'. For the subject to be able to recall a word the pathways between some starting nodes and the target node must have been marked and the list marker must have been associated to the target node. For recognition, the access to the node via marked pathways is unimportant, since the presentation of the copy of the test item automatically provides access to the corresponding node, and the recognition judgment depends on the adequacy of information about the list context, if any, attached to the node.

In a later paper, Anderson and Bower (1974) modified their theory by postulating that a word may be represented by a number of different nodes in memory, corresponding to different semantic senses or 'ideas' of the word. We shall return to this new version of the theory later.

One of the most explicit statements of the two-stage theory, and of the difference between recall and recognition, has been provided by Bahrick (1969; 1970) in an explanation of the effectiveness of extralist retrieval cues. According to Bahrick's formulation, an extralist retrieval cue (such as a word that was not explicitly a part of the presented list) can facilitate recall of a list word, because it elicits, through pre-experimentally established associative connections, the target word as an implicit response (the retrieval stage), which then can be subjected to a recognition check (the decision stage) rather like an explicitly presented 'old' test item in a recognition test. Retrieval cues are effective in facilitating recall, since, on this view, they convert a more difficult recall task into an easier recognition problem.

Several other versions of the two-stage theory have been described at greater or shorter length in the literature. They differ from one another in various details. It would be impossible to treat all of them individually in this chapter. They do, however, share sufficient commonalities to make it possible to discuss them as essentially the same. This is why we shall frequently refer to two-stage theory rather than two-stage theories.

Not all experimental facts are equally important in evaluating the nature of relation between recall and recognition. For instance, the wellknown fact that recognition is usually superior to recall is relatively unimportant inasmuch as almost any theoretical view could accommodate it. Similarly, the fact that the number of alternatives is an important determinant of the extent of the performance difference between recall and recognition is not especially critical, although the existence of the fact has sometimes been used in support of the view that recall and recognition measure essentially the same thing.

Study/Test Interactions

More relevant to the problem of the relation between recall and recognition have been data demonstrating what we shall refer to as study/test interactions. These data come from experiments in which the learning material is presented for study under at least two different input or presentation conditions and tested in at least two different test conditions, typically in free-recall and recognition tests. These data are relevant because they sharply distinguish between two-process and single-process theories. Single-process theories, which are now almost extinct, viewed recall and recognition as differentially sensitive measures of the underlying response strength, and the thrust of the two-stage argument was directed against these strength theories (Anderson and Bower, 1972; Kintsch, 1970b). Other differences between two-process and one-process theories of recall and recognition have recently been thoroughly reviewed by Tiberghien and Lecocq (1973) and Lecocq and Tiberghien (1973).

The study/test interaction of interest—observed in many experiments— is one in which performance on the recall test is different for the two input conditions, whereas performance on the recognition test is the same. A particularly thorough summary of experiments that have yielded these patterns of data has been provided by McCormack (1972), and the interested reader should consult his paper for greater details. Here we shall consider only a few examples. These will suffice to illustrate the reasoning by which the data are related to the two-stage theory of recall.

Four sets of data on study/test interaction are presented in Figure 1. The data in Figure 1A come from an experiment by Bruce and Fagan (1970) which constituted a replication, with certain additional controls, of an earlier experiment by Kintsch (1968). Subjects studied lists of 42 words. The 'related' material consisted of six words in seven conceptual categories, while the 'unrelated' materials were represented by one word from each of 42 different conceptual categories. In free recall, subjects produced as many words as they could, and then added additional words until they had written down a total of 42 words. The number of words corresponding to list words represented the free-recall score. In recognition, the 42 old words were mixed with 42 new words from the same conceptual categories as those in a given input list and the subjects were asked to select 42 words as 'old'. Recognition score was the number of 'hits'. The data depicted in Figure 1A show that the nature of the material had a substantial effect on the free-recall performance, but none whatsoever for the recognition performance.

The data in Figure 1B were reported by Dale (1966). The two study conditions were defined by the presentation of two different types of materials. The 'high-familiarity' items consisted of six names of UK counties that subjects in a previous experiment had been able to generate from memory with ease, while 'low-familiarity' materials were six county names that had been mentioned much less frequently by the subjects in the previous experiment. The critical familiar and unfamiliar county names were mixed with some other buffer items in study lists which were then presented to subjects on a single trial. In the free-recall test, subjects simply wrote down as many list items as they could. As can be seen in Figure 1B, there was a large difference in recall of familiar and unfamiliar items. In the recognition test, the subjects had to select the

46

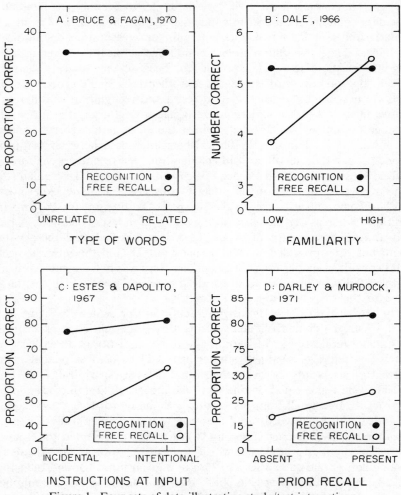

Figure 1. Four sets of data illustrating study/test interactions

list items from a total set of all 40 county names. Figure 1B shows that there was no difference whatever in the recognition of the two types of material.

Figure 1C depicts data from an experiment by Estes and DaPolito (1967). Subjects learned lists of eight CVC–digit pairs. They then either recalled response members to stimulus members as cues or attempted to identify the eight old pairs that had been mixed with eight other pairs representing re-paired stimulus and response members. One group of subjects (intentional learners) had been told prior to the presentation of the material that their task was to remember the pairs, while another group (incidental learners) were exposed to the material as part of a problem-solving task. Intentional and incidental learners differed greatly in their ability to recall the material, while differences between the two groups in the recognition task were negligible.

Finally, Darley and Murdock (1971) compared recall and recognition of words from 10 lists. Each list had been presented earlier on a single presentation trial and followed either by an immediate recall test or by a neutral activity filling the interval between the presentation of the list and the next one. The data, depicted in Figure 1D, show the effect of the prior testing of lists on the subsequent recall and recognition. In keeping with the pattern of data in the other panels of Figure 1, here, too, recall was influenced by an experimental variable, the presence or absence of an earlier recall test, while recognition scores for the two types of list were practically identical.

The Logic of Two-Stage Theory

The data appearing in Figure 1 show how four quite different experimental variables—inter-item relations, previous familiarity with items, intentionality of learning and presence or absence of prior tests—have an effect on free recall but not on recognition. While simple one-process theories would have to introduce additional *ad hoc* assumptions to make sense of these findings, the two-stage theory can readily accommodate them. All these patterns of data, according to the two-stage theory, simply illustrate the fact that recall entails two independent ecphoric stages, retrieval and decision, whereas recognition involves only the last of these two.

Probability of correct recall, according to the theory, depends both on the probability of implicit retrieval of the target item and the probability of its acceptance by the decision mechanism. Probability of a recognition 'hit', on the other hand, is determined solely by the probability of the correct acceptance of the 'old' test item by the decision system. Any experimental variable that affects *only* the probability of retrieval, therefore, will produce a difference in recall but leave recognition performance invariant. A variable that exerts an effect only at the second stage will produce a difference in both recall and recognition. The effects of a variable affecting both retrieval and decision cannot be as easily determined, except when the effects of the variable at the two stages are positively correlated, in which case the variable affects both recall and recognition similarly.

According to this logic, all the variables defining study conditions in experiments depicted in Figure 1 affected only retrieval. Consequently, they produced differences in recall but not in recognition performance. For instance, the semantic relations among list words in Bruce and Fagan's (1970) experiment, shown in Figure 1A, facilitated implicit retrieval of one list word by another; but did not affect their recognizability, which depends on the amount of occurrence information associated with each list item.

Two points are worthy of especial attention in evaluating the logic relating the data to theory. First, the argument here appears to be somewhat circular, as long as there exists no independent method of determining whether a variable

48

affects one or the other, or both, stages of processing. If we accept the two-stage theory, then the patterns of data in Figure 1 are explained. But what experimental support is there for the theory? Well, there are the data such as those in Figure 1. And how do we explain these data? Well, we assume that the theory is correct and that the study variable affects only retrieval.

In some cases it may be intuitively obvious that the input variable might have an effect only on retrievability of items and not on their recognizability, in other cases even this kind of feeble independent 'evidence' is lacking. The problem of circularity of reasoning, however, by no means applies only to the two-stage theory, and hence it does not constitute a serious criticism of the theory.

The second point of interest has to do with the assumed independence of the two stages: it must be possible for a variable X to affect one stage without affecting the other. This assumption is critical for the theory. If there were a correlation between retrievability and recognizability of items, across different levels of the variable X, then recall and recognition performances would be necessarily correlated. The data in Figure 1 are consistent with the assumed independence of the two stages, but to add extraneous strength to the assumption, the two stages have sometimes been endowed with different hypothetical properties. For instance, it has been assumed in some versions of the theory (Bahrick, 1970; Kintsch, 1968) that the retrieval process is governed by the associative structure of the memory system as it exists before the experimental presentation of the learning material, while the decision process is based on the consequences of the experimental input. In other versions of the theory, retrieval and recognition decisions are both affected by experimental input, but in different ways. In the Anderson and Bower (1972) model of free recall, for instance, retrieval depends on the associations between list tags and inter-item pathways in the memory network, while recognition decisions are based on associations between list tags and item nodes.

We shall have to keep in mind the assumed independence of the two stages as we move on to consider other sorts of data that have helped to distinguish the two-stage theory from one-process models of ecphory. For instance, one critical finding concerns the correlation between recall and recognition scores among individual subjects. Several experimenters have reported that under conditions where the same subjects are tested for both recall and recognition of different features of the same material (such as recalling *names* of picture stimuli and recognizing the actual pictures) correlations tend to be very low and sometimes not significantly different from zero (e.g. Bahrick and Boucher, 1968; Tversky, 1973; 1974). If both recall and recognition simply index some underlying memory 'strength' of the composite stimuli, then a positive correlation between recall and recognition would be expected: subjects in possession of 'strong' traces ought to get both higher recall and higher recognition scores than subjects who, for whatever reasons, have not learned the material as well.

Yet another example of the situation in which a given experimental treatment seems to produce different outcomes in recall and recognition, contrary to simple one-process theories, concerns the effect of strong associative cues on recall and recognition of target items from a list. The matter has been briefly discussed by Thomson (1972). When a list of target items is presented for study in a to-be-remembered list, with one item presented at a time, then the presence of strong extralist associates of target items as retrieval cues facilitates recall of target items (e.g. Thomson and Tulving, 1970). In contrast, the presence of such extralist cues either has no effect or even interferes with the recognition of the target items. The facts can at least partly be accommodated by the two-stage theory if it is assumed that the strong associate of the target item facilitates the retrieval of the target, whereas the recognition decision is based on the stored information to which access is provided by the 'old' test item.

Criticism of Two-Stage Theory

As we consider some of the weaknesses of the two-stage theory, we must keep in mind that different versions of the theory are not equally subject to all the criticisms that follow. Some versions of the theory can be clearly ruled out by the existence of certain experimental facts, while others suffer only from lack of sufficient detail that makes direct experimental test difficult, and sometimes impossible. The most vulnerable versions of the theory are those that postulate that retrieval processes are determined or governed by the pre-experimental (semantic) structure of memory. Other versions of the theory that assume retrieval processes to be influenced by experimental events, or the 'contents' of episodic memory, cannot be as readily rejected, but they face the problem of justifying the distinction between two separate ecphoric processes, retrieval and decision, *both* of which are guided by episodic information. These points will be elaborated later in the chapter.

Most of the criticisms of the two-stage theory are focused on the hypothesized distinction between the two stages, retrieval and decision, both of which precede the processing stage at which the product of the trace information and ecphoric information is brought into consciousness. The problem of particular interest concerns the need for the postulation of, or evidence for, the preconscious decision stage. Although no extant version of the two-stage theory makes an explicit reference to the subject's conscious awareness of a remembered event in discussing the two stages, it is assumed here that the locus of the decision stage in these theories is prior to conscious awareness. A theory of recall that postulates only a post-ecphoric decision process, designated as stage 9 in Table 1, is not subject to any of the criticisms outlined in this section. Such post-ecphoric decisions, as mentioned earlier, seem to possess an incontrovertible reality that is beyond theoretical dispute.

In this section we shall consider six specific criticisms of the two-stage theory. In the following section of the chapter a seventh difficulty of the theory is examined in the light of experimental data closely related to those providing the critical input/test interactions shown in Figure 1.

Rejection of Correctly Retrieved Items

One of the joint outcomes of the operation of two successive stages in recall is the rejection by the decision mechanism of a response candidate correctly identified by the retrieval system. This hypothesized outcome makes one wonder about the evolutionary utility of the production of wanted information by one cognitive mechanism, retrieval, that is subsequently rejected by another, decision. It also raises doubts about the reality of such a hypothesized state of affairs. Is there any direct evidence that subjects sometimes implicitly retrieve correct list items in a recall task, but fail to recall these items because the decision system does not pass the information through to the conscious stage? At the present time the answer is negative.

The problem is of considerable importance. If everything correctly identified by the retrieval process were always accepted by the decision mechanism, then the necessity for the separation of the two stages would become meaningless: cases where a correctly retrieved item is rejected by the decision mechanism would never occur, and cases where incorrectly retrieved items are rejected would never manifest themselves in the subjects' behaviour. The remaining two possible outcomes, correct recalls (correctly retrieved items accepted by the decision mechanism) and recall instrusions (incorrectly retrieved items accepted by the decision mechanism), can be specified solely in terms of the retrieval process. On the other hand, the postulation of the preconscious decision stage would become almost mandatory if it could be shown that retrievable information about target items can be prevented from reaching the stage of conscious awareness by the preconscious decision filter operating with too stringent an acceptance criterion. If, for instance, the subject in a free-recall experiment were instructed to first recall and then generate items that might have been on the list, as was done by Cofer (1967), would he ever produce any correct items that he fails to recognize as such? Appropriate controls would have to be included in the experiment, of course, but if the demonstration of recognition failure of overtly retrieved correct responses were successful, the two-stage theory would have received important support. Until such time that such evidence becomes available, the postulated preconscious decision stage in recall remains a purely hypothetical and perhaps an unnecessary construct.

'Dissociation' of Retrieval and Decision

So far there has been little direct evidence that recall entails the two hypothesized stages while recognition consists only in one. The study/test interactions and other evidence that were considered earlier are only indirect. The two-stage theory would clearly be stronger if some means existed for separate identification of, and separate measurement of the output from, the two-stages.

An attempt to differentiate the two stages has been reported by Anderson and Bower (1972, experiment III). Subjects were shown, on each of successive trials, a semi-random subset of 16 words selected from a constant total set of 32. The subset shown varied from trial to trial. The subjects had to reproduce on each trial as many words from the *total* set as they could, and for each produced word to indicate their confidence that it had appeared on the *immediately preceding* input trial. Anderson and Bower argued that the number of reproduced members from the total set reflected retrievability of the items, while the confidence with which the subject judged the membership of retrieved words in the set presented on the immediately preceding trial constituted a measure of recognition. Since the number of items produced increased over trials whereas the confidence of trial identification declined, Anderson and Bower claimed that they had 'dissociated' the two postulated components of free recall.

The argument for dissociation of retrieval and recognition in this instance is not entirely convincing. Retrievability in the experiment referred to subjects' knowledge of the membership of the total set, whereas recognition referred to the subjects' knowledge of a particular subset, the words appearing on a particular trial. On any given trial after the first, subjects had had two or more trials of practice during which they could accumulate knowledge about the membership of the items in the total set, whereas recognition decisions had to be based on the appearance of items on a single trial only. Thus, while the effects of practice could be transferred from trial to trial with respect to 're-trievability' of the items, an item's appearance on trial t could not and did not provide any useable information to the subject about its appearance on trial $t + 1$.

Anderson and Bower's reasoning underlying 'dissociation' can be extended to any situation in which a smaller subset of items (such as the words appearing in a list) is selected from a larger total set (such as all words in the language) and the subject has to decide, in a recognition test, whether or not a given item appeared in the subset. Since it is well known that under these conditions probability of recognition of an item as a member of the fixed subset increases over trials, while the subject's lexical knowledge of the words in the language (retrievability) does not, the dissociation argument could also be made on the basis of these familiar facts. Yet these facts do not appear to be highly critical for distinguishing the two-stage theory from other theories.

Sources of Recognition Failure

According to the standard two-stage theory, recognition failure is a consequence of the decision mechanism rejecting the information retrieved by the 'old' test item (e.g. Anderson and Bower, 1972; Kintsch, 1970b). The negative decision is made by the system if the representation of the test item in memory is not marked with appropriate occurrence information or list tag. This account of recognition failure follows from two assumptions: (a) test items are represented in (semantic) memory, before they have occurred as a part of a unique episode (e.g. first time in a list), and (b) a test item invariably provides access to its representation. Since there is no problem of retrieval in recognition, recognition failure can only mean that the list marker, or occurrence information, was absent or inadequate.

Such a conceptualization overlooks the possibility that negative recognition decisions can also result from the failure of access to the test item's representation, that is, using the terminology of the two-stage theory, from the failure of the retrieval process. It is easy to imagine that retrieval failure is responsible for the judgment that a test item is 'new' in a recognition situation in which the test item can have no prior representation in the memory structure and hence access to it is precluded on logical grounds. If, for instance, the test stimulus is a melody that the subject has never heard before, or perhaps an unknown olfactory stimulus (cf. Engen and Ross, 1973), the new test items must be identified by the subjects as 'new' because no representations of such stimuli exist in memory, and not because there is no occurrence information attached to the representation. Under these conditions it is also possible to conceive of similar reasons for negative recognition decisions for 'old' test items.

Theories that assume a content-addressable storage system (e.g. Shiffrin and Atkinson, 1969) could explain recognition failures in terms of the absence of appropriate occurrence information in the ('empty') location where the information about a particular stimulus would be stored had such a stimulus ever occurred. But the idea that episodic information is stored in content-addressable locations in memory is contraindicated by certain other data (e.g. Herrmann and McLaughlin, 1973; Murdock and Anderson, 1975).

Higher Recall than Retrieval

A basic and very firm prediction of the two-stage theory is that only that can be recalled that first passes the retrieval stage. Hence recall cannot be higher than retrieval.

This prediction was put to a test in an experiment conducted by Olga C. Watkins at Yale. Subjects were tested in two separate situations: (a) a semantic memory search task, in which the subject had to use certain cues to locate familiar words in memory, and (b) a simple episodic memory task, in which the subject was given similar cues as aids for recall of studied list words. The cues used were word fragments such as (a) A——AS——N, (b) A—P—N—I— and (c) HO———ON, where dashes represent missing letters. Each of these word fragments permitted only one meaningful completion, that is, each was selected to provide access to only one familiar word in semantic memory. In the semantic search task, subjects were presented with one word fragment at a time, for 15 seconds, and asked to use the fragment for the production of a meaningful word. The proportion of target words that subjects were able to generate under these conditions (the correct answers for the above fragments are ASSASSIN, APPENDIX and HORIZON) was 14 per cent. In the episodic memory task, subjects saw first a list of 17 words, with each word presented once for 1.5 seconds. The first word and the last four words in the list served as buffer items whose recall was ignored in the analysis of the data. After the presentation of the list subjects were asked to recall as many words as they could under free-recall instructions. The mean number of words recalled was 7.9, consisting of 3.5 buffer items and 4.4 words (37 per cent) from the critical, middle part of the list. Following the free-recall test, the subjects were provided with the word-fragment cues, with each cue shown for 5 seconds, and asked to recall any additional list words. In this cued recall task subjects recalled 77 per cent of the 63 per cent of the words they had failed to recall in free recall, a figure considerably higher than the 14 per cent retrieval rate in the semantic task.

Why did these word-fragment cues greatly facilitate recall of words from the studied list, in comparison with free recall? (It is reasonable to assume here that subjects could have recalled most or all of the words recalled in free recall also in response to the cues.) One might want to argue, in keeping with the two-stage theory, that the subject used the word fragment to implicitly retrieve the corresponding word from semantic memory, and then performed a recognition decision on the basis of the list tag attached to the word's representation. But this argument is ruled out by the extremely low probability of identifying the target words in the semantic retrieval task.

The results of this simple experiment require that implicit retrieval, if it is postulated as a separate stage, be either determined by the consequences of the episode of the word's appearance in the list, or thought of as constituting access to information stored in the episodic memory system (Tulving, 1972). Be it as it may, the independence of the retrieval stage from the decision stage, at least in this kind of situation, cannot be accounted for in terms of the structure of memory existing prior to the episode in question.

Context Effects in Recognition

One criticism of the two-stage theory derives from the known facts about context effects in recognition memory. A fair number of experiments have been reported showing that recognition of the study list item depends on the relation between its context at the time of the study and at the time of its test (e.g. Light and Carter-Sobell, 1970; Marcel and Steel, 1973; Thomson, 1972). Context is usually defined in terms of the presence of other items to which the subject attends. The typical findings are that the changes in the context between study and test produce an impairment in recognition performance.

Why should the context of a to-be-remembered item and its literal copy at test matter, if recognition results from a simple decision about the occurrence information attached to the item's representation in permanent memory? The two-stage theory does not have an answer to this question.

A possible revision of the two-stage theory that could handle context effects would incorporate assumptions (a) that most words have several different semantic meanings or senses, each one being represented by a separate entry in memory, and (b) that the word's context determines the sense of the word to which the list marker or occurrence information is associated at input and to which access is provided by the test word at recognition (and by the implicitly retrieved word at recall). On this view, the test word appearing in a particular context may provide access to a sense of the word different from the one that was marked at input, with the result that the recognition decision is negative. Thus, the 'old' test item in a 'new' context is judged to be 'new' for the same reason that a 'new' test item is correctly identified as such in the recognition test: lack of occurrence information in the memory location that is examined.

This kind of modification of the two-stage theory (Anderson and Bower, 1974; Martin, in press; Reder, Anderson and Bjork, 1974) assumes that recognition sometimes fails because the information available in the store cannot be found, that is, because of the failure of retrieval. Thus, the modified theory implies that recognition, too, may require both retrieval and decision. We shall return to the modified theory and some of its other implications later in the chapter.

Higher Recall than Recognition

The next criticism of the two-stage theory concerns the assertion implicit in the theory that it is impossible for a person to be able to recall an item that he cannot recognize. According to the theory, there are two potential sources of *loss* of information in recall, the retrieval stage and the decision stage, while there is only one such source, the decision stage, in recognition. Whenever an item is correctly recalled, it means that the stored information successfully passed both of these two potential bottlenecks. The logic of the theory therefore demands that recallable items must always be recognized. Experimental data showing recognition failure of recallable words, however, do exist, in direct contradiction to the theory.

Evaluation of the experimental data demonstrating superiority of recall over recognition requires that we be quite clear about the problems of measurement that the comparison entails. When, for instance, are recall and recognition performances equal? Determination of equality is a prerequisite for the determination of inequality of the two performances. Since subjects in both recall and recognition tests, and particularly in the latter, can make correct responses by 'guessing' alone, their performance has to be corrected for guessing. Statements about equality and inequality of recall and recognition, therefore, presume the adoption of some set of rules for such correction. Since agreement is as yet lacking as to what methods of correction are appropriate under what conditions, it looks as if there could be no generally acceptable solution for the problem of determining equality of recall and recognition performances.

Fortunately, it is possible to demonstrate superiority of recall over recognition in a manner that (a) leaves relatively little room for dispute on the grounds of disagreement about methods of correcting for guessing and other scaling problems, and (b) obviates the necessity to accept any particular theory of recognition memory. All that is needed is the testing of one and the same subject twice for the same set of target items, once under conditions of recall, and once in a recognition test. Each target item then can be classified for each subject into one of four mutually exclusive subsets: items both recalled and recognized (Rc, Rn), items recognized but not recalled ($\overline{\text{Rc}}$, Rn), items recalled but not recognized (Rc, $\overline{\text{Rn}}$) and items neither recognized nor recalled ($\overline{\text{Rc}}, \overline{\text{Rn}}$). If the frequency of items in the Rc, $\overline{\text{Rn}}$ category is reliably higher than that in the $\overline{\text{Rc}}$, Rn category, it can be concluded that recall is higher than recognition. A possible objection that the frequency of correct responses attributable to guessing might be higher in recognition than in recall would not apply here, since such a state of affairs could only inflate the $\overline{\text{Rc}}$, Rn score and hence only attenuate the difference on which the statement of superiority of recall over recognition is based. The argument that the higher frequency of Rc, $\overline{\text{Rn}}$ may simply reflect a higher criterion used by subjects in the recognition than in the recall test would not change the experimental fact; it only suggests one of many possible explanations of it. References in the rest of this chapter to superiority of recall over recognition are to data of this sort, higher frequency of items in the Rc, $\overline{\text{Rn}}$ category than in the $\overline{\text{Rc}}$, Rn category.

Superiority of recall over recognition has been observed in a number of experiments (e.g. Tulving, 1968b; 1974; Tulving and Thomson, 1973; Watkins, 1974; Watkins and Tulving, 1975). One of the clearest sets of data was obtained in experiments 1 and 2 described by Tulving and Thomson (1973). Subjects were shown to-be-remembered words (e.g. BABY) in an input list, accompanied by weak semantic associates of these words (e.g. *grasp*) serving as input context, or as list cues. Following the presentation of the list, subjects were given strong pre-experimental associates of target words (e.g. *infant*) as stimulus words in a free-association task, and asked to generate a number of related words to these stimuli. The generated associates included many copies of target items from the input list. The subjects were then asked to examine all words that they had generated, and to circle those words they recognized as having occurred in the previously seen input list. Finally, in an immediately following cued recall test, subjects were given the list cues and asked to recall the corresponding target items from the list. In the two experiments, the number of Rc, $\overline{\text{Rn}}$ items exceeded the number of $\overline{\text{Rc}}$, Rn items by a ratio greater than 15:1. In other words, in many cases the subjects did not recognize BABY as a list word when it had been generated in response to the extralist cue *infant*, although they could produce BABY in response to the list cue *grasp*. This superiority of recall over recognition was sufficiently large to render unreasonable any argument about chance fluctuation in the accessibility of stored information or about scaling problems. Since the recall test followed the recognition test, any forgetting that may have taken place between the two tests could have served only to attenuate the difference, thus producing an underestimation of superiority of recall over recognition.

These data, demonstrating recognition failure of recallable words, were obtained under conditions where the context of the word at the time of the test was nominally identical in recall but quite different in recognition. They can therefore be regarded as representing an extension of the earlier data demonstrating context effects in recognition memory. Regardless of theoretical interpretations of the data, the fact that a reversal of the usual superiority of recognition over recall can occur under any circumstances constitutes a weakness of the standard versions of the two-stage theory that do not permit such a relation between recall and recognition performance. The modified two-stage theory, however, that postulates many semantic senses of words determined by the context, handles the recognition failure of recallable words as adequately as it handles other context effects in recognition memory.

Further Facts about Study/Test Relations

The final criticism of the two-stage theory concerns data from experiments that have demonstrated various study/test interactions. We have already seen how the main experimental support for the standard two-stage theory is derived from these data (e.g. Anderson and Bower, 1972; Kintsch, 1970b; McCormack, 1972; Underwood, 1972). But now the criticism is offered here that the patterns of data depicted in Figure 1 represent only arbitrarily selected instances of study/test relations, and that other patterns of study/test relations must be included in the evaluation of the two-stage theory. These data are described and their compatibility with the theory discussed in this section of the chapter.

Figures 2 and 3 contain some other illustrative findings from experiments of the same general type that produced the results depicted in Figure 1. Two types of material, or one and the same type of material presented under two different input conditions, are tested in two different retrieval situations. The data shown in Figure 1 came from experiments in which one test was free recall and the other recognition, and some of the experiments represented in Figures 2 and 3 entailed the same two tests. In others, cued recall tests were used.

In the Lachman and Tuttle (1965) experiment, subjects were presented with 100 words whose order in the list constituted either a high degree of approximation to English (meaningful prose) or a low degree (random order). Retention was tested by free recall and recognition. As the data in panel A of Figure 2 show, both recall and recognition were higher for the prose than for the randomly ordered words. The two-stage theory would have to explain these data by assuming that in this particular case organization of words affected the recognizability but not necessarily the retrievability of the words. Storage of information about word-episodes, or development of list markers, may in this case have been more efficient for high than low approximation to English. It may be worth noting in passing that the problem of circularity of reasoning is relevant here, too. *If* we get an input/test interaction, retrieval processes, and hence the recall scores, are said to be affected by input conditions, while the decision processes are not; *if* we observe parallel effects in recall and recognition, the conclusion is that both processes may be affected, or perhaps only the decision process is. In either case, the data can be explained by the theory, and the theory is supported by the data.

In the Murdock (1968) experiment, subjects were presented with lists of 10 words on a single trial. The presentation was either visual or auditory. In the probe-recall test, one of the list words was presented as the probe and the subject's task was to recall the word that had followed the probe in the list. In the recognition test, a pair of words was presented. It consisted either of two words that had followed one another in the list, in the same order ('old' pair), or of two list words that had not appeared in adjacent positions ('new' pair). In panel B of Figure 2 proportions of correct responses for the words from the last two serial positions (probe positions 8 and 9) are graphed. Both probe-recall and recognition scores were higher for auditory than visual input. The two-stage theory could account for the data by assuming that the presentation modality affected only the second of the two ecphoric stages, and that the superiority of recall over recognition in this experiment is a scaling 'artefact' of some sort or another.

The next two experiments manipulated instructions to subjects at the time of input. Winograd, Karchmer and Russell (1971, experiment II) presented their subjects with 50 pairs of words on a single trial, telling them that their task was to remember the target word (right-hand member of the pair) and instructing them either to form associations between the target word and its accompanying cue word or to form a bizarre mental image combining the two words. Subjects' memory for the target words was tested in a recognition test with or without the cue words that had accompanied target words at input. The data from the experiment are depicted in panel C of Figure 2. The two kinds of instructions, associative *versus* imagery, had no effect on recognition of target words presented in the absence of the original context words, but imagery instructions did yield a considerably higher score for recognition in a test situation in which the original context words were presented alongside the target words. It is not immediately obvious how the two-stage theory would explain this sort of study/test interaction. Since the retention test entailed recognition only, differences in retrieval mechanism cannot be invoked.

The second experiment in which input instructions were manipulated is Tversky's (1974). The study materials consisted of line-drawings of objects accompanied by words labelling the objects. These object-word items were presented to the subjects on a single trial under instructions to expect either a recognition test or a free-recall test. Subjects in both instructional groups were in fact tested for both free recall and recognition. The data, shown in panel D of Figure 2, show a strong interaction between input instructions and the test mode: subjects who expected the recognition test did considerably better on the recognition test and considerably worse on the recall test than subjects who had been given the recall instructions. This type of study/test interaction cannot be readily handled by the two-stage theory without additional assumptions, since the correlation between recall and recognition

58

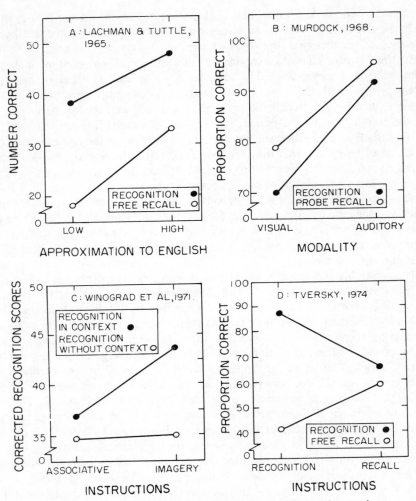

Figure 2. Four sets of data illustrating various study/test interactions

performances is negative, rather than zero, as in the data depicted in Figure 1.

The next two illustrations come from experiments that we have already mentioned earlier in connection with context effects in recognition memory. In the Tulving and Thomson (1971) experiment (only part of the data is shown here) subjects saw a long list consisting of single words or pairs of words. The pairs consisted of normatively strongly associated words. Subjects were instructed to study each presented word carefully and to expect a recognition test. In the test that followed the presentation of the list, old words were presented either alone (no context) or paired with a normatively strongly associated word (context). For the target words that had been presented as single items in the input list (input context absent) the test context was new, while for target words presented in the company of the strongly associated word (input context present) the context word at test was old. Panel A in Figure 3 shows corrected recognition scores (hits minus false positives) from the four experimental conditions. The pattern of data shows a strong interaction between input and test conditions, with the two curves, representing cue conditions at test, being crossed. The difficulties for two-stage theories in accounting for these data have already been mentioned, and need no repetition here.

Similar data from a further experiment (Thomson, 1972, experiment 4),

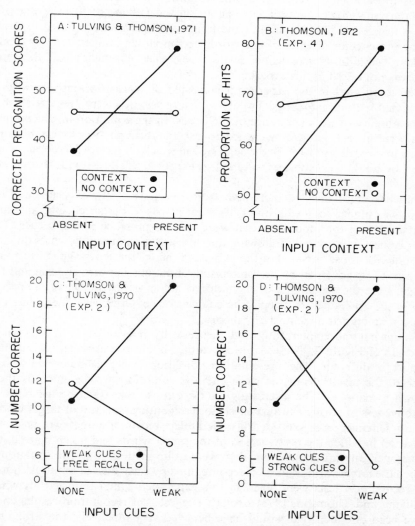

Figure 3. Four sets of data illustrating various study/test interactions

with proportion of hits as the response measure, are shown in panel B of Figure 3. The major difference between Thomson's experiment and that summarized in panel A of Figure 3 lay in the nature of the relation between words presented as pairs both at input and at test. In Thomson's experiment the words in pairs were associatively unrelated. These data thus extend the generality of the context effects in recognition memory and compound the difficulties for the two-stage theory. Even the 'homograph' theory (Anderson and Bower, 1974; Reder, Anderson and Bjork, 1974) might have to be stretched unreasonably far to handle the exceedingly large number of meanings and senses of words appearing in the context of other randomly selected words.

In the remaining two sets of data (Thomson and Tulving, 1970, experiment 2) that we shall consider, the input conditions were again differentiated in terms of the presence or absence of cue words accompanying target items at input, while test conditions were defined by the type of cues present at recall. Recognition was not tested in this experiment.

The input cues in the experiment consisted of words normatively weakly associated with target words. Twenty-four target words were presented either in the absence or in the presence of such cues. In the condition in which input cues were absent, subjects were led to expect, through two set-establishing lists, a free-recall test, while in the condition in which target words were accompanied by weak cues, subjects were led to expect a recall test with these weak cues.

Panel C of Figure 3 depicts data from one part of the experiment. Free recall was higher following input of target words in the absence of any cues than following the input of target words in the presence of weak cues. The effectiveness of weak cues following their presentation at input creates difficulties only for those versions of the two-stage theory that envisage the retrieval process to be governed by the pre-episodic relations between the cue and the target, since the probability of elicitation of the target by the weak cue is very low in the absence of their episodic co-occurrence. Otherwise, these data can be accommodated by almost any theory.

Somewhat more interesting and theoretically relevant data are shown in panel D of Figure 3. These data look rather like those in panel C, but their import is different. The presentation conditions were as described above. Indeed, the results from the weak-cue test condition are the same as those shown in panel C. The interesting data are those that describe the retrieval effectiveness of strong extralist cues, close semantic associates of target words. These semantic cues considerably facilitated recall of target words in the situation in which the presentation of the target words had taken place in the absence of any input cues, but they were quite ineffective in the situation in which the target words had been accompanied by weak cues at input. Although no recognition tests were given in this experiment, data reported elsewhere (Tulving and Thomson, 1973) strongly suggest that recognition results could have been obtained that would have behaved very much like the strong-cue recall scores.

The problem for theory here is to explain the striking crossover of the two curves. A simple two-stage theory must necessarily founder on these data. It might explain the superiority of recall in the presence of strong cues as compared with weak cues, under input conditions where no cues were presented alongside the targets, in terms of superior retrieval, more efficient recognition decisions, or both. But such assertions would be very difficult to reconcile with the weak-cue input conditions where the data show that such retrievability, recognizability, or both, of target words in the presence of strong cues was drastically diminished. We know now, on the basis of subsequent experiments (Tulving and Thomson, 1973), that it is the recognizability of target words that seems to be greatly reduced under these conditions, but this fact does not make the task of fitting the standard two-stage theory to these data any easier. The modified theory that assumes context-induced changes in the meaning of words, on the other hand, could handle these data reasonably well: different retrieval cues are differentially effective depending upon the sense of the target word stored and retrieved in various input and test contexts (Anderson and Bower, 1974; Reder, Anderson and Bjork, 1974). The major problem for this modified theory is that of justifying the retention of the idea of two successive stages in both recall and recognition, the consequence of the postulation of a retrieval process in addition to a decision process in the recognition situation. What exactly is the evidence for the two stages in the modified theory?

Episodic Ecphory

An alternative to both one-process and two-stage theories of recall and recognition is provided by the episodic ecphory view. It is not another theory— although we may sometimes refer to it as such—in that it does not predict or even really explain any empirical facts. It is a programmatic approach to the study of memory for unique events within which theoretical questions can be posed and in keeping with which they can be answered. These questions include those about the relation between recall and recognition. The framework is rather fuzzy with respect to certain issues, woefully incomplete in details, full of gaps and unsolved problems, and its main virtues lie in further questions it suggests rather than in the answers it provides. But it does help us to interpret outcomes of experiments, including those that appear to be at variance with existing theories, and it constitutes an alternative to these theories in that sense.

This section outlines those aspects of the framework that have a bearing on the issue of the relation between recall and recognition, spells out the relation between recall and recognition from the episodic ecphory point of view, considers the fit between data and theory, and briefly compares the episodic ecphory view with other theories, particularly the two-stage theory.

Unique Episodic Traces

Perception and encoding of a unique event, such as the occurrence of a word in a list, result in the creation of a unique trace in the episodic memory system (Tulving, 1972) without necessarily affecting the nature of the pre-episodic representations of the components of the event. Information in the semantic memory system is frequently used in the encoding of the event—as is information derived from other cognitive systems, including episodic memory. As a consequence, the trace of a word event may share certain features with the concepts, ideas, meanings and word senses, but it also has features not represented in the semantic system.

The role of semantic memory in the construction of an episodic trace of a word is not unlike that of, say, a person in the act of the production of a photograph of himself: the person is a necessary condition of his photograph, but not a sufficient one, and he himself is not changed as a result of being photographed. The person and his photograph obviously have certain features in common. They are in some sense very similar, and yet in other ways are also quite different. Among other things, many properties of the photograph that may be critical for its identification, or for the purpose of locating it, cannot be determined on the basis of the inspection or even questioning of the person.

The properties of the episodic trace of a word are determined not only by the perceptible properties of the word and its semantic meaning, but also by the context in which it occurs and by the specific encoding operations performed on the input into the system. Numerous experimental demonstrations exist to show that the ecphory of a target word, in nominally identical test situations, may be greatly determined by the conditions under which the word event was stored in memory. Some of this evidence has been summarized by Craik and Lockhart (1972), Tulving and Bower (1974) and Tulving and Thomson (1973). Among other things, encoding operations and the resulting traces of word events are affected by the subject's knowledge as to the method by which his memory is going to be tested. Memory performance in a recall test may be different when the subject studies a word in the expectation of a recall test than when he expects a recognition test, and the same holds for recognition (Tversky, 1973; 1974; Carey and Lockhart, 1973).

An important part of the information stored in the trace of an event has to do with the temporal date of its occurrence. In episodic memory experiments, whether they involve recall or recognition tests, the experimenter must always specify the temporal date of the event the subject is to recollect. In a situation in which a person is reminded of a past experience by some other stimulus, he also typically remembers something about the temporal coordinates of the original event. It is also possible that the contents of both episodic and semantic systems are routinely and continuously scanned as long as the organism is engaged in any perceptual or other cognitive activity. Such scanning would explain why certain inputs lead to the ecphory of previous experiences in the absence of any explicit instructions for recall or recognition.

We have no idea about the nature of the temporal code of episodic traces, although it is generally agreed that it makes more sense to talk about it in terms of temporal relations among events (e.g. event$_1$ occurred simultaneously with, or preceded or followed event$_2$ by a certain amount of time) rather than in terms of the readings of absolute values of an internal clock. The units of time in episodic memory are probably determined by experienced events and need not correspond to units of the clock and the calendar in a one-to-one relation.

Two Sources of Information

The search or scanning for information in episodic memory is guided by the subject's knowledge of the temporal date of the original events, specified in the recall or recognition instructions. The success of the search depends not only on the properties of the trace but also on the amount and relevance of ecphoric information available to the system at the beginning and in the course of ecphory. Ecphoric information is manipulated in experiments in the form of specific cues, but the assumption is that even when no such cues are explicitly provided by the experimenter, some ecphoric information that is initially separate from the trace information must be brought to bear on the trace system.

Ecphory is thus conceptualized as a joint product of information from two sources, the memory trace and the ecphoric cue. The problems of fact and theory in the study of memory consist largely in the specification of the nature of the two kinds of information and the elucidation of the laws according to which they are combined to produce conscious awareness of certain aspects of the original event.

The statement that ecphory is a joint *product* of information from two sources, the trace and the ecphoric environment, implies at least three things about the relation between the two sources of information. First, the absence of either kind of relevant information will produce a null ecphoric effect—the person cannot remember the event if either the trace information *or* ecphoric information is lacking. Second, with the amount of trace information held constant, the level of ecphoric performance is a monotonically increasing function of the amount of relevant ecphoric information. Third, with the amount of ecphoric information held constant, the level of ecphoric performance is a monotonically increasing function of the amount of trace information. It also follows that small amounts of one kind of information can be compensated for by larger amounts of the other kind to yield a constant memory performance.

Information from both sources must be compatible. A certain trace of a certain event may contain a great deal of information, but it may be unrelated to, and not compatible with, a given pattern of ecphoric information. Similarly, a given ecphoric environment can contain a great deal of information, but it may be completely unrelated to a particular trace. The probability of recollection depends on the amount of *overlapping* information between the trace and the ecphoric cues.

The presence of a specific cue has little effect on the course of memory for an event, unless appropriate information can be and is extracted from it.

The information extracted from the cue, like the information stored about an event, depends on perceptible properties of the cue, on information stored about it in memory, on the cognitive environment of the rememberer in which the cue is presented, and on encoding operations performed on it. It is possible for a cue to be lexically identical with the target word and yet fail to effect the recall of the target word, because relevant information is not extracted from the cue.

The nature of ecphoric process by which information from two sources is combined is unknown. A simple analogy, however, may help to convey the general idea of it. In Figure 4 are shown six word fragments. Each makes a complete eight-letter English word when an appropriate letter is inserted into each of the unfilled spaces. Let each word fragment represent a bundle of informational features either in a memory trace (source X, i.e. PO————IT, etc.) or in a retrieval cue (source Y, i.e. CH——CH——, etc.), and let the general retrieval instructions specify that what is being sought are 'English words'. Neither the information in the memory trace nor that in the cue alone is very likely to be sufficient for the construction of a product that matches the information given and satisfies the general criterion of 'wordness'. When information in the cue is matched to an appropriate trace, however, the resulting pattern (analogous to the remembered event) may be sufficient for the construction or selection of a response (analogous to the recalled name of the word). Thus, when we combine CH——CH——with ——IT——AT, we get CHITCHAT, when we combine PO————IT with —OR——AI—, we get POR——AIT, which readily suggests PORTRAIT. Thus, the analogy shows that something meaningful, or something that has certain general characteristics, can be created by combining components that are not meaningful in the same sense, or which in themselves do not possess the same characteristics.

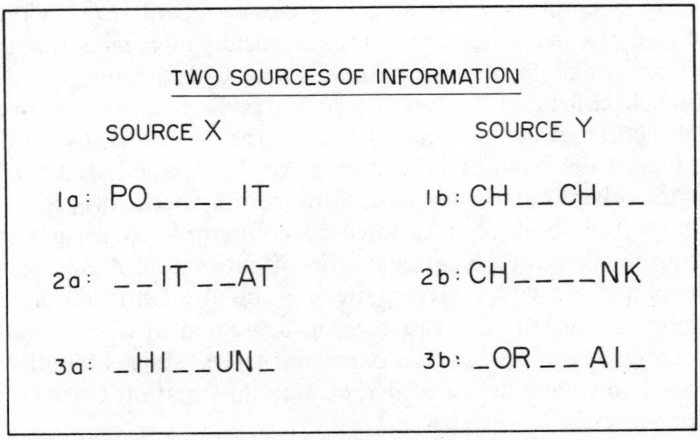

TWO SOURCES OF INFORMATION

SOURCE X   SOURCE Y

1a: PO ＿＿＿＿ IT   1b: CH ＿＿ CH ＿＿

2a: ＿＿ IT ＿＿AT   2b: CH ＿＿＿＿ NK

3a: ＿HI ＿＿UN＿   3b: ＿OR ＿＿ AI ＿

Figure 4. Word fragments illustrating information from two sources that can be combined to create meaningful products

The episodic ecphory view has many obvious shortcomings, and the absence of any specified mechanism of ecphory or retrieval is one of the more conspicuous ones. It is simply assumed that ecphory consists in somehow combining the information from two sources, and the exact mode of this combination is left open as a problem for future research. Whether such an admission of ignorance is more or less desirable than the adoption of a hypothesized mechanism consisting of implicit generation of response candidates and implicit recognition checks seems to be more a matter of one's scientific style and philosophical convictions than something that can be legislated by means of experimental facts and logical arguments.

An important consequence of the conceptualization of ecphory as a joint product of information from two sources is that the system never retrieves anything 'incorrectly'. Whatever is retrieved by the episodic system is determined by the information available in the store, by the specified temporal date of the original event, and by any additional ecphoric information that is provided. Search in the episodic memory, or some temporally defined region in it, takes place with a view to matching the ecphoric information to the trace information. The product of every successful match is entered into consciousness as a remembered event or some part of it. Recognition of certain properties of the product of ecphory is a precondition for a successful match between the trace information and ecphoric information, but there is no monitoring of the product before it is remembered. (The forced-choice recognition situation, in which the subject is always required to identify one and only one of a set of k alternatives as an 'old' item, is a more complex one, combining ecphoric processes with other task requirements, and its analysis would take us too far afield.) The system may retrieve information that does not meet certain criteria set by the experimenter, or that in fact does not correspond to a given earlier event, and the subject may decide, *after* he becomes consciously aware of the product of retrieval, that what he remembers does not fit what he wants. Such discrepancies between what is retrieved and what is accepted by a post-ecphoric decision, however, only mean that the initial ecphoric information was in some sense inappropriate or inadequate. The output from the ecphoric system is never 'wrong', only the input into the system may be.

Continuity Between Recall and Recognition

The presence of appropriate ecphoric information is as important for free recall as it is for cued recall and for recognition. When recall is compared between two situations, one entailing specific experimenter-manipulated cues and the other one containing no such cues, the contrast is not between some ecphoric information and none, but rather between some information and more information. As an illustration, consider the results of an experiment by Tulving and Watkins (1973). Subjects were shown lists of 28 five-letter words, and their retention for the list words was tested immediately after the presentation, either under conditions of free recall or with two, three, four or

66

five initial letters of words serving as specific cues. The amount of trace informa-tion was held constant by experimental design. The results are graphed in Figure 5. Probability of recall—written production of target words—is plotted against the number of letters as cues. There is a reasonably smooth monotonically increasing function between the amount of ecphoric informa-

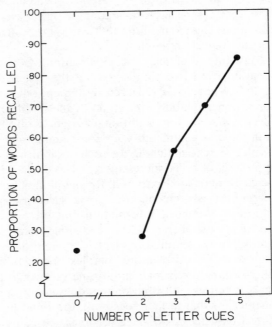

Figure 5. Proportion of five-letter words recalled as a function of number of initial letter cues. (From an experiment by Tulving and Watkins, 1973. Reproduced by permission of The Board of Trustees of the University of Illinois)

tion—corresponding to the size of the word fragment presented as a cue—and the probability of recall.

It is assumed that in all five experimental conditions recall was a product of trace information and ecphoric information. In the free-recall test only *general* ecphoric information was given, while in the conditions involving the presentation of word-fragment cues both general and *specific* ecphoric information were combined with the trace information. The situation is schematically depicted in Figure 6. The amount of general ecphoric information is assumed to have been constant in all experimental conditions, while the amount of specific additional information increased with the size of the word fragment given as a cue.

67

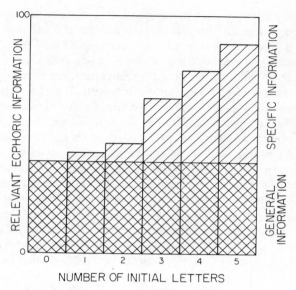

Figure 6. An illustration of the amount of general and specific ecphoric information present at recall as a function of number of initial letter cues in the experiment by Tulving and Watkins (1973)

Recall and recognition are different inasmuch as the retrieval information that is present at the time of recall is different from that at the time of recognition. They are the same inasmuch as in both cases ecphory is a consequence of appropriate combining of trace information with retrieval information. The question to the rememberer is always one and the same, 'What event or events took place at time t?', although the question can be expressed in different forms. For instance, one can ask whether or not a given event E did take place at time t, but this question only changes the ecphoric information that the subject can use in solving the problem. The 'old' test item in a formal recognition memory experiment, too, is simply another source of ecphoric information that may facilitate the utilization of the information stored in the memory trace.

If one wants to insist that free recall and recognition are different, one should, for the sake of logical and theoretical consistency, also hold that each form of cued recall is different from each other form, and that there are, therefore, as many qualitatively different ecphoric processes as there are different kinds of retrieval cues. But the postulation of such 'qualitative' differences does not help much in the ordering and summarizing of facts and hypotheses. Moreover, if one insists on a 'qualitative difference' between recall and recognition, one should know what kinds of test situations are to be classified as recall and what are to be thought of as recognition. For instance, given the data in Figure 5, where does recognition begin and recall end?

The episodic ecphory view, inasmuch as it assumes a basic similarity between recall and recognition, also implies that the process of recall does not represent any kind of a 'reversal' of the process of recognition. We saw earlier that two-stage theorists are rather fond of this idea—in recall the context is given and the task is to produce the item, in recognition the item is given and the context is to be 'retrieved'. The notion of 'reversal' makes little sense in the episodic ecphory view, since 'item' and 'context' refer to two different components, both of which are necessary for the definition of an event. The to-be-remembered event is an item-in-context. A person is not remembering an event when he thinks of only one of its components. This does not mean that the person's memory for an event cannot be incomplete. Indeed, incomplete memory is the rule rather than an exception. But if the memory of a word event is so incomplete that the person can reproduce only the word part of it, remembering nothing about the specific context of the word, then the outcome is not distinguishable from a situation in which retrieval of information takes place from semantic memory, and the whole question of whether or not the person has remembered a particular episode becomes unanswerable.

Episodic Ecphory and Experimental Data

The data we considered earlier in relation to the two-stage theory of recall can now be viewed in the light of the episodic ecphory framework. As we said earlier, the episodic ecphory view does not provide an explanation of these data, but the data can be interpreted within the general framework without any additional assumptions.

Consider the typical finding that recognition is higher than free recall. When trace information is held constant, the finding means that there was more ecphoric information present in the recognition test than in the free-recall test. Specifically, the difference lies in the information contained in the 'old' test items as specific cues, in the manner of the picture presented in Figure 6.

The data shown in Figure 1 demonstrate that the effectiveness of retrieval cues depends on specific encoding conditions under which to-be-remembered events were stored in memory. Depending upon input conditions, the informational content of the ecphoric environment in the free-recall situation was more appropriate for traces of related words than unrelated words, for high-familiarity items than the low-familiarity items, for traces resulting from intentions to learn than those produced under non-intentional conditions, following prior recall tests than following no such tests, and so on. The informational content extracted from the old test items, however, was not only greater than the informational content of the 'invisible' retrieval cues in free recall, but it was equally appropriate and overlapped the trace information equally well under both input conditions in each of the experiments considered.

The same general interpretation holds for the data summarized in Figures 2 and 3. In each case the data tell us what the relation was between information extracted from a given ecphoric cue and information stored in the trace of the original word event. This relation, as we have argued, depends on both the trace resulting from specific encoding operations and the encoded version of the retrieval cue. Indeed, sometimes it makes sense to define the trace in terms of the properties of retrieval cues that are effective in providing access to it (e.g. Tulving and Bower, 1974; Tulving and Thomson, 1973; Tversky, 1973).

The main point in these analyses of the study/test relations is that the traces created in various input conditions in all the experiments summarized in Figures 1, 2 and 3 were different, and hence the effectiveness of any two sets of retrieval cues, such as those used in different conditions of recall or recognition, were also different.

As an illustration, consider data from Tversky's (1974) experiment shown in panel D of Figure 2. Subjects anticipating the recognition test may have performed, at input, a careful analysis of the details of each picture-word item, and the information stored as a consequence of this encoding operation permitted efficient selection of the previously seen item from a pair containing a similar alternative. The same information, however, may have been less compatible with the ecphoric information in the free-recall task. Subjects anticipating the recall test, on the other hand, were encouraged to encode list items in relation to each other. Such an encoding activity is likely to result in the storage of a good deal of semantic information, and to the extent that such semantic information matched that available in the free-recall situation, recall was facilitated.

As another illustration, let us examine the data from the Thomson and Tulving (1970) experiment shown in panel D of Figure 3. The curve showing the effect of weak cues is expected by any theory, since the subject learned the associations between weak cues and target words at input in the weak-cue input condition but not in the no-cue input condition. The striking opposite effect of strong cues which were seen by subjects under neither input condition is more interesting. The interpretation offered (Thomson and Tulving, 1970) was that the subjects under the no-cue input conditions did encode to-be-remembered items in a fashion whereby associated cues became a 'part' of the encoded trace (we should now say, the informational content of the strong cues overlapped considerably with the trace information). The specific encoding of to-be-remembered words under the weak-cue input conditions, however, created traces of target words very low on the same kind of semantic information that characterized the strong cues, with the resultant low level of recall.

Similar arguments can be advanced in the interpretation of the data showing subjects' inability to recognize words that they could recall in the presence of list cues (Tulving, 1974; Tulving and Thomson, 1973; Watkins and Tulving, 1975). These data suggest that the list cue contained more relevant information for the purpose of providing access to the stored cue-target trace than did the literal copy of the target item, either because the cue-target compounds stored in memory contained little information that matched the information in 'copy' cues or because the subjects did not know what was the appropriate information to be extracted from the copy cues in the recognition test.

The interpretation of the experimental data of this sort within the episodic ecphory paradigm essentially restates the findings, but in different terms. The restatement has the value of suggesting specific questions that can be asked and experimentally investigated. Whatever the effectiveness of a cue in a given situation—whether high or low, whether surprising by whatever other standards or not—the theory points to further specific questions. Why is a given cue at recall more effective following input condition A than input condition B, given that the nominal target item is the same? Why is retrieval cue X more effective than retrieval cue Y, given that the stored information is identical? Why does a given interaction between input and test conditions come about? What is the nature of the information contained in traces of events in input conditions A and B, and what information is extracted from retrieval cues X and Y when they are presented following these conditions? These questions about the effectiveness of cues are as appropriate with respect to copy cues used in recognition tests as any other kind of cue.

Another advantage of the episodic ecphory point of view lies in its open-endedness: it can make sense, at an initial level of understanding at least, of all the data that can be produced in recall and recognition experiments. It is not at a loss when recognition performance depends on context changes, or when recall is higher than recognition. It simply converts these findings into further experimental and theoretical questions.

Comparison with Other Theories

Like all other contemporary attempts to draft the broad outlines of a general framework in which problems and phenomena of memory can be meaningfully handled, the episodic ecphory view consists of a large number of assumptions and hypotheses, each one of which can be found in some other theory, but the totality of which does not quite correspond to any other system. It would be impossible here to even mention, let alone discuss, all the points of agreement with other theories, although a small list of similarities can be given as an illustration of the relations between episodic ecphory view and other theoretical notions about episodic memory.

The idea that the memory trace of an episode is unique or is laid down in a cognitive system that is in some sense different from the semantic memory system has been mentioned or advocated by a number of writers. For instance, Hintzman and Block (1970) have pointed out the usefulness of Koffka's idea of a 'trace column', a more or less precise record of the temporal order of experienced events. Herrmann and McLaughlin (1973) have described data they interpreted as contrary to models of memory that assume episodic tagging of semantic representations of words. Atkinson, Herrmann and Wescourt (1974) have postulated an event-knowledge store (EKS) as a necessary component of the memory system and distinguished it from what they call the conceptual store. Finally, Murdock (1974) has used the metaphor of a 'conveyor belt' to describe the temporally ordered record of events that is assumed to exist in some sense separately from other memory structures.

The problem of the relation between episodic and semantic memory seems to be shaping up as an important focus of experimental and theoretical activity and perhaps controversy. Indeed, one of the major differences between the episodic ecphory point of view and most versions of the two-stage theory—Kintsch's (1974) new theory is an exception—has to do with the question of whether the trace of a word event becomes a part of the preepisodic representation of the word in semantic memory, or whether it is in some sense separate from that representation.

Rather strong evidence for the idea that the storage of episodic information is better conceptualized in a form other than tagging of existing structures has recently been found by Murdock (1974, p. 272; also Murdock and Anderson, 1975). The amount of time a person requires for a 'hit' in a recognition test is a linearly increasing function of the number of interpolated study and test items, and the amount of time needed to correctly reject a distractor item is a linear function of the position of the test item in the test sequence. These findings strongly imply a search along something corresponding to the temporal dimension in a system different from semantic memory. Since the scanning speed in episodic memory may be very high—Murdock has obtained rates close to 1 msec/item, and higher rates cannot be ruled out—the data also make more reasonable the proposition that semantic and other kinds of specific cues can be effectively and quickly used to locate information stored in episodic memory.

Correspondences between the episodic ecphory view and other theories also exist with respect to other assumptions. Thus, for instance, the proposition that recall and recognition processes are essentially identical in nature has been advanced by Shiffrin and Atkinson (1969) and by Lockhart, Craik and Jacoby elsewhere in this volume. The notion that recognition entails an access problem to the stored information, as does recall, has been accepted by many writers (e.g. Anderson and Bower, 1974; Kintsch, 1974; Light and Carter-Sobell, 1970; Mandler, 1972; Thomson, 1972; Winograd and Raines, 1972; Tversky, 1974). Retrieval process as some sort of a matching operation, or at least involving a matching process, is an old idea accepted by most theorists, and Kintsch (1972; 1974) has reminded contemporary readers of Otto Selz's idea of pattern completion as a useful metaphor to describe the retrieval process.

The episodic ecphory view incorporates the encoding specificity principle (Tulving and Thomson, 1973), which is a scheme for interpreting the relations between encoded traces and retrieval cues. The episodic ecphory view, however, attempts to encompass more than just the problem of why some and not other stimulus events serve to facilitate access to the stored information. It is concerned with the process of trace formation and the nature of representation of episodic information, with the relation between episodic and semantic memories, the relation between recall and recognition, as well as with the general problem of ecphory.

Among other theories the most similar to the episodic ecphory point of view is the new theory of Kintsch (1974). It shares with the episodic ecphory view a number of basic propositions: the distinction between episodic and semantic memory; the relevance of the encoding specificity principle; the importance of the context in the encoding of the perceived events at input and of the cues at output; the requirement that theories of memory be applicable to, and reflect the fact that memory systems can handle retention of, verbal materials as well as all other sorts of information; and the potential usefulness of the concept of pattern completion. Despite these important agreements, and perhaps paradoxically, Kintsch (1974) still maintains that it is useful to think of recall and recognition as 'essentially different' processes, and feels that the two-stage theory is a useful device for capturing the differences.

The new version of the two-stage theory proposed by Anderson and Bower (1974) is in several ways quite similar to Kintsch's. An important exception concerns the nature of stored information. In the Anderson and Bower theory, episodic information is recorded in the form of tagging of preepisodic structures, while in Kintsch's the episodic system is 'operationally distinct' from the semantic system. But like Kintsch, Anderson and Bower agree that at least in some recognition situations the access to the location in memory where the relevant episodic information is stored is not automatically guaranteed by the 'old' test word, and that there is, therefore, a significant access problem in recognition memory, as there is in recall. Thus, it looks as if the number of theorists is rapidly diminishing who believe that recall and recognition can be distinguished in terms of the presence or absence of a fallible retrieval process.

Conclusions

Whether recall and recognition are basically similar or different depends on what one means by 'basically' and by 'different'. In the early versions of the two-stage theory the meaning of both of these terms was unambiguous: since recall consisted of two stages, and recognition of only one of the two, the two processes were different and the difference was basic.

Although the distinction between recall and recognition is still made in the two-stage theory, it has become more blurred and less 'basic'. The objectives of the theory have shifted with various sorts of new experimental evidence that have been seen as presenting a challenge to the theory. The problems for the theory have also changed.

The two-stage theory originally came into existence at a time when data-based comparisons between recall and recognition involved only free-recall and standard recognition tests. Under those conditions the distinction between the two appeared sharp and the data clear. Recognition was usually superior to recall performance, and even the exceptional cases could be handled either as experimental artefacts or as otherwise theoretically uninteresting special cases. The study/test interactions constituted the most complex phenomena that were deemed to be within reach of theory, and the two-stage theory handled them admirably. The data from a large variety of cued recall experiments, the discovery (or rediscovery) of context effects in recall and recognition, and the findings that sometimes subjects can recall items they cannot recognize have now created a somewhat different world of experimental facts with which theories of retrieval have to contend.

The problems for the two-stage theory concern (a) the involvement of retrieval processes in recognition, and (b) the influence of episodic inputs on the retrieval stage. In the original versions of the the theory (e.g. Bahrick, 1970), recognition did not include the retrieval stage, and the retrieval stage in recall was independent of episodic inputs. In both Anderson and Bower's (1974) and Kintsch's (1974) new two-stage theories, retrieval is involved in recognition, and episodic inputs do determine the retrievability of the desired information. These relaxations of the initial restrictions have enabled the two-stage theory to accommodate data it could not have handled otherwise, but they have also raised the question of the necessity or usefulness of the distinction between the two stages. The problem concerns the relation between data and theory. What aspects of observable output from the memory system can be identified with each of the two stages, and how? Are there any facts left, now that the theory is changed, that still require the postulation of two successive processing stages for their explanation? The new versions of the theory are not entirely clear on these issues.

It is partly because of these difficulties with the two-stage theory that the episodic ecphory view deserves attention as an alternative way of making sense out of the phenomena of recall and recognition. This view holds that the distinction between recall and recognition, which at one time may have been indispensable, has outlived its usefulness. Successful ecphory of any kind and in whatever form depends on a large number of factors having to do with (a) the properties of information stored in traces of events, (b) the ecphoric information available in the system at any given time, and (c) the interaction of the information available in these sources. The understanding of these factors undoubtedly will require further analysis and finer distinctions with respect to the process of ecphory (Anderson and Bower, 1974), but the idea that recall and recognition represent basically different forms of recovery of stored information does not appear to be a promising vantage point in the pursuit of this understanding.

Notes

1. The preparation of this chapter has been facilitated by National Research Council of Canada Grant No. A8632 and by the National Science Foundation of the US Grant No. 40208X. I am grateful to Olga C. Watkins for the help with the manuscript.

3 Depth of processing, recognition and recall

ROBERT S. LOCKHART, FERGUS I.M. CRAIK and LARRY JACOBY

Introduction

Most attempts to characterize the essential differences between recognition and recall have made use, in one form or another, of the distinction between 'storage' and 'retrieval'. A straightforward example is the two-process theory of Kintsch (1970b), in which it is claimed that whereas recall involves both search and decision, recognition entails only the latter. Compared with earlier accounts such as those which distinguished recall from recognition in terms of a different threshold, the two-process theory appears to have several advantages. Its additional degree of theoretical freedom allows it to account readily for results (see McCormack, 1972) which show that certain variables influence recall but not recognition. Further, if a two-process theory is accepted, recognition can be taken as a relatively pure measure of storage, and recognition/recall comparisons used to establish whether a given variable exerts its effect via the retrieval or storage phase. Murdock (1968), for example, concluded that since differences between auditory and visual presentation exist in both recognition and recall, such effects represent storage differences.

Apart from its simplicity, a major factor contributing to the persistence of the two-process theory is undoubtedly the elasticity of the terms, especially terms such as 'retrieval' and 'search'. Efforts to falsify the theory have done so by attempting to demonstrate that recognition does, after all, involve 'retrieval'. But the meaning of this term (and thus the status of the evidence) is left quite vague. It is, of course, a simple matter to define retrieval in operational terms. Such a definition would identify retrieval effects with performance differences which occur as a function of conditions at time of test, all conditions prior to the test phase having been kept constant. This definition is satisfied by paradigms such as those which vary the context of recognition test items, or the availability of cues for recall. As straightforward as this operational definition is, it should be noted that it encompasses a concept of retrieval as broad as that of Melton's (1963) general notion of trace utilization. Moreover, it fails to incorporate the important point (stressed by Tulving and Thomson (1973)) that item retrieval, properly understood, involves an *interaction* between encoding processes and test conditions. For example, whether or not recall is facilitated by the presence of certain 'retrieval cues' may depend critically on the form of the item's initial encoding, and a failure to recall might just as well be viewed as a consequence of inappropriate initial coding as due to an inadequate retrieval cue.

If retrieval is defined as broadly as the operational definition above, disproving the two-process theory becomes a trivial matter; it need only be shown that recognition accuracy depends on the context in which the test item is presented. It seems likely, then, that the advocates of the two-process theory are using the term retrieval in a different, more restricted sense, but the exact nature of this restriction is far from clear. Attempts to pin down the term more precisely have most frequently introduced the concept of search and the retrieval problem as that of locating the to-be-recalled item, somewhat like locating a book in the library. There are several similar analogies that have been coined to make the same point. In a somewhat different context, Miller (1963) drew an analogy with a junk-box; inability to recover an object might be a consequence either of its not being in the box, or being in the box but effectively lost amongst the countless other objects, just as an incorrectly shelved library book can no longer be easily located. In its turn, this type of analogy draws heavily on computer models of information retrieval, for which notions of search and location can be given unambiguous meaning. The usefulness of this analysis was demonstrated by Tulving and Pearlstone (1966), who used the terms 'availability' to refer to the existence of the intact trace in the memory store and 'accessibility' to refer to the problem of locating it. A retrieval cue is then viewed as anything which serves to locate the available but hitherto inaccessible trace.

This conceptualization of retrieval has been most extensively studied within the context of categorical organization, the assumption being that the facilitating effects of such organization operate via the retrieval component. It is not surprising then that many attempts to test the two-process theory's account of recognition and recall differences have centred on the question of whether or not organization influences recognition. The results have varied from study to study, but it seems safe to conclude that there are certain conditions under which recognition increases with degree of organization (Mandler, 1972). However, it is quite gratuitous to infer that these results say anything about retrieval processes in recognition. Note that the typical experiment reported by Mandler (1972) does not conform to even the broad operational definition given above. It could be argued with equal plausibility that the task of sorting items into categories involves processing of a kind which establishes a more durable or distinctive trace and that the more categories employed, the deeper and more discriminating that processing will be. This issue is discussed in greater detail in a later section of this chapter.

The persistent difficulty with attempting to answer a question such as 'Does recognition entail retrieval?' is that as soon as one steps beyond the broad operational definition, it becomes apparent that the meaning of the question varies with one's theory of the recognition process, and that from some points of view it may not be a particularly sensible one. Under these circumstances it is preferable to set such questions aside until a more detailed analysis of the recognition process has been made. In the next section such an analysis is attempted, and using this analysis we then examine a number of basic questions of current interest. Naturally, many elements of our system have been suggested by previous workers; we make no great claims for originality, but we believe that the specific proposals advanced here fit the known facts reasonably well. In essence, we suggest that recognition of an event depends on (a) the depth of initial encoding, and (b) the similarity of presentation and test encodings. We retain Tulving's (1972) distinction between semantic and episodic memory, although we believe that these two aspects of the perceptual/memory system are more closely interrelated than Tulving supposed. In our scheme, semantic memory acts as part of a pattern-recognition system whose function is to interpret incoming stimuli by means of complex analysing and encoding operations. The product of these operations is the memory trace, which forms the latest addition to episodic memory—that part of the system comprising the temporally ordered collection of all encoded episodes and events. The deeper and more elaborately a stimulus is analysed by the perceptual system, the richer and more detailed will be the episodic memory trace. At the time of the recognition test, the probe stimulus is again encoded by the pattern recognition system and the resulting encoding is used to specify the initial trace. For recent items, retrieval information is used to select the required trace; while for remote events, the encoded probe information is used as the basis for reconstruction of the initial stimulus—this reconstructive activity is constrained and guided by information contained in the memory trace. The purpose of the next few sections is to examine in greater detail what is meant by 'depth' of processing and to suggest ways in which the recognition process may function.

Encoding of the Presentation Stimulus

Levels of Processing

Craik and Lockhart (1972) described the processing of a stimulus in terms of a continuum of analysing operations. First the physical and structural features of the stimulus are analysed, then the stimulus is subjected to progressively more elaborate semantic analyses. The phrase 'greater depth' referred to these later semantic–associative operations. It was further postulated that the memory trace was a by-product of the analysing operations and that the durability of the trace was a function of depth—deeper initial processing yields a longer-lasting trace.

We would like to modify some of these ideas. For example, if 'shallow levels of processing' comprise simple physical analyses and 'deep levels' consist of complex semantic analyses, it is difficult to see how these very different analytic operations could possibly lie on a continuum. There is no sense in which the physical analysis of visually presented words (typeface, letter form, size, colour, etc.) shades off into the meaning which the words convey. Rather, the physical, phonemic and semantic characteristics of words exist in different dimensions, or *domains*, to use Sutherland's (1972) expression. We suggest that 'greater depth' may refer to two somewhat distinct changes in processing. First, the domains themselves may be thought of as a hierarchical organization proceeding from shallow, structural domains to deep, semantic domains. Second, at one depth in this sense, the stimulus may be further analysed or elaborated by carrying out additional operations within one qualitatively coherent domain. Although the term 'depth' will be retained to describe all cases where many analytic operations have been carried out, the two senses in which the word is used should be borne in mind. Some further comments on the two kinds of depth are offered below.

In Sutherland's (1972) discussions of object recognition, he suggests that a structural description of the input pattern is formed within each analytic domain. At each level of analysis, the structural descriptions formed within one domain serve as the input to the next domain via a set of mapping rules. A slightly different way of phrasing these ideas is to say that each level of analysis provides *evidence* which is used to confirm (or reject) the structural description of the hypothesized patterns at the next level. This second way of describing the process may be preferable in that it stresses the notion that structural descriptions at any level are as much a product of expectancies and past learning as they are products of the current stimulus input. Further, descriptions of very probable events will require only minimal confirming evidence from preceding levels, since their structural descriptions have been largely preformed in anticipation. These ideas are essentially identical to Norman's (1968) discussion of the roles of sensory input and 'pertinence' in perception, and to Treisman's (1964) notion of levels of analysis, where each level is seen as a signal-detection test whose function is to allow or prevent the passage of information from one level to the next.

This analysis has several implications for practice and repetition effects. Since practice has the effect of making stimuli, or stimulus–response sequences, more probable, highly practised encoding operations will run off with a minimum of processing in each domain. That is, fewer encoding operations take place at each qualitative level of analysis. With extended practice, it may even be possible to bypass a complete domain—thus while young children and poor readers may be forced to sound out letter sequences to understand written text, the practised reader may bypass the phonemic stage entirely, for simple material at least (Hardyck and Petrinovich, 1970).

Thus while we believe that processing typically proceeds through a fixed series of qualitatively distinct stages or domains, this does not mean that *all* possible analyses are laboriously carried out in each domain. Only those analyses required to provide critical evidence for deeper levels of processing are carried out. Our views may be contrasted with the notion that practice has the effect of speeding up the *same* encoding sequence. We suggest that, with practice, fewer operations are carried out.

In general, processing proceeds until the domain relevant to the present task is reached and, quite often, it is only at the 'target' domain that sufficient processing occurs for conscious awareness of the processing operations to take place. By this latter proposition we mean that encoding operations for familiar stimuli can be effected with minimum evidence from shallower domains and that the initial analysing operations can be run off automatically, without the involvement of consciousness. However, we can become conscious of some early processing operations by directing attention to the relevant domain; in this case, further analyses are carried out within that domain and conscious awareness ensues. The difference in these two processing strategies is illustrated by skimming an easy text for gist as opposed to reading the text for typing errors. There are also exceptions to the general statement that processing proceeds only as far as the target domain—if a stimulus is highly compatible with deeper levels of analysis it may be impossible to prevent processing occurring at a deeper level even when it is not in the subject's interests to do so; the Stroop effect may be described in these terms.

We do not believe that it is very useful to talk about verbal encoding as 'automatic' except, perhaps, in certain limited contexts (Posner and Warren, 1972; Wickens, 1970). While it is true that a well-practised encoding may be accomplished by little or no conscious effort, this accomplishment seems to be a matter of degree rather than an all-or-none event. Words in a half-learned foreign language often require conscious processing before they are understood; with further practice they require less analysis, until subjectively the processing feels 'automatic'. But if the context is misleading or the subject is set to perceive a different word, or if he is fatigued or distracted, he may again be forced to invoke conscious processing before the word is understood. The apparent automaticity of encoding depends on the amount of analysis which must be performed on the word before its meaning is extracted—this in turn will depend on such factors as the material, practice, context and set.

The preceding discussion of the amount of processing carried out in each domain has important implications for our view of memory. We believe that the episodic memory trace results from those encoding operations carried out in the pattern-recognition and cognitive systems. Thus a reasonably familiar pattern or stimulus–response sequence will be analysed and encoded by a moderate number of analytic operations and will result in a moderately rich memory trace. When a stimulus becomes highly practised or expected, it is analysed more readily by fewer operations and an improverished memory trace will result. Conversely, if the stimulus is novel, or difficult to process or important, more analyses are carried out and a richer memory trace results.

The Order of Analysis

Savin and Bever (1970) showed that target syllables could be detected faster than target phonemes in acoustically presented syllables. They concluded, therefore, that syllables were not in any sense constructed from phonemes—syllable analysis seemed to be prior to phoneme analysis. In the same vein, Mistler-Lachman (1975) has shown deep structural ambiguity is apparently resolved before surface-level lexical ambiguity. These demonstrations cast doubt on the validity of a processing sequence which necessarily proceeds from simple to complex. Two comments are offered on these results. First, McNeill and Lindig (1973) report further results showing that words can be detected faster than syllables, and even that short sentences are detected faster than words. It is certainly difficult to believe that sentences are completely processed *before* any phonemes or syllables are perceived. McNeill and Lindig show that minimum reaction times occur whenever the linguistic level of the target and the search list is the same; further, given a match between target and list items, latencies tend to be faster for shallower linguistic levels. Thus they argue that the relatively long latencies shown by Savin and Bever's subjects when they detected phonemes were artefactually caused by the mismatch between the target and list items.

A second reason underlying the faster detection of apparently deeper features may be that such deeper levels of linguistic analysis (words and phrases, for example) are the levels at which conscious decision-making typically operates. We speculatively suggest that the amount of processing necessary to yield conscious perception of a spoken word may be less than that necessary to yield conscious perception of its constituent phonemes, even although evidence from the phonemic domain is a necessary input for word perception. That is, the amount of processing at the phonemic level which is necessary to provide confirming evidence for word perception is less than the processing necessary to construct a conscious phoneme percept. This shift in the level at which consciousness operates, from shallower to deeper levels, seems typical of all practised skills—a beginning piano player can run off a well-practised phrase more quickly than he can play a single note contained in that phrase; we perceive the figures and objects in a *pointilliste* painting faster than we perceive the constituent coloured dots—even though the deeper, more meaningful levels must depend on some analysis at shallower levels. Reaction-time studies are not a good source of evidence for the order in which encoding operations are performed.

Further Elaborations Within a Domain

In the same way that the processing of a well-practised stimulus proceeds rather automatically from domain to domain, further processing of a common item or event is carried out within one domain. Those analyses are performed which enable the perceiver to distinguish the event from other possible events. Again, if the event is common or expected, rather little confirming evidence may be required and few analyses need be carried out. If the event is uncommon, unexpected or ambiguous, further processing within the domain is necessary to specify the event unambiguously. Again, it is suggested that well-practised analyses are carried out with little conscious involvement; to the extent that the task requires further processing of the stimulus input, conscious effort is involved. As a further suggestion, automatic, practised encodings make use of the existing analysing routines in semantic memory; when further conscious analyses are required, the structure of semantic memory itself is altered by these new analyses. Thus, if two things appear together for the first time (a particular man and woman, let us say) it may require some conscious effort to construct a new encoding (what do they have in common?). After several such appearances, however, our encoding system contains a new 'couple' concept and the subsequent analysis of each constituent is altered accordingly.

In summary, when a stimulus is presented or an event occurs, it is analysed by the pattern-recognition processes and other 'cognitive structures' which comprise semantic memory. The essential purpose of these analytic operations is to interpret and understand environmental events—the memory trace is seen as the by-product of these cognitive operations. The bundle of analysed features which comprises the memory trace forms the latest addition to episodic memory. The richness of the memory trace depends on the number and the nature of features analyzed. In turn, the operations carried out on the stimulus depend on the interpretive task given to the subject, the context and the material. If the stimulus is expected and commonplace, few features need be noted to resolve cognitive ambiguity; if the stimulus is rare, unexpected or must be discriminated from similar stimuli, many features are analysed and a rich memory trace results. Semantic memory is seen as the system concerned with storing our knowledge of the world; it thus provides the means to analyse and interpret events as they occur. Apart from shallow sensory 'primitives', the analysing processes of semantic memory have been formed from recurring commonalities of past events—rules and relations have been abstracted from previous episodes. To the extent that further episodes conform to past rules and regularities, the structure of semantic memory remains unchanged—our interpretation of the world is confirmed. When events occur in new groupings, however, or demand different responses for their resolution, the structure of semantic memory must be amended. In this sense 'memory' can be identified as the bundle of encoded features in episodic memory, while 'learning' corresponds to a change in the structure of semantic memory.

Episodic Memory

Before moving on to a consideration of trace utilization, we would like to make a few comments concerning the episodic nature of the encoded trace. While we agree with Tulving (1972) that the distinction between episodic and semantic memory is a useful one, we question a number of the statements he makes about the nature of episodic memory. First, we would place greater emphasis on the interdependence of the two systems; on the one hand, the structure of semantic memory has been formed from a series of episodes and, on the other, an event in episodic memory can be accessed by repeating the encoding operations in semantic memory. This suggestion is amplified below. Second, Tulving suggests that episodic memory is structured in temporal and spatial terms. We would like to offer the more radical suggestion that episodic memory has *no* inherent structure. Spatial and other attributes of events are analysed and encoded at input, while the temporal properties of retrieved events are *inferred* from contextual features encoded as part of the episodic trace and from the ordinal position of the event relative to others. Thus, episodic memory is not seen as a system with a built-in time marker, but a rather structureless system which maintains the order in which episodes occur but does little else. The fact that we can perceive temporal rhythms may necessitate some modification of this statement, at least as far as recent events are concerned. In the same way that literal properties of visual and auditory events are apparently preserved for short times, so a literal record of temporal sequences may be available for a limited time after their occurrence.

We see semantic memory as a system whose function is essentially one of interpreting incoming stimuli as a basis for deciding on some relevant action. Thus, episodic memory contains copies of these interpretations or 'prescriptions for action'. While it is undoubtedly not worthwhile debating whether the memory trace is the end result of perceptual *input* processes or is the 'efferent copy', a copy of *output* instructions, some emphasis on the latter view is probably useful since it stresses the active, dynamic role of memory as opposed to the view of the memory trace as a dead, inactive residue.

After an episodic trace has been laid down, it can still be accessed from its 'home base' in semantic memory. That is, when the event recurs, and if it is processed in a similar way, this repetition of the encoding operation helps to evoke the memory of the original event. In our scheme the repeated encoding operations serve as a basis for 'reconstruction' of the encoding induced by the original event. Formation of the test encoding is constrained on the one hand by the test stimulus and on the other by information from the episodic trace. It is also suggested that traces may be accessed in a quite different way, by searching back through recent episodic memory, using the retrieval information to *select* the relevant items from other recent items. Thus episodic traces can be accessed either directly from semantic memory or by a scanning procedure through recent episodic memory.

Utilization of the Stored Trace

We suggest that the memory system has two modes of retrieval available. The first of these may be described as a process of reconstruction and the second as a search or scanning operation in which recent episodic traces are examined for the presence of some salient feature of the retrieval probe. These notions are explored further below.

Retrieval by Reconstruction—The 'Resonance' Metaphor

What happens when a stimulus pattern is recognized? Phenomenologically, a feeling of familiarity is experienced, but we can also locate the previous occurrence of the event in some specific temporal and spatial context. That is, conscious experience contains features induced by the stimulus pattern itself contextual features which were present during the first occurrence of the event. Recognition can thus be described as a process in which some approximation to the initial encoding of the event is *reconstructed* in the perceptual/cognitive system. The reconstruction is guided and constrained by the recognition stimulus on the one hand and information from the episodic trace on the other.

If good recognition depends on achieving a highly similar encoding to that induced on the item's first presentation, then it is easy to see why memory performance improves as the stimulus-plus-context presented at the time of test approximates more closely to the stimulus-plus-context presented when the item was learned initially. But this view, recognition is generally superior to recall since the recognition stimulus can evoke a similar encoding more easily. It is more difficult to see how the specific context surrounding the item's first presentation is reachieved. Initial context cannot be induced by the test context and must be derived from the episodic trace. How does the present stimulus contact traces of its previous occurrences? We have no complete answer to this central question, but offer an analogy which may help in conceptualizing the process.

It is suggested that when a particular pattern of encoding operations is induced by the test stimulus, *all* episodic traces of the pattern are contacted and help to constrain further reconstructive encoding of the stimulus. If there are many traces of the pattern, a 'familiar' encoding will be achieved easily (since it is guided by many previous traces and thus easily encoded), but the stimulus will not elicit recognition of a *specific* previous instance (since many different contexts are competing for conscious awareness). If the pattern was unique or distinctive, however, only one or a few traces of such a pattern exist—now if the retrieval information (the test stimulus) is specific enough, the previous trace will be contacted and the present encoding will contain contextual features from the initial encoding.

One metaphor for the basic mechanism of such a model of the recognition process is the phenomenon of resonance. The test encoding is viewed as analogous to the application of a specific frequency which tends to elicit, as feedback, sympathetic vibrations in all the episodic 'tuning-forks' set to that frequency. However, the parallel to physical resonance breaks down at this point since we want to say that if many episodes share the features of the test encoding, each episode will be stimulated only slightly. Thus the mixed metaphor is a 'limited energy resonance model'—if there are few tuning-forks (episodes) at that frequency, each will be stimulated to a greater extent. Of course, the resonance model is substantially more passive than the notion we wish to convey. Rather than the stimulus simply 'evoking' or 'activating' the trace, we prefer to think of the trace shaping the encoding of the test stimulus as it develops, the resonance mechanism providing the necessary feedback. It

84

follows from these notions that deeper, more elaborate encodings will be recognized better since such encodings are more unique and distinctive. By this view, too, there is nothing magical about the fact that rare words are recognized better than common words—rare words are more unique, they have occurred less often and fewer competing traces are contacted by the retrieval information. This in turn means that it is easier for the retrieval system to reconstruct the specific episode of 'occurrence in the presentation list'. If a common word is made more unique, for example if it is qualified by an unusual adjective, then it should also be well recognized—thus 'dog' is poorly recognized while 'crimson dog' may be well recognized. The interaction of word frequency with recognition and recall is discussed further below.

To this principle of distinctiveness we add two further components of good recognition. The first is the 'richness' of the encoding—the number of features analysed at input and thus laid down in the episodic trace—and the second is a 'set to recognize' factor. By the first point we mean that good recognition is partly a function of the number of features which the presentation and test encodings have in common; other things being equal, 'richer' traces will be better recognized. A trace is enriched if features of the context are encoded with it, or if it is modified or qualified in some specific way—if the same features are encoded at test, then recognition has a higher chance of success. By the second point we mean that some further factor may facilitate 'trace contact' and thus the reconstruction of an encoding similar to the initial encoding. This factor may be described as a 'set to recognize'. Although undoubtedly recognition occurs when the subject does not expect a recurrence of the event, recognition (and perhaps false alarms) may be enhanced if the subject encodes the test stimulus with a view to making a recognition decision. 'Set' in this situation may take the form of active construction of plausible contexts in an attempt to contact previous traces.

Thus, subjective feelings of recognition may accompany two types of situation. First, when a common event is presented it is encoded easily since many previous traces facilitate the present encoding. In this case recognition is a function of 'repetition of operations' as suggested by Kolers (1973). In the second case—repetition of an uncommon or distinctive event—the feeling of recognition is based on the reconstruction of the initial presentation context. One way of stating these suggestions is to say that common events will typically give rise to strong feelings of familiarity in semantic memory—the subject is extremely familiar with the meaning and connotations of the word 'dog', but cannot recall where or when he heard the word uttered on previous occasions. Unique or distinctive events have a much greater chance of being recognized as specific episodes even although they are not so familiar in the semantic sense. In point of fact, a common event may not even give rise to a feeling of recognition in semantic memory. If the event is highly probable and expected in a particular context, it can apparently be assimilated by the system with a minimal amount of analysis—thus highly familiar objects in your living-room do not typically give rise to strong feelings of recognition whenever you

glance round the room, although if conscious attention is brought to bear on
the object for some reason it is felt to be familiar. Paradoxically, it is when the
object or event is missing or out of context that consciousness is involved.
This is the phenomenon of dishabituation, described by Sokolov (1963) in
terms of a mismatch between the encoded stimulus and some internal representation. In our terms, the context induces the system to construct expectancies
which are usually confirmed by a minimal analysis of the incoming stimulus.
When the new analysis clearly does not confirm the expected patterns, conscious attention must be invoked to carry out the much more elaborate processing
now necessary to identify the unexpected event or to ascertain why the expected
event is missing. In the expected case, memory for the event will be poor since
few features were analysed, while, by the converse argument, memory for
unexpected events will be good.

In this system, recall is also viewed as a reconstructive process. Again, the
information presented at retrieval provides the basis for the reconstruction,
but since this information is typically rather meagre, more information must
now be contributed by the system—either from well-practised encoding
routines or from the episodic trace itself. Thus recall, like recognition, is
conceived of as 'guided reconstruction'. We believe that recall and recognition
do not differ in any crucial way—they are different only in the sense that in
recognition re-presentation of the stimulus provides better information from
which the initial encoding can be reconstructed. The initial encoding contains
features induced by the nominal stimulus and features induced by the context:
in recognition, the stimulus is re-presented and the system has to reconstruct
the context; in recall, some aspects of the context are re-presented or referred
to and the system has to reconstruct the stimulus. Thus, again, recall involves
contacting the episodic trace, and it is postulated that the reconstructive processes are constrained and guided by episodic information—if reconstruction is
proceeding on the right lines, further reconstruction of the same type is encouraged by feedback from the episodic trace.

We would like to distinguish our suggested recall process from two other
suggestions made by previous workers—the 'search' analogy and 'generate–
recognize' models. First, the idea of recall as a search process implies a blind
procedure in which stored events are examined either systematically or at
random until the desired information is located. In contrast, we believe that
the actual process of constructing the encoding at retrieval is guided by feedback
of an increasingly specific kind from the trace. Second, our suggestion differs
from 'generate–recognize' models in that the present system deals with partial
information, not necessarily with totally reconstructed events. Thus, if the
reconstruction is accurate in general terms, 'positive feedback' will result
and further reconstruction along the same lines is encouraged. This 'guided
reconstruction' is seen as a servomechanism in which feedback from the
target controls the reconstructive processes in semantic memory. This system
is quite different from a generate–recognize model in which complete items
are constructed and then matched with episodic events.

Both recall and recognition are superior when 'deeper', 'richer', 'more semantic' traces are formed at input. There is much evidence to support this claim at an empirical level (e.g. Hyde and Jenkins, 1969; Craik, 1973). By the present view, the beneficial effect of depth of encoding is that deeper, richer encodings are also more distinctive and unique; thus their resulting episodic traces are more easily contacted (the resonance metaphor) and the richer information may then provide more adequate feedback to guide further reconstruction.

This section has dealt with the retrieval of stored events by means of a repetition of encoding operations. It should be pointed out that this notion is radically different from a scheme which postulates one memory store with 'time-tags' to denote occurrence information. By the present view, when a probe item is encoded, it does not 'point' to an area of *time* in episodic memory, but rather to similarly encoded *events*. In this system, time is inferred from various cues (e.g. the ordinal storage of events; linking the event to well-established times and dates; etc.) in much the same way that in visual perception depth is inferred from input cues. The suggestion that the time or dating of an event is not coded directly but is inferred from other stored events is illustrated by the findings of Warrington and Sanders (1971); when subjects were asked to date various events which had been in the news, they were only able to estimate the date of an event in relation to other well-established dates in their lives.

The 'Selection' Function of Cues—Looking Back in Recent Memory

So far we have talked about using retrieval information as a means of contacting the episodic trace and as a basis for reconstructing an encoding of the original event. However, we believe that retrieval cue information (in both recognition and recall) can be used in a different fashion when the target trace has been laid down recently. In this second retrieval method, some salient aspect of the probe information is held and recent episodic traces are scanned for the presence of this salient feature. The scanning process is analogous to Neisser's (1964) visual scanning procedure, in which the subject rapidly scans a visual array of letters for some target letter. In the recent memory situation, the subject knows from the probe item that he is searching for an episode with some specific feature—it rhymes with TRAIN or is a synonym of GOOD. When the probe information is not particularly distinctive, it may be more efficient to use the information as a selector device rather than as a means of gaining access to all previous episodes which share the probe features.

When retrieval information is used in this fashion, different factors affect the success of the recognition operation. Now the most important factor is not the similarity of probe and target attributes, but the salience of the information used to pick out the target event from other recent events. Just as a target K can be very easily picked out from a context of round letters (e.g. O,P,Q,C) in Neisser's paradigm, so a distinctive event can be located in recent memory—the demonstration by Kroll *et al.* (1970) that a visual letter is better retained than an auditory letter over a period of auditory shadowing might be explained in this way. Thus, the critical feature of the scanning operation is the ease or difficulty of *discriminating* between the target and other recent traces. In this sense, 'surface structure' such as visual or phonemic features may well be as good or even better than deeper semantic features when used as selector information. This state of affairs may be contrasted with information used in the reconstruction mode—in that case semantic information is much more effective in achieving correct recognition since more features are involved and each collection of features is highly distinctive. These two ways in which retrieval information may operate are to be thought of as optional alternatives in the same system; they are modes of retrieval, much as suggested by Tulving (1968a) but with the difference that in the present system the same type of information may be used in either mode—we have no wish to equate the selector mode with phonemic information and reconstruction with semantic functioning.

Why postulate two retrieval modes? In our view, a number of experimental results make the notion a necessary one. Several recent studies have shown clearly that if a word is encoded in terms of its semantic features, it is much better recalled and recognized than if it is encoded in terms of the phonemic features; similarly, phonemic encoding is better than structural encoding (Craik, 1973; Hyde and Jenkins, 1969; Schulman, 1971). On the basis of these and similar studies, Craik and Lockhart (1972) suggested that deeper, more semantic coding yielded a more durable trace. However, there are some other studies whose results are curiously at odds with the notion that semantic encoding gives rise to a longer-lasting trace. Bregman (1968), Shulman (1970) and Jacoby (1974) all presented lists of words which were then tested by several types of probe—semantic, phonemic, structural, etc. All these authors found the 'decay rate' of recently presented words was unaffected by the type of probe used.

The apparent contradiction in these two sets of studies can be resolved by the suggestion that in the Hyde and Jenkins type of study, subjects are using the retrieval information to reconstruct the event, while in the Bregman type of study, the information is used to select the target from other recent items. The factors which induce subjects to use retrieval information in one way or another have not yet been elucidated, but one strong possibility is that subjects use the information to select the target if scanning back through recent events is feasible—that is, if the subject judges that the target item occurred fairly recently. A study by Craik and Jacoby (1975) bears out this conjecture. Subjects were induced to encode words either structurally (is the word in upper case letters?), phonemically (does the word rhyme with TRAIN?) or semantically (is the word a piece of furniture?). Interspersed with these encoding trials were recognition trials—target words were re-presented for recognition after 0–23 intervening trials. Figure 1A shows that while recognition declined with increasing lag, the type of encoding question made no

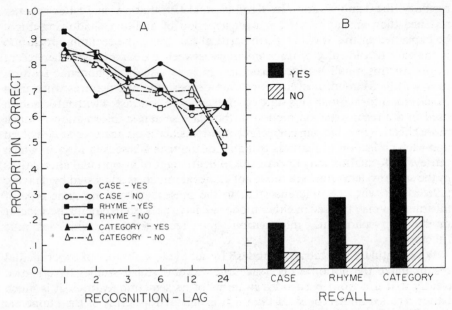

Figure 1. Initial recognition (A) and delayed recall (B) for items subjected to different initial encodings. From Craik and Jacoby (1975). Reproduced by permission of Lawrence Erlbaum Associates, Inc., Publishers

difference to the recognition rate. The study thus replicates the essential features of the experiments by Bregman, Shulman and Jacoby. However, after the encoding and recognition phase of the study was complete, subjects were unexpectedly asked to recall all the words they could; the results are shown in Figure 1B. Now there is a dramatic difference in the patterns of results—semantic encoding is better than phonemic, which exceeds structural, and at each level the questions which yielded 'yes' responses on the encoding trial gave rise to better recall than those which yielded 'no' responses. This latter pattern of results replicates the study reported by Craik (1973) and is similar to Hyde and Jenkins' (1969) and Shulman's (1971) findings. Thus, in the same study, different types of encoding may or may not yield differential memory effects. Our suggestion is that no coding differences are found when subjects use the scanning or selector retrieval strategy, but that coding differences emerge when the reconstruction strategy is used. It seems likely that at least some short-term memory phenomena may be attributed to the use of the selector retrieval strategy (Craik and Jacoby, 1975).

A final point of interest is the observation that there is at least one other example of two 'retrieval modes' in nature. We have in mind the manner in which honey bees convey information about a food source to their hive mates (Von Frisch, 1953). If the source of honey is near the hive, the bee returns and performs a particular series of movements or dance, other bees follow her and smell the odour of the honey she has brought back. In this case, the finder does not pass on location information, she simply gives the other bees the chance to smell the honey, which in turn enables them to determine the kind of flower to look for. When they leave the hive they fly in all directions, but many soon find the new food source since they have the information to *select* appropriate flowers. If the food source is far from the hive, however, a second type of dance is performed which gives information about distance and direction as well as information about the kind of flowers to look for. There is an interesting parallel here to our two suggested modes of retrieval from memory—if the event was recent, the retrieval information is used to select the desired episode from other recent events; if the event was not recent, however, retrieval information is used to locate the items directly in the memory system.

Craik and Lockhart argued that deeper, semantic processing yielded a more 'durable' code. An alternative view, which fits more readily into the present scheme, is that all encoded events are equally durable—traces are not lost from the system—but that some traces become impossible to access because they are not distinctive but similar to many other events. Thus, only very recent events of this type can be retrieved—and they are accessed by means of the scanning operation. Events which are encoded in a richer, semantic fashion may be accessed by either retrieval mode. If the event is recent or if the subject is under time pressure, he may choose to locate the item by scanning, otherwise he may use more of the retrieval information to gain access to the trace; in the first case, semantic information will not yield superior performance or evidence of a more durable trace (since semantic distinctiveness in this surface sense is not a better basis for discrimination than phonemic or structural distinctiveness), but in the second case, semantic information will be superior since the encoded event is more distinctive and the episodic trace can be contacted more readily by semantic retrieval information. This speculative account leads to the interesting prediction that if an event is encoded semantically it may or may not yield superior performance depending on the retrieval mode used. Evidence for this is provided in the studies of Jacoby (1974) and in the data shown in Figure 1.

Finally, it should be stressed that the scanning or selector retrieval mode is just as applicable to recognition as it is to recall. If a word is presented for recognition, and the subject believes that the word has been presented recently, he may abstract some salient feature of the probe word and search back through recent episodes using the abstracted features as selector information. In this sense, short-term probe situations (where some feature is given as the retrieval information) may yield as good performance as short-term recognition, where the whole item is provided—an example is Shulman's (1970) study, in which homonym probes yielded as good performance as identical probes.

Some Empirical Issues Reexamined

Before considering certain theoretical questions, we should like to examine several direct consequences of the preceding analysis for some empirical issues of current interest.

Organization and Recognition

Our analysis permits a relatively straightforward account of the role played by organization in the recognition process. The term 'organization' is being used in its most general sense to refer to the incorporation of a nominal item into a larger perceptual or conceptual unit. Thus we wish to include the incorporation of an item into a superordinate category, the grouping or association of subsets of items within a list, and the interaction between nominal items (such as *head* and *light*) to form a functional item which may bear no simple relation to its component parts. It is doubtful whether these three forms of organization represent any important theoretical differences, and elements of all three might be operative in the encoding of any particular item.

The first point to be noted is that there can be no general answer to the question of whether or not organization facilitates recognition; it may facilitate, hinder or have no effect at all, depending on the relationship between such organization and the conditions at the time of the test. Insofar as organization represents increased depth and distinctiveness of processing, and test conditions are such to encourage identical processing of the probe, recognition should be enhanced. For one retrieval mode, such conditions would lead to a rapid reconstruction of the episodic trace, while if the scanning mode were adopted, they would ensure the selection of an effective cue. However, in recognition, the test-cue conditions are very much under the experimenter's control, and it is this fact that permits the deliberate manipulation of the similarity between the organizational processing of the item as originally presented and when re-presented as a probe.

It has become popular in recent years to demonstrate that the manipulation of probe processing can result in substantial decrements in recognition performance. Such results are scarcely surprising, and the techniques used are similar to those employed by Gestalt psychologists to demonstrate the effects of context, stimulus segmentation, embedding, etc. Thus ambiguous figures are replaced by ambiguous words (Light and Carter-Sobell, 1970; Tulving and Thomson, 1971) or the test word represents a component of the original item whose separate identity was embedded in a larger whole, as in Kohler's (1947) demonstration that elements of a previously seen figure may not be recognized if subsequently shown in isolation (Horowitz and Manelis, 1973; Tulving, 1968b).

It has been more difficult to demonstrate positive effects of organization on recognition. One reason for this is that the similarity between item and probe encoding is likely to be very high, even in a control or 'neutral' condition in which the experimenter does not explicitly set out to manipulate the relationship between the encodings. Several experiments have shown that encouraging organization during list presentation enhances recognition (D'Agostino,

1969; Jacoby, 1972a; Bower, Clark, Lesgold and Winzenz, 1969; Mandler, 1972). These effects probably reflect the deeper processing necessary to achieve the categorization, such processing being effective for recognition unless the encoding of the test item is explicitly biased in the manner described in the previous paragraph. There is some evidence that if test order is varied recognition is highest when the order most closely approximates study order (Jacoby, 1972a; Jacoby and Hendricks, 1973; Light and Schurr, 1973). This facilitation is interpreted in terms of the reinstatement of the study context at the time of test, thereby inducing greater similarity between the two encoding operations.

A further reason for the difficulty of showing positive effects is that recognition can be enhanced by organization only to the extent that other sources of information do not provide an adequate basis for recognition. Retention of physical or sensory characteristics may provide an alternative basis for recognition and may, in certain circumstances, prove to be more reliable. For example, an experiment by Horowitz and Manelis (1973) found that a context change between study and test was ineffective when items were presented visually rather than auditorally. This elimination of context effects was attributed to the additional source of physical information gained from visual presentation. Recognition on the basis of physical characteristics would also help explain the results reported by Davis, Lockhart and Thomson (1972), who found that recognition performance increased with item repetition, even when such repetitions occurred in a semantically misleading context. If physical or sensory characteristics become ineffective as a basis for recognition more rapidly than do semantic elements, then the influence of semantically based organization should become more evident with longer retention intervals. Such a result has been reported by Mandler (1972).

Optimal Encoding

An issue which has received recent attention is the question of test-appropriate strategies—that is, the notion that subjects process items differently depending on the type of test anticipated. This idea leads to the concept of *optimal encoding*, which refers to that encoding of the stimulus which anticipates (and thus makes maximum use of) those retrieval cues available at the time of test. (See, for example, Cooper and Monk, Chapter 5.) Most discussions of retrieval processes have considered the differential effectiveness of retrieval cues relative to a fixed, stored trace; but it is possible to consider the matter in reverse—the relative effectiveness of encoding operations for a given set of retrieval conditions. Insofar as the nature and availability of retrieval cues is fixed by the experimenter, performance may be enhanced by encoding operations which take these conditions into account.

Because recognition and free recall represent very different retrieval conditions, these paradigms provide a natural starting point for the investigation of test-appropriate strategies. Evidence that subjects adopt different encoding strategies depending upon whether a recall or recognition test is anticipated is still rather scant. However, there are now a few experiments showing that recognition is more rapid (Frost, 1972) and accurate (Carey and Lockhart, 1973; Tversky, 1973) when recognition rather than free-recall testing is anticipated. If cued recall represents an intermediate retrieval situation relative to free recall and recognition, then an intermediate form of encoding should be optimal. This idea was confirmed by Jacoby (1973b); cued recall performance was higher when subjects anticipated cued recall rather than free recall or recognition. Thus, there is evidence that subjects develop encoding strategies that are appropriate for cued recall and recognition tests.

In free-recall studies, the evidence is less clear. A frequent finding has been that the overall probability of free recall is independent of the form of retention test anticipated (Carey and Lockhart, 1973; Jacoby, 1973b; Tversky, 1973, exp. I). This overall similarity may mask subtler encoding differences, however. For example, in Jacoby's (1973b) study, further analyses revealed that subjects who had been led to expect a cued recall test recalled fewer categories but more instances of each category than the subjects who correctly anticipated the free-recall test. In the Carey and Lockhart experiment, more detailed analyses showed that the probability of free recall declined across intracategory serial positions when subjects were anticipating a free-recall test but remained stable across positions when a recognition test was anticipated. Thus, it appears that the same overall level of free recall was attained in different ways dependent upon the form of retention test that was anticipated.

In contrast to the studies cited above, Tversky (1973, exps. II and III) has demonstrated an overall free-recall advantage for subjects anticipating a free-recall rather than a recognition test. However, in Tversky's experiments, the words used were unrelated, not members of a limited number of categories with category instances presented together, as in the studies by Carey and Lockhart (1973) and Jacoby (1973b). In addition, Tversky's subjects who were told to expect a free-recall test were encouraged to organize the study material. Thus, it seems possible that Tversky's different results are due to the greater latitude her subjects had in organizing the material; in both the Jacoby and the Carey and Lockhart experiments, organization was heavily constrained by the presentation conditions.

As well as anticipating the retrieval environment, optimal encoding must also take into account the length and nature of the retention interval. This aspect is particularly important under the conditions where study time is limited, and some strategy of distributing study time and effort must be adopted. There is good evidence that subjects adopt different encoding strategies as a function of the anticipated retention interval. When retention was tested after a long delay, performance was higher for those subjects who expected the delay than for subjects anticipating a shorter retention interval (Götz and Jacoby, 1974). Also, Evans and Jacoby (1973) have shown that the provision of additional study time is more beneficial for memory over the long term if a delayed rather than a shorter retention test is anticipated; in the 'delayed' case subjects may indulge in deeper, semantic processing.

Similarly, several recent studies have shown that 'primary memory' items are poorly retained in a second, delayed recall test (Craik, 1970; Craik and Watkins, 1973) unless a delayed test is anticipated (Jacoby and Bartz, 1972). The processing which maximizes long-term retention may actually be less than optimal for immediate or short-term recall—that is, if subjects are induced to form deeper, elaborative codes, such encoding appears to be less efficient for immediate recall than shallower phonemic encoding (Mazuryk and Lockhart, 1974). In the case of negative recency in free recall, the poorer long-term retention of terminal items appears to be a direct consequence of an encoding strategy which optimizes *immediate* recall.

Much research remains to be done before a detailed account of optimal processing can be given. In the meantime, however, the possibility of test-appropriate encoding strategies should be considered before it is assumed that nominally identical study conditions are also functionally equivalent.

The Effects of Recognition on Subsequent Retrieval

We have suggested that recognition is executed via one of two possible retrieval modes. Even within each of these modes, however, the amount of processing necessary to make the recognition decision can vary considerably. In a very short-term recognition test, for example, it may be possible to make a 'same' decision on the basis of a few, relatively superficial (sensory) features and thus to make the decision quite rapidly. At longer retention intervals such features may no longer be effective, and deeper, more extensive analysis of the probe may be necessary. Thus, the act of recognition itself can demand varying depths of processing, depending on such factors as the retention interval, the similarity of surrounding items and the distinctiveness of the original episodic trace.

One method of indexing this increased processing is to measure decision latencies (Okada, 1971; Murdock and Dufty, 1972). For our present purposes this method has a number of disadvantages. It is frequently difficult to distinguish the time occupied by processing within the memory system from that spent in making the actual decision, and this division of time is likely to be sensitive to trade-off effects between speed and accuracy. Moreover, it cannot distinguish between the quality, as opposed to the quantity of processing, and in the context of the present discussion this distinction is crucial.

A preferred method of evaluating the process involved in recognition is to examine the effects of such processing on subsequent retrieval. That is, it should be possible to index the depth of processing involved in a given act of recognition by examining its effects on a subsequent retrieval. This approach is tantamount to treating recognition as an incidental orienting task and using it in the manner suggested by Craik and Lockhart (1972).

Consider an experiment in which subjects are given a series of single-item Brown–Peterson recognition trials. A word is presented, the subject counts backwards for 0, 2 or 8 seconds and then is presented with a probe word to which he must respond 'same' or 'different' as rapidly as possible. Under these conditions virtually no errors occur, but after 45 such trials an unexpected final free recall is given. The question of interest is whether final recall is a function of the length of the retention interval between the initial presentation of the item and its probe.

The results from such an experiment are shown in Figure 2 and the answer is clearly affirmative; when the probe is the same word, final free recall increases with the duration of the filled interval. No such increase occurs if the probe is a new word, a result which rules out an explanation in terms of covert rehearsal during the retention interval.

While the detailed explanation of these results may take many forms, their general interpretation seems quite clear; as the initial retention interval increases

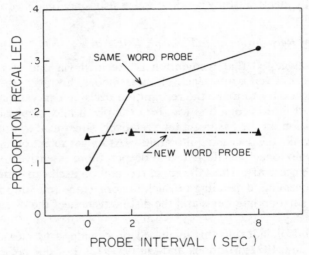

Figure 2. Delayed recall as a function of the probe (retention) interval in initial recognition

(and with it the degree of forgetting of the item) the depth of processing of the probe necessary to arrive at a 'same' decision also increases and thus, as a by-product, subsequent retrieval is facilitated.

Several points concerning these results can be made. Firstly, they suggest that even over the restricted range of retention intervals considered (0–8 seconds) there are substantial differences in the qualitative aspects of the retrieval processing involved in making the recognition response. Accounts of recognition memory which ignore the analysis and processing of the probe itself are missing what is perhaps the major aspect. It is important to remember that it is some encoded version of the probe and not the probe itself that is utilized to contact the stored trace.

Secondly, the results add weight to the conviction that examining the consequences of recognition for subsequent retrieval may be a fruitful approach to analysing recognition itself. It should be possible to establish systematic relations between the conditions under which recognition occurs (probe context, lure similarity, etc.) and subsequent retrieval (free or cued recall, recognition, etc.). A recent study by Bartlett and Tulving (1974) further exemplifies this approach.

The Word-Frequency Effect

It is well established that whereas common words (like TABLE, DOG) are better recalled than rare words (like GIMLET, ATOLL), the superiority is reversed in recognition—that is, rare words are recognized better than common words (Kintsch, 1970b; Gregg, Chapter 7). From the standpoint of the present system, two factors are invoked to account for the recognition result. First, common words are relatively easily encoded and thus the resultant episodic trace is not particularly rich; rare words demand more analysis and result in a richer trace. Second, the attributes comprising the trace of a rare word form a more distinctive and unique event in episodic memory; thus when the word is re-presented for recognition, the encoded probe word evokes the episode more easily. It seems likely, also, that rare words give rise to more nearly identical encodings on successive occasions—ATOLL or GIMLET thought of in the same way on each exposure, while TABLE or DOG may lead to somewhat different encodings from one occasion to the next. Another way of expressing this difference is to say that the meaning of low-frequency words is less sensitive to changes in context. By this view, the encoded attributes of a low-frequency (rare) probe are more likely to 'overlap' the attributes of the encoded first presentation. It is suggested, then, that rare words are better recognized since their traces are richer and more unique, and since successive presentations yield highly similar encodings.

Furthermore, since the meaning of a low-frequency word is less obvious and since the word itself thus demands more processing before its gist is extracted, more attention will be paid to the word's surface features—its constituent letters, phonemes and syllables. Thus the encoded trace of a low-frequency word may contain a substantial 'physical' or surface-features component. One experimental result which fits this view was reported by Schulman (1967); he found that polysyllabic words (compared to shorter words) boosted recognition performance for low-frequency words but not for high-frequency words—the polysyllabic words may have resulted in a richer physical trace for the rare words.

In the present system, recall is conceptualized as the guided reconstruction of the original encoding from the basic information provided by the retrieval information. On the other hand, recognition relies less on the reconstructive efforts of the system since more retrieval information is provided by the stimulus; in this case, the uniqueness and distinctiveness of a low-frequency word are the factors which give rise to its superior recognition.

We would like to get away from Kintsch's (1970b) proposal that recall consists of search and decision phases while recognition involves only the latter phase. As Tulving and Thomson (1973) point out, this model rules out the possibility that recall could be superior to recognition but, in fact, this outcome is demonstrated by these authors. However, rather than talk about recognition and recall being 'on a continuum', we prefer to think of the processes reflecting *different aspects* of the same system. Recall and recognition have some operations in common; the similarity between the procedures will depend on the particular situation. Thus, since recall and recognition reflect different questions being asked of the system, it should not be too surprising that some variables, such as word frequency, affect the processes in different ways.

Some Theoretical Issues Reconsidered

The Effects of Expectancy on Encoding

It has been argued that the episodic trace is a by-product of the perceptual operations carried out on the stimulus input. Since these operations themselves may be modified by various factors, it follows that the episodic trace will be rich or impoverished depending on the amount of perceptual processing necessary to carry out the original perceptual task. One factor which influences the ease of perception is expectancy. If a particular word is expected (due to prior experience, immediate context or instructions, for example) then it will be recognized easily, with a minimum of perceptual analysis; if the word is not expected, more processing will be necessary to identify the word. Thus the end product—word identification—is the same in both cases, but since fewer perceptual operations are required in the first case, the resultant episodic trace will be less rich than the second trace.

Expectancy serves much the same role for encoding as set does in problem-solving. Set may facilitate or retard problem-solving, and similar effects are expected with the encoding of verbal material. Facilitating effects usually stem from increasing efficiency as intermediate steps are deleted in a manner similar to practice at a skill. We should like to carry this parallel one step further by examining its consequences for retention. Increasing the efficiency of encoding by the dropping out of steps will have the consequence of excluding these steps from the episodic trace. Thus, paradoxically, when expectancy facilitates initial encoding, it reduces the richness, and later effectiveness, of the resulting memory trace.

Before going on to deal with some negative effects of expectancy on encoding, one positive example will be cited. One function of expectancy is to focus attention on those aspects of the stimulus that are important for confirmation or denial of the expectancy. This focusing of attention has the effect of reducing the number of aspects of the stimulus that are processed and affects memory in that only those aspects of the stimulus that have been given attention will be remembered. One example of this principle comes from an experiment by Quartermain and Scott (1960). Subjects were instructed to find a key that had been hidden in the room. In a later test of their retention for the contents of the room, subjects were best able to remember those things that could have contained a key. Instructions to find a key led subjects to deal with only particular aspects of the total stimulus situation, and it was only those aspects that had been dealt with that were well remembered.

The negative effects of expectancy are really further examples of the same general principle. When context makes a word highly expected, it is necessary to deal with only a few of the word's physical features in order to identify it. Thus if the word is embedded in a context of continuous prose, physical features such as misspellings, type font, and so on, can go unnoticed and will form little or no part of the episodic trace.

In addition to limiting the physical aspects of a stimulus that are dealt with during encoding, expectancy or prior experience in a situation may also reduce the number of cognitive operations required to arrive at an encoding. This point is best illustrated with an example. Suppose that a subject has been given the problem of adding 35 and 17. After he has produced 52 as a correct answer, he is immediately given the same problem. On this second occasion, the subject is likely to give the sum from memory rather than constructing a solution by adding the two numbers. The external stimuli, 35 and 17, have served only to bring the sum to mind, so that the relationships intermediate to the final solution have been completely bypassed. As a result, the intermediate relationships will not be represented in the memory trace of the second problem occurrence and cannot be used later to aid in reconstruction of either the problem or the solution. Again, the same principle is likely to apply to the encoding of verbal material. Retention over the long term requires more than simple pronunciation of an item. If an item is to be remembered, it must be placed in relationship with other events so that a structure involving the item is constructed. As in the arithmetic example, prior experience can limit the number of operations required in the construction. A case in point is the transition of a metaphor to a cliché. As a result of frequent use, the components of a metaphor are no longer compared in order to construct a meaning. Rather, the metaphor leads directly to a meaning in the same way that the two numbers in the arithmetic example led to their sum.

Examples given above have illustrated two ways in which prior experience or expectancy can influence the encoding of a stimulus. First, stimulus priming may occur so that few physical aspects of the stimulus are attended to in order to identify it. In addition, the operations required to give the stimulus a place in a structure may be abbreviated or totally bypassed due to the reproduction of a prior encoding from memory. In contrast to an interference theory of forgetting (e.g. Postman and Underwood, 1973), the present position emphasizes the encoding of a stimulus input as well as the process occurring during the retention interval. The failure to recognize or recall particular details of a stimulus may be due to failure to deal extensively with those aspects during encoding as well as an effect of interference during the retention interval or at the time of test. The next few paragraphs will illustrate how our position can be applied in the interpretation of several memory phenomena.

The first data areas to be examined are those of learning to learn and proactive inhibition. Increased efficiency in performing a task after practice on similar tasks is a common observation in both verbal and non-verbal situations. For example, when several unrelated lists of paired associates are learned, fewer trials are required to reach a performance criterion on lists presented later in the series. One interpretation of this improvement (Warr, 1964) is that subjects are performing the same operation for all lists but quickening the performance of those operations with practice. That is, subjects are learning the same thing about words in later lists as those in earlier ones but doing it faster. This appears to be the interpretation of learning to learn that underlies attempts to control degree of original learning in studies of proactive inhibition. The notion is that degree of original learning must be controlled by equating performance levels on an immediate test before differences in rate of forgetting can be detected (Underwood, 1964). When multiple lists are learned, later lists are presented for fewer trials since a performance criterion is reached more rapidly due to the effects of learning to learn. Proactive inhibition is then shown by the rapid forgetting of lists learned later in the series and explained in terms of interference between lists at the time of test. According to our view, attempts to equate degree of original learning have been unsuccessful and proactive inhibition is at least partially due to subjects learning less about later lists in the series.

Rather than a quickening of operations, learning to learn can be seen as the result of a reduction in the number of operations performed. Words in earlier lists are dealt with more extensively in order to meet the same performance criterion as words in later lists. Some operations performed on earlier lists are unnecessary to satisfy the performance criterion imposed on the immediate test so they are eliminated from the learning of subsequent lists. However, some of those operations that have been eliminated are important in aiding the reproduction of list items in the long term. If this view is correct, the amount learned is not equated by continued training on successive lists until a common criterion is gained or by the more elaborate techniques proposed by Underwood (1964). A performance criterion can be gained in a number of ways, so an equivalence in immediate recall performance does not imply equal learning in the sense of equally rich encodings. An alternative approach would be to equate lists on the number of exposures or study time rather than on a performance criterion. When this is done, proactive inhibition is largely eliminated (Warr, 1964). However, equating study time is not a totally satisfactory solution either. There are still likely to be differences in the particular operations performed as a function of learning to learn, although study time is equated. A subject who has gained experience with a task is unlikely to act as if he were naive simply because he is required to spend the same amount of time on the task as he did originally. If we are to understand proactive inhibition, we must first understand the operation of learning to learn. Proactive inhibition is likely to be a consequence of changes in operations performed on the study material as well as interference between lists at the time of test.

The notions described earlier can also be applied to the effects of proactive inhibition in the Brown–Peterson paradigm. Our analysis would emphasize the effect of prior lists on the encoding of items in later lists. When instances of the same category are presented on successive trials, subjects may come to expect instances of that category, so that the operations necessary to identify a presented category member are abbreviated. In this regard, the situation is analogous to the example of presenting the same addition problem twice in succession. For items presented later in the series, dimensions or attributes that are common across lists can be given directly from memory, and require little new construction.

The last data area to be examined in this section is that of the spacing of repetitions. Both recall and recognition are generally found to be enhanced when repetitions of an item during study are spaced rather than continuous. Our interpretation of the spacing effect is that the continuous repetition of an item leaves the analysing processes so highly activated or 'primed' that further encodings of the item involve very few operations. This view is very similar to that presented by Lockhart (1973). That is, the final product can be repeated or rehearsed without constructing that encoding anew when repetitions are massed. Again, the situation is quite similar to the example of solving the same arithmetic problem twice in a row. The sum of the numbers or a final encoding can be repeated without repeating all of the operations which were originally necessary to construct the sum or final encoding.

Data supporting our interpretation of the spacing effect come from several sources. First, there is now a large body of data showing that reaction time to a stimulus input is decreased if that input is a repetition of an immediately prior event (e.g. Remington, 1969). Thus, massed repetitions either quicken the operations or, as we would prefer to argue, reduce the number of operations that are required, prior to responding. In the retention literature, the effect of spacing of retentions has been attenuated when each repetition is accompanied by a different modifier (Jacoby, 1972b; Gartman and Johnson, 1972; Madigan, 1969). This effect has been interpreted as showing that retention is enhanced by increasing the number of access routes to an item in memory. However, it is just as reasonable to conclude that a change in modifiers is important because it requires the subject to go through constructive acts prior to arriving at a final encoding of a repetition. That is, for massed repetitions without a new modifier, the subject may go directly to an earlier final encoding rather than constructing it. With spaced repetitions, the encodings of a repeated item might be quite similar, but due to forgetting during the interval between presentations, the subject has constructed the encodings for each of the repetitions. One very nice piece of evidence for this position comes from an investigation by Hintzman, Block and Summers (1973). In that investigation, each presentation of an item was presented in a different modality, auditory or visual. A later test for modality of input then allowed retention to be traced to each presentation of an item. Application of this technique revealed that it was retention of the second presentation of a repeated item that suffered under conditions of massed repetition. This result is precisely what would be expected if encoding of a massed repetition was highly primed so that a subject paid little attention to the physical characteristics of the item in order to identify it.

The STM/LTM Distinction

Does the present system retain the distinction between short-term and long-term memory? In their previous model Craik and Lockhart (1972) proposed that memory is essentially one system, but that subjects can also retain information by maintaining activity in some part of the analysing structures. This 'maintenance processing' at some specific level of analysis was seen as equivalent to keeping the item in consciousness, paying attention to the item, rehearsing the item or retaining the item in primary memory. The characteristics of short-term memory defined in this way would thus not be absolute but would depend on the level of analysis at which processing was maintained—at deeper levels, encoding would be more semantic in nature, 'capacity' would be greater in that more use could be made of learned rules, and the rate of forgetting would be slower since deeper processing yields a more durable code.

In the present model we want to keep the notion that retention in primary (or short-term) memory is equivalent to continued activation of some part of the analysing structures, but also incorporate Jacoby's (1974) suggestion that many short-term memory phenomena are attributable to the retrieval strategy used—that is, recent items are scanned, and the target selected on the basis of some characteristic specified by the retrieval question. The main point we wish to make is that the notion of one short-term memory mechanism with a range of specific characteristics (limited capacity, acoustic coding, etc.) may be an oversimplification—rather, we should think of the phenomena of recent memory and ascribe these phenomena to the different questions asked, and to the different strategies employed by the system.

First, some short-term phenomena are ascribed to the continued activation of the analysing structures, with the subjective concomitant that the items are still 'in mind'; memory-span tasks and the Sternberg reaction-time task (when small set sizes are used) may be described in these terms. Other phenomena of recent memory, involving matching or probe techniques may be tapping the scanning or 'looking back' strategy (Jacoby, 1974)—Shulman's (1970) results and Waugh and Norman's (1965) probe-digit technique are examples of this mode of operation.

As a further suggestion, the reconstruction strategy may also be more effective for recently presented items—since the specific processing operations have recently been performed and possibly because recent traces provide more effective feedback and guidance to the reconstructive processes. Recency effects with this retrieval strategy should be relatively 'long-term' in nature (that is, not transient fragile effects), and such recency phenomena have been reported by Bjork and Whitten (1972) and by Tzeng (1973). In summary, we believe that it still makes sense to distinguish 'short-term' from 'long-term' memory, but the characteristics of short-term retention will depend not only on material and task (which in turn will influence the depth of encoding), but also on the retrieval strategy utilized by the subject.

Recognition and Recall—Concluding Comments

We are now in a position to make some concluding comparisons between recognition and recall. In the first place, it seems clear that there is little to be gained by attempting to answer such global questions as whether or not recognition involves a search or retrieval phase and whether or not it can be distinguished from recall on this basis. Such questions presuppose a view of memory which is altogether too simple. The only sensible approach is to examine the form of processing necessary to execute the recall or recognition and then to document their similarities and differences.

We have argued that two basic modes of retrieval exist for recognition—reconstruction and scanning. The same two modes exist for recall, and in this sense it is possible to argue that recognition and recall are basically the same process. However, within each mode (whether it be recall or recognition) the processing may differ with task conditions. In the case of the reconstruction mode, the amount and depth of processing necessary to construct an encoding which will 'resonate' with the episodic trace can vary considerably, and if the term 'retrieval' is to be assigned a meaning which is more specific than the operational definition given in the introduction, it should be in reference to this process of reconstruction. In the case of recall, the reconstruction mode can be seen to operate in a similar fashion, the only difference being in the nature of the experimenter-provided information. In the case of recognition, the reconstruction process necessary to achieve resonance may be no more than the normal, and highly practised, analysis of meaning that typically occurs when a word is read or heard. In such cases recognition or familiarity would seem, in subjective experience, to be direct and involuntary—without the conscious awareness of a search process. In fact, if such analysis of the probe yields little or no resonance, the item will typically be rejected as new. Thus, if the context of the probe is such as to bias a very different meaning (as in Tulving and Thomson's 1971 study) a miss will frequently result. If resonance is present but weak, additional processing of the probe may be executed in an attempt to resolve the ambiguous status. Mandler's post-recognition retrieval check can be viewed as one form that this additional processing might take. As the degree of such processing extends beyond the initial 'reading' of the item, processing may be under more conscious control and a subjective sense of search memory may result.

In the case of recall, reconstruction of the episodic trace will typically demand more extended processing simply because the experimental situation provides less retrieval information. We have argued that this extended processing is not one of 'generate and recognize' but rather a continuous interplay between the reconstruction process and the episodic trace. Of course, a compelling feature of the 'generate and recognize' model is that recalled items must, in some sense, have been acknowledged as 'old' prior to overt recall; after all, subjects do not typically emit items they judge not to have been in the list. According to the views presented here, however, such final editing would usually be trivial, if indeed it occurred explicitly at all. Items which are generated as candidates for recall are not fortuitously old or new in a way analogous to a yes/no recognition test. The retrieval process itself ensures a high probability that such items will be list members. The important editing occurs, not *following* an item's retrieval, but as an integral part of the processing (which we have labelled 'guided reconstruction') involved in the item's production in the first place.

Recognition and recall, then, are not related by the former being a subcomponent of the latter; rather, one is typically a more extended—and in that sense more complex—version of the other. Moreover, the terms represent rather loose labels for what in fact is a variety of retrieval conditions, and the development of a comprehensive theory of human memory would be better served, not so much by direct comparisons of recognition and recall, but by a more detailed analysis of the processing involved in each.

Notes

1. This research was supported by grants from The National Research Council of Canada, No. A0355 to R. S. Lockhart and No. A8261 to F. I. M. Craik. We would like to thank P. Kolers, B. B. Murdock, Jr. and E. Tulving for their critical and helpful comments.

4 *Imagery in recall and recognition*

ALLAN PAIVIO

Imagery variables affect performance in a wide variety of recall and recognition memory tasks. This chapter is concerned primarily with the nature of the memory coding process responsible for such effects. Specifically, are the effects best explained in terms of perceptual images, verbal representations, a combination of both, or some kind of abstract semantic representation which is neither imaginal nor verbal? Still another possiblity is that the effects are mediated by some general factor such as depth of processing, as opposed to qualitatively distinct memory codes. These alternatives apply equally to recall and recognition, but it is possible that different codes, or at least a different combination of coding processes, would be involved in the two tasks at some stage between stimulus input and memory performance. If so, the information would bear generally on the distinctions (if any) between recall and recognition, and specifically on such issues as the role of encoding specificity in memory retrieval. Such possibilities will be explored to the extent permitted by the available facts.

The chapter is organized into the following sections: (a) a description of imagery variables, i.e. the procedures that have been used to manipulate or operationally define imagery, (b) a review of relevant theories, (c) an overview of the effects of imagery variables in various memory tasks, (d) a more detailed comparison of recall and recognition effects as a function of relevant variables, and (e) a summary of the empirical and theoretical conclusions suggested by the research to date.

Imagery as an Empirical Variable

Imagery is generally inferred from or manipulated in terms of stimulus attributes, experimental manipulations and individual difference tests. The most relevant stimulus attribute is the image-arousing value of stimulus material, with pictures or perceptual objects regarded as highest in imagery value, concrete words or sentences intermediate, and abstract verbal material lowest in imagery. The empirical and theoretical validity of such a continuum has been documented elsewhere (Paivio, 1971a), and imagery and concreteness ratings are available for a large number of nouns (Paivio, Yuille and Madigan,

1968). The most widely employed experimental method for manipulating imagery is the use of mnemonic instructions, in which subjects are asked to learn words, phrases or sentences by generating mental images of the objects or events suggested by verbal material. In addition, such procedures as fast rates of presentation and distracting visual tasks have been used as attempts to interfere with image arousal at some stage of memory performance. (For reviews of such experimental procedures, see Bower, 1972a; Paivio, 1971a, Chapters 10 and 11.) The third empirical approach relies on individual differences in imagery as inferred from spatial manipulation tests, subjective ratings of vividness of experienced imagery, and so on (see Marks, 1972; Paivio, 1971a, Chapter 14; Sheehan, 1966).

The three general approaches are designed to affect the availability of imagery, or the probability that such a process will be involved in some phase of the memory task. The probability of such involvement is presumably increased by the use of high-imagery material, instructions to use imagery, slow presentation rates, or subjects who are high in imagery ability. To the extent that similar results are obtained using the different procedures, they can be regarded as convergent operations in the empirical study of imagery. Such a view seems partly justified on the basis of available evidence, particularly in regard to item attributes and experimental manipulation. The predictive and theoretical status of individual difference variables is more uncertain and for that reason somewhat less attention will be paid to the literature in that area in the present review.

Some Theoretical Alternatives

The empirical effects of imagery variables on recall and recognition need not be interpreted only in terms of imagery as a theoretical process. Indeed, it seems unlikely that non-verbal imagery alone could account for memory effects when words serve as items, although it is a logical candidate and we shall consider it along with four other theoretical approaches, including verbal coding, dual coding, abstract representations and depth of processing.

Image Coding

A strong imagery interpretation would assert that any effects attributable to imagery variables are due entirely to the mnemonic properties of the image code. Such a code presumably would contribute to the distinctiveness of items or function as a mediator of response retrieval. If the response is verbal, it must also be assumed that it is retrievable from the non-verbal image without necessarily having been stored along with the image during encoding. Thus, a strong image hypothesis would appear to be inconsistent with Tulving and Thomson's (1973) encoding specificity hypothesis and with Rohwer's (1970) suggestion that imagery storage facilitates learning only when the image is accompanied by a verbal representation of the same event. Standing and Smith

(1974) have recently proposed a model for recognition memory of pictures or descriptions of pictures which appears to be essentially a strong image-coding theory. The model postulates specifically that both pictorial and verbal stimuli are encoded in a pictorial (or functionally equivalent) form to which subsequent transformations (e.g. verbal decoding) can be applied as required by the experimental task.

Verbal Coding

A second possibility is that the effects of imagery variables are mediated entirely by verbal processes. This was once a popular approach to the interpretation of both recall and recognition memory involving either words or pictures as items. It is clear now, however, that a strong verbal-coding hypothesis has difficulty explaining such simple facts as the superiority of pictures over words and of concrete words over abstract in many memory tasks. The theory could accommodate such findings only if it is also assumed that pictures evoke more elaborate verbal processes than do words (and concrete words more elaborate than abstract), and that such elaboration somehow enhances the memorability of stimuli. Such a theory has been effectively ruled out in a series of experiments which controlled the nature of verbal coding in free-recall tasks (Paivio and Csapo, 1973). It has also been rejected by Ellis (1972) as a sufficient explanation of recognition memory for non-verbal stimuli. For these reasons the strong verbal-encoding hypothesis will not be seriously considered in the present paper. Nonetheless, verbal processes undoubtedly play an important role in both recall and recognition tasks in collaboration with imagery or other factors. This possibility is given due weight in the following theoretical alternative.

Dual Coding

A third approach would explain many of the effects of imagery variables in terms of both imaginal and verbal processes. I have suggested (e.g. Paivio, 1972a) that these processes involve independent but partially interconnected systems for encoding, storage, organization and retrieval of stimulus information. The units of the imagery system are memory representations corresponding to concrete things. The units of the verbal system consist of stored representations corresponding more directly to linguistic units. Independence of these codes implies that either one can be available and activated in varying degrees, depending on stimulus attributes and experimental task conditions. One of the more important memory implications of this assumption is that the two codes can have additive effects on performance. The assumption of interconnectedness implies that one code can be transformed into the other, so that pictures can be named, words can evoke non-verbal images, and similar transformations can occur entirely at the cognitive level.

The dual-coding theory also incorporates the notion of distinct levels of information processing, which have been termed representational, referential and associative levels (Paivio, 1971a, Chapter 3; Paivio and O'Neill, 1970). Processing to the representational level refers to the activation of imaginal representations by non-verbal stimulus events and of verbal representations by linguistic stimuli. Referential processing refers to the activation of an established interconnection between images and verbal representations, so that a word arouses a non-verbal image, an object is named, or such exchanges occur entirely at an implicit level without being expressed in overt responses. The term 'referential' indicates that the interconnection corresponds to the semantic relation between words and things. This does not imply a one-to-one relation between a verbal representation and a particular image. It implies instead something analogous to a verbal-associative hierarchy: a word generated different images or an object different verbal descriptions depending on the subject's past experience and the context in which the referential reactions occur. Finally, associative processing refers to the activation of associations involving representational units within each of the two postulated systems. Verbal stimuli presumably elicit verbal reactions in an associative chain, and non-verbal perceptual images activate other imaginal representations through their interconnections within the imagery system.

The theory also assumes that the two representational systems have distinct functional properties. The most relevant of these for present purposes is that imagery is assumed to be specialized for spatial organization and synchronous integration of stimulus information. It is not specialized for sequential organization. Conversely, the verbal system presumably organizes units of linguistic information into higher-order sequential structures. This feature of the theory has implications for the relative effects of imagery variables in sequential and non-sequential memory tasks, and in associative as compared to non-associative ones.

Abstract Codes

A fourth theoretical approach to memory coding has become increasingly popular in recent years. According to this view, both verbal and non-verbal information is represented in some common abstract form, which can be described in terms of logical propositions (e.g. Anderson and Bower, 1973; Chase and Clark, 1972; Pylyshyn, 1973; Rumelhart, Lindsay and Norman, 1972). These theories have been able to account for certain data involving comparison tasks and memory tasks involving verbal material, but so far they have not been formulated in such a way that they could account for or predict many of the empirical findings which involve distinct effects of verbal and non-verbal stimuli or linguistic and imagery variables. Thus it is not clear whether this kind of approach is relevant to most of the phenomena under consideration here. Nonetheless, because of its present prominence, the abstract-entity theory will be referred to from time to time in the context of specific findings.

Levels of Processing

The final theoretical model to be considered is the levels-of-processing hypothesis, as proposed by Craik and Lockhart (1972; see also Chapter 3). The concept of processing levels was mentioned in relation to dual-coding theory. The Craik–Lockhart approach differs in principle from the dual-coding model in that memory performance is assumed to be a function of the depth to which an item has been encoded in memory, without any necessary reference to specific structural or functional differences between memory codes at any given level. Within the dual-coding theory, memory representations corresponding to non-verbal perceptual units and to linguistic units are assumed to be at the same (relatively superficial) level. Deeper processing is presumably involved whenever an interconnection is activated, but the process is equally deep whether it involves verbal coding of perceptual objects or image coding of words. Associative reactions within codes is still another kind of processing where the cognitive activity is not necessarily deeper than in the referential case but involves representations within the same coding system (e.g. word–word associations in the case of verbal associative coding and image–image association in the case of the imagery system). Whereas the depth-of-processing hypothesis attributes effects to the hypothetical depth or level variable, the dual-coding theory attributes effects to the functional distinctions between imaginal and verbal codes and to the number of codes activated in a given task. The different implications of the two types of depth theories have not been systematically tested in very many studies to date, but some relevant findings will be mentioned in the final section. The results also bear on a process approach to memory that has been put forward recently by J. J. Jenkins and his collaborators (e.g. Hyde and Jenkins, 1973; Walsh and Jenkins, 1973), in which the crucial task variable affecting memory is whether the task is semantic (deep?) or non-semantic (superficial?).

General Effects of Imagery on Recall and Recognition

This section presents a general overview of the effects of imagery variables on recall and recognition performance. Few of the studies to be reviewed here have been concerned with direct comparisons of recall and recognition (such studies will be considered in a later section). Nonetheless, allowing for considerable variation in the procedures involved in different studies, the literature indicates that imagery variables generally have comparable effects in recall and recognition tasks. Much of the early literature has been reviewed elsewhere (Paivio, 1971a; 1972a,b), and it will suffice here to cite some examples of the effects, especially those from recent studies, and to suggest what their implications are for the theories reviewed above. The research will be reviewed under the headings of non-cued memory for items, cued recall and recognition, and memory for sequential order.

Item Recognition and Recall Without Associative Cueing

Memory performance is better with pictures than with concrete words, which in turn are superior to abstract words both in free recall (e.g. Bevan and Steger, 1971; Kirkpatrick, 1894; Paivio and Csapo, 1973; Paivio, Rogers and Smythe, 1968; Sampson, 1970; Scott, 1967) and in item recognition (e.g. Davies, 1969; Gorman, 1961; Jenkins, Neale and Deno, 1967; Paivio and Csapo, 1969; Shepard, 1967; Standing, Conezio and Haber, 1970). The general impression is that the patterns of concreteness effects are rather similar for the two kinds of tasks. In one direct comparison of the relation between concreteness of nouns and memory in the two tasks, Olver (1965) found that dichotomous concrete–abstract scores correlated (biserial r) 0.41 with recall and 0.45 with recognition. Both correlations are highly significant and obviously comparable in magnitude.

Instructions to use imagery mnemonics also have been shown to have positive effects in both recall and recognition, although the effects are somewhat less consistent than that of imagery as an item attribute for the two tasks. Positive effects of imagery have been reported for free recall of concrete nouns by Kirkpatrick (1894) and for two-word phrases by Gupton and Frincke (1970) and Mueller and Jablonski (1970), but Rogers (1967) and Groninger (1972) failed to obtain significant effects. When recall is tested only incidentally, however, imaging to individual concrete nouns resulted in much higher recall than if the subject merely verbalizes to the items (Paivio and Csapo, 1973); in fact, imaging under such conditions raises word recall to the same level as pictures recall. In contrast to his free-recall results, Groninger (1972) did find that the accuracy of recognition memory for items was increased by imagery instructions (see also Groninger, Bell, Cymer and Wess, 1972). Such an effect has also been reported by Simpson (1972).

Imagery as measured by tests of individual differences has yielded a rather complex empirical picture that will not be discussed here in detail (see Paivio, 1971a, Chapter 14). Suffice it to note that the results of some studies conform to the straightforward expectation that high imagery ability should be associated with superior memory for 'pictureable' material. Stewart (1965) found that high imagery-ability subjects were superior to low imagers in picture recognition, while low imagers were better than high imagers on word recognition. Similar results were obtained by Ernest and Paivio (1971), but only for female subjects. Since Stewart used only females, it may be that the sex difference applies to both recognition and recall tasks, but the generalization is yet to be tested directly. On the negative side, Stewart (1965) found that low imagery subjects were superior to high imagers in the free recall of words, regardless of the imagery value (vividness) of the words. Similarly, Ernest and Paivio (1971) found that low imagery females were superior to high imagers in recalling words. These and other findings involving individual differences are difficult to interpret in terms of any straightforward theoretical model.

Aside from the individual difference results, the data on item recall and recognition are generally consistent with the dual-coding model. Specifically, they support the idea that independent imaginal and verbal codes have additive effects in memory tasks in which both can be aroused. This aspect of the theory accounts for many of the performance differences between pictures, concrete words and abstract words in terms of the simple assumption that the probability of dual coding is highest in the case of pictures of familiar objects (they are likely to be labelled by the subject), next highest in the case of concrete nouns (many subjects will imagine the objects suggested by the nouns) and lowest in the case of abstract nouns (subjects are least likely to image to such words because they lack direct linkages with corresponding non-verbal representations). This hypothesis also accounts for some effects involving mnemonic instructions in a straightforward manner: such instructions presumably increase the probability of, or prime, encoding activity in one systerm at the same time as the to-be-remembered items themselves evoke a memory representation in the other. Thus, imagery instructions will increase the probability that concrete nouns will arouse a non-verbal image as well as a verbal representation, thereby enhancing recall. Such interpretations have been strongly supported by a series of experiments in which free recall of pictures and words was tested under imaginal and verbal encoding conditions (Paivio and Csapo, 1973). The theory also accounts for interactions that have been observed between stimulus concreteness and rate of presentation (e.g. Paivio and Csapo, 1969). That is, a fast rate of presentation reduced the performance differences that are normally observed as a function of concreteness when slower rates are used, presumably because the fast rate impeded the associative arousal of images to words (as well as verbal labels to pictures). Other evidence consistent with functional independence of pictorial and verbal memory codes has been presented by Bahrick and Bahrick (1971) and Nelson and Brooks (1973).

The above findings are not so readily explained in terms of any uniprocess theory, whether expressed in terms of verbal coding, image coding or abstract semantic representations alone. A combination of factors is possible, of course. For example, the Paivio and Csapo (1973) experiments suggested that the superiority of pictorial and image-coding conditions over verbal conditions is best explained in terms of a combination of dual coding and image superiority. That is, the non-verbal image contributes more than the verbal code to their additive effect on memory. Dual-coding effects may also depend on active generation of one code under some circumstances (e.g. Davies, Milne and Glennie, 1973). Depth of processing remains another plausible alternative at this point, since it could always be argued that dual coding and imagery conditions simply ensure a deeper level of processing. The alternative interpretations will be considered again in a later section.

Studies Involving Associative Cueing

As in the case of free recall, performance in cued-recall tasks increases with item concreteness (e.g. Paivio, 1965; Paivio and Yarmey, 1966). This effect is stronger and more consistent when imagery is varied among items that function as retrieval cues for associative recall than it is when imagery is varied among the to-be-recalled response items. Two observations support the conclusion that this asymmetry in the effectiveness of imagery in associative recall is a retrieval phenomenon. First, if no retrieval cue is explicitly presented and subjects are instead asked to free recall both members of each pair of items, there is no differential facilitation by concreteness favouring either the left- or right-hand member of the pair (Yarmey and Ure, 1971; Yuille and Humphreys, 1970). Second, the concreteness effect is greater for the nominal 'response' (i.e. the right-hand or second member of the pair) when it serves as the retrieval cue, as in a test of backward association (e.g. Lockhart, 1969; Yarmey and O'Neill, 1969).

The asymmetrical retrieval function of imagery as a stimulus attribute also has implications for recognition tests of associative memory. Specifically, there should be no differential effect favouring concreteness of either member of a pair when a recognition test is used, inasmuch as either the nominal stimulus or the nominal response could function as the retrieval cue. Consistent with this view, Paivio and Rowe (1971) obtained an equivalent facilitative effect of word concreteness for both members of a list of pairs when associative learning was assessed by a matching test. Raser and Bartz (1968) presented their subjects with a list of word–word, word–picture, picture–word or picture–picture pairs once, and tested associative learning by a recognition procedure in which the stimulus member was presented along with seven response alternatives, one of which was the correct one. The results showed a significant facilitative effect of pictures as 'response' terms but not as 'stimulus' terms. The authors point out that the recognition procedure places more emphasis on the response term than does the usual paired-associate learning procedure. That is, subjects must differentiate among the response members. Under these conditions, it is not surprising that picture superiority was greater among the so-called response members.

Imagery mnemonic instructions also increased cued recall relative to standard control or rote-learning conditions (e.g. Bower, 1970; Schnorr and Atkinson, 1969; Yuille and Paivio, 1968) and sometimes in comparison with verbal mediation instructions as well (e.g. Paivio and Foth, 1970). Imagery instructions have also been shown to increase the accuracy of recognition memory for items under conditions in which subjects were presented pairs of words and were asked to generate compound or interactive images to the pair, but where recognition memory was tested for only one member of the pair (M. J. Peterson and Murray, 1973; Winograd, Karchmer and Russell, 1971). Bower (1970), however, failed to observe any positive effect of interactive imagery instructions on stimulus recognition, although the instructions strongly facilitated response recall. Peterson and Murray suggested that the discrepant results might be due to the fact that subjects in their experiment were given more time in both the study trials and stimulus recognition–response recall tests than was the case in Bower's experiment. Peterson and Murray concluded that interactive imagery instructions (as well as rated imagery value of items) enhance both the individual items and the associations. Peterson and McGee (1974) demonstrated further that interactive imagery instructions facilitated response recall as well as recognition of items and pairs. Curiously, however, item imagery (concreteness) did not aid response recognition or pair recognition although it did facilitate response recall. Thus, item imagery and imagery instructions had different effects on recognition and recall when subjects were presented with noun pairs. This contrasts with the comparable positive effect of noun imagery on both recognition and recall when items are presented individually rather than as pairs. These various discrepancies remain to be explained.

The relation between individual differences in imagery and cued memory tasks appears to be somewhat more consistent than in the case of non-cued memory for items. Hollenberg (1970) found that high imagery subjects, as defined by spatial manipulation tests, learned the nonsense-syllable names of objects faster than did low imagery subjects. Stewart (1965) similarly found that high imagery subjects learned picture–digit pairs more quickly than low imagery subjects, whereas the reverse was true when words served as stimuli for the digits. Ernest and Paivio (1969) found no difference between high and low imagery subjects in intentional learning of a paired-associate list in which some stimulus members were Stroop items, i.e. colour names printed in incongruent colours, such as the word RED printed in green ink, whereas other stimuli were congruent in regard to name and colour. For some subjects the functional stimulus for learning was the colour and for others it was the colour word. High imagers were superior to low imagers, however, in their incidental recall of the irrelevant component of the compound stimulus, particularly under certain combinations of colour–word congruency and functional stimulus. The finding was replicated in a second experiment in the same study, but not in a later one by Ernest and Paivio (1971). The latter differed in that the task was free-recall rather than associative learning and subjects were tested incidentally for their memory of an attribute of the pictorial items that had been used for intentional recall. There is no obvious explanation for the discrepant findings. No comparable data seem to be available on recognition memory using associative memory tasks and subjects differing in imagery ability.

Dual coding provides a partial explanation of the facilitative effects of imagery variables on associative memory. High imagery conditions simply augment the probability that an association will be stored imaginally as well as verbally. As in the case of item memory, however, dual coding is insufficient to account for many of the available findings without the additional assumption that the imaginal and verbal codes differ in their functional properties. The crucial assumption in this context is that images are uniquely specialized for spatial organization and integration of stimulus information, whereas the verbal code is specialized for sequential organization. The idea that imagery effectively integrates stimulus information has been supported by the results of numerous studies in which instruction to imagine the referents of concrete nouns in some kind of interactive relation or compound image benefited cued recall more than instructions to image items separately (for summaries, see Bower, 1972a; Paivio, 1971a, Chapter 10). Such facilitation has also been observed when the integrated relation is provided by pictorial materials (Epstein, Rock and Zuckerman, 1960; Wollen, Weber and Lowry, 1972).

Two studies by Begg (1972; 1973) have provided the strongest evidence to date for the imagery-integration hypothesis. The earlier study showed essentially that subjects could free recall as many adjective-noun phrases as individual words when the items were concrete (e.g. white horse) but only half as many phrases as words when the items were abstract (e.g. basic truth). Moreover, cued recall exceeded free recall only in the case of concrete phrases. These findings were predicted from the reasoning that image coding in the case of a concrete phrase provides a unitary representation from which both words can be retrieved. Presentation of one word from the phrase as a retrieval cue further enhances recall because it redintegrates the entire image. Each abstract phrase, on the other hand, is presumably stored as a sequence of two verbal units, each of which takes up separate 'space' in memory. Cueing provides no additional facilitation because the items are not mnemonically integrated. Begg's 1973 experiment involved concrete noun pairs and imagery instructions. He predicted and obtained an interaction, so that cued recall surpassed free recall significantly more when subjects imaged the pair members as an integrated unit than when the members were imaged separately. Begg and Robertson (1973) have subsequently shown that imagery integration is equally relevant to long-term retention.

Begg's findings are particularly interesting because they provide new evidence on the conditions under which explicit retrieval cues are effective. They indicate that an explicit retrieval cue enhances item recall only if the encoded representations of the retrieval cue and the to-be-remembered word are integrated or unitized during input. This appears to be an important qualification of the retrieval process as envisaged in the encoding specificity hypothesis of Tulving and Thomson (1973). We return to this issue again in the final section of this chapter.

It has also been suggested that the associative effects of imagery variables can be explained in terms of abstract representations. Specifically, Bower (1972a) suggests that we may have a common generative grammar that underlies our verbal production of sentences and our imaginal production of visualized scenes, and that the properties of such base grammars may determine the mnemonic value of interactive imagery. A similar view has been extended and formalized in the propositional approach to associative memory proposed by Anderson and Bower (1973). They have documented the explanatory and predictive power of such a model, but it remains difficult to see how it can explain such effects as superior associative memory for concrete as compared to abstract word pairs, or of pictures over words, or the differential potency of concreteness when varied among retrieval cues as compared to the items to be recalled.

Presumably a propositional approach could explain such findings in a *post hoc* fashion by the added assumption that the underlying propositions become increasingly complex as materials increased in abstractness, and that pairs in which an abstract item functions as the retrieval cue for a more concrete associate are more complex than concrete–abstract pairs. Anderson and Bower (1973, p. 458) suggest two specific possibilities of this kind. First, abstract nouns are generally more complex than concrete nouns in the sense that the former are more often derived from verbs or adjectives by the addition of affixes. Second, abstract words generally have more dictionary meanings than concrete words. The implication is that either of these variables might account at least partly for the greater difficulty of learning abstract items. Both possibilities have been disconfirmed. Kintsch (1970a) found that lexical complexity and concreteness had independent effects in paired-associate recall, and Peterson and McGee (1974) showed similarly that number of dictionary meanings could not explain the positive effect of imagery concreteness in paired-associate recall. These variables can be added to a list of more than 20 word attributes that have been ruled out empirically as confounding correlates of imagery concreteness (Paivio, 1968).

The abstract representation theory is further strained by other findings. For example, Paivio and Foth (1970) obtained an interaction between mnemonic instructions and concreteness of noun pairs, so that imagery mnemonics resulted in higher recall than sentence mnemonics when the pairs were concrete, whereas imagery was inferior to verbal mediation when the pairs were abstract. The finding is easily accommodated by the dual-coding theory in terms of two empirically supported assumptions. The first is that it is more difficult to generate images than sentences to abstract words. Thus the inferiority of the imagery condition in this case is attributable to differences in code availability, affecting the encoding stage of learning. Second, imagery is superior with concrete pairs because it encourages dual coding and because imagery provides a more integrated memory representation than does a sentence. This explanation seems more plausible than one expressed in terms of abstract representations, as well as the levels-of-processing model, which seems not to have any straightforward implications that would account for the Paivio and Foth data.

Sequential Memory Tasks

The above studies generally showed positive effects of imagery variables with tasks involving memory for items. The results are quite different when the tasks involve only memory for sequential order of unrelated items. The imagery value or concreteness of items does not facilitate sequential memory as measures by immediate memory span (Brener, 1940; Paivio and Csapo, 1969), serial reconstruction (Paivio and Csapo, 1971) or discrimination of recency (Paivio, 1971a, p. 237). Indeed, sequential memory was poorer in the above studies under 'pure' imagery conditions created by presenting pictures at rates too fast to permit implicit labelling than it was for words under similar conditions. Further support for these conclusions appeared in a recent study by

Del Castillo and Gumenik (1972), in which familiar and unfamiliar forms were used as items. It should be emphasized that these findings refer to immediate sequential memory, and not to serial learning in which the items are presented in the same order over repeated trials. In serial learning, pictures were not found to be significantly inferior to words even at the fast rate, and concreteness facilitated serial learning at a slower rate (Paivio and Csapo, 1969). However, the interaction has been observed even with serial learning as the sequential task when environmental sounds serve as the non-verbal stimuli (Philipchalk and Rowe, 1971): sounds were inferior to their auditory labels in serial learning but not in free recall.

The inferiority of pictures relative to words in sequential memory tasks at fast presentation rates was predicted from the theoretical assumption that the verbal code is specialized for sequential organization whereas imagery is not. It is difficult again to see how the alternative hypotheses could predict or explain the negative or null effects of concreteness in immediate sequential memory, and the uniform positive effect of this variable in item memory tasks.

Some recent findings appear to be inconsistent with a strong form of the hypothesis that imagery is not specialized for sequential memory. The hypothesis implies that imagery variables should never facilitate immediate sequential memory for discrete items. Contrary to this implication, Nelson, Brooks and Borden (1973) found that serial reconstruction scores were higher for pictures than for words presented at a 1.5 sec rate. Snodgrass and Antone (1974) presented picture and word pairs to their subjects either in a spatial or a temporal relationship. This was followed by a recognition test consisting of the same pairs with half in a reversed and half in the same order. Subjects indicated on a rating scale which pairs were reversed and which were in the same order. The results showed that pictures were superior to words in both the temporal memory and spatial memory tasks. Both of these studies suggest that the pictorial code can enhance memory for the sequential order of items.

It is difficult at the moment to reconcile the contrasting findings from the different studies. One possibility is that the results of the Nelson *et al.* and Snodgrass and Antone studies involved conditions that permitted subjects to infer sequential order from correlated cues. For example, subjects in the Nelson *et al.* study may have coded some of the items as a linear array or compound spatial image from which the sequential order could be derived. Alternatively, subjects might have tagged items in distinct positions verbally (for example, first and last), which would constitute a kind of dual coding that would contribute to the superiority of pictorial items in those locations. Whether such factors can explain the discrepant findings or the imagery hypothesis needs to be modified remains to be determined.

Relative Effects of Imagery in Recall and Recognition

Most of the studies considered thus far investigated either recall or recognition memory as a function of imagery without attempting to compare performance under the two test conditions. In this section we shall review studies that permit such comparisons to be made. We shall also consider whether the various hypotheses have any differential implications for the effects of imagery variables in the two kinds of tasks. The dual-coding hypothesis suggests, for example that verbal coding of pictures should have less effect on recognition memory performance than on recall because, logically, it is not necessary for the name of the picture to be retrieved in a recognition test whereas it is obviously essential in verbal recall. Nonetheless, some facilitation from dual coding would be expected even in the case of recognition because such coding would increase the probability that one code would be retained and available during the recognition test. In the case of pictures, if only the verbal code were retained at the time of test, the subject need only label the pictorial test items in order to achieve a correct match. The analogous argument applies to verbal input items that have been coded as images. Verbal encoding would also be expected to affect the way pictures are perceptually encoded during input, thereby influencing subsequent recognition (Ellis, 1972; Wilgosh, 1970). With these and other similar possibilities in mind, we shall examine evidence on possible distinctions between recall and recognition memory as a function of imagery variables.

Olver (1965) was apparently the first to attempt a systematic comparison of recall and recognition as a function of word concreteness. As mentioned earlier, she found that concreteness–abstractness correlated about equally with recall and recognition scores for items. Equivalent correlations might nonetheless conceal interactions between memory task and concreteness. In fact, Olver had predicted that item concreteness should have a greater effect in recognition memory than recall on the basis of an analogy between test conditions in the two tasks and the stimulus–response distinction in paired-associate learning. Remember that concreteness is typically related more strongly to paired-associate learning when varied amongst stimulus members (that is, items that function as retrieval cues during the test trial) than when varied among the to-be-recalled response members. Since the items also are presented in a recognition test but not in recall, Olver reasoned that the effect of concreteness should be greater in the former than in the latter. This would be reflected impirically in an interaction, so that the superiority of concrete over abstract items would be greater in recognition than in free recall. The trend of the results was as predicted, but the interaction fell short of significance, $p < 0.10$. The study obviously deserves to be replicated using a larger sample of stimulus words than were available at the time that Olver conducted her experiment.

Interactions involving item concreteness and frequency are also relevant to the issue. Indices of item familiarity or frequency typically have different effects in recognition than in recall tasks. In recognition, low-frequency items are usually recognized better than high-frequency items, whereas frequency often has a positive effect in free recall (see McCormack, 1972; Paivio, 1971a, Chapter 7). Kintsch (1970a, p. 277) used these observations as partial evidence that recall and recognition involve different processes. The evidence that frequency has a positive effect on recall is not as consistent as is generally assumed (see the review by Paivio, 1971a, Chapter 7), and the exceptions are particularly interesting because they implicate item concreteness. Gorman (1961) orthogonally varied concreteness and frequency and found completely independent effects of the two variables: concrete words were recognized better than abstract regardless of frequency; conversely, low-frequency words were recognized better than high-frequency regardless of the level of concreteness. Paivio and Madigan (1970), however, found that item imagery-concreteness and frequency interacted in free recall. High-imagery words were recalled better than low-imagery words regardless of frequency. However, frequency facilitated recall only when the items were concrete. When the items were abstract, low-frequency words were easier to recall. Thus frequency has contrasting effects in recall and recognition only when the items are concrete and high in imagery value. Frequency has a comparable negative effect in both tasks when the items are abstract. These complex findings suggest that different processes are involved at some stage of processing in the two tasks, but it is not immediately apparent what the differences might be. For possible answers, we turn to other studies.

Recent Experiments

The writer has recently conducted several experiments explicitly designed to compare recall and recognition performance as a function of imagery and verbal encoding variables. The type of coding was controlled by the use of incidental memory tasks patterned after those introduced by Paivio and Csapo (1973). One task involved a comparison of pictures and words under conditions that did not require the subjects to code the items in any way. They needed only to recognize whether the presented item was a picture or a word. Thus, subjects were presented a mixed list of 72 randomly ordered pictures and words with the instructions that this was a probability learning experiment. Their task was to guess whether the next item was going to be a picture or a word. They recorded their guess during a 5-sec interval between items and also checked whether their previous guess had been right or wrong. The pictures were line drawings of familiar objects such as a pipe, clock, stove, etc., and the words were the common labels of the objects (for examples, see Paivio, 1971a, p. 202).

The second incidental orienting task explicitly required subjects to encode the items by imagery or by naming. Thus they were asked to generate a mental image to, or implicitly pronounce, the name of each picture or printed word during the 5-sec inter-item interval. During that interval they also indicated how easy it was to image or pronounce the item using a seven-point rating scale. The task involved homogeneous lists of 72 pictures or words. During list presentation, each item was accompanied by the spoken cue 'image' or 'pronounce', in a random sequence which corresponded exactly to the sequence of pictures and words in the probability learning experiments. Since the lists used in the two kinds of tasks involved the same concepts presented in the same order, it was possible to compare the effects of picture–word presentation with imaginal and verbal coding of the same concepts.

Some of the recall and recognition experiments involved a further test in which subjects were presented all of the correct input items and were required to indicate the mode in which each item had been presented (picture or word) or the way it had been coded (imaged or pronounced) during input. First we shall consider the average memory performance as a function of the different experimental conditions, then we shall discuss the results of a correlational analysis involving memory scores and various other characteristics of the items.

Free Recall Performance. Free recall was tested in each case by having subjects write down the names of as many of the items as they could remember during a 4-min interval. The results for the free-recall experiment involving the mixed list of pictures and words under probability learning conditions come from the study by Paivio and Csapo (1973, experiment 4). Memory was tested under both incidental and standard free-recall instructions. The recall proportions were much higher for pictures than words under both incidental (0.162 and 0.088, respectively) and standard conditions (0.440 and 0.283). The comparison of incidental and standard conditions established the generality of the findings and the standard control condition was not repeated in all of the subsequent experiments.

The extensions involving imaginal and verbal coding have thus far been conducted only with words as input items, and only under incidental conditions. The results of this study revealed much higher recall proportions for imaged than for pronounced items (0.31 and 0.17, respectively). This highly significant difference contrasts with the failure to obtain significant effects of imagery instructions in free recall of concrete items under standard (intentional) conditions by Rogers (1967) and Groninger (1972), as well as with the smaller though significant effect reported by Kirkpatrick (1894). A probable explanation of this apparent discrepancy is that the standard free-recall condition does not control for the type of coding strategy that a subject is likely to use. University students in particular tend to use whatever strategy best enables them to remember verbal items, including imagery (for further discussion of the point, see Paivio, 1971a, p. 362).

The test of memory for how the items had been encoded during input revealed that subjects were 86 per cent correct in the case of both imaginally and verbally coded items. This might mean only that subjects remembered the instructional tag (image and pronounce) associated with each item during input. The fact that recall of items was almost twice as high for those accompanied by 'image' than by 'pronounce' argues against such an interpretation, however, since there is no reason to expect that the two verbal tags alone would differ in their potency as implicit retrieval cues. It is reasonable to conclude, therefore, that subjects coded the items in accordance with their instructions and that imagery contributed much more than pronunciation to item recall. But if this is true, why was memory for the input code equally good in the case of verbal and imagery coding? The question will be discussed following the recognition memory results, since the same results were observed in that task as well.

Recognition Memory Results. The recognition experiments involved a forced-choice test in which each old item was paired with a new distractor. For one group of subjects, the test alternatives were all words whereas for another group they were all pictures. Thus, it was possible to compare performance under conditions in which the input item was in the same modality as the test item (picture study–picture test and word study–word test) with conditions in which the modality changed from study to test trial (picture–word and word–picture). The pattern of results could then be compared with those of previous studies which involved the same combination of conditions under standard learning instructions (e.g. J.R. Jenkins, Neale and Deno, 1967; Snodgrass, Wasser, Finkelstein and Goldberg, 1974). The present experiment also included standard control conditions. The analogous imaginal and verbal encoding experiment has thus far been done only with words as input and test items.

Table 1. Proportion correct recognition of pictures (P) and words (W) when tested with pictures or words under incidental or intentional conditions

Conditions	Picture test		Word test	
	P	W	P	W
Intentional	0.972	0.882	0.960	0.896
Incidental	0.731	0.612	0.713	0.624

Table 1 shows the correct recognition proportions as a function of picture–word input and picture–word test conditions, under the probability learning incidental condition and the standard recognition memory instructions. Analyses of these results reveal two significant effects: input pictures were recognized much better than words, $p < 0.001$, regardless of the test mode; and recognition memory was higher under intentional than incidental conditions, $p < 0.001$. The interaction did not approach significance.

The general superiority of pictures over words as input items simply replicates what has been repreatedly obtained in previous experiments. The observation that the effect is equally strong under incidental learning conditions is new. The absence of a significant interaction of input and test mode is inconsistent with the results reported by Jenkins *et al.* (1967) and Davies (1969), although the trends in the present study are in the same direction as the previous ones. That is, recognition tends to be slightly higher when test items were in the same mode as the input items. The absence of an interaction nonetheless indicates that input mode was clearly the more potent determinant of recognition in the present experiment. That this occurred even under incidental conditions, where the subjects were not required to encode the items in any particular way, seems to be at variance with what would be expected from Tulving and Thomson's encoding specificity hypothesis. According to that hypothesis, recognition should be better when input and output modes match, unless subjects encoded in both modes during input. There is no reason to suppose that such coding occurred consistently in the present experiment, under the incidental condition at least. Thus the results are more consistent with a dual-coding hypothesis in which it is assumed that subjects can retrieve the input item correctly by translating the test item into the input code when necessary, without any requirement that the translated code be present at input as well.

The test of memory for the input code revealed equal accuracy of memory for pictures and words. Each was remembered correctly for 67 per cent of the items regardless of the test mode. There was, however, a difference in the relation between item recognition and code recall. The contingencies are shown in Table 2. It can be seen that the recognition scores and memory for input code are strongly associated in the case of pictures, but the two types of memory are much less related in the case of words. These observations suggest an interpretation that may be applicable also to the finding that memory for imaginal and verbal encoding was equally high in the case of free recall. Subjects presumably had high item-recognition scores in the case of pictures because they remembered them as pictures. This was reflected also in an association

Table 2. Relation between incidental item recognition and memory for the input code (picture or word). Cell values are proportions of items of each type

Pictures		
	Recognition	
Code memory	Correct	Incorrect
Correct	0.543	0.126
Incorrect	0.176	0.155
Words		
	Recognition	
Code memory	Correct	Incorrect
Correct	0.380	0.283
Incorrect	0.238	0.099

between correct recognition and memory for the input code. In the case of words, however, subjects could sometimes infer that an item had been presented as a word because they did not remember it having been presented as a picture, but such knowledge would not necessarily ensure a correct choice between that item and its distractor during the test of item recognition. Essentially the same argument can be applied to the finding (discussed earlier) that image coding resulted in much higher free recall than did verbal coding, yet the two codes were remembered equally well given the correct items as cues. Apparently memory for the coding was partly an inference based on those instances in which the subject felt confident that a particular item had not been coded imaginally during input. A direct test of this explanation requires a different procedure for measuring memory for the input code than was used in these experiments.

The results for the intentional recognition condition also showed that memory for the input code was very high, 90.6 per cent correct for pictures and 88.7 per cent correct for words. With both item recognition and code memory so high, the two are bound to be related and no further analyses were performed on these data.

The parallel experiment in which the encoding cue was varied and words served as items has been conducted only under incidental conditions, primarily because this condition was run first and the performance levels were so high that a similar experiment done under intentional conditions would be unlikely to reveal any higher performance. The proportion of items that were correctly recognized was 0.970 in the case of imaginally coded words and 0.914 in the case of pronounced items. Even with such high scores, the difference was clearly significant ($p < 0.01$ by a sign test), inasmuch as 32 out of 43 subjects recognized more imaged than pronounced items while only one subject did better with the pronounced items (10 subjects performed equally well with both codings). The test of code recall again showed high accuracy, 82.5 per cent correct overall, with no significant difference between the accuracy for imaged and verbalized items. These observations further indicate that differential encoding was involved, and that one code is mnemonically superior to the other.

Recall and Recognition Compared. The above experiments strongly confirmed some earlier studies in showing that pictorial presentation and imagery coding substantially facilitate both recall and recognition memory. However, these data alone do not provide a basis for distinguishing any subtle differences that might exist in the nature of the effective coding processes involved in the two tasks. Some relevant information is available from a correlational analysis involving memory scores and available data on certain characteristics of the 72 items used in the studies. The analysis included the recall and recognition data for the picture–word and imaginal–verbal encoding experiments described above, as well as recall data from the earlier experiments by Paivio and Csapo (1973). Since each item had been presented to different subjects under different conditions (as a picture or a word, imaged or verbalized, under incidental and intentional conditions) there were a number of memory scores (proportion of subjects showing correct memory) for each item. The other item attributes included scores on various indices of word familiarity (familiarity ratings and frequency counts), age of acquisition ratings for the labels obtained by the method described by Carroll and White (1973), consistency and latency of labelling for the pictures, structural attributes of the words (number of letters and syllables), ratings of word imagery and concreteness, etc. Correlations were computed between the variables over the 72 items and the matrix was factor analysed and subjected to a varimax rotation.

The correlational data will be reported elsewhere in detail. Here we shall emphasize only those features that are relevant to the comparisons of recall and recognition and to the theoretical interpretations of these data. The first important point to note is that the correlations between recall and recognition scores were small and generally non-significant. This was reflected in the fact that the memory scores from the two tasks loaded on independent factors. Where significant correlations did occur, they involved words more often than pictures. The values of r ranged up to 0.435. These findings are consistent with those of Bahrick and Boucher (1968), who found no correlation between visual recognition and verbal recall of pictures. Tversky (1973) also found only a small positive correlation between recognition and recall scores for pictures when the same subjects were tested on recall first and then on recognition, but no correlation when the recognition test was given first. Since the latter studies involved correlations between recall and recognition scores for subjects rather than items, the data are not exactly comparable to the present ones, but they do support the same general conclusion, namely, that recall and recognition memory scores tend to be unrelated.

The second important point is that recall and recognition scores are generally related to different characteristics of the items. Specifically, recall tends to be correlated positively with verbal and imaginal associative variables (verbal attributes in the case of pictures and imagery attributes in the case of words) whereas recognition is essentially uncorrelated with such attributes. Conversely, recognition scores are correlated somewhat more often with structural variables and familiarity of the stimuli, but the correlations in this case are more often negative than positive.

Consider first the relation between the associative variables and memory scores. Word attributes such as rated familiarity, frequency counts, labelling latency and age of acquisition reflect the availability of verbal associative (or in terms of the dual-coding model, referential) reactions when pictures serve as items or when retrieval is from a non-verbal image. The correlational analysis showed that such variables correlated positively with recall scores for pictures or for words encoded as images more often than with scores for words that presumably were encoded only verbally. This was revealed most strikingly in the case of memory scores for pictures and words obtained under the incidental conditions of the probability learning task that did not require any elaborative coding of the items (Paivio and Csapo, exp. 4—see above). The rated familiarity, frequency and age of acquisition scores correlated with free-recall scores for the pictures, with r values ranging from 0.26 to 0.54. That is, recall was higher for early-learned and familiar items than for the opposite. Paradoxically, however, none of these variables correlated significantly with recall scores when words served as items in these experiments.

These results strongly suggest a dual-coding effect in the case of picture free recall. The reasoning is as follows: although the incidental orienting task did not require picture labelling as a general strategy, uncontrolled (implicit) labelling would be expected to occur occasionally, particularly to items that are easy to name, i.e. those with early-learned or high-frequency labels. This was reflected in significant correlations between those variables and recall scores where pictures served as items. The same variables were ineffective in word recall because they were irrelevant to dual coding i.e. image arousal to words). Dual coding also accounts for the correlations between the familiarity attributes and recall scores obtained under conditions deliberately designed to encourage dual coding.

The relations discussed above involved memory scores obtained under incidental learning conditions. Under intentional conditions, the familiarity and frequency attributes did not correlate significantly with recall scores for pictures, and only the Kučera–Francis frequency count showed a significant correlation of 0.34 with free recall of words. Age-of-word acquisition showed an appropriate negative correlation with free-recall scores for both pictures and words ($rs = -0.27$ and -0.23)—items with earlier-learned labels were recalled relatively better than those with late-learned labels.

In sharp contrast with free-recall, recognition scores were essentially uncorrelated with label familiarity and age-of-acquisition variables when pictures served as items, but recognition sometimes showed the usual negative correlation (the rs ranged up to -0.25) with familiarity when the items were words. These results again suggest that dual coding is less relevant in the case of recognition memory than recall. However, recognition scores did show a small significant correlation with one verbal attribute under conditions that suggest an effect attributable to dual coding during retrieval. Under incidental learning conditions, with words as input items and pictures as test items, recognition scores correlated -0.28 with labelling latency. Items that can be named quickly were recognized relatively better on the average than ones that take longer to name. Since the input items were words, the finding suggests that subjects relied partly on labels evoked by the test pictures, especially if the picture elicited the label quickly. This correlation, though small, is noteworthy because both the recognition scores and label latency scores had small variances (the items had originally been selected to be easily named) which probably attenuated the true relation between the variables. Perhaps for the same reason, label latency did not correlate significantly with performance scores under any other condition.

On the reverse side of the dual-coding coin, ratings of image-evoking value were also available for the verbal items. These imagery scores also showed little variance, presumably because all of the words were selected to be highly concrete and pictureable. Despite this limitation, rated imagery correlated significantly with many of the free-recall scores for both pictures and words, this general relation being reflected in the fact that imagery loaded 0.283 on the free-recall factor. The only exceptions were that rated imagery did not correlate with recall of words under the incidental orienting task in which subjects pronounced the items, nor with incidental picture recall following the probability learning task that did not require any elaborative coding of the items. These are precisely the conditions that were least likely to involve verbally evoked imagery as a coding strategy. Thus, despite a restricted range of variation, the imagery value of words correlated significantly with recall under those conditions in which associatively aroused imagery could function as a memory code. These data are quite consistent with a dual-coding interpretation of recall.

Recognition scores again contrasted with free-recall. None of the recognition scores correlated significantly with rated imagery of the labels, and what trends there were tended more often to be negative rather than positive in direction. These findings, like those involving the familiarity and age-of-aquisition variables, suggest that dual coding is less relevant in recognition than in free recall. The results do not mean that *imagery* is irrelevant, however, only that small variation in the imagery value of highly pictureable words is insufficient to effect recognition. That image coding is generally effective in recognition memory was indicated by the superiority of pictures over words, and of imaginally coded words over those that were merely pronounced. Moreover, several studies reviewed earlier showed that high-imagery words were recognized better than low-imagery words. These positive effects of imagery variables together with the relative absence of correlational evidence for dual-coding effects in the case of picture or word recognition suggest that the superiority of pictures or imaginally coded items is due primarily to the superiority of the non-verbal image as compared to the verbal code in a recognition task. This interpretation is consistent with Standing and Smith's (1974) suggestion that both pictorial and verbal stimuli are encoded in a pictorial or functionally equivalent form in a recognition memory task.

It must be emphasized, however, that the above conclusion concerning the role of dual coding in the two tasks is a relative one. Dual coding is apparently more important in the case of free recall than in the case of recognition memory. Moreover, this functional difference seems to apply more to the encoding and storage of items than to their retrieval. This qualification is necessary because it is difficult to explain the recognition memory data without assuming that subjects sometimes based their recognition choices on associative reactions to test items. It will be remembered that items presented as pictures were recognized better than those presented as words regardless of whether recognition was tested using words or pictures. Therefore, under the incidental condition at least, subjects must have recoded test items into their input mode in order to recognize them. These findings differ from those on which Standing and Smith based their theoretical analysis, as well as earlier findings by Jenkins *et al.* (1967) and Davies (1969). Presumably the precise experimental procedures involved in these studies determined the extent to which dual coding was functional or image coding alone sufficed in recognition memory, but the relevant procedural differences cannot be specified at this time.

The final comment on the correlational data concerns the role of structural attributes in recognition memory. The word attributes included word length (number of letters and syllables) and rated pronunciability of the words or labels. The word-length variables correlated positively and rated pronunciability of the words negatively with recognition memory scores, but only when the items were words. Thus word recognition was better when the words were long and difficult to pronounce than when they were shorter and easier to pronounce, suggesting that recognition is positively related to the structural complexity of the words. The results for free recall were generally the reverse of those for recognition: significant correlations occurred more often for pictures than words (or imaged words rather than ones that were verbally coded), and the relations were such that shorter and more easily pronounced words were easier to recall than the reverse. These contrasting patterns suggest that recognition memory is based partly on the visual word pattern or its phonemic representation—longer words presumably contain more lexical information than shorter words, thereby enhancing the probability of correct recognition. Conversely, free recall of pictures or imaged words depends on how easy it is to generate an appropriate verbal response during recall, and less complex words are presumably generated more easily than more complex ones.

Comparable structural measures were not obtained for pictures. The only variable that might be relevant is the rated ease of imaging to pictures, obtained from experimental subjects by Paivio and Csapo (1973, experiment 3). This variable showed positive correlations in two instances with free recall and two with recognition memory. In the case of free recall, both instances involved memory for pictures coded by imagery. In the case of recognition memory, one involved pictures as input and test items, the other words as input items and pictures as test items. These relations simply implicate imagery in the sense of pictureability in both recall and recognition.

What conclusions can be drawn from these data in regard to the distinction between recognition and recall? First, the fact that recall and recognition scores are generally independent or only slightly correlated suggests that different processes are involved. Second, the correlational data suggest that free recall is relatively more affected by dual coding in the sense that variables indicative of the availability of a verbal code to pictures and an image code to words correlated more with free recall than with recognition. Third, recognition memory seems to be relatively more dependent on the surface properties of the stimulus itself, such as the number of syllables or pronunciability of words, or the ease with which pictures can be imaged. The latter relation can be interpreted in terms of coding at the representational level: recognition is enhanced by the extent to which the stimulus arouses distinctive representations of the same modality as the input and test stimuli. Free recall, on the other hand, seems to be dependent more on the availability of word-image interconnections in long-term memory, involving what I have termed referential processing.

These distinctions appear to be generally consistent with proposals made recently by Tversky (1973). Using intentional tasks with pictures and words presented together as stimuli, she found that subjects performed better on a recognition test if they expected such a test at the time that the items were presented, and better on a recall test when this was expected. Here data also suggested that subjects used different information from the stimuli depending on which test they anticipated. According to Tversky, successful recognition depends on encoding enough detail about the appearances of the stimuli to discriminate them from similarly appearing stimuli during the test. In the case of free recall, her results showed that recall was enhanced by conditions that encouraged for formation of associations and interrelations among the items. The present analysis emphasized the associative attributes of individual items rather than inter-item relations, but in a general sense the analysis agrees with Tversky's: recognition depends relatively more on discriminative attributes, and recall relatively more on associative attributes of items.

The preceding statement emphasized the distinctions between recall and recognition, but the experimental results reveal strong similarities as well. Thus, performance on both tasks was facilitated by presenting items as pictures or encoding words as images. This evidence implicates dual coding at some stage between encoding and retrieval. This is particularly so in regard to the recognition conditions in which input pictures were tested with words and words were tested with pictures. Successful recognition in this case demands that the appropriate code be retrievable from the transformed test item. Moreover, the potentiating effect of imaging to words directly implicates dual coding during item input as well as during the recognition test.

Alternative Interpretations and Some Further Evidence

Here we shall reconsider two alternatives to the dual-coding analysis of the above effects. The first is the common abstract representation hypothesis, and the second is the levels-of-processing hypothesis or the somewhat similar semantic interpretation of coding effects.

It could be argued from a strong abstract entity theory that a common abstract representation (e.g. proposition) is the functional memory code underlying imaginal and verbal variables. As already indicated in relation to the earlier research literature, such a theory cannot easily account for the superiority of pictures over words or imaginal over verbal coding instructions in recall and recognition. Moreover, without additional assumptions, the theory cannot explain the subject's memory for the input code in the recognition tasks. It could do so by assuming that subjects simply store a differentiating tag along with the abstract entity, but this would not explain why item memory is higher with one tag than with the other. The conclusion seems unavoidable that pictorial (or imaginal) and verbal codes must have different memory properties associated with them at some point in the stream of information processing. Such a conclusion is tantamount to acceptance of some form of dual-coding theory.

According to the levels-of-processing approach, pictorial presentation and imaginal coding would favour memory performance because they involve a deeper level of processing than words that have been coded only by the verbal procedures used in the above experiments. A firm choice between that interpretation and dual coding may be difficult on the basis of the preceding experiments alone, but other recent studies have yielded relevant evidence. Simpson (1972) reported a recognition memory experiment in which different groups of subjects were asked to encode words by generating an image to each, or a verbal association, or simply repeating the item. This encoding variable was crossed orthogonally with test conditions in which subjects were required to choose the correct input item from a pair of synonyms (e.g. wigwam, teepee), antonyms (e.g. king, queen), homophones (e.g. profit, prophet) or unrelated pairs. On the basis of the dual-coding hypothesis, Simpson predicted an interaction so that recognition errors would be highest when tested with synonym pairs in the imagery condition, antonym pairs in the verbal association condition and homophones in the repetition condition. These predictions were qualified by a third variable, rate of presentation, but for present purposes this variable can be ignored.

Despite very high recognition performance, the results were generally as predicted in the case of imagery and verbal association conditions. Synonym errors were most frequent in the case of imagery and antonym errors most frequent in the case of verbal association. In the case of repetition, homophone errors were clearly more frequent than either synonym errors or errors with unrelated pairs of items, but the highest number occurred to antonym pairs. Simpson had recently replicated these results (personal communication) using incidental rather than intentional instructions, with very similar results. Thus the pattern of effects can be regarded as reliable. The qualitatively different error patterns under imagery and verbal association conditions in particular support dual-coding theory, especially when considered in conjunction with the fact that imagery resulted in better recognition accuracy. Depth of processing could predict the general superiority of imagery by assuming that imagery coding is deeper than verbal associative coding, but it is difficult to see how it would directly predict the differences in the types of error that were most frequent in each condition.

Groninger (1974) also reported results more consistent with dual coding than depth of processing. His subjects rated concrete and abstract nouns on familiarity, ease of eliciting a word association or clarity of evoked imagery prior to a surprise recognition memory test. Recognition was unaffected by the coding conditions when the words were abstract, but recognition was highest under imagery coding and lowest under the familiarity condition when the words were concrete. Recognition was also generally better for concrete (high-imagery) than for abstract nouns. These results seem inconsistent with the depth hypothesis for the following reason: if imagery coding increased recognition simply by inducing deeper processing, it should have done so with abstract as well as concrete items.

Further compelling evidence comes from a recent (unpublished) free-recall study conducted by the author in collaboration with Andrew Yackley and Wallace Lambert of McGill University. The study was set up as a direct test of two alternative versions of dual-coding theory. One is the version described above, which assumes qualitatively different imaginal and verbal codes, one of which has greater memory value than the other. The alternative is to assume that the two codes, though independent and qualitatively different, have equal mnemonic value. The alternatives were tested by comparing bilingual coding of words with labeling of pictures. Thus bilingual subjects were presented a list containing equal numbers of pictures, French words (concrete nouns) and English words. They were required to encode these items during list presentation by writing down the name of each picture, translating the French word into its English equivalent or writing down the English word. Therefore the encoding task was the same for all items, viz., writing an English word. Following this task, subjects were unexpectedly asked to recall the words they had written. Since these were all English nouns, any recall differences would have to be attributable to differences in the input items, or to processes involved in translating these into a common output code. No difference would be expected if the additional pictorial and bilingual codes contribute equally to recall. Moreover, since there is no reason to suppose that the processing involved in language translation is any shallower than picture labeling, the depth hypothesis would also predict no difference between these conditions.

The results showed highly significant and approximately equal differences in recall between the three conditions. Recall was highest for pictures (the proportion of items correctly recalled was 0.51), next for translated words (0.34) and lowest for copied words (0.17). Two important points should be noted. First, the mean of the translated items was almost exactly twice the mean of words that were simply copied, suggesting that the verbal code had been exactly duplicated and that the two verbal codes were therefore independent in storage. The fact that the picture–label condition significantly exceeded the translation condition appears to be clear evidence that the pictorial code is more memorable than an independent verbal one. The second point is that these results can be safely generalized to the experimental designs and encoding conditions of the picture–word experiments reported earlier. The generality of the results is supported by the observation that the recall proportions for the picture–write and word–copy conditions are very similar to those reported by Paivio and Csapo (1973) for homogeneous lists rather than mixed-list conditions. Moreover, Paivio and Csapo found that imaging to words resulted in recall levels equivalent to that produced by seeing a picture and labelling it. Therefore it can be concluded that imaging to words (by drawing a picture) would exceed the translation condition by about the same amount as did the picture–label condition in the experiment just described. These observations are most consistent with a dual-coding theory in which it is also assumed that one code is more memorable than the other. The observations are inconsistent with undifferentiated dual-coding, depth-of-processing and semantic coding theories that make no differentiation between the types of semantic codes that might be involved.

Conclusions

The following general conclusions are suggested by the studies reviewed in this paper.

(1) Conditions that encourage non-verbal imagery generally result in higher levels of recall and recognition memory for items and associations. They do not generally enhance memory for sequential order of unrelated items.

(2) The similarities in the facilitative effect of imagery on recall and recognition are more striking than the differences. This is evidenced by the observations that the patterns of effect using different memory paradigms are generally similar whether memory is tested by recall or recognition.

(3) The correlational data involving item attributes and memory scores reveal subtle differences which suggest that dual coding may be relatively more important in recall than in recognition tests. Since input and coding conditions were generally comparable in these experiments, the different correlational patterns must result from processes operating during retrieval. The results make sense if we assume that, in a recognition test, the items function as cues which first arouse a representation corresponding to the items themselves. Only if a decision is not possible on the basis of that representation will the subject rely upon further associative (verbal or imaginal) coding. In the case of recall, however, with no explicit retrieval cue available, the subject will tend to use whatever memory information is available. Thus all conditions that enhance dual coding will be more likely to reveal their effect in recall than in recognition.

(4) Although many of the studies in this area are equally compatible with dual-coding, levels-of-processing or semantic *versus* non-semantic coding interpretations, some recent evidence suggests qualitative differences in the memory representation which are more consistent with the imaginal–verbal dual-coding model than with the others.

(5) Finally, some of the evidence appears to be inconsistent with a strong form of Tulving and Thompson's encoding specificity hypothesis. In particular, the finding that incidental recognition memory is higher for input pictures than words even when the mode of representation was reversed during test (that is, picture input items became words and words became pictures on the test trial) is difficult to reconcile with that hypothesis unless one assumes that subjects always encoded the items in the other mode even though the task did not require it. This seems unlikely in some instances at least, so the hypothesis needs to be qualified in some way. One possibility is that the encoding specificity hypothesis applies particularly to the situation where the retrieval

cue has a verbal associative relation to the to-be-remembered items. This was the case in the tests of the encoding specificity hypothesis reported by Tulving and Thomson (1973). The hypothesis may not be as applicable to the picture–name (or image–verbal code) relation because it is so direct that the input information can be effectively retrieved from either code during test even if that information was not explicitly associated with the item during its presentation. Even this qualification, however, does not eliminate all of the difficulties for the encoding specificity hypothesis. Remember that Begg (1972) found that cued recall exceeded free recall for adjective-noun pairs when the nouns were concrete but not when they were abstract. The effect with abstract pairs is contrary to what would be expected from the encoding specificity hypothesis. It would be tempting to conclude from this that imagery is implicated even in the encoding specificity hypothesis, but the evidence is as yet too sparse to warrant such a generalization.

Notes

1. The author's research reported in this paper was supported by grants from the National Research Council of Canada (A0087) and the University of Western Ontario Research Fund.

5 Learning for recall and learning for recognition

ALDWYN J. R. COOPER and ANDREW MONK

1. Introduction

Verbal learning studies are concerned with the ability of subjects to store information about previously presented verbal material. In list-learning experiments the verbal material is presented as a list of discrete units, usually words, so that performance may be assessed by counting the number of words remembered. In a recall test the subject is asked to reproduce the units, in a recognition test he is presented with a second list containing items from the original list with distractors, usually similar verbal units, and has to indicate which items are which. This chapter is concerned with comparing the effects of various instructions and manipulations at presentation on these two performance measures.

In line with current theoretical thinking, it will be suggested that performance on any list-learning task reflects learning in a number of component processes. For this reason the same performance increment under different conditions may be due to different stored information. By using a number of performance measures, especially recall and recognition, and looking at the detail of the results obtained it is possible to get some idea of what is learned. The chapter is partly concerned with study/test interactions. More generally, it is concerned with differentiating the learning that occurs on test trials from the learning that occurs on study trials. The specific conditions under which such differential effects may or may not occur will be considered in some detail. Before going on to discuss this work, the processes assumed to underlie learning for recognition and recall will be outlined to provide a context to which the rather complex results may be related.

The recognition test requires discrimination of list words from non-list words. Thus, at presentation, the subject must be performing two basic tasks. Firstly he has to build up a specification of the list. This is likely to include overall properties, 'All the items were nouns', 'This is the second list I have learned'. There is also the possibility that subjects will find associations between the list items, 'I have been able to form a sublist of animal names'. All this information may be loosely described as context information, the parts of which one might call context elements (Anderson and Bower, 1972). This first task then is to specify the context elements which define the list as an event in the subject's history. The second task is, of course, to associate these context elements to the individual list items so that at test the context information becomes accessible to be checked off against the list specification in the test phase. Each test item is assumed to have a familiarity value, the basic continuum assumed to underlie recognition. The familiarity of the test item will be a function of the proportion of its associated context information which may be taken as evidence of list membership. Some context elements will have more weight than others in determining familiarity. In the extreme, properties such as 'They are all nouns' have infinite weight for negative instances, since distractors which are not nouns will easily be recognized as such. This phenomenon, dubbed 'class recognition' by Kintsch (1968), might be more usefully considered as by-passing this part of the decision process. When the familiarity of the test item has been determined, a criterion is applied to make a decision list or non-list. This part of the test phase may be described by various decision models.

It is clear that the experimental recognition test has little similarity to the layman's concept 'to recognize' meaning to identify as seen before. In this sense the recognition of a stimulus may be considered in isolation. For example, one might recognize a face in that one feels one has experienced those features at some time in the past. This is not true of the recognition test. Here the task is one of discrimination and the subject's responses to the distractors must also be considered. It has clearly been demonstrated (Murdock, 1965; Brown, 1965a,b; Brown and Routh, 1968) that recognition is not an all-or-none process, and one cannot simply consider the distractors as catch trials and apply a guessing correction.

The recognition task then is one of discrimination. The recall task is one of retrieval and the problem is to form some sort of cueing system. Work on free-recall learning (see Tulving and Donaldson, 1972) has shown it is plausible to consider that a subject 'organizes' a list in learning for recall. It appears that previously established associations, meaningful relations such as taxonomic categories as well as more idiosyncratic relationships, are used to guide the retrieval process. The subject's task in learning for recall is to specify some associative pathway to act as a retrieval plan. This is likely to contain concepts corresponding to non-list words as 'mediators', for example category headings, so that a second task in learning for recall is to differentiate the list items from plausible intrusions generated by the retrieval plan. It also means that the recall test includes a recognition task, comparable to the experimental recognition test, as a subprocess.

Table 1 summarizes the current ideas on subprocesses involved in recall and recognition. On this basis we may speculate as to how much the two tasks have in common and to what extent learning for recall will benefit recognition, and

Table 1. Tasks involved in recall and recognition

	Presentation	Test
Recognition	List specification Item-to-context association	Familiarity estimation Criterion placement

Recall	Retrieval plan formation
	(Item-to-item association)
	Item discrimination
	  List specification
	  Item-to-context association
	  Distractor discrimination
		Retrieval plan elicitation
		
		Item recognition
		  Familiarity estimation
		  Criterion placement

vice versa. The major difference is that recognition does not necessarily involve the item-to-item association needed to form a retrieval plan. This is equivalent to the widely held view that recognition measures 'registration' in memory whereas recall measures 'accessibility'. It is not to say that recognition will not benefit from strategies which improve recall, or vice versa. A retrieval plan will provide additional context information for the list items, though at the same time non-list concepts will be associated with context elements in the list specification, making related distractors more confusable. However, the item differentiation which is generally successful (there are few intrusions in free-recall protocols) is aimed at making related distractors more discriminable. Similarly, learning for recognition will improve recall. The recognition subprocess in recall may be facilitated, even though the 'internal' nature of the distractors will make the tasks rather different. A comprehensive list specification and some types of list item-to-context association may also facilitate retrieval plan formation. Despite or perhaps because of this close relationship, input procedures which differentially affect recall and recognition are of interest as they give some insights into the properties of the subprocesses.

2. Learning on test trials—a review

It has long been realized that no sharp distinction can be drawn between the processes being carried out in study and test trials (Ballard, 1913). The test phase cannot be thought of as merely a passive measure of performance. The act of testing, *per se*, appears to alter the behaviour it sets out to measure. However, it would be surprising if the processes involved were entirely parallel in these two rather different tasks. In this section we shall review the literature which has examined the differential effects of study and test trials on performance in three verbal-learning tasks—free recall, paired-associate learning and recognition. It is hoped that this will afford some insight into the processes involved.

Recall

The simplest sequence of test and study trials is to present a list once and then to test it once, either immediately or after some delay. Table 2(a) signifies this paradigm. To examine the differential effects of study and test phases this simple sequence is elaborated. There must, of course, be at least one study trial and at least one test trial. Table 2(b)–(f) shows some of the possibilities. Table 2(b) signifies a simple paradigm in which a single study trial is followed by two consecutive test trials. Ballard (1913) noted that performance on a second test was sometimes superior to that on the first test although there was no intervening experience with the list. It often happened that items not recalled on test one were correctly recalled on test two. He termed this phenomenon 'reminiscence', the occurrence of which was confirmed by many of his contemporaries (Abbot, 1909; Norsworthy, 1912; Huguenin, 1914; Gates, 1917). Over the following half-century a wide variety of theories were put forward to account for this, at first, surprising result.

Warner Brown (1923) noted the two most obvious possibilities. Firstly, 'A recall test does not give an exhaustive measure of all items remembered'. Chance factors affect recall. The context of testing will on one occasion favour one subset of words while at a later date another subset may be advantaged. Secondly, as pointed out by many of the early authors (Witasek, 1907; Kuhn, 1914; Gates, 1917), the initial test provides the subject with the opportunity to view and practise one subset of the items. It is suggested that a combination of chance fluctuation combined with the consolidating effect of the first test is sufficient to explain the phenomenon. A second recall trial may elicit more items than the first because repetition tends to fix those items recalled on the first test while chance tends to introduce new additional ones.

A more detailed analysis of those factors affecting reminiscence was attempted by Rohrer (1949). He suggested that two major types of theory had been advanced. The first requires that some factor is operative that increases the 'associative strength' of the non-recalled items during the interpolated period. The second is that some inhibitory factor affecting non-recalled items in the first test is somehow dissipated before the second. There is little support for the first class of model, though various mechanisms for increasing the 'strength' of non-recalled items were postulated. Rohrer points out that models involving formal rehearsal (Ballard, 1913; Williams, 1926; Woodworth, 1938; Buxton, 1943) must assume covert rehearsal of items which cannot be recalled. Similarly, Skaggs' 1920) suggestion that the first test may point out the lacunae in the recall profile, allowing the subject a more efficient search in the second test, is only plausible if the recall time is limited. Since unlimited time was given for recall in some of the studies demonstrating reminiscence (e.g. Raffel, 1934) this cannot be the whole story.

Rohrer concludes that there is no evidence for any model in which associative strengths are increased between tests. This includes models involving 'maturation' (Piéron, 1913; Wheeler, 1929; Doré and Hilgard, 1937; Wright and Taylor, 1949) and 'associative strength change theory' (Hovland, 1940). He was able to obtain experimental evidence for his inhibition dissipation, also suggested by Dashiell (1928), McLelland (1942) and Hull (1943), by interpolating acti-

Table 2. Some examples of study/test manipulations

(a) S T
(b) S T T
(c) STSTSTSTSTSTSTSTSTSTSTST
(d) STTTSTTTSTTTSTTTSTTTSTTT
(e) SSSTSSSTSSSTSSSTSSSTSSST
(f) STTTTTSTTTTTSTTTTTSTTTTT

S indicates a study phase, T a test phase. (c), (d) and (e) are the conditions S, R and P in Tulving (1967).

vity between the two tests. An intervening task unconnected with the learning situation gives greater benefit than attempted formal rehearsal of the list. A possible explanation has been detailed by Rundus (1973), though in a different context. The idea, attributed to Brown (1968), is that retrieval is like sampling with replacement. Each time a retrieval cue is used an item is retrieved which may or may not have been already recalled. Each time an item is retrieved its probability of being retrieved is increased. It is clear that items which have only a moderate likelihood of being recalled become even less likely to be recalled as the process of retrieval proceeds. Using this model Rundus was able to predict the effect of having list items present at recall and Brown was able to predict the effect of 'priming' a subset of the list on the recall of non-primed items. To explain reminiscence we must assume that the effect of the highly retrievable items is dissipated before the second test. It is not clear why this should happen, though the area would seem promising for future research.

It is possible to repeat the simple sequences of study and test trials that have been considered. Table 2(c) illustrates the paradigm used in standard multi-trial free recall. Table 2(d)–(f) demonstrates more complex cycles embodying the same principles.

Skaggs (1920) noted that all previous work carried out in this area had failed to use any standard type of paradigm. He decided that the most efficient way to investigate the phenomenon was to equate the lengths of study and test periods. He also decided to look for differential effects with a variety of materials. It was hoped by this means to ascertain whether some schedules of study and test trials led to superior retention over others. The conclusion drawn from his study was that, provided a minimum level of familiarity with the material had been achieved, the most efficient type of sequencing was to alternate study and test. This was true with either sense (poetry) or nonsense materials. Trow (1928) adopted the basic design and found that, when using sense materials, study and test trials interspersed produced considerably superior recall to study alone. In addition he found that, provided that the number of study trials was held constant, the probability or recall after delay was a function of the number of test trials given. Raffel (1934) confirmed this by studying the effect of introducing one, five or seven extra test trials after presentation on the delayed recall of 100 familiar words. Delayed recall was considerably enhanced by the introduction of more test trials.

This consolidation due to testing was also manifested as a stereotyping of recall. The same items tend to be recalled whether they are correct or incorrect (Bartlett, 1932; Zangwill, 1937; 1939; Rohrer, 1949). More recently some authors have been considering whether a test trial can be thought of as directly equivalent to a study trial in free-recall learning (Lachman and Laughery, 1968; Tulving, 1967; Birnbaum and Eichner, 1971; Donaldson, 1971). Essentially, they have been investigating an extension of the 'total time hypothesis' for verbal learning (Bugelski, 1962; Cooper and Pantle, 1967; Zacks, 1969). The original hypothesis stated that, 'The amount learned is a direct function of study time regardless of how that time is distributed'. Tulving and others were considering whether it would be reasonable to extend the hypothesis to read, 'The amount learned is a direct function of the time spent manipulating the material, regardless of how that time is distributed between study and test'. With very few exceptions (Borkowski, 1967), the original hypothesis holds true for immediate free recall. There is little effect of massing and spacing of time. Likewise, the modified total-time hypothesis seems to hold for immediate free recall. Tulving (1967) used the three sequences represented in Table 2(c), (d) and (e). At the end of the complete sequence of cycles recall on each of the three conditions was equivalent. The amount learned appears to be independent of the way in which the total time is divided up between study and test.

The literature on the massing and spacing of study time with delayed free recall shows many instances of the breakdown of the total-time hypothesis (Rothkopf and Coke, 1963; 1966; Melton, Reicher and Shulman, 1966; Melton, 1967; Madigan, 1969; Underwood, 1969b; 1970). Likewise, it appears that test trials can no longer be seen as equivalent to study trials when one considers delayed free recall. An experiment by Hogan and Kintsch (1971) typically demonstrates this breakdown. In their experiment 2, conditions one and three, subjects were initially required to learn a list of 40 monosyllabic words. The initial learning trial was either followed by three further learning trials or three attempts at recall. All subjects were tested on delayed free recall after 48 hours. Those subjects who had been tested on the original learning session performed significantly better than those subjects who only had study experience of the material. This is the result that is generally found (Brown, 1923; Trow, 1928; Raffel, 1934; Postman and Phillips, 1961; Donaldson, 1971; Darley and Murdock, 1971).

The major effects of test trials on immediate and delayed free recall may be summarized as follows.

Provided that some minimum level of performance is reached:

1. Performance on a second recall test may be superior to that on the first although there is no intervening experience of the list. This is reminiscence.

2. In a long sequence of study and test trials, the learning on test trials is as effective as the learning on study trials for immediate recall. This is the total-time effect.

3. A test trial consolidates the learned material in some way leading to resistance to forgetting in delayed recall and a stereotyping of the responses.

These three effects will be dubbed reminiscence, potentiation and consolidation. Reminiscence has already been discussed in some detail. The second effect has been described as potentiation as it is not the recall trial itself which increases performance. The total-time effect only applies to a complete sequence of study/test cycles. If one considers Tulving's condition R (Tulving, 1967, see Figure 2, p. 178), the recall curve has a sawtooth appearance. Performance on the second test trial of each cycle (STTT) is slightly lower than that on the first (STTT). Recall on the third test phase of each cycle (STTT) is the same as that on the second. It is only on the test trial following the next study trial (STTTST) that the potentiating effect of the test phase becomes apparent and recall is considerably increased. Donaldson (1971) has investigated the boundary conditions of this potentiating effect. He found that after three consecutive test trials the potentiating effect began to wane. Going back to our Table 2, this would mean that (f) would be less effective as a complete sequence than, say, (d). Similarly, Patterson (1972) found that Tulving's experimental conditions gave the same results when unlimited time was given for recall.

So much for the potentiating effect of test trials in immediate free recall. Let us turn to the consolidation effect. Two obvious candidates for explanations of the effects may be described under the headings rehearsal and organization. They will discussed in turn.

It has been suggested (Sanders, 1961) that testing by recall is in some way equivalent to formal rehearsal, i.e. self-presentation. However, this suggestion is not as simple as it first appears. There are a number of demonstrations that the effect of rehearsal on recall performance may be negligible (Woodworth and Schlosberg, 1954; Broadbent, 1958). Similarly, overt repetition has been shown to have no effect on recall (Tulving, 1966; Glanzer and Meinzer, 1967; Atkinson and Shiffrin, 1971), and a considerable body of evidence has built up which implies that some forms of rehearsal have no effect at all on long-term recall (Meunier, Ritz and Meunier, 1972; Jacoby, 1973 (a); Mandler and Worden, 1973; Craik, Gardiner and Watkins, 1970; Rundus, Loftus and Atkinson, 1970; Shiffrin, 1973; Davis and Okada, 1971). On the basis of these findings it has been claimed that there are two entirely separable functions of rehearsal (see Woodward, Bjork and Jongeward, 1973; Craik and Watkins, 1973). The first of these has been termed the 'maintenance' function. In this role, rehearsal merely maintains the availability of items in short-term store, with no active organization or transfer to long-term store. If any transfer to long-term store occurs, it is simple autonomous registering of occurrence. The second function is termed 'elaborative'. This is an active role in which the material is organized into logical structures by the subject. As has already been pointed out, it is this type of processing that is essential for building retrieval plans to make possible delayed recall. Further support for this view comes from Rundus, Loftus and Atkinson (1970) and Rundus (1971).

We may relate this distinction to study and test trials. In a study trial the subject is faced with the complete set of items. Depending on the experimental conditions and his level of motivation, a larger or smaller proportion of the list will be exposed to elaborative rehearsal strategies and the rest will experience only maintenance rehearsal. In a recall trial he is forced to think about inter-item relationships in the process of retrieval. Also, given time, he is likely to run over the words he has recalled and their associations in an attempt to retrieve further items. This is very much akin to elaborative rehearsal. The proportion of the list actively processed at recall depends on the number of words actually recalled. Thus we see that a study trial may be more or less effective than a test trial depending on the levels of performance and motivation and the other experimental conditions which govern the proportion of the list actively processed.

This leads us into the second consideration, organization. The learning on a recall trial is constrained in that only the words recalled may be actively processed. Since this makes the words more likely to be recalled, it is clear that largely the same set of words will be recalled on each trial. Thus, after test sequences a restricted set of the possible item-to-item associations will be especially accessible at the expense of the rest of the list. In contrast, after study sequences the inter-item associations which make up a retrieval plan will be diffuse but rich. Postman (1972) has pointed out that this is an implication of Thomson and Tulving's (1970) encoding specificity effect. If the order of presentation is randomized for each study phase, as is typical in these experiments, contiguity will emphasize different inter-item associations on each presentation. Investigators have looked for evidence of such organizational effects in the order in which the words are recalled.

Rosner (1970) attempted to analyse whether there were any differences in the organizations induced by the types of learning sequence used by Tulving (1967). Three main types of organization measure were taken–the ITR measure (Bousfield, Puff and Cowan, 1964), assesses the number of items recalled together and in the same order on consecutive trials, commutative ITR, which assesses the number of pairs that occur together regardless of order (Mandler and Dean, 1969), and S-units, a measure of subjective organization based on introspection. The simple ITR seems to depend on the amount of test in the sequence of practice trials, the condition containing the largest number of test trials giving the highest value. However, the measure of commutative ITR showed no difference across conditions. It would seem therefore that both study and test trials form the same number of 'units' but that the test trials somehow consolidate a particular order within the pairs. After the experiment, subjects were asked to identify the groups of words that they thought they had used to recall the list. The number of such S-units that the subjects believed they had formed did not vary between conditions, but an inspection of the individual protocols showed that the S-units of the subjects in the test condition were more coherent. Further evidence of organizational consolidation is provided by Donaldson (1971). In experiment 2 he uses a categorized list and finds that the improvement in inter-trial recall following test trials is due to the consolidation of higher-order units (words per category recalled) rather than the accessibility of the categories themselves (number of categories recalled). Birnbaum and Eichner (1971), again using categorized lists, obtained evidence for the contention that after test sequences the organization will be limited but powerful. Subjects learned the list using standard (STSTSTSTS) or test (STTTSTTTS) sequences. After delayed recall they were cued with the category headings. The cueing elicited nearly twice as many words from the standard group as the test group.

In summary, the learning on a recall trial is evidenced by three effects in free recall. In reminiscence the learning on a recall trial makes recalled items more retrievable, so that on a second recall trial the retrieval processes are somehow freed to retrieve additional items. This may be due to additional time or the avoidance of inhibition on non-recalled words. In potentiation this learning makes more time available for active processing of non-recalled items in the following study trials. The consolidation implied in the above two effects may be observed in the organization of the output and the perseveration of intrusions but it is most evident in delayed recall. As learning in recall is restricted to a subset of the list, this subset is particularly resistant to forgetting.

In discussing paired-associate learning and recognition, we shall be looking for effects parallel to the reminiscence, potentiation and consolidation effects found with free recall.

Paired-Associate Learning

The controversy engendered by the change in Estes' position from one of support for incremental learning theory (Estes, 1959) to one supporting all-or-none theory (Estes, 1960) stimulated a profusion of studies attempting to corroborate one approach or the other. These experiments may have done little to clarify the all-or-none/incremental learning polemic (Underwood and Keppel, 1962; Wollen, 1962) but they provide a considerable body of data on the effects of unreinforced test trials on the acquisition and retention of paired-associate material.

A point of major interest to all-or-none/incremental theorists was the shift in recall probability between consecutive test trials with no intervening study trial (reminiscence). As appears usual in cases where two extreme positions are being defended, a variety of contradictory results have been obtained. A number of authors have found that there is an increase in the probability of recall above chance level on the second and subsequent unreinforced test trial (Goss, Morgan and Golin, 1959; Goss, Nodine, Gregory, Taub and Kennedy, 1962; Wollen, 1962; Postman, 1963; Richardson and Gropper, 1964; Butler and Peterson, 1965). The effect though is generally small, indeed so small that a large number of authors, utilizing a wide variety of designs, have failed to detect any improvement in performance across sequences of up to 19 consecutive test trials (Izawa, 1966b, 1968a, b; 1969; 1970c; Peterson and Brewer, 1963; Jones, 1962). Thus it seems there is no reliable parallel to the reminiscence effect observed with free recall.

There is, however, a potentiating effect. Test trials following a study phase make for a greater performance increment after the next study phase (Izawa,

140

1966a; 1967; 1968b; Allen, Mahler and Estes, 1969; Bregman and Wiener, 1970). It has been shown that the maximum effective sequence was of seven consecutive test trials. Additional tests failed to increase the potentiation, but in no way interfered with either learning or retention (Izawa, 1970a).

Consolidation effects are also evident in paired-associate learning. As sequences of test trials progress, both correct and incorrect responses become more consistent (Estes, Hopkins and Crothers, 1960; Richardson and Gropper, 1964; Bregman and Wiener, 1970; Jones, 1962). Not only do the responses become more consistent, but they are also made more rapidly (Allen, Mahler and Estes, 1969; Eimas and Zeaman, 1963). The effect on delayed recall is dramatic. Allen, Mahler and Estes found that five study trials plus five imme- diate test trials produce long-term retention much superior to that observed after 10 study trials with no immediate test. The addition of a single test after 10 study trials reduces the number of errors after a 24-hour delay by 50 per cent as compared to 10 study trials without the immediate test. This result is confirmed by Izawa (1970a), who found the consolidation effect did not decline even when the series of trials was as long as 19 consecutive tests.

A summary of the main effects of test trials on paired-associate learning is then as follows.

1. Little if any change in response probability is noticed across sequences of test trials (no reminiscence).

2. Test trial sequences potentiate future learning trials, the maximum potentiation being achieved with sequences of seven unreinforced test trials.

3. Stereotypy of both correct and incorrect responses is developed across sequences of test trials, accompanied by a decrease in the latency of the response, and a resistance to forgetting evolves. The retention becomes more impervious to delay the longer the series of trials.

Thus in many ways paired-associate learning is similar to free recall in the way it is affected by study/test manipulations. However, when we come to interpret these results an additional factor must be considered. Studies of massing and spacing show that the total-time hypothesis (Bugelski, 1962) which held for free recall does not hold for paired-associate learning (see Bjork (1966; 1970) and Potts (1972) for reviews of this literature). This means that there is the possibility that the effects of test trials may be explained as special cases of massing and spacing, the so-called neutral test trials providing the spacing. However, substituting blank and neutral trials into study/test sequences shows that blank trials are not equivalent to test trials (Izawa, 1967; 1970b). These experiments also rule out any other explanations based on the fact that test trials delay the study trial. This includes accounts involving formal rehearsal, delayed reinforcement (Jones and Bourne, 1964) and simple stimulus fluctuation models (e.g. Estes, 1955).

There are, however, no obvious objections to the explanations put forward in connection with the free-recall results. A study trial will involve the active processing of a larger or smaller proportion of the pairs according to the conditions. Similarly, recall will involve the active processing of those items which are recalled. The consolidation of stimulus item-to-response item links of recalled pairs frees the processors in the following study phases so that new pairs can be linked and makes them resistant to forgetting. The lack of reminiscence effects implies that additional time for retrieval has little advantage in paired-associate learning, or alternatively that the inhibition of non-recalled items, demonstrated by Rohrer, is not operative in paired-associate learning. This is consistent with an 'all-or-none' interpretation of paired-associate learning.

Recognition

Few authors have attempted to study the effects of a recognition test on later recognition performance. With recognition it is more obvious that one test will affect performance on later tests. A recognition test necessarily involves the presentation of the list. Furthermore, this second presentation will usually be in the original presentation mode and in the presence of distractors. This contrasts with the partial self-presentation implicit in a recall test. The distractors are necessarily presented in the same way as the targets. Thus context elements concerning the presentation of test items will be associated with the distractors as well as the targets. This means that if the same distractors are used in the second recognition test they may be extra potent and down any increment due to consolidation. On the other hand, if different distractors are used, there is the possibility of discriminating targets without initially presenting the list, simply by noting which items occur on both tests. These factors make it difficult to interpret results involving repeated recognition tests.

As one would expect, there is an increase in performance between two recognition tests if different distractors are used on each test and a decrease if the same distractors are used (Hogan and Kintsch, 1971; Richardson, 1974). Richardson notes that the positive effect is almost entirely due to a reduction in the number of false alarms, while the negative effect is due mainly to a reduction in the hit rate. It is apparent that the subjects notice the relation between the two distractor distributions and alter their criteria accordingly.

Considering the recognition test in the light of our interpretation of the free-recall and paired-associate learning results, one might expect parallel effects. In these tasks the test phase differs from the study phase in that elaborative processing is necessitated or at least encouraged for the items recalled. In recognition all the items are present at testing and there is less reason for a subset of the items to receive special attention. However, the retrieval of context links for items in the recognition process may strengthen these links and thus, other things being equal, one might expect reminiscence, potentiation and consolidation effects.

We have not been able to trace any attempt to discover a potentiating effect in recognition, probably because of the problems of repeating recognition tests. The possibility of consolidation has been investigated, though not very satisfactorily for our purposes. False alarms become consistent with repeated recognition (Mandler, 1972; Richardson, 1974). Hogan and Kintsch found that delayed recognition performance was essentially the same whether an initial study trial was followed by two more study trials and a recognition test or simply three recognition tests. This applies whether the recognition tests in the training phase used the same or different distractors each time. This result is difficult to interpret because only one cycle was used and a different set of distractors to those used in the training phases was employed in the delayed recognition test. Under these conditions recall shows a similar effect, and so one may conclude tentatively that there are consolidation effects in recognition.

Transfer

Perhaps more interesting are the studies where recall and recognition are used in mixed sequences. These may be regarded as studies of the transfer of reminiscence or consolidation. Postman, Jenkins and Postman (1948) tested both recognition and recall performance for the same learning task. Group 1 had a recognition test followed by recall. Group 2 had recall followed by recognition. A recognition test preceding recall improves recall performance. More surprisingly, a preceding recall test inhibits recognition performance. The first result is interpreted as a transfer of reminiscence from recognition to recall. It has been replicated by Richardson (1974), who found that distractors from the recognition test tend to be carried over into the recall test as intrusions. Their second result was unexpected and is confounded by delay. Belbin (1950) and later Kay and Skemp (1956) examined the effect using pictorial material and a design in which delay is not confounded. After study the experimental group recalls while a control group performs some unrelated task. Both groups then perform the recognition task. Strong inhibitory effects of recall on recognition were observed. Unfortunately, their results are open to a number of criticisms, particularly the possibility of large criterion effects. They used neither a forced-choice recognition task nor a measure that separates criterion from discrimination effects. To correct this, Hanawalt and Tarr (1961) repeated their experiment using a forced-choice recognition test and verbal material. They found a small but significant positive effect which increased with the delay between the recall test and recognition. They also repeated the experiment of Postman *et al.*, using this paradigm, and got no significant effect, though the mean values were very similar to those originally obtained. At this point one might have concluded that the inhibitory effect is artefactual, or at least confined to a criterion effect, and that a preceding recall test in fact improves recognition. However, Brown and Packham (1967) using Brown's Ā measure (Brown, 1965b), which is designed to avoid criterion effects, found that recognition was decreased by a preceding recall test as compared to discrimination in a control group without recall. Recall levels in these two studies were comparable (45 per cent in Hanawalt and Tarr and 55 per cent in Brown and Packham). The major difference is in the nature of the recognition tests.

In the former it was a five-alternative forced-choice test, while Brown and Packham had their subjects rank all the test items for plausibility. $\bar{A}$ is calculated from the average number of distractors which are ranked higher than each target. Packham (1968) has suggested that their result was due to the highly plausible recalled words conveying the impression that only crude discriminations were required, whereas in fact fine judgments are required to discriminate non-recalled words from distractors. This explains why the result was confined to the low-confidence items and why a forced-choice task with a limited number of alternatives will cancel the effect. To test his hypothesis, he presented subjects with recognition tests which contained no recalled words. All the subjects had a recall test followed by two recognition tests. Group 1 had a recognition test which included five recalled words followed by a recognition test, using different items, which included no recalled words. Group 2 had the reverse arrangement. Discrimination was better in Group 2, i.e. the set induced by the first recognition test, due to the presence or absence of recalled items, is critical in determining the overall level of discrimination. In this connection it is worth mentioning that Broadbent (1973) reports an experiment in which recognition following recall, but with no recalled items in the test, was equivalent to recognition of the whole list by subjects experiencing no preceding recall test. This might be interpreted as strong evidence for Packham's explanation. It is concluded that, other things being equal, recall has no inhibitory effect on the discrimination of targets and may have a small facilitory effect, i.e. reminiscence transfers from recall to recognition as well as from recognition to recall.

Turning from reminiscence to consolidation, there being no studies of potentiation, there is evidence of positive transfer from recognition to recall but again less clear-cut results concerning transfer from recall to recognition. The former result was obtained by Hogan and Kintsch. A study trial followed by three recognition tests, using the same distractors each time, gives better delayed recall than three study phases and one recognition test. Since recognition trials are more effective than study trials, it cannot only be the additional study time, afforded by a recognition test, which gives this consolidating effect. Turning to the effect of recall on delayed recognition, Hanawalt and Tarr found that a recall test immediately following presentation had a clear positive effect on recognition after two days (see also Rundus, Loftus and Atkinson, 1970). However, it is unclear whether an additional study trial would have been just as effective. Darley and Murdock (1971) used a delayed recency paradigm in which 10 lists were presented and tested immediately, and finally after the presentation of all 10 lists. Some lists were tested immediately, some were not. Though there is a clear effect of immediate recall in final recall there is no effect on recognition. Hogan and Kintsch (1971) used standard study/test cycles (SSSS, SSST and STTT) and looked at the effect on recall and recognition after a 48-hour delay. A sequence of one study trial followed by three recall trials gives better delayed recall than a sequence of four study trials. However, the opposite is true for delayed recognition. One problem with this experiment is due to the extreme nature of the training conditions. Subjects in the study condition had no experience of any test trials whatsoever. This may have a motivational effect in that the subject is allowed to behave in an entirely passive manner and may virtually ignore the material. In the test condition the subjects had only one study trial. Recall was around 25 per cent. Since there were no following study trials these few items were the only ones practised. Although they used a two-alternative forced-choice recognition test, the extreme differences in plausibility between these items and the rest of the list might be expected to produce an effect of the type discussed by Packham. If there had been more than one cycle so that final immediate recall on both conditions was comparable, the results might be more easily interpreted. The experiments presented in the next section were designed to examine these points. They also look at the effect of different study/test cycles on recognition latencies. Before going on to describe them, the interpretation of these transfer effects will be discussed. Taking the approach described in the Introduction to this chapter, there are two possible areas of overlap between the processes and information used in recall and recognition. Firstly, a recognition test is assumed to be a subprocess of recall. Secondly, 'organizational' item-to-context links are assumed to provide evidence for recognition and to form part of the retrieval plan used in recall. It was pointed out in the Introduction that the list specification used in recognition will contain some information which is used in forming a retrieval plan for recall (e.g. 'There were four animals'). A similar distinction is made by Schulman (1973), who distinguishes between the context elements concerned with the presentation of a list and those concerned with the properties of the list itself.

If one is to explain transfer by an overlap in the information used in these two performance tasks one would expect symmetric results. Consolidation on recall trials should transfer to delayed recognition to the same extent as consolidation on recognition trials transfers to recall. Hogan and Kintsch's asymmetric results—recognition transfers to recall but not recall to recognition—are not explicable within this approach. In experiment 2 we shall see that learning on recall trials can transfer to delayed recognition under the right conditions.

3. Learning on Test Trials—Two Experiments

The aim of these experiments was to provide performance data concerning the effect of a number of study/test schedules under conditions rather different from those used by previous investigators. It was noted by Lachman and Laughery (1968) that the nature of the transition from study to test, test to test, etc., will affect the possible learning strategies. The type of between-subject designs used by previous investigators will mean that some subjects will experience predominantly study trials while others will experience predominantly test trials. This may lead to the formation of learning sets that will affect performance in ways quite separate from the effects of study or test phases *per se*. For this reason we used a repeated measures design in which all the subjects learned several sublists, one for each of the five S/T sequences used (two in experiment 1).

Although the sublists received different proportions of study and test, each subject received the same overall sequence of study and test trials. By appropriately spacing the presentation and recall of each sublist it was possible to construct a sequence such that during the critical part of the experiment the subject was exposed to alternating study and test trials. While the subject knows that the study and test phases will alternate, he does not know which list will be presented or tested on any given trial. In addition to thereby controlling the formation of learning sets, this design also eliminates the phase-transition effects, especially those of recency, by interposing other S/T activity between the consecutive experience of any given sublist.

Experiment 1

The sublists were made up of 12 common nouns and were indexed by the initial letters of the words. This has been shown to be an effective cue in free recall by Earhard (1967) and avoids the disadvantage of categorized lists, which is that all items within a category are necessarily well associated.

A pool of 25 lists of 16 common nouns was constructed, each list beginning with a different letter. The only letter excluded was X. Two sublist structures were used in the experiment. The first was made up by taking 12 words from one alphabetic heading (1/12 structure). The second was made up by taking three words from each of four headings (4/3 structure).

For example, 1/12: Hamster Hippo Holiday Heater Home Hill Hate...
4/3 : Atom Apple Archive Doctor Dairy Dictator Umpire...

It was hoped that any differential effects of the study/test schedules on these structures would help to localize the organizational effects of the training sequences.

Since the recall was to be cued by initial letter, one initial letter was provided for the 1/12 condition, for example H, and four, for example ADUW, were provided in the 4/3 condition.

A total of five study/test conditions were used and these are shown below.

STTTTT	STSTST	STTSST	SSSTTT	SSSSST
1	2	3	4	5

Each begins with a study phase and ends with a test phase. 1 and 5 represent the extreme recall and study conditions respectively, while 2 represents a standard learning condition. Lachman and Laughery found that later test trials are marginally more effective than early ones. This may be due to an inappropriate organization being consolidated early in the sequence. For this reason it was predicted that condition 4 might prove superior to condition 3.

In order to fulfil the earlier mentioned constraint that, after the initial study phase and before the final immediate test phase, study and test sequences would alternate, two order blocks were constructed. Block 1 is given below. (S2 was followed by S5, etc.)

Block 1

Initial presentation:	S2	S5	S1	S4	S3
	T2	S5	T1	S4	T3
	S2	T1	S5	T3	S4
	T2	S5	T1	S3	T4
	S2	T1	S5	T4	S3
Immediate recall	T2	T5	T1	T4	T3

S indicates a study phase and T a test phase. The numeral indicates which list is being studied. To identify any possible order effects, Block 1 is as near as possible the inverse of Block 2.

It should be noted that:

(a) the pattern in each block is SSSSS TSTSTSTSTSTSTSTSTS TTTTT;

(b) the conditions 1–5 have the requisite S/T sequencing;

(c) the interval separating consecutive experience with a given list is as even as possible, the average being four trials with a maximum of five and minimum of three.

All the subjects were asked to attend on two sessions. At the first, after two familiarization and warm-up tasks, they underwent the learning procedure outlined above.

At the second session, after the necessary warm-up, they were given a recall test on all the material. This was followed by a recognition test. Four words were selected from each of the presented sublists to act as targets in the two-item forced-choice test. The distractors were made up from the original pool of items. Subjects were asked to express their confidence in their recognition decision on a five-point scale.

The recall data were analysed by a five-way split plot fully crossed design. Three of the variables are within subject and two between. The two between-subject variables, block order and list structure order, are nuisance variables. Neither produced a significant main effect or interaction with any other variable. The three within-subject variables are list structure (1/12 or 4/3), study test condition (5 levels) and time of test (immediate or delayed). The triple interaction of these three variables is significant ($p < 0.05$). To interpret this result separate analyses were performed for the data associated with each of the two list structures. Figures 1(a) and 1(b) summarize these data. The triple interaction is due to an interaction between time of test and study/test condition which occurs only in the 4/3 lists. For the 1/12 lists all the conditions suffer about the same decrement due to delay. However, for the 4/3 list this is not the case. Sheffe tests show that condition 1 (all test) is inferior to the other conditions and in the case of the 4/3 lists suffers less from delay than the other conditions.

The recognition results appeared to show the same relationships between the conditions with respect to both hit rate and confidence. However, it is difficult satisfactorily to interpret the data as they are confused by ceiling effects.

In summary, there are two major recall results in this experiment. Firstly, under extreme conditions such as these the usual recall-consolidation effects

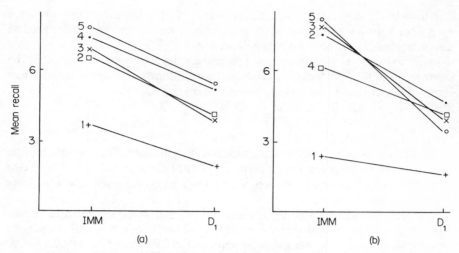

Figure 1. Experiment 1. Conditions × delay interaction. (a) 1/12 list structure; (b) 4/3 list structure

may not be apparent. The low level of performance in the training stage means that the words recalled, though well learned, are not sufficient in number to rival delayed recall in the other conditions. Secondly, there is an interaction with list structure. The more subdivided lists are more impervious to delay after recall training. This latter rather complex result requires further exploration and replication.

Though these results are interesting, they do not answer satisfactorily our original questions—namely, when learning set effects are removed by using a within-subject design and level of performance is suitably manipulated, is it possible to get transfer from recall consolidation to delayed recognition? In particular, the recognition results from experiment 1 are not interpretable because of obtrusive ceiling effects. In experiment 2 the same design is modified to rectify this state of affairs.

Experiment 2

The design of experiment 2 used the same mixed-list structure as had already been used in experiment 1. The number of conditions was reduced to three: study, test and standard. The conditions 3 and 4 in experiment 1 had not contributed any significant information and were therefore dropped. The immediate recall following all conditions was also dropped in order to obtain purer results of the all-study condition in delay. Four delayed-recall trials were given, one before the recognition test and three after. Forty-word sublists were used, each cued by initial letter. Three letters were chosen and 80 words were selected for each. For all the words frequency of occurrence was between one and 20 in the corpus of Kucera and Francis (1967); they were all tri-or quadri-syllabic concrete nouns. Forty words were selected at random from each pool to provide the sublists for presentation and the other 40 were used as the distractors in the delayed-recognition test.

In order to ensure that there was a reasonable level of initial learning, all the items received four presentation trials at the beginning of the sequence and then received five critical trials, as may be seen below.

Study	SSSS	SSSSS	Delay	T	Rg	TTT
Test	SSSS	TTTTT	Delay	T	Rg	TTT
Standard	SSSS	TSTST	Delay	T	Rg	TTT

All trials in the first session were blocked into the mixed-list design and the average interval between consecutive experience on a given sublist was two trials. A presentation rate of two seconds per item was used and the delay period was one week.

The recognition test was carried out by a signal-detection method (Egan, 1958; Parks, 1966). Single items were presented for recognition and the subject was required to decide whether the item was NEW (non-list) or OLD (list) and then to indicate his confidence in that decision on a three-point scale (sure, fairly sure, guess). Recognition reaction time was measured from the onset of the stimulus until the initial decision response by means of a timer/voice key.

Analysis of the recall data (Figure 2) showed that there was a significant main effect of S/T conditions ($p < 0.001$) and time of test ($p < 0.001$). Further analysis showed that the test condition was significantly better than the other two and that the standard condition was better than the study condition. The time-of-test effect represents a strong reminiscence effect in all three conditions.

The results confirm that, even in a situation where the subject is expecting test on all conditions and the uncertainty of the situation is sufficient to maintain interest, it is the test condition that consolidates retention and leads to a higher score on delayed recall.

The recognition data are perhaps best expressed as the operating characteristics, criterion placements and recognition reaction times for the three conditions. In a signal-detection analysis it is assumed that targets and distractors form two separate but overlapping distributions of 'strength' (in our case, familiarity). The model assumes one may estimate the probabilities that a test item came from the target or distractor distributions respectively on the basis of its familiarity. A criterion familiarity level is assumed to be set such that items with familiarity levels above it elicit the response 'Old'. The responses made in a recognition test depend on the degree of overlap between the two distributions and the criterion. The former is measured by a family of parameters, the commonest being denoted d' (we shall also use d'_a and d'_e). These parameters indicate the degree of discrimination. For a given d' the criterion may be set in a number of positions. In the extreme it may be set to exclude all false alarms, at the cost of missing some targets, or to include all targets, at the cost of increasing the false alarm rate. The d' and criteria are deduced

149

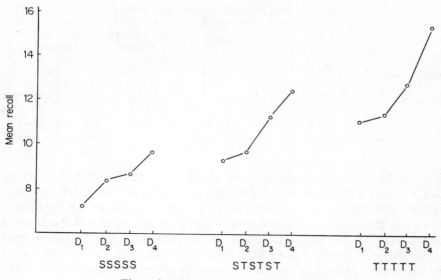

Figure 2. Experiment 2. Delayed recall

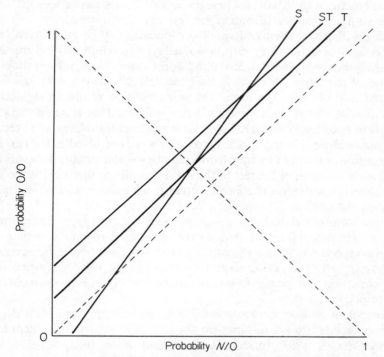

Figure 3. Experiment 2. Mean operating characteristics (normal–
normal plot)

Table 3. Recognition data from experiment 2

	d'_a	d'_e	β	Yes responses Targets	(maximum 40) Distractors
Study	0.721	0.722	0.76	31.42	16.53
Standard	1.110	1.130	0.97	31.33	10.50
Test	0.644	0.692	0.90	28.66	13.92

from an ROC (receiver operator characteristic). The probability of saying 'Old' to a target (hit) is plotted against the probability of saying 'Old' to a distractor (false alarm) for a number of criteria. In the recognition test the criteria are represented by the confidence ratings. For a full explanation of this analysis see McNicol (1972). Figure 3 shows the mean operating characteristics, derived from mean d'_a (Simpson and Fitter, 1973) and mean slope of the individual characteristics, plotted on normal coordinates. It can be seen that the mean separation of the target and distractor distributions is approximately the same for the study and test conditions but that greater separation is achieved in the standard condition ($p < 0.017$). These d'_a and d_e' values can be seen in Table 3 together with the criterion (β) values, hit and false alarm rates.

These results show the usual recall consolidation effect on delayed recall. There is also evidence for transfer to delayed-recognition discrimination. Comparing the study and standard conditions, there is a significant difference in favour of the latter. However, unlike the delayed-recall results, this is not continued into the test condition. The test condition results in significantly poorer discrimination than the standard condition. This is again explicable as a performance-level effect. Delayed recall may be consolidated when recognition is not because of the different number of words involved in the two tests. In recognition, a few well-learned words may be a disadvantage if they are well learned at the expense of the rest of the list. From the comparison of the study and standard conditions it is concluded that recall consolidation does transfer to delayed recognition.

The reaction-time data for the four possible response types are plotted in Figure 4. The normal result that correct responses require less time than incorrect responses is shown (Sternberg, 1969). It is noticeable, however, that the time required for an OLD response, correct or incorrect, is shortest in the 'study' condition and longest in the 'test' condition. The reverse is true for the NEW responses.

A number of authors have suggested that the time required for a decision is inversely related to the distance on the strength axis from the item to the criterion (McGill, 1963; Bindra, Williams and Wise, 1965; Sekuler, 1965; 1966; Hall, Sekuler and Cushman, 1969). Smith (1968) has demonstrated that, for most practical purposes, it is reasonable to envisage the system as being

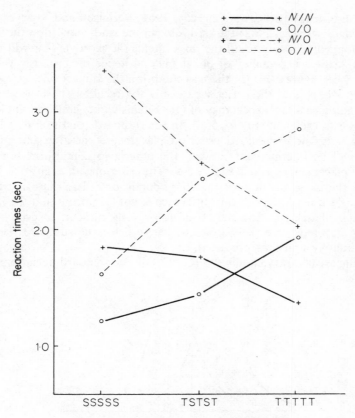

Figure 4. Experiment 2. Recognition latencies

divided into two areas, one of high cost, close to the criterion, and the other of low cost, where cost is reflected in time to make a decision.

This idea is remarkably similar to the recognition models of Atkinson and Juola (1973) and Atkinson, Herrmann and Wescourt (1974). Consider Figure 5(a). Outside the area bounded by the subsidiary criteria, C_0 and C_1, a rapid decision is possible, but inside this area extra processes, reflected in increased reaction times, are required for decisions. The actual bandwidth of C_0–C_1 is governed by a speed/accuracy trade-off (Weaver, 1974). It is our contention that a mechanism of this type is operating in our experiment.

Smith (1968) has suggested that in situations of low d' a biased criterion placement is the most cost effective, while in a high-separation situation an unbiased placement is most economic. As can be seen in Table 3, the d_a and d_e' values (which are approximately equivalent to d' in the equal-variance case) are low and almost equal for the test and the study conditions. This would suggest that a biased criterion might prove to be the most practical. It is our suggestion that the direction of the criterion shift will be determined by the subjective expectancies of target frequencies involved and that this will affect

152

the reaction times (LaBerge and Tweedy, 1964; Bertelson and Tisseyre, 1966; Bertelson and Barzeele, 1962; Parks, 1966). In the study condition the subject has a prolonged exposure to all the target items (40 words). This will lead to there being a high expectancy of old items and hence the criterion will shift to the left (see Figure 5(b)). In the test condition the subject only experiences all the items once and thereafter views only the recalled subset (average 15 words), leading to a low expectancy of OLD items with a concomitant shift of the criterion to the right (Figure 5(c)). In the standard condition d' is higher, suggesting a possibly unbiased criterion placement, and the subjective expectancy will be intermediate between the other two conditions, suggesting the type of placement shown in Figure 5(a). The criterion values given in Table 3 show that the mean β value for the study condition is less than that for the test trials as required, though this difference is not significant and the latter is still just less than one. However, β is notoriously difficult to estimate and averaging may have unexpected effects. Mean β for the standard condition is approximately unity, as predicted.

Assuming an arbitrary bandwidth $(C_0 - C_1)$ of one standard deviation (of the

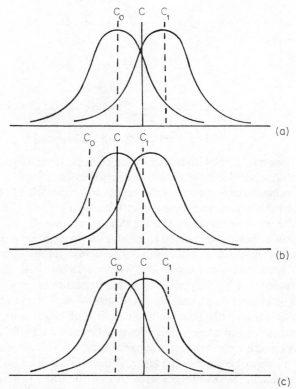

Figure 5. Experiment 2. Hypothetical criterion placements. (a) TSTST; (b) SSSSS; (c) TTTTT

distractor distribution) it is possible to predict the proportion of each type of response that will fall into the high-cost area, using the d' and β values obtained in the experiment. The ordering of these proportions fits the reaction-time data well for the study and standard conditions. The fit is not so good for the test condition. However, the bandwidth of C_0–C_1 may be governed by factors that do not hold constant over conditions. Likewise, C_0 and C_1 may not be equidistant from β. One of the next tasks is to determine how this search area is defined and what factors affect its width and placement, and whether the extra search time required holds constant across all types of material.

Summary and Discussion

Two experiments were performed using a within-subject design to remove any possible effects of learning set. The important results come from experiment 2, in which recall-test phases were found to facilitate delayed recognition as well as delayed recall. The transfer effect is more limited in terms of the condition under which it is obtainable than the simple recall-consolidation effect. This is explained on the basis of level of performance as an additional variable.

The latency results were interpreted in a two-stage recognition model of the kind used by Atkinson and Juola (1973; 1974). This model was extended to explain criterion placement in the experiment.

The transfer of learning on recall trials to delayed recognition indicates a degree of overlap in the information used in recall and recognition. Two possible areas have been suggested where this overlap might occur. Firstly, there is the recognition test postulated to be a subprocess in recall. The correspondence between this kind of recognition and the experimental recognition task depends on the correspondence of the covert distractors in the former to the overt distractors in the latter. The covert distractors are assumed to be mediators associatively related to the targets, the latter are chosen by the experimenter and may be more or less related to the targets.

Considering the distinction drawn earlier between context elements concerning the presentation of the list and context elements concerning the properties of the list, both may be affected. Recall is a type of presentation, and new context elements will be associated to an item as the result of producing the item at recall. Covert recognition at recall may also increase the accessibility of item-to-context associations concerning the properties of the list. This is related to the second area of overlap between item-to-context associations concerning properties of the list and item-to-item associations used for retrieval. For example, a context element of the form 'there were four animals' may be part of the association between 'Lion' and 'Giraffe' in the retrieval plan. Thus any increase in accessibility due to practice will facilitate both recall and recognition. It is clear from this discussion that this approach requires that semantic factors should play a part in recognition as they do in recall. It was once assumed that this was not the case (Kintsch, 1970b); however, there is now a growing body of evidence that semantic factors do affect recognition memory (see, for example, Chapters 2 and 3).

4. Conclusions

In the second section the nature of learning during a test sequence, in terms of its effect on recall and recognition performance, was examined. It was concluded that under the right conditions learning on recall trials may transfer to recognition, and vice versa. This allowed us to hypothesize that the information used or the processes involved in recognition and recall must overlap to some extent. In the previous section a framework was described within which possible areas of overlap might be identified. Learning is split up into a number of hypothetical subprocesses. Learning for recognition has been considered as list specification and item-to-context association. Learning for recall depends mainly on item-to-item associations which are used to build up a retrieval plan.

The context elements used in recognition are divided into two kinds: those which are concerned with the presentation of the list and those concerned with the properties of the list itself. The latter will in many cases be part of the item-to-item associations used in retrieval. The two areas of overlap considered are those context elements which double as associations between items for retrieval and the recognition subprocess of recall postulated to distinguish mediators from distractors in a retrieval plan.

There has been some emphasis on theory in this chapter and it should be said that none of the evidence discussed proves that the approach taken is the most suitable. All that can be said is that the evidence is consistent with the approach and, hopefully, the approach allows the complex results to be assimilated more easily. The experimental data are as yet far from complete. Quite a lot is known about item-to-item association from studies of organization, but relatively little about the processes involved in recognition or the difference between the experimental recognition test and the recognition subprocess of recall. New paradigms are required to examine these points. However, we feel that the ideas and concepts involved have some potency.

Consider first the distinction between context elements concerned with the presentation of the list and those concerned with the list itself. This is related to the dichotomy commonly drawn between 'sheer familiarity' and 'organization' as contextual information used in recognition. For example, Mandler (1972) distinguishes between 'occurrence information' and 'organizational variables'. The former is used to make an initial judgment and the latter, if necessary, as a 'retrieval check'. Similarly, Atkinson and Juola (1973; 1974) distinguish between a simple judgment on the basis of familiarity and an 'extended memory search' on the basis of information from the 'event knowledge store'. We have no theoretical commitment to a dichotomy rather than a continuum of 'sensuousness'. We prefer to consider a continuum based on number of context elements sampled in making a familiarity estimation, and for that reason a corresponding continuum of sensuousness may be more useful.

The model proposed to explain the recognition latencies following study and test sequences has a number of merits. Firstly, it provides a link between the various performance measures obtainable from a recognition test. It also gives detail to our approach by indicating what determines the most effective placement for the criterion and rules to predict how much context information needs to be sampled in a familiarity estimate.

It is proposed that the amount of information considered when estimating the familiarity of a test item is dependent on the relation between the item's familiarity and the criterion-familiarity level above which the subject responds 'Old' and below which he responds 'New'. If the familiarity is close to the criterion, more context elements are sampled in an attempt to provide a more accurate value. The evidence for this approach is provided by the response times gathered in experiment 2.

Atkinson and Juola (1973; 1974) propose that a simple judgment on the basis of 'familiarity' is always performed first, and if the resultant familiarity estimate falls within some critical area either side of the criterion the extended memory search is instituted. Though this may often be the case there is no *a priori* reason why the more sensuous context elements should always be sampled first. We have also seen how one may predict the optimum placement of criteria so as to minimize 'cost'—in this case response time. Smith (1968) has shown that a two-value model will produce essentially the same results as a more complex one where the cost is a continuous function of the distance from the criterion. Thus, in many respects, there is no great difference between the two models.

Summary

The paper discusses learning on test trials in the light of resultant recall and recognition performance. Comparing recall and recognition performance, these manipulations may produce differential effects, though it is generally possible to arrange the conditions so that recall and recognition performance are affected in the same way. These conflicting results are resolved by a detailed examination of the experimental conditions, especially level of performance.

The results rule out any interpretation in which recognition and recall are based on the same unidimensional strength. Instead, they are incorporated into an associative viewpoint of the kind favoured in the current list-learning literature. Learning and performance are divided into a number of hypothetical subprocesses. Learning for recognition consists of list specification and item-to-context association. Recognition performance depends on comparing context elements associated with the test item to the list specification so as to obtain a familiarity estimate.

Two experiments are presented incorporating a within-subject design which avoids some of the problems faced by previous investigations of learning during

156

test trials. The second demonstrates transfer from learning during recall trials to delayed recognition. Recognition latencies are interpreted using a model which predicts the amount of information sampled in producing the 'familiarity' estimate as well as the criteria set to evaluate it from a signal-detection model.

Acknowledgments

We wish to thank John Brown for advice in the planning of the experiments and David Routh for help during the preparation of this chapter. Full details of the experiments are given in the doctoral thesis of one of us (Cooper, 1974), who held a studentship from the Social Science Research Council.

6   *Interference theory revisited*

LEO POSTMAN

Are recall and recognition equally susceptible to retroactive and proactive inhibition (RI and PI)? This question has assumed increasing importance in recent discussions of interference theory, particularly with reference to the conditions and characteristics of RI; it has also potentially important implications for current conceptions of the differences between the processes of recall and recognition.

Historical Background

Classical interference theory was developed to explain the impairment of associative recall by interpolated learning (IL). There are several historical reasons why the measurement of RI in associative recall became the reference operation in experimental tests of principles of interference. First, retention losses attributable to interference were originally demonstrated for associative recall (Müller and Pilzecker, 1900). Early investigations failed to find evidence of RI when retention was measured by recognition rather than recall (Heine, 1914). Second, and most important, the concept of interference took on major systematic significance by virtue of its compatibility with a stimulus–response analysis of acquisition and retention, and with the extension of principles of conditioning to the domain of verbal learning and memory (e.g. Gibson, 1940; Osgood, 1946). Thus, interference came to denote a conflict of habits, or competition between responses to identical or similar stimuli. The A–B, A–D paradigm became the standard procedure for examining the operation of interference in transfer and recall. Finally, the emphasis on RI was sustained by the fact that this form of interference could be placed in direct opposition to the principles of decay and disuse (McGeoch, 1932). The phenomenon of PI was identified relatively late (Whitely, 1927), and interpreted as a matter of course within the framework of theories of retroaction. The fundamental importance of PI as a determinant of long-term forgetting was brought to the fore only many years later (Underwood, 1957). The assumption that RI and PI represent complementary manifestations of the same processes of interference was never called into question.

Two-Factor Theory

These historical developments were crystallized in the two-factor theory (Melton and Irwin, 1940; Melton and von Lackum, 1941), which for a long time provided the basic conceptual underpinning for the bulk of experimental studies of interference in recall. The two factors determining the amount and the observable characteristics of interference are unlearning and response competition. Unlearning of A–B occurs during the acquisition of A–D and is a process which is akin to experimental extinction (or, more precisely, counter-conditioning). The weakening of the A–B associations during IL is a consequence of negative transfer: B continues to be elicited by A and fails to be reinforced. While response conflict is a condition of unlearning, it was not assumed that A–B must be extinguished before A–D can be acquired (for a detailed discussion of this point, which becomes important in the assessment of recent tests of the hypothesis of associative unlearning, see Postman and Underwood, 1973). If an A–B association escapes unlearning, for whatever reason, it is subject to competition from the newly acquired A–D association when recall of the first list is required. The postulation of two loci of retroactive interference—one during IL and the other at the time of recall—reflects the assumption that two or more responses can coexist as associates of the same stimulus and clearly implies that the acquisition of A–D is not contingent on the prior unlearning of A–B.

The analogy between unlearning and extinction entailed the prediction that retroactive losses are transitory: unlearned associations should show spontaneous recovery over time. Given this assumption, the conditions of PI could be derived directly from the two-factor theory of RI. Since the most recent task is not subject to unlearning, there remains, by subtraction as it were, only competition at recall as a determinant of PI. It follows that PI should be smaller than RI as long as the unlearned first-list associations have not fully recovered. As spontaneous recovery proceeds, the retroactive losses caused by unlearning are reversed and the competitive power of first-list associations increases. Consequently, RI should decrease, and PI increase, as the retention interval is lengthened. Early evidence confirmed the prediction that RI exceeds PI after relatively short retention intervals (Melton and von Lackum, 1941) and that this difference is reduced as a function of delay (Underwood, 1948a,b). At that time, there was no evidence for absolute spontaneous recovery; consequently, it remained uncertain whether the decrease in RI and the increase in PI were interdependent processes. More recently, absolute first-list recovery has been demonstrated in several experiments, for the most part after intervals of the order of half an hour (Forrester, 1970; Kamman and Melton, 1967; Martin and Mackay, 1970; Postman, Stark and Fraser, 1968; Postman, Stark and Henschel, 1969; Shulman and Martin, 1970). In some cases, increases in first-list retention have been reported after delays of a day or more (Abra, 1969; Ceraso and Henderson, 1965; 1966; Silverstein, 1967). A causal link between first-list recovery and increases in PI has, however, not been established (Postman, Stark and Fraser, 1968).

Competition

When the two-factor theory was formulated, neither of the postulated processes of response competition and unlearning was firmly anchored to empirical observations. The expected manifestation of competition is the overt intrusion of conflicting responses attached to a given stimulus—B responses during the acquisition of A–D, and D responses during the recall of A–B. Such intrusions do occur, but only very infrequently, certainly not in sufficient numbers to account for the observed levels of negative transfer and retroaction. In general, the same is true for the intrusion of responses from prior lists on tests for PI. Furthermore, frequency of intrusions is not related monotonically to the observed level of interference. To maintain the position that competition plays a significant role in recall interference, it became necessary to assume that many intrusions are recognized as errors and consequently remain implicit. The ability to identify the list membership of responses was designated as list differentiation (Underwood, 1945). It was proposed that list differentiation varied directly with both the absolute and relative strengths of the competing associations and inversely with the length of the time interval since the end of IL. These hypotheses subsequently received independent verification (Winograd, 1968; McCrystal, 1970).

The introduction of the concept of list differentiation represented an important elaboration of two-factor theory. It was important, first of all, because it specified the conditions governing the overt manifestation of response competition. More generally, the door was opened for the incorporation into interference theory of concepts that do not derive directly from traditional principles of stimulus–response association and conditioning. When this development is viewed from the vantage point of contemporary orienting attitudes, one finds here an early recognition of the influence of discriminative and decision processes on recall performance. This point is worthy of emphasis because it is a mistake to view classical interference theory, as represented by the two-factor approach, as a static expression of S–R and conditioning principles.

The role assigned to non-associative factors in determining interference at recall was broadened when Newton and Wickens (1956) introduced the concept of generalized competition. To account for the substantial RI they observed under the A–B, C–D paradigm, i.e. in the absence of conflicting associations to identical or similar stimuli, these investigators suggested that subjects carry over to the test of first-list retention a disposition to restrict themselves to the responses from the recently practised interpolated list. This form of competition was designated as generalized because it occurs not between the alternative responses to specific stimuli but rather between the response repertoires in the successive lists. Attention was thus called to the fact that interference at recall could be a consequence of the subject's set as well as of the elicitation of conflicting responses by individual stimuli. Generalized competition is to be distinguished clearly from list differentiation: the former refers to the persistence of a set to give the responses learned last, the latter to the ability to identify the list membership of individual responses. The two may often be correlated, but in principle they need not be. In any event, it is clear that with the introduction of the concepts of list differentiation and generalized competition the original view of competition as habit conflict was substantially extended. Competition became a theoretical construct of which overt intrusions are only one observable manifestation.

Unlearning

For a long time, the evidence for unlearning remained highly circumstantial. Such a process was postulated in the first instance because the overt effects of competition, i.e. interlist intrusions, apparently could not account for the observed retroactive losses. Actually, a pure competition theory of RI, such as that advocated by McGeoch (1942), remained tenable if one were willing to make appropriate assumptions about the influence on performance of implicit intrusions (Thune and Underwood, 1943). However, the difference in magnitude between immediate RI and PI, and the change in this difference over time, could be explained most economically by the two-factor theory. Even this evidence remained uncertain, however, since increases in PI could not be linked directly to the spontaneous recovery of unlearned first-list associations.

The status of the concept of unlearning changed drastically with the introduction of the MMFR test by Barnes and Underwood (1959). This procedure— requiring the subject to reproduce both the B and the D response to each stimulus in either order and at his own pace—made it possible to assess the availability of first-list and second-list associations independently of specific competition. The availability of first-list associations was found to be reduced progressively as IL continued. This finding has been reproduced consistently in many subsequent studies and is by now a firmly established fact.

The MMFR test has proved to be a powerful analytic device for the investigation of the conditions and characteristics of unlearning. Granted that the results obtained by this procedure demonstrate unlearning in a descriptive sense, the question arises of what components of the original memory are weakened or lost as a consequence of IL. Since unlearning is linked to negative transfer, it appeared likely that the components of prior learning responsible for transfer were also subject to unlearning. This deduction was verified in an important study by McGovern (1964) which showed that the retroactive losses found under various paradigms of transfer could be assigned, in an essentially additive fashion, to the unlearning of forward, backward and contextual associations. In this analysis, contextual associations represent response learning, i.e. the formation of associations between the several responses in a list and the experimental situation. With each of the components of transfer specified in terms of a set of associations, it became possible to conclude that a given component would be unlearned if the A–B, A–D paradigm obtained for it in the successive lists.

To isolate the contribution to RI of the unlearning of contextual associations, i.e. the decrement attributable to response loss, McGovern examined the reductions in RI under various paradigms when the test procedure was changed from MMFR to associative matching. As expected, the gains were greatest when the original and the interpolated responses were different and unrelated (A–B, A–D; A–B, C–D); the changes were relatively minor when the responses remained the same (A–B, C–B; A–B, A–Br). The pattern of scores obtained on the two tests of first-list retention indicated that both specific (forward and backward) and contextual associations are unlearned. In view of subsequent developments, it is important to make explicit the logic of measurement which led to this conclusions. It is assumed that performance on a test of recall depends on both the availability of the responses and the integrity of the specific associations. Associative matching requires only recognition of the correct stimulus–response pairings and hence will be successful to the extent that the specific associations remain intact. Thus, the inference about what is unlearned hinges on the validity with which the retention of specific associations can be assessed by a test of associative matching.

Measurement of Associative Unlearning

Can it be taken for granted that a matching test administered after the acquisition of successive lists under a paired-associate recall procedure provides a valid measure of associative loss? There are several considerations which suggest that it would be hazardous to do so. First, after a fixed amount of practice recognition normally surpasses recall. Thus, the attainment of a criterion of recall performance represents overlearning with respect to the same criterion on a test of recognition. When recall and matching are compared directly, the relative susceptibility of specific associations to unlearning may, therefore, be underestimated because of functional differences in the degree of original learning. If that were the only probable source of bias, estimates of retroactive losses in associative matching could be accepted as conservative. The fact that such losses are usually small in absolute terms (e.g. Delprato, 1971; Garskof, 1968; Garskof and Sandak, 1964; Greenberg and Wickens, 1972; Sandak and Garskof, 1967) would have no critical implications, nor would occasional failures to observe any RI at all (e.g. Merryman, 1971).

The problems of interpretation that arise in comparisons between tests of recall and of associative matching are not, however, limited to probable differences in the effective degrees of learning. A potentially important source of confounding is that after paired-associate learning associative matching introduces a drastic change in the method of testing, whereas recall represents a continuation of the procedure used during acquisition. One must ask, therefore, how likely it is that a subject shifted to a matching task after a protracted period of recall practice will in fact completely change his mode of responding. The arrangements of the matching task do not force him to do so. He can, if he so chooses, attempt to recall the response to each of the stimuli, and then search for the response he has retrieved among the alternatives presented to him. The failure to recall a response may result in the false rejection of a correct alternative. Even when the subject sets out to carry out the matching instructions by choosing among the possible pairings, he may well use his ability to recall the response as a checking device when he is uncertain (cf. Mandler, 1972). Under these circumstances a failure of recall may again lead to the rejection of the correct alternative.

To the extent that the subject's matches are influenced by his ability to recall the responses, the test of associative matching fails to eliminate response availability as a determinant of performance. Since the probability of recall is substantially lower for the experimental (say, A–B, A–D) than the control (rest) group, the difference between them could thus be maintained, even if there were no associative loss. (Here, and in the discussion that follows, associative loss refers to decrements in intrapair association.) Such an explanation is not necessarily strained, since the absolute difference to be accounted for is small, usually of the order of one item. The experimental subjects have, of course, twice as much recall practice during acquisition as the control subjects, and hence should be more disposed to mediate their matches by response recall or to resort to recall checks prior to making their choices.

An even more basic question of interpretation must be considered when there is a shift from recall during acquisition to recognition on the test of retention. There are growing indications that the way in which material is processed at the time at input, and in particular what features are selectively encoded, is systematically influenced by the subject's expectations about the test of retention that is to follow (Bernbach, 1973; Carey and Lockhart, 1973; Loftus, 1972; Tversky, 1973). Of special importance for purposes of the present discussion is the findings that recognition performance is superior when the subject anticipates a recognition test than when he prepares for a test of recall (Carey and Lockhart, 1973; Tversky, 1973). The implication is, of course, that a test of associative matching after paired-associate practice may not provide conclusive information about the resistance of specific associations to unlearning because the subject did not encode the stimulus–response contingencies so as to maximize the probability of success on such a test.

On a matching test the subject must discriminate between correct and incorrect associations; on a test of recall the stimulus term serves as a retrieval cue for the response. It is only reasonable to suppose that the maximally efficient processing strategies differ for these two tasks. In anticipation of matching, attention might well focus on differences among intact pairs. For purposes of recall, the retrieval route from the stimulus to the response is of primary importance. In terms of Underwood's (1969a) analysis, recall is dependent primarily on the associative attributes of memory, and recognition on the discriminative ones. Advance knowledge about the nature of the test of retention will encourage the selective storage of the appropriate class of attributes. Furthermore, the subject will become increasingly efficient in the retrieval of these attributes during the test trials of original learning. These skills become irrelevant, or may indeed be a source of interference, when a new method of testing calling for the utilization of different attributes is used in the test of retention.

We have identified two closely related difficulties that arise when recall and recognition are compared after conventional paired-associate practice: (a) performance is likely to be depressed because of the persistence on the test of retention of modes of responding established during acquisition; (b) when there is such a change, what was originally stored may not be optimally focused on the information required at the time of test. The magnitude of the resulting biases may well be related to the amount of paired-associate practice and the level of negative transfer in acquisition. The first of the difficulties can be eliminated by keeping the conditions of acquisition and testing the same. When purely associative losses are to be measured, a matching procedure is then used on the acquisition trials as well as on the test of retention. The difference between recall and matching scores is again used to estimate the contribution of response losses to RI in recall. The estimate can, however, be only approximate at best because the scales of measurement for recall and recognition are not the same.

If there is no RI in recognition, it becomes reasonable to infer that reduction in response availability is largely responsible for the unlearning observed in recall. On the other hand, if both tests show RI, the implication is that associative as well as response losses contribute to the losses in recall. The relative weight of the two factors cannot be gauged precisely because of the difference between the two scales of measurement. Even such qualitative conclusions must remain tentative, however, because the second systematic difficulty remains unresolved: associative matching and access to available responses in the presence of specific cues may be based on different attributes of memory and mediated by different retrieval processes. Thus, there may be associative losses in recall, in the sense that a response in the subject's repertoire cannot be placed appropriately, even when a recognition test under comparable conditions of IL fails to show RI.

The constraints on inferences drawn from comparisons of retroactive losses in recall and matching may be summarized as follows. Taken by themselves, measures of associative matching yield evidence about the susceptibility of purely associative information to unlearning. Provided there is no unexpected change in procedure, variations in performance on the two types of test permit a gross assessment of the components of interference in recall. Because of inherent differences in the task demands, however, such assessments must remain tentative and eventually have to be verified in the context of recall.

Retroactive Losses in Recognition

We consider now the results of experiments on retroaction in which performance was measured by recognition both during acquisition and on the test of retention. This arrangement was introduced by Postman and Stark (1969), who used a multiple-choice procedure throughout. Each multiple-choice item consisted of the stimulus term and four alternative responses from within the list being learned or tested for retention. Retroactive inhibition was assessed under several paradigms of transfer, but attention will be limited here to three conditions: A–B, C–D; A–B, A–D; and A–B, A–Br. The only paradigm under which there was a significant amount of RI was A–Br. There was only a small difference (half an item) between C–D and A–D, and neither differed from the single-list control treatment. It is important to note that relative to C–D there was substantial negative transfer in the learning of A–D as well as A–Br. Thus, specific associations appeared to be highly resistant to unlearning (A–D) except under conditions of heavy and persistent negative transfer during IL (A–Br). These results were in sharp contrast to those obtained with the same material and at comparable levels of original and interpolated learning under a recall procedure. In the latter situation, RI was greater for A–D than for A–Br, i.e. first-list recall was poorer when the responses changed than when they remained the same. The pattern of retention losses observed under the two procedures was taken to imply that RI in recall reflects primarily a loss of response availability when successive lists conform to the A–B, A–D paradigm.

Questions inevitably arise about the validity of a conclusion based on acceptance of the null hypothesis. The finding that multiple-choice tests of recognition show little or no RI under the A–B, A–D paradigm is no exception. The results reported by Postman and Stark (1969) have been replicated by other investigators (Anderson and Watts, 1971; Sanders, Whitaker and Cofer, 1974). Nevertheless, it is necessary to consider the objection that the null effect is attributable to a lack of sensitivity of the measures of performance. In a recent review, Wickelgren (1973) makes the claim that 'in the Postman and Stark study, the difference between AB–AC and AB–CD paradigms was quite large (*sic*!), though too near the 100 per cent correct ceiling to be statistically significant' (p. 435). Such an argument begs the question. It is a fact that significant RI was observed under another paradigm (A–Br); hence, the sensitivity necessary to detect interference was present in principle. To explain the absence of significant losses under other conditions by reference to a ceiling effect is to assert that the performance was, as it were, higher than it should be. However, that is precisely the point at issue, namely, whether specific associations are relatively resistant to unlearning. If they are, then an acceptance of Wickelgren's argument would make it impossible ever to establish this fact.

One can, of course, manipulate the degree of original and of interpolated learning, to see whether a significant difference emerges when the overall level of retention declines. However, such a pursuit of statistical significance is beside the point. The theoretically important fact is that at comparable levels of learning there is substantial RI in recall but not in recognition. The implications of this finding would not be changed drastically by a demonstration of significant RI in recognition under a particular set of circumstances. In any event, acceptance of the null hypothesis—that there is never any associative loss on tests of recognition under the A–B, A–D paradigm—has not been advocated and need not be refuted. As the results obtained with the A–B, A–Br paradigm show, there is substantial unlearning of specific associations when negative transfer is heavy and persistent. It is not likely that there is a sharp discontinuity of processes as one moves from one paradigm to another. The argument is rather that under the classical arrangement for producing associative interference the retroactive losses on tests of recognition are small relative to those observed in recall.

Tests of associative matching are normally designed so as to eliminate other sources of interference, in particular failures of list differentiation. The opportunity for such failures to occur can, however, be created by including the second-list as well as the first-list response among the alternatives presented along with a given stimulus. As was shown in an early study (Postman, 1952), the juxtaposition of original and interpolated items significantly increases the amount of RI. This increase is attributable directly to failures of list differentiation.

Recently, Anderson and Watts (1971) reintroduced this manipulation in an experiment in which the multiple-choice procedure was used in acquisition as well as on the test of retention. Both the A–B, A–D and the A–B, A–Br paradigms were included in the design. A significant amount of RI (relative to the A–B, C–D control treatment) was obtained under both experimental paradigms when the two successive associates to a stimulus were juxtaposed on the retention test, but not when the alternatives were restricted to responses from within the list. The authors interpret these results as evidence for competition or specific associative interference in recognition. They suggest that in the presence of the second-list response the first-list association may be 'displaced'. The reference to a mechanism of displacement is obscure, but if it is implied that the first-list association cannot be recognized as correct, the conclusion is clearly not warranted. The absence of RI under the non-competitional treatment shows that IL does not by itself lead to a decline in recognition. Thus, the findings of Anderson and Watts demonstrate only that failures of list differentiation can occur on matching tests when the correct choice requires identification of list membership.

To the extent that recognition choices are mediated by recall, processes akin to competition can influence matching performance at least indirectly. This expectation is borne out by the results of a recent study by Sanders, Whitaker and Cofer (1974), in which the multiple-choice procedure was employed in all phases of the experiment. As measured by the number of of correct choices on the test of first-list retention, there was no RI for either the A–B, C–D or the A–B, A–D paradigm. However, there was clear evidence for interference under the latter condition when response latencies were considered. The authors suggest that the increases in latency may reflect response competition, which serves to delay the identification of the correct alternative. When the subject sees a stimulus term, the second-list response,

166

which has become dominant during IL, may be elicited. That response is not, however, one of the available alternatives. The subject might thereupon attempt to recall the first-list response and locate it among the possible choices, or carry out the matching operation proper, i.e. base his decision on the relative familiarity of the alternative pairings.

How seriously the final matches are affected by such intervening processes probably depends on the conditions of acquisition. In the experiment of Sanders *et al.*, virtually all the matches remained correct in spite of the increases in latency. When acquisition is by the anticipation method, responses that fail a covert recall test may, in some cases at least, be erroneously rejected. The potential influence of response competition should be greatly reduced, if not eliminated, when a multiple-choice procedure analogous to the MMFR test is used. That is, the subject has to identify both the first-list and the second-list associate to each stimulus, and the set of distractors includes equal numbers of alternatives from both lists (Postman, Stark and Burns, 1974)

The Search for Artefacts in Recognition Measures of RI

The results of matching tests have failed to provide a definitive answer to the question of whether and to what extent specific associations are subject to unlearning under the A–B, A–D paradigm. After acquisition by the recall method, tests of associative matching usually yield significant evidence of RI. On the other hand, when a recognition procedure is used throughout, the amount of retroactive loss is minimal. In view of the theoretical importance of the issue, it is not surprising that there have been attempts to press for a less equivocal conclusion—to discount the absence of RI as an artefact on the one hand, and to urge acceptance of the null hypothesis on *a priori* grounds on the other.

In defence of the traditional hypothesis of associative unlearning, it has been argued that the virtual absence of RI on multiple-choice tests under the A–B, A–D paradigm is attributable to mediation of the correct choices by intact backward (B–A) associations. Evidence in support of this interpretation has been presented by Merryman (1971) and by Greenberg and Wickens (1972). While the two studies differ in many details, they share the common feature of comparing recognition performance under unidirectional and bidirectional conditions of unlearning. Thus, Merryman used a mixed-list design in which the paradigm of transfer was A–B, A–D for some pairs and A–B, A–D and B–E for others. In the latter case, there were two interpolated pairs corresponding to each first-list pair to provide for the extinction of forward and backward associations, respectively. The design of Greenberg and Wickens was superior to that of Merryman because it avoided the complications of a mixed-list procedure and equated the amount of interpolated activity under the unidirectional and the bidirectional treatments. Nevertheless, there are serious methodological reservations about this design as well as Merryman's. In each case, the manipulations used to produce bidirectional unlearning are, probably of necessity, confounded with other potentially important task variables. These problems have been discussed in detail elsewhere (Postman and Stark, 1972; Postman and Underwood, 1973). It should be noted that in both studies original and interpolated learning were by a recall method, and the multiple-choice procedure was first introduced at the time of the retention test. As for the results, RI was found to be greater after bidirectional than after unidirectional unlearning in both experiments—increasing from near zero to about 20 per cent in Merryman's study, and from about 10 to about 20 per cent in the critical conditions of Greenberg and Wickens' investigation. The latter difference fell short of statistical significance. In a replication of Merryman's experiment (Postman and Stark, 1972), in which an attempt was made to eliminate some of the more serious confoundings, the difference was substantially reduced and was far from significant.

A design that permits an unbiased comparison between unidirectional and bidirectional unlearning remains to be developed. Taken at its face value, the available evidence suggests that the contribution of backward associations to matching performance on a test of first-list retention is quite limited at best. No special importance need be attached to these empirical findings, however, not only on methodological grounds but also because the rationale of the experiments is open to serious question. To explain the absence of RI, it is necessary to assume that backward associations are learned sufficiently well to mediate correct recognition and are not weakened at all during IL. Associative symmetry in acquisition is certainly not an established fact. It is also far from clear that there is no generalization of unlearning from forward to backward associations. Results consistent with this hypothesis have been reported by Johnston (1967) and Petrich (1970; 1971), but there is also strong evidence to the contrary (Birnbaum, 1966; Houston, 1964; Keppel, Bonge, Strand and Parker, 1971). Thus, it is improbable that at the end of IL an intact backward association can fully compensate for every forward association that might have been unlearned. Perhaps more important, the distinction between forward and backward associations becomes blurred when original and interpolated learning are carried out under a multiple-choice procedure. Matching is inherently not a unidirectional process. The pairings among which the subject must decide are likely to be scanned in both the forward and backward direction (cf. Wolford, 1971). As a consequence, the conditions of interference become bidirectional. When the forward associations in the successive lists are A–B and A–D, the relationship between the backward associations is B–A, D–A. The latter paradigm is known to produce associative interference and RI (e.g. McGovern, 1964). Thus, both A–B and B–A associations are subject to disruption when there is bidirectional mediation of matching responses during acquisition.

Whereas mediation by backward associations has been invoked to preserve the generality of the principle of associative unlearning, Martin (1972; 1973) has argued that the existing evidence for RI in recognition should be discounted on methodological grounds. He considers the results unacceptable 'because of the problematic nature of such tests, involving as they do unassessed confusion and decision factors that need to be partialled out' (1973, p. 495). This criticism is sweeping but not very specific. As for decision factors, the subject's choices on a matching test are forced, so that criterion differences should not influence the level of performance. (As was noted previously, correct response terms may be rejected erroneously when they cannot be recalled, but this source of bias is assumed to be minimized when a matching procedure is used in acquisition.) An indication of what is meant by confusion factors is given by Martin (1972, p. 80) in his comments on the finding that there is significant RI for the A–Br paradigm on a multiple-choice test. He suggests that because of the inclusion of the second-list associate of the stimulus among the incorrect alternatives in approximately one-third of the items, 'the subject was simply faced with a tougher multiple-choice decision....Subjects were on some proportion of the tests conned into a second-task recognitive encoding of the stimulus because of the presence of certain responses'. The concept of stimulus recoding will be considered later. For the moment, the matter of primary concern is whether the juxtaposition of first-list and second-list associates accounts entirely for the retroactive losses under the A–Br paradigm.

The empirical questions at issue are whether (a) performance is appreciably lower when second-list associates are included among the distractors than when they are not, and (b) there is a bias towards choosing the second-list associate when an error is made. Data bearing on both these questions are available from the study of Postman and Stark (1969). The multiple-choice items in which only the currently correct associate was present will be designated as 1A, and those in which two associates were juxtaposed as 2A. During IL the overall percentages of correct choices for the two types of items were quite similar—68 and 64, respectively. In the case of the 2A items, however, choices of the first-list associate accounted for an increasing proportion of all errors, rising from about 30 to more than 50 per cent, as IL continued. This trend suggests that at the beginning of the transfer task the first-list associates can be readily discriminated as incorrect on the basis of their high frequency of past occurrence in the experimental situation. The frequency differential diminishes progressively as a function of second-list practice, and a bias in the opposite direction develops when the numbers of occurrences for the two associates approach equality. To the extent that the subjects' choices were, indeed, influenced by frequency differences, the mechanism is similar to that in verbal-discrimination learning (Ekstrand, Wallace and Underwood, 1966). On the test of first-list retention, the percentages of correct choices were 75 for 1A items and 70 for 2A items. Of the errors made on 2A items, 33 per cent were choices of second-list associates, which is exactly at the chance level. The discriminative practice during IL appears to minimize failures of list differentiation on the test of retention. (These results appear to disagree with those of Anderson and Watts (1971) mentioned earlier. However, the latter investigators used different distributions of distractors during acquisition and on the test of retention. Furthermore, they failed to obtain control measures for the different types of retention test, so that the exact amounts of RI obtained under each of the conditions are not known.) Thus, there is no empirical support for Martin's interpretation, and the hypothesis that specific first-list associations are weakened under the A–Br paradigm remains tenable.

So far, only conventional studies of paired-associate learning have been considered, in which multiple trials are given on both the original and the interpolated list. It is important to note that for pairs bearing an A–B, A–D relation to each other no RI (or PI) has been found in short-term recognition memory. In the experiment of Bower and Bostrom (1968) each pair was studied only once, and retention was tested by binary recognition judgments. Lack of sensitivity to interference could be ruled out, since repetition of items produced significant gains in recognition. The authors concluded that the results cast doubt on 'any simple notion of destructive storage' (p. 212). Along similar lines, Wickelgren (1967) found that recognition of adjacent pairs of digits in a series was not impaired by the presence of competing associations in the series to which the subject had been exposed. According to Wickelgren, 'there is no indication that A–C associations have any systematic effect on the measured strength of A–B associations, when a recognition test is used' (p. 170). In a recent review, Wickelgren (1973) contrasted this finding with the results obtained in long-term retention (e.g. under conditions of list learning), which he interprets as providing consistent evidence for storage interference (cf. Wickelgren, 1972). Differential susceptibility to unlearning is taken to be one of the characteristics in terms of which short-term and long-term traces can be distinguished. Our own assessment of the evidence differs from Wickelgren's. Under appropriate conditions of measurement the evidence for RI in recognition under the A–B, A–D paradigm is weak in long-term as well as in short-term memory situations. On the other hand, as the results obtained under the A–B, A–Br arrangement show, acceptance of the null hypothesis is not justified.

Response-Set Interference

Statement of the Hypothesis

The large discrepancy between the amounts of RI observed in recall and in recognition was the point of departure in the formulation of the principle of response-set interference (Postman and Stark, 1969; Postman, Stark and Fraser, 1968). The principle is designed to account for the heavy retroactive losses in recall that occur when new responses are attached to old stimuli during IL. These losses are attributed in large measure to the operation of a mechanism of response selection which results in the suppression of the repertoire of first-list responses. The hypothesis brings together two previous formulations of the conditions governing response restriction in acquisition and recall. (a) Underwood and Schulz (1960) inferred the existence of a selector mechanism from the notable ability of subjects learning a verbal list to confine their responses to the prescribed items. (b) According to the concept of generalized competition introduced by Newton and Wickens (1956), the subject's set to limit himself to responses from the interpolated list is carried over into the test of first-list recall. Building on these assumptions, the hypothesis of response-set interference holds that the activation of the selector mechanism during IL entails the suppression of the repertoire of first-list responses; the selector mechanism cannot operate effectively in the transfer phase unless such suppression does, in fact, occur.

Generalized competition depresses first-list recall because the selector mechanism is characterized by a certain amount of inertia. That is, having limited himself to the responses from the interpolated list during transfer, the subject experiences difficulty in shifting back to the first-list repertoire. The dominance of the most recently learned list of responses is assumed to be a reversible process, and absolute rises in first-list recall are to be expected as the interval between the end of IL and the test for RI is lengthened.

Response suppression during IL and generalized competition in recall are viewed as complementary processes. In principle, generalized competition could occur in the absence of prior response suppression, as long as there is a set to continue giving the responses learned last. It is reasonable, however, to treat response suppression as an antecedent of generalized competition. Given response suppression, generalized competition becomes, as it were, obligatory. Furthermore, response suppression is an essential link in the explanatory chain because it is assumed to be related directly to the level of negative transfer; taken by itself, generalized competition cannot account for differences in RI as a function of paradigm of transfer. Thus, while the concepts of generalized competition and response-set interference at recall are closely related, the latter carries the additional connotation that suppression of earlier responses ensures the dominance of those learned last.

Within the framework of a component analysis of unlearning (cf. McGovern, 1964), response-set interference is taken to be responsible for reduced availability of the responses *per se*. The proposed mechanism was thus substituted for the unlearning of contextual associations to which such losses had been previously attributed. There are several considerations that favour such a reformulation. (a) RI usually develops quite rapidly, i.e. there is substantial unlearning even when the number of acquisition trials is considerably higher on the original than on the interpolated list (e.g. Barnes and Underwood, 1959; Delprato, 1972). This fact is more easily reconciled with a mechanism acting on the list as a whole, or on a subgroup of items, than with a process of gradual extinction. (b) First-list recovery is accompanied by systematic shifts in the order of output of the responses from the original and the interpolated lists. The first list moves forward in the recall sequence as the interval between the end of IL and the test of retention is lengthened (Postman, Stark and Henschel, 1969). This shift is reasonably interpreted as reflecting a change in the relative dominance of the alternative-response repertoires. (c) Comparison of the amounts of recovery observed under various paradigms of transfer indicates that rises in first-list recall are attributable primarily if not entirely to increases in response availability (Postman and Warren, 1972). (d) Heavy amounts of unlearning are found in free recall, with both unrelated and categorized lists (e.g. Postman and Keppel, 1967; Shuell, 1968; Strand, 1971; Tulving and Psotka, 1971; Tulving and Thornton, 1959; Watts and Anderson, 1969). Again, RI sets in rapidly as a consequence of IL. In the case of categorized lists, the members of a category tend to be recalled or forgotten together. Those that are lost can be made accessible by categorical cueing (Tulving and Psotka, 1971). Such phenomena cannot be understood in terms of changes in the strength of associations between individual words and experimental context; rather, they appear to reflect changes in the accessibility of circumscribed groups of items. In that sense the findings are consistent with the principle of response-set interference.

In view of subsequent developments, it will be useful to delimit explicitly the scope and empirical implications of the principle of response-set interference. The primary focus is on the mechanism responsible for the loss of responses *per se*. It is proposed that such losses reflect the operation of a process of response selection, which is carried over to the test of retention, rather than the gradual unlearning of contextual associations. The principle does not entail the assertion that specific associations are immune to unlearning. Comparisons of the amounts of RI on tests of recall and recognition suggested that, under the A–B, A–D paradigm at least, response selection carries much greater weight than associative unlearning. Evidence for strictly associative decrements may require a modification of this conclusion but does not bear directly on alternative assumptions about the conditions of response loss. If it were shown that all RI is reducible to associative unlearning, there would obviously be no need to postulate separate mechanisms to account for the reduced availability (or, probably more appropriately, accessibility) of responses. That would apply equally to the unlearning of contextual associations and to response-set interference. Given the validity of the analytic distinction between response losses and associative decrements, the concepts of response-set interference and associative unlearning are fully compatible with each other. They should not, therefore, be put in opposition to each other as alternative and mutually exclusive mechanisms of RI.

Experimental Tests

The implication of the principle of response-set interference that is most directly vulnerable to experimental disproof is that the processes of selection and suppression operate at the list level. Several experiments have shown that the difference between the A–B, A–D and A–B, C–D paradigms is maintained under mixed-list conditions, i.e. when both paradigms are represented in the interpolated list (Delprato, 1971; Weaver, Rose and Campbell, 1971; Wichawut and Martin, 1971). Similar findings have been obtained under an arrangement in which some proportion of the first-list stimuli is omitted from the interpolated list. The omission of the first-list stimuli reduced the amount of RI for the corresponding pairs (Birnbaum, 1972; 1973; Delprato, 1972). A related demonstration of cue-specific RI was reported by Weaver, Duncan and Bird (1972). During original learning, each response was associated with two different stimulus terms. In the transfer phase, a new response was attached to one but not to the other of these stimuli. There was significant RI only when the stimulus paired with a new response was used as the recall cue on the test of first-list retention.

These experiments agree in showing that retroactive interference does not fall indiscriminately on all the items in a list and in that sense is paradigm- or cue-specific. Do such results invalidate the principle of response-set interference? To draw such a conclusion would be premature, although the findings certainly call for a specification of the boundary conditions of the hypothesized mechanisms of response selection and suppression. The early evidence that led to the postulation of such mechanisms was obtained under conditions of transfer in which all the items in the interpolated list conformed to the same paradigm. Suppression of the total repertoire of first-list responses is an appropriate strategy under these circumstances. The optimal method of coping with the conditions of interference during transfer obviously changes when there is more than one paradigmatic relation between the items in the successive lists. It is reasonable to suppose that the subject readily recognizes the mixed nature of the interpolated task, e.g. the presence of new stimuli or the omission of half of the original ones. Suppression of the first-list responses may still occur, but it may be selective with respect to a distinctive subgroup of items, namely, those for which the A–B, A–D paradigm obtains. There is independent evidence that during transfer learning subjects can reliably differentiate items with old stimuli from those with new ones (Postman, 1966). The dichotomy between interference effects that operate at the list level and those that are entirely cue-specific does not exhaust all the possibilities.

In the analysis of interference processes, as in other areas of inquiry, it is important to ask about the generality of the conclusions that should be drawn from the results obtained under a particular experimental arrangement. It would be rather surprising if exactly the same mechanisms came into play regardless of whether all or only half of the first-list stimuli were repeated in the second list. What would one expect to happen if the interpolated list consisted of just one A–D pair? The obvious point here is that mechanisms of interference are necessarily tied to task demands. It may be theoretically inelegant but realistic to speculate that interference effects operate at the level which represents an identifiable transfer unit for the subject; depending on the experimental arrangement, that may be the entire list, subgroups of items within the list or specific individual pairs. The search for mechanisms of interference that are entirely independent of task structure may prove unproductive. This view is reinforced by the observation that there are experiments in the literature in which the A–B, A–D paradigm failed to produce RI (DaPolito, 1966; Underwood and Ekstrand, 1966; 1967) or indeed was found to be a condition of facilitation (Bruce and Weaver, 1973). The reasons for these exceptions will not be considered further here. Suffice it to say that neither response suppression nor cue-specific RI is inevitable. Equally relevant is the fact that information about an impending test of first-list recall can effectively reduce the amount of RI (Postman and Stark, 1962; Schwartz, 1963; Tell and Schultz, 1972). Clearly, control processes (cf. Atkinson and Shiffrin, 1968) can serve to modify the operation of mechanisms of interference.

Before concluding this section, we return briefly to the relationship between response-set interference and recognition performance. The low level of associative unlearning observed on tests of recognition focused attention on the contribution of response losses to RI in recall, and also suggested that these losses may reflect the operation of a non-associative mechanism. The validity of the concept of response-set interference is not, however, tied to the absence of associative RI in either recognition or recall. How viable the concept, or some modification of it, will prove depends on whether (a) the distinction between associative and response losses continues to be analytically useful and (b) the processes that render responses inaccessible can best be represented as operating at the level of higher-order groupings such as total lists or determinate subgroups within lists.

Stimulus Encoding and Interference

The last few years have witnessed a major critical assault, led by Martin (1971; 1972; 1973), and Greeno and his associates (1971), on the existing conceptual framework of interference theory and a call for a drastic reformulation of the processes underlying transfer, retroaction and proaction. The refutation of existing theories was based largely on the analysis of retrieval dependencies in recall, which were viewed as disconfirming critical predictions derived from the principles of associative unlearning and response-set interference. The proposed new formulations place major emphasis on the conditions of stimulus encoding as the basic determinants of transfer and interference. These arguments have been examined in detail elsewhere (Postman and Underwood, 1973). Only some of the central points at issue, and the implications for differences between recall and recognition, will be considered here.

Independent Retrieval Phenomena

According to Martin and Greeno, the hypothesis of associative unlearning implies an inverse relation between the availability of the first and of the second response to a given stimulus on a terminal test of retention. Such a conditional pairwise relation between B and C recall follows from the assumption that the acquisition of A–D is contingent on the unlearning of A–B; hence, the more strongly A–D is learned, the more thoroughly A–B has been weakened or extinguished. Chi-square tests based on the data of numerous experiments (see Greeno, James and Dapolito, 1971; Martin, 1971) failed to bear out this prediction. Instead, the probabilities of recall of B and D were found to be essentially independent. It was concluded on the basis of these tests that 'neither proaction nor retroaction can be attributed to associative interference or unlearning' (Wichawut and Martin, 1971, p. 320). The conclusion is unacceptable for the following reasons. (a) As was pointed out earlier, the two-factor theory of RI does not include the assumption that learning A–D 'entails' (Martin, 1971, p. 316) the unlearning of A–B. Rather, the attachment of a new response to an old stimulus provides an opportunity for the unlearning of the response. The two associations may, however, coexist. In fact, it is expected that both will remain intact at least part of the time, and the factor of competition is added to that of unlearning to allow for the interference that develops when both responses remain available. (b) Whatever the theoretical basis for the prediction, the assessment of retrieval dependencies is seriously complicated by potentially important biases favouring a positive relation between B and C recall, namely, differences in stimulus difficulty and subject ability (cf Hintzman, 1972). (c) Virtually all the statistical tests of pairwise relations in recall are inconclusive, since the retention of second-list responses is typically so high as to ensure independence of B and D availability. Thus, the so-called independent retrieval phenomenon has little or no bearing on the validity of the hypothesis of associative unlearning.

A different kind of retrieval dependency was deduced by Martin from the principle of response-set interference. This hypothesis was taken to imply categorical organization of the successive response ensembles. On this assumption it was predicated that after the acquisition of two paired-associate lists (A–B, A–D) there should be significant clustering on the basis of list membership in a terminal test of free recall for both sets of responses. This prediction was disconfirmed in an experiment by Martin and Mackay (1970). There was, instead, stimulus-defined clustering, i.e. responses paired with the same stimulus tended to be reproduced together. (Similar results were subsequently reported by Petrich, 1973). The results were considered as conclusive evidence against the principle of response-set interference, or, as the authors prefer to designate it, list-differentiation theory. Once more, however, the conclusion is not justified because the original deduction does not follow from the hypothesis. What is at issue is the mechanism of response loss, not the conditions governing order of output in free recall. When learning is by the paired-associate method, there is no reason to suppose that response suppression entails a weakening of stimulus control over those responses that are available. Furthermore, clustering in free recall of the responses is an extremely doubtful measure of whatever memorial organization might have been achieved during paired-associate learning. Clustering reflects an output strategy which may or may not be adopted by the subject. Since identification of list membership is quite accurate, there is little doubt that a high degree of list clustering could be induced by appropriate instructions. Such a result would no more support the hypothesis of response-set interference than the absence of list clustering refutes it.

It is apparent that an examination of retrieval dependencies fails to provide critical evidence regarding the validity of alternative mechanisms of inter-ference. However, for those who attach especial importance to this class of phenomena the existing results pose a paradox. When recall is cued, the retrieval probabilities of the responses to a common stimulus are presumably indepen-dent. When recall of the responses is free, there is stimulus-defined clustering, which implies that retrieval of the two responses is not independent. In fact, a rather strong dependency can be inferred, since the stimulus is not presented and must be recovered implicitly. Martin (1971) has suggested that responses may be linked in free recall by a mediational chain of different encodings of the same stimulus. But if such mediation occurs in free recall in the absence of the stimulus, it should certainly take place in cued recall as well. The dilemma may be more apparent than real, because there is little usable evidence on conditional response relations in cued recall. In the meantime, the general theoretical conclusions based on retrieval dependencies can be discounted as tangential to the verification of principles of interference.

Encoding Variability and Interference

Current discussions of memory have centred increasingly on the role of coding processes which determine the nature of the stored representations of events and the effectiveness of retrieval cues. This emphasis is reflected in the recent analyses of transfer and interference by Martin and Greeno. The thrust of their arguments is that these phenomena can be best understood in terms of the changes that occur in the functional encodings of the to-be-remembered items.

Martin (1971; 1972; 1973) has summarized the guiding assumptions that lead to a reformulation of the basic principles of transfer and interference. (1) A nominal stimulus possesses multiple components; each component comprises an independent set of attributes or features. (2) only a subset of stimulus components is likely to be sampled on any given occasion. This sampling operation constitutes stimulus encoding. Which features are selected is deter-mined largely by the characteristics of the response. Each stimulus–response pair is eventually represented in memory as a single integrative code. (3) In the initial stages of a learning task, stimulus encoding is variable; the probability of correct responding increases as encoding variability declines. (4) When the nominal stimulus remains the same but a new response is required, the stimulus must be recoded. A different subset of stimulus components must be sampled to make possible the formation of a new code. Thus, when the response changes, so does the functional stimulus. 'If R_1 and R_2 are two distinct behaviors and if S_1 is the presumed stimulus for R_1, then any assertion that S_1 can be also the stimulus for R_2 is a mistake' (1972, p. 71). Negative transfer reflects the failure to establish a distinctive new encoding. Furthermore, when the stimulus is not recoded, the new and the old response cannot both be maintained. In such a case, the subject 'dumps' (sic!) A–B and retains only A–D. (5) Retro-active inhibition results from the persistence on the test of recall of the feature-sampling bias established during A–D learning; consequently the A–B code has a low probability of being sampled. (Presumably the 'dumping' of A–B also contributes to retroactive losses.) (6) Spontaneous recovery is observed because the feature-sampling distribution flattens out over time. (7) Proactive interference occurs because some of the features dominant during the acquisition of A–B continue to be sampled during the recall of A–D. It is important to note that in this account both the A–B and A–D codes are assumed to be intact at the end of IL; interference is entirely a matter of a persistent bias in the sampling of features or codes. The first-list and second-list codes are sampled independently; hence the probabilities of recall of the two responses to a given stimulus are not correlated (the independent retrieval phenomenon).

Greeno *et al.* (1971) likewise emphasize persistence of inappropriate encodings as a source of negative transfer; a second source is the need to replace the retrieval plan developed during original learning. There are two ways in which the latter process can evolve. (a) The earlier plan is suppressed but remains intact and available for future use. The possibility of such temporary suppression hinges on the presence of distinctive cues to list differentiation, e.g. a change in either stimulus or response terms. (b) In the absence of cues to differentiation, the development of a new retrieval plan entails the 'disorganization or breakdown' of the earlier one. Interference is greater in the second than in the first case. The fact that negative transfer is greater for the A–B, A–Br than the A–B, A–D paradigm is explained in these terms. Retroactive inhibition is attributed to failures of retrieval. While the stored representations of A–B remain intact, retrieval is hindered by the suppression or degradation of the appropriate retrieval plan during the transfer phase. No explanation of PI is offered.

These speculative models are open to numerous criticisms, on both logical and empirical grounds. The major objections have been detailed elsewhere (Postman and Underwood, 1973), and for present purposes only a few brief comments will be sufficient. In principle, the emphasis on the potentially important role of encoding and recoding operations is fully justified. Few would wish to quarrel with the assertion that identical nominal stimuli can be encoded in different ways. The hard fact is, however, that when subjects are given the opportunity to change their functional encodings, they more often than not fail to do so. This conclusion emerges from numerous studies in which compound stimuli were used in successive lists, so that recoding required no more than a shift from one distinct and separate component to another (for a detailed review of these studies see Martin (1972)). Subjects may, of course, be conservative in their coding strategies for a very good reason: abandoning familiar encoding devices in favour of new ones may not in the end be profitable even though there is a reduction in associative interference. If this situation prevails with compound stimuli, any *a priori* assumption that single nominal stimuli are routinely recoded is open to serious doubt. The fact that negative transfer, RI and PI are as ubiquitous as they are strongly reinforces this doubt. Given this state of affairs, the new formulations reduce to a negative, and essentially empty, assertion: interference occurs because subjects fail to recode stimulus and response terms appropriately. That gets one back to the point of departure of earlier interference theories which made precisely this assumption, though not in the same terms: interference develops when new responses must be attached to old stimuli.

No useful purpose is served by the revival of the old conundrum of whether two different responses can be attached to the same stimulus. The well-known problems of definition that are involved here are not limited to transfer but arise whenever one tries to specify exactly what is learned. It may be taken as axiomatic that no stimulus or response is ever repeated exactly. A long time ago, Hull (1943, p. 195) tried to solve the paradoxes of stimulus learning and stimulus evocation by appealing to gradients of generalization; likewise, response variation was subsumed under the heading of response generalization. Behaviour theorists have often defined responses producing the same outcome as equivalent. Thus, how many different responses can be associated to the same stimulus becomes in the first instance a matter of how one defines 'same' and 'different'. What limitations there are on the network of associative contingencies during transfer is an empirical and not a logical question. We know that subjects can recall multiple responses to the same nominal stimulus. Without begging the question, it cannot be inferred that the changes in stimulus encoding during transfer exceed the normal variability during original learning. The subject does have the problem of differentiating between the first and second response when the nominal stimulus is presented. It is likely that he does so on the basis of contextual information (cf. Anderson and Bower, 1972). Contrary to what Martin suggests (1972, p. 71), the storage of contextual information with each pair is not equivalent to a recoding of the pair itself. In short, an encoding variability principle of transfer cannot be proved on logical grounds.

Theoretical formulations such as Martin's and Greeno's fail to resolve the question of whether and to what extent mechanisms of interference operate on individual pairs, on subgroups of items, or total lists. The assertion is that interference must always be item-specific. 'Neither associations nor responses are somehow set aside on a task membership basis; rather, the accessibility of the memorial representation of a given A–B contingency is altered only to the extent that a subsequent contingency must be learned that is specifically related to the original A–B contingency' (Martin, 1973, p. 497). However, to account for RI, both Martin and Greeno have to invoke what amounts to a generalized, non-specific mechanism of interference—the persistence of a sampling bias in favour of the features selected during the transfer phase, or the suppression of a retrieval plan for the list as a whole. All measurable manifestations of interference are item-specific, since we observe responses to individual stimuli. The critical theoretical question concerns the level at which the inhibitory mechanisms operate. In that respect, there are no essential differences among a feature-sampling bias, suppression of a retrieval plan and response suppression. The latter may have an heuristic advantage because it is applicable to other than paired-associate situations, e.g. free recall. It is only fair to say that all extant accounts of interference share the weakness of making *ad hoc* assumptions. No basic advance is made, however, by recasting old and poorly understood problems in new and timely terms.

Encoding theories of interference have little to say about interference in recognition except to rule it out flatly. The assertion is that at the end of IL the composite codes from the two tasks remain 'distinct and intact entities' (Martin, 1973, p. 497). As we have seen earlier, existing evidence for RI in recognition is dismissed out of hand. The matter can obviously not be settled on such an *a priori* basis. Furthermore, if a feature-sampling bias is, indeed, carried over from IL to the test of retention, one might well expect failures of recognition when stimulus components appropriate to the second list are sampled during a test of recognition for the first list. Martin (1967a,b) demonstrated earlier that cued recall fails when the subject fails to recognize the stimulus as old. Should not recognition fail likewise under these circumstances? We must leave the matter here, because the problem has not been explored by the theorists themselves. At this point it is far from clear, however, that the premises upon which encoding formulations of interference are developed imply that recognition should be immune to retroactive and proactive effects.

Proactive Inhibition in Recall and Recognition

Our discussion of theoretical analyses of interference has been limited almost entirely to mechanisms of RI, and little has been said about PI. There are two major reasons for this asymmetry in the consideration of empirical results. First, experiments on retroaction have remained the major testing ground for alternative conceptions of interference. Second, and more important, there is today no coherent account of the conditions and characteristics of PI, and this state of affairs signals a major weakness of current theories of interference. Classical interference theory attributed PI to competition and failures of list differentiation. As was noted previously, recent studies have provided more impressive evidence for the decrements in recall than can be produced by the latter factor. The major interpretative difficulties stem from the fact that PI continues to be observed when competition and differentiation are ruled out or minimized as sources of interference, namely, on MMFR tests (Ceraso and Henderson, 1965; 1966; Houston, 1967; Koppenaal, 1963; Postman, Stark and Fraser, 1968). The results can be attributed to the recovery of the set to give earlier responses, on the assumption that the simultaneous arousal of two response repertoires generates output inteference. Some independent evidence for this assumption was obtained in a study of long-term PI in free recall (Postman and Hasher, 1972).

Investigations of PI on matching tests of recognition are few and far between. When acquisition is under conditions of associative recall, no PI has been found (Ceraso and Henderson, 1966; Postman, Stark and Fraser, 1968). Because of the shift in the method of testing, the implications of such findings are uncertain. In a recent experiment (Postman, Stark and Burns, 1974), the multiple-choice procedure was used in acquisition as well as on the test of retention. A significant amount of PI was observed under the A–B, A–D paradigm, but the proactive losses failed to increase over time. The pattern was essentially the same when cued recall was used throughout. It appears, therefore, that associative as well as response losses can contribute to proactive decrements. The absence of progressive temporal increases in interference suggests that PI may reflect a learning deficit. One possibility is that for a given stimulus, the optimal associative mediators are preempted during first-list learning. Consequently, the second association may be less stable and more vulnerable to interference than the first, even though the terminal level of performance is equated to that under the control treatment. These speculations must be regarded as highly tentative, but it is advisable to consider seriously the possibility that RI and PI may not be in all respects complementary processes reflecting the operation of the same mechanisms. The fact that PI is found on multiple-choice tests of recognition, whereas RI under the same procedure is typically negligible, lends some face validity to these speculations.

Conclusions: Interference in Recall and Recognition

The available evidence shows that recall and recognition differ in susceptibility to RI, although the same may not be true for PI. One plausible inference from these findings is that response loss is a major source of RI whereas specific associations are relatively immune to unlearning. There is some reason to believe that the relative weight of these two components of interference is more nearly equal in PI, but there is only some preliminary evidence in favour of the latter conclusion. It is fair to say that the total picture is complex and beset by many uncertainties, not only as far as differences between recall and recognition are concerned, but with respect to the general conceptualization of the underlying mechanisms of interference. One cannot help but wonder why after so many years of patient experimental effort interference theory today finds itself entangled in so many empirical inconsistencies and theoretical complications.

The reason may be that we have been aiming at the construction of a general theory of interference which can be applied to any and all paradigms of learning and retention. That is, we have proceeded from the assumption that principles of interference are trans-situational, e.g. that they do not change in any fundamental sense as we move from recall to recognition, or from paired-associate learning to free recall. This assumption, and hence the strategy of the research, may be mistaken. Perhaps the analytic efforts should proceed in the other direction: from the exploration of the characteristics of storage and retrieval in a given class of memory task to the formulation of principles of interference that are indigenous to that class. A plurality of theories of interference may be propaedeutic to the emergence of a truly general theory.

There are indications that theoretical developments and the shape of the evidence are encouraging the exploration of pluralistic principles of interference. Studies carried out within the framework of the frequency theory of verbal discrimination (Ekstrand, Wallace and Underwood, 1966) are a case in point. The theory holds that verbal discrimination, like item recognition, is mediated by judgments of frequency. A higher situational frequency accrues to the correct than to the incorrect members of the pairs between which the subject can choose. Thus, the frequency difference provides a reliable basis for discrimination. It follows that under a reversal paradigm, in which the correct and incorrect members of the pairs are interchanged, RI should be maximal when the numbers of trials on the successive lists are equal. This prediction was confirmed in an experiment by Underwood and Freund (1970a). When there were substantially more trials on the interpolated than on the original list, retroactive facilitation was observed, apparently reflecting the increase in the frequency difference. As the authors point out, this trend contrasts sharply with that for associative tasks where there is little or no reduction in RI with high degrees of IL. In the relearning of the original list, error reduction is slow because the frequency differential present at the time of recall is progressively reduced; however, performance fails to decline to a chance level when frequency ceases to be an appropriate cue (Underwood and Freund, 1970a; Underwood, Shaughnessy and Zimmerman, 1972). It is possible that the subject can distinguish between near and remote frequencies (cf. Hintzman and Block, 1971), or that attributes other than frequency are utilized in the discrimination. (There has been considerable discussion of the question of whether incidentally formed associations between right and wrong items play a role in discrimination learning, and whether the unlearning of these associations is implicated in RI for verbal discrimination tasks (Eschenbrenner, 1969; Kausler, Fulkerson and Eschenbrenner, 1967). This problem will not be examined here. Recent evidence suggests that such associations do not influence verbal-discrimination learning significantly (Zimmerman, Shaughnessy and Underwood, 1972). Wallace, Remington and Beito (1972) have shown that the patterns of RI under different paradigms do not coincide for verbal discrimination and incidentally learned associations.)

Interference is less clearly related to frequency differences when PI rather than RI is measured (Underwood and Freund, 1970a), although the pattern again diverges from that found for associative tasks: after a fixed number of trials on the first list, the amount of proactive loss was found to be independent of the number of trials on the second list. There is also a striking difference between verbal discrimination and associative tasks in susceptibility to cumulative PI. When successive paired-associate lists are learned and recalled in the laboratory, there is progressive drastic decline in the level of retention (e.g. Keppel, Postman and Zavortink, 1968). By contrast, there is little change in the retention of successive verbal-discrimination lists (Underwood, Broder and Zimmerman, 1973). This difference becomes understandable when the conditions of successful performance in the two types of tasks are considered. Recall of paired associates depends on the availability of the responses and the integrity of the individual associations. Cumulative PI reflects the depression of one or both of these components of performance as a result of prior learning. According to frequency theory, neither of these components is essential for verbal-discrimination learning. Acquisition depends on the establishment of reliable frequency discriminations, and forgetting occurs to the extent that these discriminations are lost. There is no reason to suppose that the learning of prior lists composed of different words should speed the degradation of the frequency discriminations in the most recent list. The authors' analysis is fully supported by the results.

It is becoming apparent that the conditions and characteristics of inter-ference change with the attributes of memory (cf. Underwood, 1969a) that must be utilized on the test of retention. It is probably not too early to say that the principles of RI and PI are not likely to be the same for discriminative and retrieval tasks. In recent years, Underwood and his associates have presented a substantial amount of evidence in support of the thesis that recognition is mediated in large measure by frequency discrimination (cf. Underwood, 1971). If this thesis is upheld, we may expect an increasing divergence between the laws of interference that apply to recognition on the one hand and to the retrieval of responses on the other. Thus, plural theories of interference may already be in the making. If this trend gathers momentum, then some of the points of contention on which we dwelled in the body of this paper may become moot.

Acknowledgment

The preparation of this report was supported by grant MH-12006 from the National Institute of Mental Health.

7 Word frequency, recognition and recall

VERNON GREGG

Introduction

Considerable arguments have been advanced against the classical trace-strength theory of recognition and recall. The theory seeks to explain superior recognition compared to recall in terms of a lower threshold of response for the former compared to the latter. This approach is inadequate for reasons which include findings that recognition performance is not invariably superior to recall (Davis, Sutherland and Judd, 1961; Lachman and Field, 1965; Tulving, 1968b), items which are recalled are not necessarily recognized (Tulving and Thomson, 1973) and the differential effects of certain variables on recognition and recall scores (Kintsch, 1970a). Among the findings contrary to the threshold model is the widely accepted frequency paradox (Anderson and Bower, 1972; Kintsch, 1970a; McCormack, 1972). The paradox is created by the superior free recall of common words relative to uncommon words, while in recognition the opposite is true; this poses problems for the classical trace-strength theory, which predicts a constant ordering of performance in both recall and recognition tests. The retrieve–edit model of recall proposed by James (1890) offers a means of resolving the paradox.

According to the retrieve–edit model, recall consists of two stages, a retrieval process in which items are made available as responses, and an editing process in which the subject decides whether each available item is appropriate as a response. These ideas have been taken up in several forms (e.g. Anderson and Bower, 1972; Underwood and Schulz, 1960). Kintsch (1968; 1970a), subsequently supported by McCormack (1972), has described the retrieve–recognize version of the model. In this model retrieval of the item from the memory store takes the form of a search which is directed by organizational rules utilized by the subject in storing them. The editing of items retrieved by the search is equivalent to recognizing in that it utilizes recency or familiarity information. This information, which is independent of the list context in which the item was presented, is assumed to be directly accessible when the item is presented at test in recognition or retrieved by the search in recall. The frequency paradox is neatly handled by this model if the recognition process is more effective for uncommon words but the retrieval process more productive for common words.

The retrieve–recognize model has come under attack because recognition appears to involve retrieval processes (Light and Carter-Sobell, 1970; Tulving and Thomson, 1971). That is, if the subject interprets an item differently on the presentation and test occasions he will fail to recover the information necessary to make a correct decision about that item. Also, Mandler's (1972) conclusion that organizational factors do indeed affect recognition performance suggests that recency and familiarity are not the only bases for recognition decisions. The retrieve–recognize model and the data cannot be reconciled simply by adding a retrieval requirement into recognition; to account for the frequency paradox the information retrieved must lead to superior recognition of uncommon words. This can be achieved, to some extent, [by adopting Underwood's (1969a) distinction between discriminative and retrieval attributes of memory. These sets of attributes serve to discriminate one memory from another and to retrieve memories from storage. Underwood's approach differs from Kintsch's in that the sets of attributes utilized by discriminative and retrieval processes may overlap, the former being mainly temporal, the latter largely associative. Such a formulation explains the frequency paradox by proposing that retrieval attributes are more effectively established for common words than for uncommon words and discriminative attributes are more effectively established with uncommon words than for common words. If this view is adopted, the challenge is to reconcile models of word storage, in the generic (Howell, 1973b) or semantic sense (Tulving, 1972), with specific or episodic phenomena. This does not seem difficult because, as we shall see, common words possess properties which are generally favourable to associative and organizational encoding; also, increments in familiarity should be more discriminable against a background of few rather than many previous occurrences (Noble, 1963).

Several considerations prevent us from immediately adopting the view just outlined. The extent of the paradox is by no means certain; common words do not invariably give rise to better recall nor uncommon words to better recognition. Also, before attributing the paradox to an interaction between word frequency and retrieval demands it is necessary to consider the comparability of recall and recognition conditions, giving rise to the paradox; its presence is generally inferred from the results of separate studies of recognition and recall. The central issue appears to be the extent to which the paradox can be used to clarify the distinction between the processes underlying recognition and recall performance. Alternatively, given certain assumptions about processes underlying recognition and recall performance the paradox can be used to examine the properties of common and uncommon words. Since acceptance of both the paradox and the distinction between recognition and recall processes involves strong assumptions, this chapter reviews the work on word-frequency effects in recognition and recall and attempts to reconcile models of these memory processes with explanations of word-frequency effects in general. The terms common and high frequency (HF) are used interchangeably, as are uncommon and low frequency (LF). They are general terms and will be used unless precise values of frequency are necessary for the argument.

Assessment of Word Frequency

The Thorndike–Lorge (1944) and Kučera and Francis (1967) word counts are the primary sources of normative frequencies for studies of verbal behaviour. All such norms suffer from ageing and the necessarily limited range of material upon which they are based. The Thorndike–Lorge (T–L) norms contain tables of frequency of occurrence per million words from various sources of written material. The G count is an amalgam of the separate source tables. These norms suffer specific inadequacies, including the lack of precise frequencies of common words in the G count (they are listed as A, 50 occurrences per million words but not as many as 100 per million, and AA, 100 per million or more) and the failure of some very rare words in separate source tables to appear in the G count. Also, entries do not represent words as such but combinations including plurals and other variations.

Despite the extensive collection of frequency norms for written and spoken English listed by Shapiro and Gordon (1971), it is possible that particular experimental requirements combined with local patterns of linguistic usage and individual differences will find these norms unsatisfactory. An alternative approach is to obtain subjective estimates of frequency, this having the distinct advantage that assessments can be made of frequency of usage (spoken, heard and read) and familiarity rather than merely frequency of occurrence in written material. Kučera and Francis (K–F) frequencies are highly correlated with subjective estimates based on multiple rank orders (Shapiro, 1969) and subjective magnitude estimation (Carroll, 1971; Shapiro, 1969), but, as Carroll points out, subjective estimates are consistently lower than objective frequencies at the rare end of the spectrum due to the lower limits on probability of occurrence imposed on the latter by sample size.

Evidence from several other sources confirms that objective frequency and subjective estimates are positively correlated but not always highly so, for example rated familiarity and T–L frequency (Postman, 1961; Rubenstein, Garfield and Millikan, 1970) and estimated frequency of use and T–L frequency (Tryk, 1968). Galbraith and Underwood (1973) report the interesting findings that the correlation between subjective and objective estimates differs for concrete and abstract nouns, as indeed does the correlation between T–L and K–F counts. Furthermore, subjective estimates of frequency were significantly correlated with judgments of contextual variety, this being greater for abstract than for concrete nouns.

The discrepancies between subjective and objective measures of frequency raise serious problems concerning which is more appropriate for a particular investigation. In general, investigations of verbal memory have utilized objective measures, and the reader must consider this throughout the chapter.

Word Characteristics Related to Frequency

A major difficulty in the study of word-frequency effects arises from the large number of other word characteristics related to it. The existence of these reliable, although not perfect, correlations suggests that frequency itself may not be a potent factor but that its effects are mediated by these related characteristics. Considering this problem of 'fundamentality', Underwood and Schulz (1960) have argued the opposite view. That is, frequency of experience is a fundamental variable. It is not intended to pursue here the arguments advanced by Underwood and Schulz concerning the effects of frequency on learning where non-word units are involved. However, their Spew hypothesis is of direct relevance. This states: 'the order of availability of verbal units is directly related to the frequency with which the units have been experienced' (Underwood and Schulz, 1960, p. 86), and holds good in a variety of situations which are touched on later.

Word frequency is positively related to several measures which may be termed indices of inter-relatedness. For example, common words are more meaningful as defined by Noble (1963), i.e. compared to uncommon stimulus words they give rise to more associative responses per subject as measured directly (Cofer and Shevitz, 1952; Paivio, 1968; Saltz, 1967; Winnick and Kressel, 1965) or by rated associative ease (Brown and Ure, 1969; Silverstein and Deinstbier, 1968). Similar results are obtained when rated familiarity rather than counted frequency is used (Noble, 1963).

When subjects are required to produce only one response to each stimulus, responses tend to be common words (Howes, 1957). Also, the variety of responses given by all subjects is a decreasing function of stimulus frequency (Hall and Ugelow, 1957). Hall and Ugelow also found associative response times to be inversely related to stimulus frequency, which suggests that although common stimulus words possess a wide range of associative responses their dominant responses are relatively directly retrieved.

Noble's measure of meaningfulness, m, is often assumed to assess the number of different meanings possessed by a word. This assumption and the positive correlation of m with T–L frequency is the basis of Underwood and Schulz's (1960) suggestion that the two measures reflect the same dimension. While word frequency and the number of dictionary definitions (dm) are related (Saltz and Modigliani, 1967; Zipf, 1945), the correlation between m and dm is not significantly large (Saltz and Modigliani, 1967). The word frequency–dm relation agrees with Paivio's (1968) finding that the correlation between word frequency and rated complexity is positive and for word frequency and rated specificity is negative. Paivio (1968) agrees with Brown and Ure (1969) in finding no correlation between word frequency and concreteness. Paivio also agrees with Frincke (1968) that concreteness–imagery and meaningfulness–familiarity factors should be distinguished.

Affective characteristics positively related to word frequency include goodness and pleasantness (Brown and Ure, 1969; Paivio, 1968; Silverstein and

Deinstbier, 1968). Emotionality gives significant positive (Brown and Ure, 1969) or negative (Paivio, 1968) correlations with frequency, the difference presumably reflecting a general as opposed to specific definition of emotionality.

The pattern which emerges when common words are compared with uncommon is that the former are more complex in terms of meaning and associative inter-relations; also, they tend to evoke 'good' evaluative judgments and, predictably, are less interesting. Any attempt to control related characteristics while varying frequency almost inevitably leads to the use of small samples of words. Because the number of co-varying characteristics is large, there is the ever-present possibility that some uncontrolled characteristic will be confounded with frequency.

Lexical Access and Word Retrieval

Common words are dealt with more rapidly, and given as responses more readily, in several situations including word discrimination, picture-naming, anagram solution and word identification. These tasks are generally considered to involve access into a lexicon or word store on the basis of various amounts of information in order to map the information on to a corresponding unit, or to determine the presence of such a unit. Lexical organization and access rules are often of principal interest. Also involved is the function and content of the lexicon as contrasted with the encyclopaedia or semantic memory (Lachman, 1973), or the logogen system contrasted with the cognitive system (Morton, 1970).

Many explanations of frequency effects in this area can be traced back to the statistical word count made by Zipf (1935), from which the expression $N = kf^2$ may be derived, where N is the number of word tokens occurring with frequency f. Starting from the assumption that dealing with a word has a cost to the processing system, Mandelbrot (e.g. 1965) has shown how Zipf's law of frequency distribution follows from Zipf's principle of least effort (Zipf, 1949). Put simply, Mandelbrot showed how the statistical theory of communication maintains that the minimum average cost per word is obtained by ensuring that the most frequently used words are the least costly. This statistical statement does not, of course, shed much light on the means whereby words become less costly. It is likely that they do so through use due to reorganization of the lexicon and semantic system, but also easily processed words may be chosen to represent frequent events on the basis of characteristics such as length, pronounciability (Stanners, 1970) and phonemic complexity (Frederiksen, 1971). Whatever the causes and effects, Mandelbrot's demonstration gives a fundamental reason to expect more rapid processing of common, as opposed to uncommon words. Some of the findings relevant to this issue are now briefly described.

Verbal-Response Latencies

In reading, where stimulus–response mapping is relatively direct, verbal-response latencies to discrete stimuli are shorter for common than for un-common words (Berry, 1971). This relation holds when specification of the response is less precise, as, for example, when subjects are required to produce category exemplars with a constraint on the initial letter, e.g. Animal–Z (Freedman and Loftus, 1971). Also, exemplar production is more rapid with increasing word frequency of the category name (Loftus and Freedman, 1972), which indicates that articulatory factors are not the only cause of the short latencies associated with HF responses.

Word/Non-Word Discrimination

Common words are associated with faster response times than uncommon words in word/non-word discriminations, and Rubenstein, Garfield and Millikan (1970) attribute this effect to the earlier inclusion of common words in the marked set of lexical units. Stanners and Forbach (1973) suggest a somewhat similar model.

The dangers of grouping different meanings of homographs in frequency norms are pointed to by the study of Rubenstein, Lewis and Rubenstein (1971). The stimuli consisted of nonsense and English words, with the latter divided between non-homographs (only one meaning, e.g. thigh) and homographs, which have more than one meaning. For systematic homographs the various meanings are functionally close (e.g. plough, which can be an implement or the act of using that implement), but for unsystematic homographs the different meanings are not related in any systematic way, e.g. yard. They found that unsystematic homographs gave rise to shorter latencies than either non-homo-graphs or systematic homographs, with this effect being most marked when the various meanings of the unsystematic homographs have similar frequencies of occurrence. This suggests that unsystematic homographs have separate lexical entries for each meaning and that marking occurs first for those of high frequency. Importantly, if the frequencies of separate meanings are influencing decision times, the effect cannot be due primarily to differences in rates of initial perceptual analysis.

Picture-naming

Oldfield (1966) showed how the inverse relation between time to name a pictured object and the logarithm of the name's T–L frequency could be explained by combining Zipf's model of frequency distribution with marking of the name's frequency class. Since class size is inversely related to frequency, HF names will be located and hence emitted faster than LF names. Initial perceptual analysis of the stimulus is eliminated as the locus of the word-fre-quency effect because this effect is much reduced when recognition thresholds of picture–objects are determined and in same–different judgments where the name is followed by the picture.

Carroll and White (1973) extended the Oldfield and Wingfield study, using more stimuli and working with the Standard Frequency Index (SFI) derived from the log-normal model of word-frequency distribution. The correlations of naming latencies with SFIs derived both from T–L and K–F norms failed to reach significance. However, age of acquisition of the name was a reliable predictor of latency when estimated from subjects' ratings and objective sources of vocabulary acquisition.

We have already seen that correlations between subjective estimates of familiarity and objective counts are generally not high. Since Carroll and White based their SFIs on objective counts, it is just possible that the smallness of the frequency effect was due to the inadequacy of the counts for assessing the underlying frequency dimension. Indeed, Lachman (1973) found subjective estimates of frequency of usage to constitute a reliable predictor of naming latency, whereas SFIs based on K–F frequencies did not. Lachman proposed a separation of the lexicon and encyclopaedia or semantic memory. Frequency effects appear both in the encyclopaedia during semantic analysis of the stimulus and during access to the lexical unit corresponding to the results of this analysis. The point is that both Oldfield and Lachman advocate more rapid access to lexical entries of HF rather than LF names.

Anagram Solution

Anagrams may be solved by several methods, but a consistent finding is that solution words having high T–L frequencies are easier to solve than those having low frequencies (Mayzner and Tresselt, 1958). This suggests that subjects do not simply work through a systematic series of permutations of the letters but rather utilize the anagram as a source of information by which to access the lexicon. Words thus generated are tested as solutions.

Mayzner and Tresselt explained the frequency effect in terms of the Spew hypothesis (already referred to) and this receives support from studies by Duncan (e.g. 1970). In these subjects were given only a few letters rather than a complete anagram and required to produce words containing them. More common than uncommon words were retrieved.

Duncan (1973) suggested that some solution words may not be in subjects' vocabularies, while others may be present but difficult to retrieve. Working with all five-letter English words beginning with specified bigrams, he required one group of subjects to recall them following a single presentation; a second group generated as many words as possible, beginning with the initial bigrams; a third group indicated whether they had ever seen the words in print before the experiment. All three measures increased with frequency of occurrence. When the number of words generated is expressed as a percentage of words recognized as seen in print this rises from 18 to 25 per cent with increasing frequency. Thus, even when words are in the lexicon those of low frequency are more difficult to retrieve. Clearly, these results have important implications for models which assume that the entire item population is scanned in recall (e.g. Davis, Sutherland and Judd, 1961; Ingleby, 1973).

Word Identification

Interesting similarities exist between memory and perceptual recognition paradigms when open and closed forms of the latter are distinguished. In open tests the population of potential stimuli is effectively the subject's entire vocabulary or some large subset of it; under these conditions HF words are more readily identified than LF words (Howes and Solomon, 1951). The effect is much attenuated in closed tests which employ small, and often prespecified, item populations (Pollack, Rubenstein and Decker, 1959). Since the free-recall situation is usually similar to open tests in terms of stimulus population specifications, some explanations of frequency effects in perceptual recognition may be relevant to memory phenomena.

The pure guessing theory maintains that subjects assume the experiment reflects the 'real' world and respond with an HF word when in doubt. Sophisticated guessing theory acknowledges that stimulus information which is insufficient to unambiguously specify one word may enable a set of likely words to be marked. The urn model of Pollack, Rubenstein and Decker (1960) deals with the frequency effect by postulating a random draw from word tokens within the marked set. Since each word is considered to be represented by tokens in proportion to its frequency, such a draw will more often yield HF than LF words.

Broadbent (1967) rejected both guessing theories because, contrary to their predictions, the ratio of erroneous HF responses to erroneous LF responses is independent of stimulus frequency. Instead, he proposed that HF words have a bias operating in their favour such that they are output on the basis of less evidence than LF words. Somewhat similar mechanisms have been incorporated into Morton's model (1969). It is possible that similar processes are operating in free recall, i.e. given a limited amount of retained information this would be more likely to make available HF rather than LF responses.

Controversy between Catlin (1969) and Broadbent (1967) over the prediction of sophisticated guessing theory has resulted in Treisman's (1971) conclusion that Catlin's position is unjustified and both models should incorporate the requirement that stimuli convey information about their frequency class before identification, i.e. HF and LF words are not acoustically equivalent. This requirement, based on the ratios of HF and LF errors, has been justified by the direct demonstrations that equivalence does not hold for auditory (Frederiksen, 1971) and visual (Landauer and Streeter, 1973) modalities.

The overall picture emerging from the research discussed in this section is one in which words are processed more rapidly with increasing frequency of usage; also, under a wide range of uncertainty, HF words become available as responses more readily than LF words. It seems that these effects are mainly attributable to differences at the level of semantic analysis and lexical access rather than peripheral perceptual and response factors.

The concept of marking a subset of words on the basis of available information, rather than searching the whole lexicon for an appropriate unit, emerges as a cohesive theoretical principle: within marked sets HF words take priority of processing.

Recall

Free Recall

In the Introduction to this chapter it was pointed out that the retrieve–recognize model of recall is able to account for the frequency paradox if the retrieval process is more effective with HF words and the recognition process more effective with LF words. However, any explanation of the frequency paradox in terms of greater effectiveness of retrieval processes in the case of HF words is embarrassed to the extent that HF words are not recalled better than LF words. As we shall see, such situations exist and provide information concerning the nature of retrieval processes and retrieval attributes.

Before going further, it is necessary to discuss one obvious explanation of the frequency effect which we encountered in connection with perceptual identification experiments, namely, guessing. Our knowledge of word-frequency distributions indicates that a guess is more likely to be correct if it is made amongst all HF nouns rather than all LF nouns, since there are more of the latter than the former. Because of the large populations involved, it seems that a purely random guess would not lead to any apparent increase in recall scores. In any case, evidence which we shall discuss later suggests that mixing HF and LF words in the presentation list leads to an increase in LF recall and a decrease in HF recall relative to homogeneous lists. Guessing within the specified populations would necessarily lead to reduced performance for both classes of words since the population is increased for both on mixing. What may be termed 'directed guessing', i.e. within a set of words marked in some way by intra-list relations, could conceivably aid HF recall more than LF. Some such strategy may be used when categorized lists are employed, since HF lists not only give better recall than LF lists but categorical clustering is greater and appears earlier in recall protocols in HF lists (Bousfield and Cohen, 1955). This can be taken to indicate that category names are utilized as retrieval cues and that HF words, being high rank-order exemplars, are emitted more readily by enumeration.

The manner in which retrieval of list items is achieved is the concern of the immediately following sections. It will be seen that neither simple Spew principle nor priority of access notions are very helpful in explaining the data, largely because recall is not invariably superior for HF words relative to LF.

Organization

Several findings indicate that the general superior recall of HF word lists is due to the greater facilities for organization which they possess, compared to LF lists. For example, Sumby (1963) was able to attribute the superior recall of HF lists to the easier formation of meaningful associations between list items because changes in serial position curves accompanying learning of HF lists were similar to those exhibited by lists of high sequential approximation to English; LF lists showed changes similar to low-approximation lists.

Tulving and Patkau (1962) took a more direct approach to the assessment of organization. They found that recall of HF lists increased markedly with approximation to English, while the increase for LF lists was small. However, the number of output groupings corresponding with sequences in the presentation lists (adopted chunks) were similar for all types of lists; differences in number of words recalled were attributable to the number of words per chunk, this increasing with word frequency.

The adopted chunk measure taps a form of encoding which, possibly, is only utilized when the input has some sequential redundancy. That adopted chunks appeared with low levels of approximation to English in Tulving and Patkau's experiment may have been because subjects were tested at one level of word frequency but at all levels of approximation to English. This allows the possibility of strategy carry-over effects from one list to another. When only lists of low approximation to English are used the adopted chunk measure may well be inappropriate, since chunking of adjacent list items is unlikely to provide the optimal basis for constructing retrieval units. The problem, which is essentially one of deciding how to measure the subjects' organization of items, is highlighted by Postman's failure to find any convincing relationships between measures of subjective organization and recall.

Postman (1970) measured free-recall learning and immediate and delayed (seven days) retention of lists of high-(HF), medium-(MF) or low-frequency (LF) nouns with very low inter-item associative strengths. On learning trials HF lists gave consistently superior recall to LF and HF lists. On retesting after seven days the same pattern of results was maintained. If subjects were organizing the materials into chunks which were utilized at retrieval, the same consistency in the output order across trials would be expected. Rather than assume that these organizational units need correspond with input sequences, Postman employed the index of subjective organization, SO (Tulving, 1962), which indicates the relative probability with which the same ordered pairs occur in successive recalls. Although SO scores were significantly greater for HF lists compared to MF and LF, the differences were small absolutely. Also, correlations between SO and recall scores were small and insignificant for both acquisition and retention trials, this arguing against organizational interpretations. However, it could be that the pairwise basis of SO fails to take account of reorganization taking place across trials. Postman's results are not inconsistent with the notion that the facility for organization increases with word frequency even when the index of inter-item associative strength is low.

Inter-item Associations

The view that word-frequency effects are at least partially mediated by inter-item associations is strongly supported by several studies, Here the emphasis is on specific linguistic habits, the strengths of which depend on the frequency of their practice rather than the general usage of the individual words entering into them. Word-association data and numbers of word meanings suggest that the frequencies of occurrence of individual LF words are distributed across a small number of habits, thus admitting the possibility that the average strengths of these habits are greater than those of the more numerous habits entered into by individual HF words. If this is a contributing factor in free recall then appropriate manipulation of intra-list association should produce superior LF performance.

Deese (1960) reports several findings relevant to this issue. From knowledge of associative response distributions he predicted that the index of inter-item associative strength (IIAS), and hence free recall, should increase with list length, with this increase rising with word frequency. Deese confirmed these predictions using separate subjects to determine IIAS and recall. However, many of the IIAS values were zero and this restricted determination of the recall–IIAS relation to lists of the highest frequency classes, within which the measures were positively related. Importantly, when list length and IIAS were held constant, word-frequency effects were reduced or eliminated.

Additional evidence on the role of inter-item associations in the word-frequency effect comes from Matthews and his associates (Matthews, 1966; Matthews and Hoggart, 1970; Matthews and Manasse, 1970). In these experiments the unidirectional associative frequencies within specific word groups were varied factorially with word frequency. The starting point was the observation that Deese's IIAS gives a misleading assessment of the associative relation within a list. This is so because subjects are permitted only one response to each stimulus so that high communality responses drastically reduce the associative frequencies of other words high in the response hierarchy. The method of continuous, controlled associations, similar to Noble's method, avoids this problem.

Matthews (1966) constructed 12-word lists containing triplets of a core word and two responses elicited by it with one of four levels of frequency. Half the lists contained HF (T–L) words, the remainder contained core words, HF (T–L) and LF (T–L) responses. Thus word frequency and associative frequency were varied factorially. Recall was positively related to associative level but LF lists gave better recall than HF, this being explained by the more specific associative relationships of LF words. This explanation is supported by the greater clustering of associated triplets in LF lists and by association tests conducted with separate subjects which showed that LF triplet members elicited each other more often than did members of HF triplets.

An interesting point emerged when Matthews unpacked the triplets, distributing the members throughout the lists. Recall of HF lists was superior to LF lists on the first trial but this was reversed by the third trial suggesting that the more diffuse associative networks of HF words permitted the initial development of less-than-optimal encoding. This, in turn, suggests that the increased flexibility of encoding accompanying higher average word frequency proves a disadvantage when the list structure already encourages effective encoding. Matthews and Hoggart (1970) produced further evidence supporting this view by manipulating the number and size of associative clusters. When either or both of these is large the difficulties of encoding are magnified (Mandler, 1967), and under these conditions HF words were recalled better than LF words of similar associative level.

Recall from Matthews' unrelated control lists does not vary with word frequency, as was the case with Deese's lists of zero IIAS. The conclusion that 'word frequency alone does not facilitate recall' (Matthews and Manasse, 1970, p. 183) is unwarranted for at least two reasons, however. First, because Matthews' LF control lists contained HF words matched with core words in the associated lists, the average frequencies of HF and LF lists (1966, Table 1) are similar to those of the two highest-frequency classes employed by Hall (1954); these did not differ in recall. Second, the control lists differed with respect to word characteristics other than frequency, thus admitting the possibility that some potent factor was offsetting the effects of frequency. This applies to Deese's study also. We shall now turn to this problem in detail.

Isolating Word-Frequency Effects

We have considered a number of findings which strongly implicate the role of organizational and associative processes in the word-frequency effect. Descriptions of these processes have involved word characteristics which co-vary with word frequency, and when these are manipulated independently, as with Matthews' control of specific associative frequencies, common words do not invariably give superior recall. It is fundamentally important to determine whether any effects of frequency remain when related characteristics are controlled or partialled out. A number of studies which have attempted to determine the separate effects of frequency and concreteness, imagery value or meaningfulness are now discussed.

Dukes and Bastian (1966) varied concreteness and frequency while equating meaningfulness (m) determined by Noble's method. They employed a single lists consisting five words from each of the four combinations of word frequency and concreteness low-frequency words were recalled best at both levels of concreteness but the effect was reliable only with abstracts. Similar results were obtained by Winnick and Kressel (1965), but both experiments can be criticized for the use of small samples of words. This allows the possibility that other word attributes were confounded with the main variables. Indeed, Dukes and Bastian note that their LF abstract words were particularly high on emotionality. Also, equating m with such small samples of words does not necessarily equate associative or conceptual overlap of the items comprising the samples. The usefulness of these results for unravelling the means whereby word-frequency effects may be mediated is limited, therefore. However, an interaction between word frequency and imagery value (I) was obtained by Paivio and Madigan (1970) using larger word samples. With concretes, HF nouns gave consistently more effective recall, while with abstracts, LF nouns had the advantage in the initial five trials. Here, all the effects were significant.

Paivio (1971a) and Paivio and Madigan have discussed several explanations of the frequency by imagery interaction, including the joint effects of imaginal and verbal coding and differences in response availability, but these explanations have difficulty dealing with the poor performance of high-frequency–low-imagery items. It is possible that subjects presented with a list mixed with respect to levels of frequency and imagery adopt an encoding strategy which favours concrete words. Thus high-frequency–high-imagery items have the advantage of high-response availability, but the advantage of encoding compatibility is offset somewhat by verbal interference arising from their large, unspecific associative networks. High-frequency–low-imagery words suffer because of both verbal interference and encoding incompatibility.

While Paivio and Madigan maintain that word frequency and imagery have reliable and separate effects on free recall, both Frincke (1968) and Paivio (1968) failed to obtain significant correlations between word frequency and recall performance. Despite the wide range of frequencies used by Paivio (1 to 100 per million), the correlation with recall was near zero; rated familiarity gave a small negative correlation with recall. Frincke also obtained a near-zero correlation between free recall and T–L frequency, but the negative correlation with rated familiarity was significant.

The findings of Paivio and Frincke are not necessarily at variance with those of Paivio and Madigan, since the latter study found that HF words were recalled no better than LF words, overall, on early trials. The frequency effects only revealed themselves in the interaction with imagery. The different correlations with recall obtained for objective and subjective estimates of frequency are to be expected since, as we have already noted, the two are themselves only moderately correlated. Also, the direction of differences in correlation coefficients follows from the findings that abstracts are judged more frequent than concretes when equated on T–L frequency (Galbraith and Underwood, 1973), while concretes are recalled more often than abstracts (Paivio and Madigan, 1970).

The studies referred to above bring into focus the considerable problems involved in isolating word-frequency effects. If a factorial design is adopted then word samples become small, thus increasing the likelihood that some other factor is confounded with frequency. Furthermore, all these studies, both factorial and factor analytic, have employed mixed lists containing HF and LF words. Because of this, and because recall of individual words depends on the conceptual and associative relations within the list as a whole, conclusions that recall has either a negative or no relation with frequency must be restricted to the mixed-list situation. This view is supported by the superior recall of HF words when homogeneous lists are used with words matched on meaningfulness (Kanungo and Mohanty, 1970). The use of mixed and homogeneous lists has a major influence on the word-frequency effect and deserves further consideration.

Mixed Lists

In general, homogeneous lists give rise to superior HF recall while mixed lists yield superior scores for LF words. Explanations of the effects of mixing frequencies include diversion of attention from familiar to unusual words, changes in associative and conceptual overlaps, and elimination of guessing advantages enjoyed by HF words in homogeneous lists.

It is unsatisfactory to assess the effects of mixing by comparing across experiments, especially because of the varied and limited word samples employed where related factors have been controlled. A direct comparison of free recall from homogeneous and mixed lists was made by May and Tryk (1970). Drawing on rather small samples of two-syllable HF (AA) and LF (3 or less per million) words, taken randomly from the T–L count, they constructed homogeneous lists of 20 items; the mixed list was constructed by alternating HF and LF words. Trials to the criterion of two correct free recalls were least for the mixed list and most for the LF list. While LF words took longer to learn than HF words in homogeneous lists, the opposite was true in the mixed list. May and Tryk explain their results in terms of 'stimulus variability', i.e. alternating HF and LF words maintains orientation towards the list. In addition, LF words in the mixed list 'stand out' against the background of familiar words. Taken together, these explanations account for the superior recall of mixed lists and of LF words within these lists. However, the finding that mixed lists are learned more easily than both types of homogeneous lists is not supported by other findings to which we shall now turn.

It follows from Deese's arguments concerning associative relations that mixing should increase IIAS and conceptual overlap for LF words while decreasing them for HF words relative to the homogeneous situation. Thus, mixing should improve LF recall while reducing HF recall, the overall effect leading to recall scores from mixed lists intermediate to those of HF and LF homogeneous lists. These predictions differ from the results obtained by May and Tryk.

Fergus Craik and I tested these predictions using a more extensive design than that of May and Tryk (Gregg, 1970, experiment 1). We constructed 15 HF lists by randomly drawing sets of five abstract and 15 concrete words from a pool of 300 monosyllabic nouns. Fifteen lists of LF words were similarly formed. Mixed lists contained equal numbers of HF and LF words and the order within all lists was randomized. Eighteen, eighteen and twenty subjects received the 15 HF, LF and mixed lists, respectively. Presentation was auditory at a two-second rate and each list was followed by immediate written free recall. The number of words recalled, averaged across homogeneous lists, was 8.46 for HF and 6.04 for LF, the difference being reliable. In mixed lists the figures were 3.13 for HF and 3.26 for LF. Correcting these figures for opportunity it can be seen that the HF words suffered as a result of mixing while LF words gained. Also, the overall performance of mixed lists (6.39) lies between the scores of the homogeneous lists. Interestingly, the LF scores are slightly greater than those of HF words in mixed lists, this agreeing with the general findings already discussed.

Some interesting points emerge if we reconsider the studies of Tulving and Patkau and of Matthews. Tulving and Patkau employed one set of lists containing only HF words while the other set was composed of both HF and LF words. At the lowest level of AE these lists are similar to the HF and mixed lists employed in our experiment just described. The same point has already been made in connection with Matthews' control lists; the LF lists were mixed since they contained HF words matched with core words. In both studies the mixed lists were slightly inferior to the HF lists on the first trial.

It appears that mixed lists do not generally give rise to better recall than HF lists, contrary to May and Tryk's findings; the increased orientation towards mixed lists which formed part of their explanation is not generally applicable, therefore. The diversion of attention from familiar to unusual items may contribute to the effects of mixing, but turning again to Matthews' work we find evidence favouring the associative/organizational interpretation. Matthews was able to produce superiority for the mixed lists (LF-associated) by manipulating the strengths and specificity of association between items, and this can be seen as a controlled version of what takes place in random mixing. The relevance of the effects of mixing for the guessing explanation of the recall–frequency relation has already been discussed.

Frequency effects in free recall are not explained by the straight-forward Spew principle; rather it appears best to consider them arising from the wider encoding facilities offered by HF relative to LF words. This encoding flexibility is not necessarily an advantage, especially where the list structure already offers specific bases for encoding (e.g. Matthews, 1966). The Spew principle has been widely used to explain results in paired-associate and serial recall learning but difficulties arise in separating item availability from associative hook-up as is made clear in the next two sections. A better conceptualization maintains that performance depends on the ease with which items enter into specific encodings which are themselves incorporated into the task context.

Paired-associate Learning

Underwood and Schulz (1960) conceived of paired-associate learning as a response integration stage, in which responses are made available, and an associative stage, in which these are hooked up with stimulus items. They further maintained that familiar responses become available earlier than unfamiliar ones and this has received support from several sources. For instance, Postman (1962) found speed of acquisition to be directly related to response frequency; also, percentage errors due to misplaced responses increased with response frequency, suggesting that HF responses become available more readily than LF responses but are more likely to be misplaced.

That the HF superiority is due to greater response availability is indicated by the finding that low, not high, response frequency yields faster learning in paired-associates recognition where response availability is presumably equated (Holborn, Gross and Catlin, 1973). However, the subjects of Holborn *et al.* were expecting a recognition test and the results are not entirely helpful in distinguishing between integration and association stages of recall. Indeed, Hall (1972) found that high response frequency facilitated paired-associate recall but not stimulus–response matching nor free recall, all following paired-associate recall instructions. All three measures increased with stimulus–response associative frequency, suggesting that pairs of items are encoded as single units and making it difficult to maintain the widely accepted distinction between integration and association stages.

Hall's results can be accommodated within Postman's view that unit sequence interference and facilitation arising from pre-experimental linguistic habits, depend not on frequency *per se*, but on the positively correlated property of meaningfulness. While Postman (1962) attributed the curvilinear relation between *stimulus* frequency and speed of acquisition to the interplay of facilitating and interfering associations, Saltz (1967) considered it to be the outcome of the positive but not perfect correlation between frequency and meaningfulness each of which has distinct effects.

Saltz sees the effect of word usage as strengthening linguistic habits, but he distinguishes between frequency of word usage and the frequency with which each meaning of the word is used. Speed of acquisition is held to be inversely related to resistance to unlearning of old habits, therefore the crucial factor in paired-associate learning is average frequency per meaning rather than gross word frequency. Saltz's model is successful in dealing with manipulation of frequency and meaningfulness of both stimuli (Modigliani and Saltz, 1969; Saltz, 1967) and responses (Saltz and Modigliani, 1967). Impressively, it also predicts the average frequency per meaning above which speed of acquisition is a negative function of response word frequency (Saltz and Modigliani, 1970).

That low stimulus frequency sometimes facilitates learning could be due to more specific stimulus–response encoding than occurs with high stimulus frequency. Such a proposal holds the frequency effect to result mainly from opportunities for encoding variability (Martin, 1968) and accommodates Saltz's contention that gross word frequency is, in itself, not an adequate measure. The encoding notion may offer an explanation of the interaction between imagery and word frequency reported by Paivio and Madigan (1970). Amongst the complex interactions was the finding that high-imagery pairs with low stimulus frequency produced highest recall, and low-imagery pairs of high stimulus frequency produced lowest recall. While imaginal coding may be operating as a factor distinct from frequency, it is also possible that abstracts, having occurred in more varied pre-experimental contexts (Galbraith and Underwood, 1973), are richer in encoding possibilities than concretes. Thus, Stimulus–response encoding should be relatively unspecific when HF abstracts are involved.

Serial Recall

Investigations of serial recall as a function of word frequency have largely centred on the predictions of the unit-sequence interference hypothesis (Underwood and Postman, 1960). This hypothesis maintains that pre-experimental linguistic habits will facilitate learning to the extent that the experimental sequence conforms to these habits. Where the sequence diverges from these well-established habits they must be unlearned and hence will interfere with new learning. For example, Postman, Turnage and Silverstein (1964) considered that unit-sequence interference should increase faster than unit-sequence facilitation with word frequency, so that random sequences of LF words should yield longer-running memory spans than HF sequences. This expectation was confirmed on the first trial (subsequent trials suffered from unequal repetition of items), but more HF words were recalled regardless of order. Thus, the greater span for LF lists is not due to the greater availability of LF responses.

The small values of running memory span obtained by Postman *et al.* with auditory presentation—about two items—raises the possibility that modality-specific interference, rather than unit-sequence mechanisms, gives rise to the frequency effect. While HF and LF word populations differ phonemically (Frederiksen, 1971), it is not clear whether HF words are less distinctive amongst themselves than LF words, but this is true if one-letter substitution neighbourhoods are considered (Landauer and Streeter, 1973).

Support for the unit-sequence hypothesis has been claimed by Turnage and McCullough (1968) and Turnage and Steinmetz (1971) on account of the curvilinear relation between word frequency and both forward and backward serial recall, assessed by terminal span and pair score (number of pairs recalled in correct order, regardless of preceding or subsequent errors). However, these results constitute only weak evidence in favour of the unit-sequence hypothesis since incorrect spellings constituted errors. This is obviously to the disadvantage of LF lists, particularly as paralogs formed the lowest frequency class.

Taking a different approach, Baddeley and Scott (1971) failed to obtain differences in forgetting rates for short sequences of HF and LF words, contrary to the predictions of unit-sequence interference. They point out that the greater LF span obtained by Postman *et al.* could arise from the difficulty of ordering the larger number of HF words retained.

In order to equate response availability and storage load I have employed a serial-ordering procedure. Subjects were presented visually with lists of 12 HF (A and AA) or LF (1 per million) nouns of low inter-item associative strength, at a two-second rate. An interfering letter-reading task then followed to prevent ordering by initial letter. Subjects then attempted to order the words, written on cards, into the prescribed sequence. Four measures of ordering were taken: (a) number of words in correct serial position; (b) sum d^2, where d is difference between placed and original serial positions; (c) Kendall's P, which takes account of cumulative correct relative placements; and (d) number of correct pairings irrespective of serial position. None of these measures revealed differences between HF and LF lists over 10 learning trials. Turnage

(1970) also obtained no effect of frequency when he presented subjects with sequences of 10 items (paralogs, 10 per million and 50 per million, T–L) and on testing required them to indicate each item's serial position.

While it seems clear that response availability increases with word frequency in serial recall, it is not clear how serial order is encoded and how, if at all, word frequency affects this encoding. When item availability is equated word frequency has no effect on ordering, but these findings may not be relevant to explanations of serial recall because subjects may be expected to engage in different encoding operations in the two situations. Differences in serial recall of HF and LF lists may be due to various consequences of differences in item availability or procedural artefacts and not to facilitation of, or interference with learning of specific sequences due to existing linguistic habits.

Editing Processes in Recall

The retrieve–recognize model of recall maintains that word retrieval is followed by an editing process with the same characteristics as recognition. This implies that while more HF words are retrieved, the editing process is more effective for LF words.

The evidence concerning these predictions is mixed: in serial recall, Underwood and Postman (1960) and Postman (1961) report slightly more extra-list intrusions with LF compared with HF lists; in paired-associate recall, Postman (1962) found intrusions increased with word frequency but Saltz (1967) found no such relation. In free recall, to which the retrieve–recognize model directly refers, few authors report intrusion incidence, but this has been found to increase with frequency (Postman, 1970) or to be unaffected by it (Bousfield and Cohen, 1955) although in both studies the number of words correctly recalled increased with frequency. These various results plausibly derive from differences in encoding leading to the storage of information more or less useful to the editing process.

To examine further the predictions of the retrieve–recognize model Fergus Craik and I conducted the experiment referred to earlier (Gregg, 1970, experiment 1). Subjects were given 15 free-recall trials with non-overlapping lists and indicated how confident they were that recalled items were in the most recent list. It was assumed the ratings reflected trace strength, recency or other information utilized by the editing process. This view receives support from a study by Turnage (1967) in which the relations of confidence ratings and number recalled with word frequency showed different changes over retention intervals of 2 to 30 seconds; this suggests that confidence ratings and number recalled do not reflect the same information.

In our experiment, as expected, recall was superior for HF words from homogeneous lists and for LF words from mixed lists. Confidence ratings ranged from 5, 'certain word is current list member' to 1, 'guess'. The results are given in Table 1. Differences are significant in homogeneous lists but not in mixed lists. Contrary to our expectations, the rating data showed the same

Table 1. Mean No. of correct recalls and mean confidence ratings
(Gregg, 1970, expt. 1)

		Mean No. recalled	Mean conf. rating
Pure lists	HFW	8.46	4.90
	LFW	6.04	4.80
Mixed lists	HFW	3.13	4.85
	LFW	3.32	4.86

Table 2. Total No. of PLIs (corrected for opportunity) and mean
confidence ratings (Gregg, 1970, expt. 1)

		No. of PLIs	Mean conf. rating
Recent	HFW	74	3.59
	LFW	27	3.33
Distant	HFW	16	3.00
	LFW	29	3.23

pattern as proportion recalled, one interpretation of this being that the retrieve–recognize model is correct but accessible trace strength falls more rapidly for HF than LF words, thus eventually producing the situation indicated by the superior recognition of LF words. This explanation does not account for the effects of mixing on confidence ratings, however. A more adequate explanation is that list contexts are utilized in both retrieval and recognition processes (Anderson and Bower, 1972) and this would permit the inclusion of a recursive search in which information relevant to one process facilitates the other. This suggestion requires that the information utilized by the decision process is defined with more complexity than 'trace strength' or 'recency'.

As may be expected, our experiment produced a number of previous list intrusions (PLIs). These are items from previously presented lists which occur in the current output and therefore represent a failure of the editing process. As such they are of interest to the present discussion, particularly the manner in which their numbers and confidence ratings change over time. When comparing the numbers of PLIs arising from various sources it is necessary to take into account differences in opportunity for obtaining them from increasingly distant lists. Because of this we considered only intrusions occurring during trials 6 to 15 and having origins in lists 1 to 10 trials distant. The small number of PLIs forced us to combine them with respect to source into recent (1 to 5 lists distant) and distant (6 to 10 lists distant) and to restrict analysis to homogeneous lists. The number of PLIs, corrected for opportunity, produced by 18 subjects at each frequency are given in Table 2, together with their mean confidence ratings. More HF than LF intrusions occur from recent lists but the position is reversed for distant lists. This suggests that list discrimination, or estimation of recency, is poor amongst recently presented HF lists but rapidly improves relative to LF lists. This is supported by the ratings which show that subjects are more confident that recent intrusions are current list members when they are HF rather than LF. The position is reversed for distant intrusions, suggesting that editing is more effective for HF words at long intervals, whereas recognition studies show that editing is generally more effective for LF words.

Anderson and Bower (1972) proposed that occurrence of a word as a list member leads to the linking of the word to a set of contextual elements via a list marker; decisions concerning list membership are based on the evidence attached to the marker. Importantly, list discrimination depends on the overlap between the elements of different lists. The large number of HF intrusions from recent lists in our experiment can be accounted for if HF lists have greater overlap in contextual elements than do LF lists. This is reasonable since the recall data have already been explained in terms of the large encoding flexibility possessed by HF words. The situation at distant lists is difficult to deal with because of the small number of intrusions involved.

Our failure to obtain differential effects of word frequency on the number recalled and confidence ratings led us to look at recall from very long lists (Gregg, 1970, experiment 2). The primary reason for this was the use of such lists in recognition studies where performance was superior for uncommon words. Briefly, we presented subjects with homogeneous lists of 160 HF (AA— 20 per million, T–L) or LF (1 per million or less) two-syllable nouns, visually at a three-second rate. Six lists were constructed at each frequency level by drawing from a pool of 320 words. Immediate written free recall was required with a confidence rating for each word. A 10-point rating scale was used with 1 representing a guess.

The data are represented in Figures 1 (a) and 1 (b), where input blocks represent 20 successive serial positions. Each curve is based on 60 subjects. Significantly more HF than LF words were recalled. The confidence ratings were higher overall for LF words but inequalities in the number of ratings available for each block make statistical assessment difficult. However, Mann– Whitney tests showed the differences at blocks 2,3,4 and 5 to be significant.

The results are in line with our expectations and contrast with those of the earlier experiment where confidence ratings were highest for HF words when homogeneous lists were employed; there are several plausible explanations of this reversal. It is possible that with long lists subjects were able to base their decisions on familiarity or some such temporal information similar to that plausibly used in recognition memory; in the earlier recall experiment, however, this information would not be sufficiently fine to discriminate between current and other list membership. The confidence-rating serial position curves could then reflect more rapid loss of familiarity with HF than with LF words over the interval between presentation and recall. This explanation is difficult to test because with the long lists this interval is largely confounded with serial position.

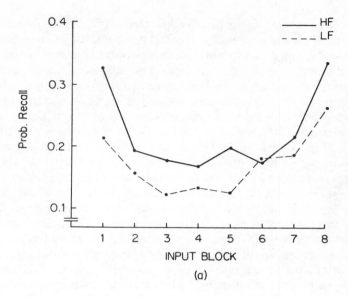

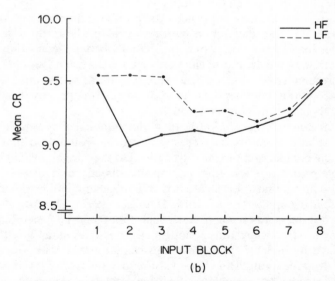

Figure 1. (a) Proportion of items recalled. (b) Mean
confidence ralings for recalled items

A further possibility is that the confidence ratings reflect differences in bias,
i.e. subjects are more reluctant to recall LF words than HF words. The use of
confidence ratings in the manner just described does not permit a formal
treatment of this point. Ingleby (1973) approached the problem by applying
Luce's choice model to recall and recognition of common and uncommon

surnames. The starting point was Dale's (1967) conclusion that unfamiliar English county names were poorly recalled relative to familiar names because they were not scanned at retrieval. In a recognition test unfamiliar names were recognized slightly better than familiar ones, suggesting that trace strength was greater for the unfamiliar names. Ingleby's approach is within the tradition of models of recall which embody undirected scanning of the whole set of potential and available items and reveals several problems which arise when a direct comparison of decision processes in recall and recognition is attempted.

Ingleby sampled the London Telephone Directory to estimate the number of names occurring in six frequency classes. The number of names (N) in each class were inserted into Luce's choice model to obtain estimates of the bias and strength parameters. Subjects were required to remember anecdotes featuring five characters with different names. After 20 seconds of backward counting they attempted to recall the names when given the anecdote with them missing. Probability of recall was monotonically related to commonness of the name but the number of intrusions was independent of frequency class. This situation, translated into decision parameters, reflects a bias against responding with uncommon names while their accessible trace strength was greater than that of common names. Similar results were obtained when response availability was equated in a recognition test.

Ingleby argues that there is no need to resort to differences in availability between common and uncommon names to explain the recall data. Instead, he concludes that uncommon names are 'actually better preserved or retrieved than familiar ones, but are more reluctantly emitted as responses' (1973, p. 386). While his results agree with the general findings that uncommon words give superior recognition compared to common words, the proposed mechanisms underlying them require consideration.

The conclusion that the inferior recall of uncommon names is due to subjects' reluctance to emit them as responses requires the assumption that all items enter into the comparison of trace strengths, i.e. they are all available as responses. Ingleby did not test this assumption directly and there is evidence from other sources that subjects are not able to generate all members of quite closely specified populations of words (Duncan, 1973). Duncan showed that the proportion of words recognized as such that could be generated fell with decreasing word frequency, thus permitting the possibility that the effective N is overestimated by Ingleby's procedure, this being more so with lower frequencies. Since the trace strength and bias measures derived from the yes–no recognition procedure did not involve N, they may not be comparable with those derived from recall. If we assume that retrieval of words from storage proceeds according to plans developed at input, the more extensive relations between, and encoding opportunities offered by, HF words could plausibly lead to retrieval of more correct *and* incorrect names relative to LF names. Thus *more* HF names than LF names may be involved in the decision-making.

A second reason why the measures derived from the two types of test may not be comparable stems from a procedural difference. In the recognition test, names which had appeared in the anecdotes always appeared in the same location at test if they appeared at all. Thus decisions could be based on whether the words had appeared in the experiment or not. In recall, names were only scored correct if they were recalled in the correct location. Also, intrusions in recall were not divided into items misplaced rather than imported from outside the original set of names. Thus it is impossible to ascertain what proportion of intrusions were due to subjects' inability to assess occurrence, rather than position, in the anecdotes, as would be necessary in order to compare the measures of bias and trace strength with those derived from recognition.

The difficulties of assessing the decision process in recall are numerous; direct comparison of these processes in recognition and recall is more difficult still because different test expectations lead to different storage strategies (see Chapter 5 by Aldwyn Cooper and Andrew Monk); in recognition, strength and bias measures are often not independent (Parks, 1966; Donaldson and Murdock, 1968) and the implications of movements in bias during recall may be different from those in recognition.

Recognition

The retrieve–recognize model of recall maintains the context-free nature of information utilized by recognition processes thereby forcing an explanatory dependency on concepts such as recency or familiarity. Such explanations of frequency effects seem reasonable in that these concepts are intimately bound up in frequency of usage; also, the relation between rated familiarity and situational frequency has similarities to the Weber function (Noble, 1963). However, studies of verbal-discrimination learning (Paivio and Rowe, 1970) and frequency discrimination (Underwood, Zimmerman and Freund, 1971) have provided only marginal support for the notion that situational frequency is additive with, and assimilates into background frequency. It has already been made clear that the frequency paradox is inferred from comparisons across experiments and that problems exist for direct comparison of accessible trace strength in recognition and recall. Before speculating on the nature of the stored information utilized in recognition, the consistency of frequency effects will be assessed and several explanations considered.

The Effects of Mixing Frequencies

Mixing HF and LF words in presentation lists has a marked effect on recall; indeed, the superiority of common words in homogeneous lists is eliminated or even reversed by mixing. It is plausible that the use of mixed lists in recognition studies has been a major contributory factor to the paradoxical situation, just as attention to only studies employing homogeneous lists is necessary to arrive at the conclusion that recall of HF words exceeds recall of LF words. This explanation is made plausible by the finding, mentioned earlier, that mixing increases the confidence ratings assigned to recalled LF words while decreasing those assigned to HF words.

The effects of mixing are also relevant to the status of the retrieve–recognition model of recall, since it implies that list structure and organizational factors should affect the retrieval of items but not the recognition process. The uncovering of organizational effects has forced the acceptance of retrieval processes in recognition (e.g. Mandler, 1972) and this adds credibility to the point made earlier that contextual information could be contributing to the effects of mixing on confidence ratings in recall. While such considerations do not rule out the possibility that the decision processes entered into at recall are similar to those involved in recognition, they do demand, at least, that such decisions make use of information in addition to recency or a simplistic trace strength.

The possibility that the frequency paradox arises from the use of mixed lists in recognition can be dismissed, since LF words are recognized better than HF words both in homogeneous lists (Gorman, 1961; Gregg, 1970; McCormack and Swenson, 1972; Schulman and Lovelace, 1970; Underwood and Freund, 1970b) and in mixed lists (Allen and Garton, 1968; Garton and Allen, 1968; Schulman, 1967; Shepard, 1967).

The occurrence of a similar effect in both types of lists counters the argument that it is due to the diversion of attention from familiar to unfamiliar words. Further evidence against this explanation includes the finding by Allen and Garton (1968) that physics students performed better than arts students not only on uncommon words but also on the common words contained in same lists; also, the frequency effect is not removed nor reversed when a few common words are embedded in lists consisting mainly of uncommon words (Garton and Allen, 1968). Even if it is accepted that familiar words do not become unusual by being in the minority, a reduction in LF performance would still be expected since more LF words are competing for attention compared to the situation in which the two classes of words are equally represented.

Clearly, determining the influence of mixing on the frequency effect by comparing mixed and homogeneous lists across experiments is unsatisfactory and a direct comparison is called for. In such an experiment (Gregg, 1970, experiment 3) subjects received 96-word inspection lists of HF (AA or A), LF (15 per million or less) or equal numbers of HF and LF randomly mixed. All words were monosyllabic and visual presentation was at a three-second rate. The test sequence followed after a 15-second interval and contained the 96 targets and 100 distractors drawn from the same populations as the targets. The effect of mixing was to improve LF performance from a d' of 1.34 in homogeneous lists to 1.44 and to reduce HF performance from 0.92 to 0.91. The effect of frequency and the interaction between frequency and type of list are significant, but the differences within each level of frequency are not so.

Although the superiority of LF recognition is increased slightly in mixed lists relative to homogeneous lists, this is not sufficiently great to explain the frequency paradox; such an explanation would require a reversal of the frequency effect in homogeneous lists relative to mixed lists.

207

Retention Intervals

Despite the problem associated with the assessment of accessible trace strength in recall situations, the data arising from the recall of long lists suggest that it may fall more rapidly over time when HF rather than LF words are involved, thus raising the possibility that similar effects may appear in recognition. If this were to happen, the case for equating the decision component of recall with recognition would be strengthened and the frequency effect in recognition could be attributed to differences in rates of forgetting. This, in turn, would provide a basis for relating properties associated with common and uncommon words to recognition processes.

Prediction of differential changes over time in recognition of HF and LF words can be extracted from Shepard's 'diffusion' principle (1961) and Bower's encoding variability model (1972b). If we speculate that Shepard's diffusion of conditioned elements takes place via overlapping word attributes or associative pathways, then our knowledge of such features suggests that the rate of diffusion will be greatest for HF words. Similarly, the more varied meanings and greater meaningfulness of HF words will give rise to more opportunities for encoding variability than will those of LF words. Both models offer scope for predicting that hits will fall, and false positives increase with retention intervals more rapidly for HF than for LF lists.

The ordering of recognition performance is consistent over a number of different procedures and definitions of HF and LF classes. It is possible to calculate mean retention intervals for individual items in several experiments, and when this is done it is found that LF words are recognized better than HF words at mean intervals of six minutes (Gregg, 1970), 10 minutes (Shepard, 1967; Schulman, 1967) and 12 minutes (Allen and Garton, 1968). Shepard's subjects were self-paced, so the interval is based on the assumption that they took two seconds per item.

Gorman (1961) used 18-word lists followed by test sequences of six targets and 12 distractors to give a mean interval of only 18 seconds; even at this short interval performance was best for LF lists. Gorman's method of scoring involved allotting scores of $+1$ to correct responses and -1 to errors and summing algebraically. Unfortunately, this does not reveal the separate effects of frequency on hits and false positives and gives rise to the possibility that differences in decision criteria, between frequencies, could distort the scores; this is particularly so with imbalance in the numbers of targets and distractors.

McCormack and Swenson (1972) recorded hits and false positives separately and were thus able to assess changes in proportions of hits taking place with increasing retention intervals. They presented subjects with lists of 21 HF or LF words followed by a 75-second backward-counting task and a 42-item recognition test. Most hits were achieved with LF lists, but HF distractors gave rise to most false positives; both measures indicate superior LF recognition, therefore. A detailed analysis showed the proportion of hits for both classes of words did not change over the 75 to 210 seconds between presentation and testing of specific items.

The last finding does not necessarily reflect a constant level of discrimination between targets and distractors across retention intervals, since it is known that criterion changes occur with progress through a testing sequence (Donaldson and Murdock, 1968; Shepard and Chang, 1963); indeed, when this problem is avoided by using the forced-choice procedure, forgetting over comparable intervals is found (Underwood and Freund, 1970b). McCormack and Swenson did not ignore the false positives and this aspect of their analysis will be considered later.

It is clear that the assessment of retention intervals for individual items within the Egan paradigm, in which an inspection sequence is followed by a test sequence, leads either to confounding of interval and proportions of inspection and test items occupying the interval or, if these are equated, confounding of interval and position in both inspection and test sequences.

Underwood and Freund (1970b, experiment 2) avoided these problems by varying the interval between inspection and test sequences to look at forgetting rates of HF (AA) and LF (1 per million) words. Homogeneous, 50-item inspection lists were followed by a symbol-cancellation task of 0.5, 3 or 6 minutes' duration. Then followed 50 two-alternative, forced-choice trials containing targets and distractors from the same frequency class. In this way they measured recognition at mean intervals of 80, 230 and 410 seconds. Low-frequency lists gave superior performance at all intervals, with the overall level falling over time. Although the interaction between frequency and interval was not significant, the increase in errors with interval was greatest for LF words, contrary to our predictions derived from the diffusion and encoding variability models.

Underwood and Freund drew attention to the fact that as the retention interval increases, new items become newer. Common distractors should benefit more from increasing intervals than uncommon ones since pre-experimental occurrence of the former will be more recent than of the latter. The operation of such a principle is indicated by the faster increase in LF errors with interval, but the extent of its influence is difficult to determine because as the authors themselves demonstrate, interference effects, also dependent on frequency, were present.

The continuous-recognition procedure (Shepard and Teghtsoonian, 1961) makes it possible to fill the retention intervals of individual items with specified numbers of presentation and test events. Furthermore, by employing a long enough sequence of events a 'steady state' can be achieved in which the complications of primacy and practice effects are minimized. Two experiments which I have conducted using the two-alternative, forced-choice and yes–no versions are relevant here (Gregg, 1970, experiments 4 and 5).

The forced-choice procedure, similar to that introduced by Shepard and Chang (1963), involved homogeneous sequences of HF (A, AA) or LF (1–15 per million, T–L) nouns. Seventy-two single-presentation items were followed by 180 test groups each consisting of two stages: (a) distractor and target, requiring recognition of the target; (b) the distractor alone to indicate that this item would be tested later. Half the targets had mean lags of 40 test groups, the remainder mean lags of 80, these being evenly distributed throughout the sequence and corresponding to retention intervals of 120 and 240 seconds. Performance was assessed over the last 80, steady-state, groups. Performance was superior for LF words, the d' values being 1.58 and 1.27 for LF at lags 40 and 80 respectively, and 1.13 and 1.02 for HF. Although the interaction between lag and frequency was not significant, forgetting was significant for LF but not for HF words, this agreeing with Underwood and Freund's results.

The yes–no task was based on that of Shepard and Teghtsoonian (1961) and slso employed homogeneous HF and LF lists. The lags of 10 and 40 items corresponded to intervals of 35 and 140 seconds. Forgetting was reliable for both classes of words and slightly faster for HF, the mean values of d' falling from 2.64 to 1.63 for HF and 3.41 to 2.51 for LF.

The recognition superiority of LF words is consistent across retention intervals ranging from 18 seconds to 12 minutes both within and across experiments involving a variety of procedures. Also, the similarity of forgetting rates different frequency classes is not affected by the content of the interval.

What is shown to be true for recognition of HF and LF words is generally true for other procedures and variables; rates of forgetting are remarkably constant (Postman, 1972), whereas level of performance is dependent on such variables. It is surprising, therefore, that little emphasis has been placed on acquisition rather than decay of, or interference with stored information, or on retrieval and decision aspects of recognition. Schulman and Lovelace (1970) found that increased presentation rates reduced inter-subject variability in recognition scores, suggesting that elaboration of encoding was curtailed. However, reductions in performance were similar for HF and LF words and these results offer little towards explanation of the LF superiority.

Intra-experimental Sources of Interference

The effects of mixing frequencies and differences in rates of forgetting are too small to account for the frequency paradox and to provide much positive evidence on the cause of LF superiority in recognition. One further possibility is that interference from presentation and testing events is greater when HF, rather than LF, words are involved. If such interference were to build up rapidly it would explain why the frequency effect appears when small numbers of words are involved (Gorman, 1961). McCormack and Swenson (1972) looked at these possibilities.

McCormack and Swenson argued that if the frequency effect is due to differences in the build-up of proactive interference, the performance should deteriorate more rapidly for HF than LF words over three inspection and test sequences of non-overlapping lists of the same frequency class. Recognition was superior for LF lists, with similar falls across lists, for both frequency classes. The proportions of hits fell slightly with progress through each HF and LF test sequence but the false positives, initially similar, increased most rapidly in HF sequences. These results indicate two loci of interference, both more potent for HF words: since differences in hit rates were apparent within the initial seven test items, and thereafter fairly stable, target interference must have occurred during storage; on the other hand, interference on distractors builds up as the test sequence progresses. This interference interpretation of the frequency effect is attractive, suggesting as it does that presentation-sequence interference builds up within lists of only 21 words while test-sequence interference appears after only seven test trials.

McCormack and Swenson's separation of presentation- and test-sequence interference assumes that responses to targets are independent of responses to distractors. However, subjects generally attempt to keep the proportion of 'Old' responses at some explicit or implicit level (Donaldson and Murdock, 1968; Parks, 1966). As a consequence, when discriminability is low subjects may adjust an initially high proportion of 'New' decisions to the true proportion of new items. The proportion of 'Old' responses (hits plus false positives) in McCormack and Swenson's study approached the true level of 50 per cent from the second sixth of the test sequence onwards, and the data are consistent with a fall in d' due to test-sequence interference alone, or forgetting over time. However, if this were so it is surprising that subjects should consistently start lists with a preponderance of 'New' responses.

One suggestion as to the mechanisms by which interference is produced derives from the finding that a distractor is likely to be recognized as a target if it occurs as an implicit associative response (IAR) during target processing in the inspection phase (Anisfeld and Knapp, 1968; Underwood, 1965). In the explanation of the word-frequency effect proposed by Underwood and Freund (1970b) the occurrence of a word as an IAR is equivalent to its presentation in that both events lead to the incrementation of the word's situational frequency count (SFC) by one unit. In a two-alternative, forced-choice test subjects are assumed to select the item with the highest SFC as the target. An important feature of this model is that SFC does not sum or interact with pre-experimental frequency of occurrence, the emphasis then resting on associative characteristics. Relative numbers of SFCs accruing to targets and distractors from HF and LF inspection lists can be assessed from knowledge of associative response distributions.

In a test of the model, Underwood and Freund presented subjects with 50-item HF or LF lists followed by 50 forced-choice pairs all consisting of one of the four possible target–distractor frequency combinations (HF–LF, etc.). The SFC model correctly predicts the ordering of conditions, from least to most errors, as HF–LF, LF–HF, LF–LF, HF–HF and it is not possible to attribute the HF–LF superiority simply to discrimination of frequency class since they gave significantly fewer errors than LF–HF pairs.

Underwood and Freund's results agree extremely closely with those of Shepard (1967), with the exception of the HF–LF condition. Shepard employed very long inspection lists containing both HF and LF words and test sequences containing all four target–distractor combinations. The probability of correct response to HF–LF pairs is given as approximately 0.98 by Underwood and Freund and as 0.867 by Shepard. Thus, Shepard found that pairs in which the target was LF invariably gave better recognition than those with HF targets. One possible explanation of this discrepancy lies in the use of mixed lists by Shepard. The predicted effects of mixing frequencies are to reduce IARs involving HF targets and distractors while increasing those involving LF items. Comparing mixed against homogeneous lists we find that performance on LF–LF pairs should be little affected, as was the case. The observed fall for HF–LF pairs is predicted because target IARs will decrease while distractor IARs, already low in homogeneous lists, will fall very little. Mixing should improve HF–LF performance because both target and distractor IARs will fall, but SFCs arising directly from item presentation will be maintained, thus leaving a favourable balance. Also, LF–HF pairs will receive additional distractor IARs due to the inclusion of HF items in the presentation sequence and this should lead to a decrement in performance.

It is difficult to predict the magnitude of change due to mixing, but the last two predictions were not borne out and the SFC model thereby weakened. However, the experiments of Shepard and of Underwood and Freund differed in features other than mixing; for instance, Shepard's test sequences contained all types of pairings and his presentation sequences were very long. These differences alone may account for the discrepancies between predictions of the SFC model and the presumed effects of mixing.

The failure to find substantial mixing effects with the old–new procedure (Gregg, 1970) could be due to the non-independence of 'Old' and 'New' responses and the consequential inability to separate effects on targets and distractors.

It is interesting to note that whereas Underwood and Freund emphasize interference effects arising at storage with false positives arising from IARs at this stage, McCormack and Swenson conclude that false positives arise from interference originating in the test phase.

The SFC model is attractive because it predicts the unusual findings of very high recognition of HF targets, and taken with McCormack and Swenson's suggestions, offers an explanation of the appearance of the frequency effect when short lists or lags are employed. Further, it offers a parsimonious explanation of the frequency paradox by resorting to the relation between word frequency and associative probability which goes some way to explaining the effect of frequency on recall. Unfortunately, there are several considerations which limit the model's attractiveness. For instance, SFC units are discrete and appear unable to deal with list discrimination situations referred to by Anderson and Bower (1973); but there is no reason why the units should not be made less discrete, thus taking the form of list elements in Anderson and Bower's model. Other difficulties are posed by the finding that hypothesized implicit associative frequencies do not contribute to the difficulty of discriminating actual frequencies of presentation (Howell, 1973a), and the inability of IAR occurrence to explain certain failures of recognition (Tulving and Thomson, 1973).

An alternative approach which avoids most of the problems arising from the discrete nature of the SFCs is to be found in the theory of encoding variability (Bower, 1972b). Briefly, each word is considered as a collection of attributes or features held in memory. During inspection some subset of features corresponding to the stimulus are incremented, or in some other way distinguished from unencoded features. Failure to recognize target words is determined by the extent of encoding variations between inspection and test and consequent failure to retrieve stored information. Decay of incrementation also produces forgetting. False positives occur to the extent that distractors share features with targets. Semantic and associative relations suggest that HF words share more features with each other, and have larger sets of features, than do LF words. Thus HF lists should produce most false positives; they should also produce fewer hits than LF lists since the opportunities for encoding variability should increase with frequency. The extent of encoding variability may also be determined by the processing of other targets and distractors.

It is tempting to conclude that LF superiority in recognition is due to the more restricted set of encoding variations compared to HF words. The equality of forgetting rates found for HF and LF words is possibly due to equal decay rates of all feature incrementations. However, encoding variability seems to extend over intervals equal to those considered here (Madigan, 1969) and rates of forgetting may therefore be expected to depend on frequency. Despite this shortcoming the encoding variability theory has the advantage of being able to deal with the combined effects of frequency and meaningfulness, homography and abstractness. Also, accepting access processes in recognition helps explain some of the available data on recognition latencies.

Frequency and Other Word Characteristics

Both Gorman (1961) and Olver (1965) obtained superior recognition for LF compared to HF words and for concretes compared to abstracts, the effects being additive. While concretes should benefit from imageability, their more specific meanings, and consequent lack of encoding variability, should also give them advantage over abstracts. By similar argument, high meaningfulness should be associated with poor recognition, but Paivio (1971a) reports that Olver (1965) found no effect of m using a limited range of items. Interestingly, Allen and Garton (1968) found that physics students were much better than arts students in recognizing physics words, but only slightly better at recognizing common words, even though physics students should find physics words more meaningful than would arts students. Thus familiarity or word knowledge facilitates recognition, presumably because for arts students physics words are semantically indistinct and share their few encoding features. These findings suggest that at low levels of word frequency recognition improves with word knowledge whereas with high frequency the reverse holds. The finding by Allen and Garton that physics students did slightly better at recognizing common words than did arts supports a curvilinear relationy between familiarity (word knowledge) and recognition.

The stimulus encoding model is also able to deal with Winograd and Conn's (1971) findings that polysemous nouns presented without context are usually encoded in terms of their most frequent meaning. We have already encountered this aspect of frequency of usage in paired-associate learning (Saltz, 1967) and word discrimination (Rubenstein *et al.*, 1970).

Recognition Latencies

The trace-strength model of recognition latencies (Norman and Wickelgren, 1969) predicts that the larger values of d' obtained with LF words relative to HF should be reflected in shorter recognition latencies. This prediction has been confirmed by Atkinson and Juola (1973).

The attributing of differences in latency to differences in trace strength assumes that access to the stored information is direct. On the basis of evidence discussed earlier it appears that representations in memory of HF words are accessed more rapidly than those of LF items; it is possible, therefore, that some component of the differences in recognition latencies could be due to differences in access time. When short lists are used trace strengths may be sufficiently similar to reveal differences in access, i.e. latencies for HF probes should be shorter than for LF; the results of three experiments confirm these expectations (Gregg, 1970, experiments 6,7,8). Typically, subjects received homogeneous sequences of 13 HF or LF monosyllabic words with auditory presentation at a two-second rate. Two seconds after the final word a probe was presented requiring an old–new decision; manual response latencies were recorded. Some representative results are given in Table 3. The entries represent mean latencies for target probes, where targets occupied serial positions 4,8,11 and 13, and for distractors, which constituted 50 per cent of the probes.

Apart from the short HF latencies, several interesting points emerge from all three experiments. The shapes of the serial position curves and the relation of latencies for distractor and target probes rule out serial exhaustive and serial self-terminating scans and support the trace-strength explanation of Baddeley and Ecob (1970). The shorter latencies of HF probes in relation

Table 3. Mean latencies (msec) for correct responses (Gregg, 1970, expt. 6)

	Serial position				
	4	9	11	13	Distractors
HF	763	760	634	571	765
LF	884	882	740	626	879

to LF, however, could be due to distinctive effects arising from auditory presentation. The findings, already discussed, in relation to phonemic distinctiveness and one-letter-substitution neighbourhoods do not readily support such an explanation. Alternatively, the effect could be dependent on the use of a single probe rather than many probes in each list, a view which implicates test-item interference as the cause of the usual LF superiority. These various explanations are currently under investigation at Birkbeck College.

Conclusions

The starting point of this discussion was the effects of word frequency in recall and recognition, and the extent to which they support the retrieve–recognize model of recall. Of principal interest was the frequency paradox, which several writers have taken as evidence for the retrieve–recognize model of recall, but which we have seen to be an inadequate representation of the data; recall is not always positively related to frequency and although the LF word superiority in recognition is very consistent there are exceptions. Denial of the paradox on these grounds does not necessarily demand rejection of the retrieve–recognize model provided it can be shown that changes in the relation between frequency and recognition performance are matched by similar changes in the editing process of recall, with other changes in frequency effects in recall being attributable to the retrieval process.

The retrieve–recognize model is difficult to test largely because of problems in separating the retrieval and editing phases of recall; we have seen that attempts to assess the editing phase by confidence ratings and direct comparisons of decision parameters in recall and recognition run into problems of interpretation. In turn, this situation makes it difficult to test the suggestion that retrieval attributes of memory are more readily established for HF words while discriminative attributes are more readily established for LF words.

The findings that recall is not invariably positively related to frequency reduce the applicability of the notion, derived from several other situations, that HF words have priority of access and hence are emitted more readily than LF under conditions of uncertainty. Instead, the free-recall data can best be explained in terms of organizational and associative encoding; compared to LF words, HF words offer more encoding options and this gives them a greater likelihood of being readily encoded within the list context, i.e. of being incorporated within an effective retrieval scheme. However, the more specific relations of LF words can often be advantageous. The advantages and disadvantages of a narrow rather than a wider range of possible encodings are seen, for example, in the effects on free recall of manipulating associative relationships within specific item clusters, and in the consequences of variations in stimulus and response frequencies in paired-associate recall.

These explanations of recall emphasize response retrieval but pay little attention to editing. However, we have seen that the confidence ratings given to items recalled from successive, non-overlapping lists appear to reflect the same contextual information used in retrieval. This suggests that decisions on current list membership may utilize some of the information used to retrieve items. Similar suggestions have been made by Mandler, Pearlstone and Koopmans (1969). Such considerations lead to the conclusion that decisions on list membership in recall are not identical with those in recognition, if only because different information is available to the decision-maker depending on the form of encoding entered into at presentation.

The multi-component word model maintains that words are collections of components (Bower, 1972b) or attributes (Wickens, 1970) each of which is capable of being encoded. Although the mechanism of such encoding is obscure, it must enable encoded attributes to be distinguished from unencoded ones. This model accommodates the hypothesized encoding opportunities offered by HF and LF words and in so doing accounts for much of the recall and recognition data; it acknowledges access/retrieval processes in both tasks and can account for differences in retrieval demands by assuming that the name is one attribute of a word (Brown and McNeill, 1966) and constitutes the basis for interrogation of the memory system in recognition. The purpose of this interrogation is to retrieve information concerning whether or not word attributes to which the name refers had been encoded in terms of the list context. In recall it is the name itself which must be retrieved. Presumably the latter is achieved by converging operations among encoded attributes, taking the list context as a starting point.

The multi-component model also provides a basis for dealing with the combined effects of frequency and related word characteristics. In order to do so, however, it has to be acknowledge that word frequency may not be the crucial variable; rather, the manner in which gross word frequency is distributed across the various word meanings or attributes appears to be more appropriate. Also, word frequency and its distribution across experiential contexts is critical in determining the number of attributes possessed by a word, its relations with other words and the likelihood that a particular context leads to any one of the set of possible encodings being utilized.

The retrieve–recognize model is too simple in that it fails to acknowledge that decisions made at retrieval depend on the encoding performed at input. Also, it fails to accept that procedural differences, such as the inclusion of experimenter-selected distractors in recognition, may lead to interactions between type of test and frequency. It is submitted that the multi-component word model in conjunction with the encoding variability notion accommodates the complexity of recall and recognition processes and acknowledges the various ways in which word frequency has its effects. However, much still remains to be done in determining the appropriate way of estimating frequency, of assessing the editing component of recall and in bringing recall and recognition together in comprehensive studies, thus avoiding the necessity of arguing across experiments.

Summary

This chapter is concerned with the effects of word frequency on recognition and recall and their implications for models of these memory processes. Two points are of particular interest: first, the extent to which it is possible to maintain the widely accepted frequency paradox, i.e. recall is better for common than for uncommon words, while in recognition the opposite is true; second, the support given to the retrieve–recognize model of recall by frequency effects. The pursuit of these issues forces consideration of the methods of assessing frequency, isolation of frequency effects from those of related word characteristics and the problems of comparing effects in recognition and recall across experiments. In addition, testing the retrieve–recognize model proves difficult due to problems in separating retrieval and editing processes. As a result of these considerations it is proposed that a multi-component word model incorporating the encoding variability notion best accounts for the data.

Dedication

This chapter is dedicated to the memory of Brenda Hallam.

8 Recognition and recall in amnesia

ELIZABETH WARRINGTON

Introduction

Neuropsychology offers a potentially powerful technique for examining both the organization of brain function and the properties of cognitive systems. In the field of memory the most obvious example has been the neuropsychological evidence for a double dissociation between long-term memory and short-term memory, the implications of which are far reaching for the organization of normal memory processes (Warrington and Weiskrantz, 1973). The analysis of the amnesic syndrome has for the most part focused on the sequential component stages of memory: deficits of registration and transfer of information, storage of information and retrieval of information have all been considered in the genesis of the amnesic syndrome, the assumption being that if one could specify in terms of information processing the point of breakdown, then the properties of that system could be investigated, and inferences would then generalize to normal memory function.

The subject of this volume is to discuss the distinction between recall and recognition, and it is clear from the preceding chapters that there is a wealth of data and theorizing on this problem. In studies of human memory disorders there are surprisingly few data pertaining to this issue. There is to my knowledge no study specifically addressed to this point, although some indirect evidence is relevant. This chapter will present a short summary of the data relating to recall and recognition and other methods of testing retention in amnesic patients, and the implications for the operation of normal memory mechanisms will be briefly discussed.

The amnesic syndrome is characterized by a severe impairment of memory and learning for on-going events in patients whose performance is normal on tasks demanding attention and reasoning. The deficit may range from almost total loss of memory and a complete inability to learn new material to a state in which the only noticeable difficulty is an unreliable memory and a slowness in learning new material. Ever since the amnesic state was first described by Korsakoff in 1887 as part of a polyneuritic syndrome, the pathogenesis of the syndrome has been known to be quite variable (Talland, 1965). The amnesic syndrome is now recognized to occur following encephalitic illnesses and after bi-medial temporal lobe lesions, as a sequel of severe head injuries and in association with alcoholism and deficiency states. Consequently the anatomical concomitants of the syndrome are complex and it seems likely that two separate but interconnected regions of the brain are involved: the mamillary bodies and thalamus in the diencephalon (Victor, Adams and Collins, 1971) and the hippocampus (Scoville and Milner, 1957). This lack of a firmly established unitary lesion has perhaps contributed to the slow transition from qualitative to quantitative investigations in this field; the selection of amnesic patients is perforce by the very symptom under consideration. At present, there are no independent criteria such as site of lesion for the selection of experimental groups. This imposes severe limitations and restrictions on the inferences which can be drawn from any single investigation; in particular, multiple lesions may cause associated symptomatology which may not be a necessary or an integral feature of the emnesic state. Until double dissociation of deficits is achieved, all conclusions must be provisional.

Recall and Recognition in Short-Term Memory Tasks

The immediate memory span, one measure of the capacity of the short-term memory system, has been consistently reported to be normal in amnesic patients. Drachman and Arbit (1966) using a recall measure found span for both digits and spatial position of pairs of light were normal in a small group of amnesic patients. Wickelgren (1968) found that one severely amnesic patient (H.M.) had normal short-term memory for digits and tones, using a recognition probe technique.

On short-term forgetting tasks the evidence to date is somewhat conflicting. Baddeley and Warrington (1970) compared the performance of six amnesic subjects and six control subjects on an adaptation of the Brown–Peterson short-term forgetting task, testing recall of word triplets, using intervals of up to 60 seconds. Here and in subsequent experiments reported with which the author was associated, the control subjects were patients with extra-cerebral neurological disease matched for age and intelligence with the amnesic group. They found no difference whatever at any interval (including 60 seconds) between the two groups. A comparable test of the short-term forgetting of the spatial position of a dot similarly showed no difference between the experimental and control groups (Warrington and Baddeley, 1974). Multi-choice (three-choice) recognition memory for surnames (chosen to be a verbal control for short-term memory for faces which was the subject of the investigation) was normal after a 30-second filled interval in this same population of amnesic patients (Warrington and Taylor, 1973). On the other hand, Cermak and his collaborators (Cermak, Butters Goodglass, 1971; Cermak and Butters, 1973) have reported consistent deficits on verbal short-term forgetting tasks, whether retention is tested by recall or by recognition. That performance on short-term forgetting tasks is not normal in all amnesic patients subjected to investigation cannot detract from the significance of the findings that short-term memory can be unimpaired in some severely amnesic patients and that impairment of short-term memory is not an intergral part of the amnesic syndrome.

However, it is undoubtedly the case that no qualitative differences between recall and recognition using short-term memory paradigms have been detected in amnesic patients. Indeed, this is also the case in patients with selective impairment of short-term memory; with both recall and recognition measures much the same degree of deficit is obtained (Shallice and Warrington, 1970). Perhaps these data may be taken as further evidence for there being a valid distinction between short-and long-term memory systems.

Recall and Recognition in Retrograde Amnesia

Retrograde amnesia, the forgetting of events prior to the onset of illness, is a constant feature of the amnesic syndrome, though estimates of its extent are very varied. Clearly, there are difficulties involved in assessing the duration and other properties of retrograde amnesia, and up to recently much of the evidence comes from anecdote and unsystematic observation. Public events and personalities provide a common source of experience for most people and can thus be used as a source of items to test remote memories. In an exploratory investigation Warrington and Silberstein (1970), using a 40-item questionnaire relating to events of the previous year, tested retention by recall and multi-choice recognition on three occasions at intervals of six months in independent groups of subjects. Recall memory tasks are held to differentiate between young and old subjects better than recognition memory (e.g. Schonfield and Robertson, 1966), and this general conclusion was supported; the oldest subjects scored nearly as well as the younger subjects on the recognition (there was not a ceiling effect) but not on the recall version of the task.

Warrington and Sanders (1971) extended this method to include both a greater time span and also a visual memory version by using photographs of well-known people. Performance of normal old people and amnesic patients as compared with younger subjects and a control group matched by age, respectively, on a recall and recognition version of the verbal questionnaire test (40-year time span) and recall and recognition version of photographs of personalities (25-year time span). In contrast to the previous study, there was little indication of a differential effect between recall and recognition with age of subject on either the verbal or visual test. Whatever the origin of this different pattern of results, it cannot be attributed to memories for remote events having different properties from those of on-going events, since almost without exception performance on the contemporary events was a good predictor of performance on items relating to more remote events. In the amnesic group a comparison of recall and recognition was less illuminating. On both the recall version of the questionnaire and the 'faces' test they were almost unable to score, their remote as well as recent memories being apparently non-existent. On the multi-choice version of the tests their scores were no better than chance, again at any time span sampled. Apart from demonstrating a profound retrograde memory defect in these amnesic patients, the likelihood of a 'floor' effect precludes drawing any inferences regarding the relationships of recall and recognition of remote memories in amnesic subjects. The same technique applied to less severe amnesics could well be worthwhile.

However, a dramatic improvement in performance was obtained in the amnesic patients by adopting a different method of retrieval; namely, prompting recall with the initial letters of a proper name (Sanders and Warrington, in preparation). For each item of the faces test a prompt of the first two or three letters (whichever was appropriate to prevent generating the correct answer without direct experience while remaining an effective cue, e.g. ST for Stalin, WIL for Wilson) was given. The three amnesic patients tested with this method obtained scores as good as normal subjects tested by recall (see Figure 1). A normal decay function was obtained, there being no evidence of any relative sparing of remote memory. Only incomplete data are available for normal subjects comparing prompted recall with the standard recall and recognition scores on the test. Nevertheless, pilot studies indicated that prompted recall in normal subjects was only marginally superior to recall scores for each time period sampled, a similar decay function being obtained, but was still inferior to the recognition measure. Thus it is highly likely that there is a differential effect of method of testing retention in the normal subjects and the amnesic patients.

Recall and Recognition in Anterograde Amnesia

Impaired retention of on-going events is the central component of the

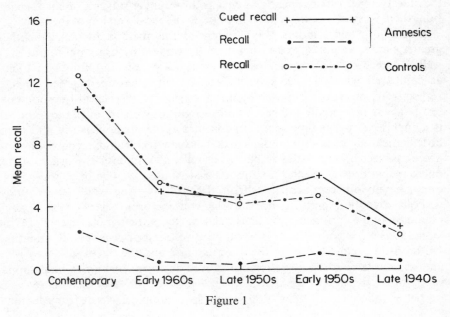

Figure 1

amnesic syndrome. A multitude of studies have consistently recorded severe deficits of retention tested by recall and recognition, and only a few can be cited here. Drachman and Arbit (1966) demonstrated a severe rote-learning deficit for both verbal and visual stimulus items. Talland (1965) has collated an extensive body of empirical data in his monograph *Deranged Memory*, which includes evidence that rote learning, paired-associate learning, recall and recognition of verbal material are all impaired in amnesic patients. Milner, Corkin and Teuber (1968) have reported detailed investigations of a single patient (H.M.) and emphasized the global nature of the memory deficit, only new motor learning being spared. These early quantitative studies tend to stress the global nature of the deficit both as regards the modality of stimulus and the method of testing. Perhaps the sheer density and apparent pervasiveness of the deficit led to the general acceptance of the failure of consolidation as an explanation of anterograde amnesia (Whitty and Zangwill, 1966).

The first hint of a qualitative difference in amnesic memory emerged from an investigation of forgetting rates in amnesic patients (Warrington and Weiskrantz, 1968). The normal relationship between recall and recognition was not found, there being a somewhat greater deficit on the recognition task than on the recall task. Subjects were tested on a yes / no recognition and on free-recall test using one, five and 10 learning trials after intervals of five and 15 minutes. Under all conditions there was a greater divergence between the amnesic patients and the normal subjects on the recognition test than on the recall test. The design of this experiment did not permit a direct quantitative comparison of retention tested by recall and recognition, but what was clearly established was that the amnesic patients had a very severe deficit on both recall and recognition tasks; even after 10 learning trials the amnesic patients showed less retention than the control subjects after one learning trial.

Strikingly different results were obtained with the same group of patients tested by cued recall. Learning using a technique of cueing with fragmented words or cueing with the first three letters of a five letter word was relatively efficient, and although they required more trials to learn compared with the control subjects, it proved possible to teach the amnesic patients to the same criterion. Moreover, there were significant 'savings' in the amnesic group when retested after relatively long intervals (Weiskrantz and Warrington, 1970a,b). It therefore became possible to compare directly retention tested by different methods of retrieval after a constant learning procedure.

Different methods of retrieval were used to test retention of word lists. Free recall, yes/no recognition, cueing recall with the initial letters of the word or cueing recall with a fragmented form of the words were compared for an eight-word list after a filled interval of one minute (Warrington and Weiskrantz, 1970). The results of this experiment are shown in Table 1, and they provide the only firm evidence that the normal relationship between recall and recognition does not hold in amnesic patients. Though both recall and recognition were impaired in the amnesic group compared with the control subjects, retention tested by recognition was significantly better than recall in the control

Table 1. Mean per cent correct (Warrington and Weiskrantz, 1970. Reproduced by permission of *Nature*, Macmillan (Journals) Ltd.)

	Controls $N=8$	Amnesics $N=4$
Recall	54.2	33.0
Recognition	77.9	43.7
Fragmented words	46.2	47.9
Initial letters	66.7	60.4

group but not in the amnesic group. Furthermore cued recall, either by the first three letters or by fragmented words, was not impaired in the amnesic group, the small differences in performance between the experimental group and control group on cued recall with initial letters not approaching significance. In no condition were the findings confounded by 'floor' or 'ceiling' effects.

First, this finding establishes that the efficacy of the cued-recall technique is not a trivial consequence of task difficulty, and second, a differential effect of method of testing retention obtains in the amnesic patients (i.e. the subject groups × method of testing interaction term was significant at the 5 per cent level). A partial replication of this experiment has been reported using a longer word list (16 words) and a longer retention interval (10 minutes) (Warrington and Weiskrantz, 1974). Yes/no retention of eight of the words was tested by cued recall (the first three letters) and eight of the words by yes/no recognition. Again, the amnesic group were unimpaired on the cued-recall task and very impaired on the yes/no recognition task. There is thus clearly a differential effect of the method of testing retention in amnesic patients.

Theoretical Considerations

Normal retention in amnesic patients when tested by cued recall is a robust phenomenon which must be taken into account in any interpretation of the amnesic syndrome. One special property of retrieval by cued recall is that a subject can eliminate incorrect responses. The number of stimulus items which would match the fragmented words must be very limited if not unique, and in the case of the first three letters the number of alternatives is limited and can be counted. Indeed, it has not only been shown that the number of response alternatives was an important variable in a cued-recall task but also that the performance of the amnesic patients was more influenced by the number of response alternatives than the control group (Warrington and Weiskrantz, 1974). In the extreme case where a word is uniquely specified by the first three letters (JUI——, ORP——, OIN——, etc.), cued recall 24 hours after 'learning' was somewhat superior in the amnesic patients to that in the matched control group (Warrington and Weiskrantz, in preparation). It might be objected that a two-choice recognition test on which amnesic patients perform very badly (Warrington, 1974) should be equally effective in reducing response alternatives. But this assumes that for memory the processes achieving recall and recognition are similar; that is, one must assume that to recall one of two possible stimulus items involves the same operations on the memory systems as to recognize one of two stimulus items. There is ample evidence provided in this volume to the contrary, and this point will be considered in more detail below.

It is generally agreed that a consolidation theory of the amnesic syndrome has difficulty in incorporating recent findings (Baddeley, 1975). Though the author at present favours an explanation of the amnesic syndrome in terms of interference phenomena, without at this stage any firm commitment as to mode of operation, two alternative hypotheses have been advanced, which apart from their intrinsic merit have the advantage of being able to account for the cued-recall phenomenon. These are inadequate encoding of stored information, and impairment of the recognition memory. Each of the three major hypotheses will be considered briefly.

Interference Hypothesis

Warrington and Weiskrantz (1970; 1974) have consistently interpreted the cued-recall phenomenon in terms of interference effects. They have suggested that information in storage is not inhibited or not dissipated normally so that competing or *irrelevant* material is interfering. It is outside the scope of this chapter to consider in any detail the different formulations of the role of interference in normal memory. Nevertheless, interference phenomena are a powerful source of forgetting in the normal subject whatever the mechanisms of operation; it is thus plausible that damage to the systems controlling such mechanisms could have the devastating effect on memory seen in the amnesic patient. The interference hypothesis has been put to a more direct test by manipulating cued-recall techniques to enhance rather than reduce interference from prior learning experiences (Warrington and Weiskrantz, 1974). Interference paradigms were adapted so that the cues for recall were common to more than one set of items to be recalled; two experiments provided some support for the notion of increased interference effects in amnesic subjects. In one experiment the word lists comprised items from the same taxonomic categories with relatively few exemplars (e.g. *yellow flower*—daffodil, primrose; *shellfish*— crab, prawn, etc.) and retention was tested by cueing recall with the category information. Testing of list 1 words was immediately followed by testing on list 2 words, each of which had a category cue in common with list 1. There was no significant difference between amnesics and controls on the first-list retention, but the amnesics were impaired on the second interfering list. The finding was not sufficiently clear-cut to produce a significant interaction term on the analysis of variance.

Perhaps more illuminating was the experiment designed to be analogous

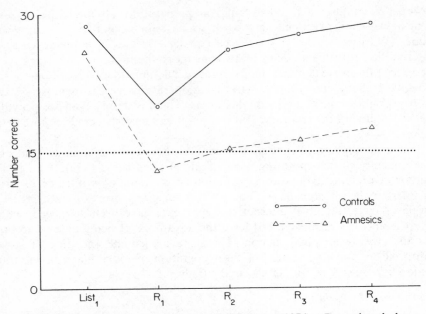

Figure 2. From Warrington and Weiskrantz (1974). Reproduced by permission of Pergamon Press Ltd.

to reversal-learning experiments in animals; the test stimuli were words having the property that only two words in a dictionary of basic English begin with the same first three letters (e.g. puddle—pudding, soft—sofa, etc.). Thus for the cue of the first three letters there were only two possible response alternatives. After testing retention for first-list learning (one trial) subjects were given four trials on the second list, which comprised the only alternative word beginning with the same initial three letters. Again, there was no significant deficit in the amnesic patients in the retention of the list 1 words. Although the percentage decrement between the amnesic group and the control group did not reach significance on the first reversal trial, there was a significant difference on the second and subsequent reversal-learning trials (the interaction term was highly significant) (Figure 2). These results are clearly consistent with the interference hypothesis and show that under certain conditions prior learning has enhanced effects in amnesic patients, resulting in this case in the persistence of wrong responses. Presumably the high incidence of prior-list intrusions by amnesic patients derives from the same mechanism (Warrington and Weiskrantz, 1968; Baddeley and Warrington, 1970; 1973).

The reversal-learning experiment has been replicated using longer word lists and allotting the lower-frequency word of each pair to the first list (e.g. peony—people); an almost identical result was obtained (Warrington and and Weiskrantz, in preparation). At the end of this experiment the subjects were required as an additional task to generate two words given the cue of the first three letters. There is a striking qualitative difference between the amnesic

Table 2. Mean number of words generated

	Controls $N = 8$	Amnesics $N = 4$
List 1	30.8	37.5
List 2	40.2	33.0

patients and the controls; the words from the first list, despite their lower frequency, were generated more often than the words from the second list by the amnesic patients, and conversely the controls generated more words from the second list than the first list (Table 2). This task, which to some extent avoids the effects of list differentiation (whether by time or by context cues), provides a relatively good measure of availability (or strength) of the first and second list responses, respectively. It appears that there may be a pre-empting effect by the first list which prevents subsequent relearning. Insofar as there is an inverse relationship between list 1 and list 2 in the two-subject groups, response strength may have a critical role in this task. These preliminary findings are described in some detail as further exploration of this type of paradigm might clarify the origin of these interference effects in amnesic patients.

It is necessary to consider whether the probable breakdown of the normal relationship between recall and recognition presents a problem for the interference hypothesis. There is accumulating evidence that recognition is at least in part itself mediated by associative retrieval mechanisms (Anderson and Bower, 1972) or subjected to a retrieval check (Mandler, Pearlstone and Koopmans, 1969). The author would, in fact, argue that such mechanisms are even more critical for recognition than for recall. In an investigation of the effects of orienting tasks on forced-choice recognition memory for words, faces and pictures, it was found that a semantically relevant orienting task (judging each stimulus item as pleasant or unpleasant) improves performance compared with the control condition of no orienting task (Warrington and Ackroyd, 1975), whereas earlier studies have shown this not to be the case for recall, no differences in performance being obtained with and without semantic orienting tasks (Hyde and Jenkins, 1969; 1973). It was argued that the semantic orienting task could provide a relatively easily retrieved associate for the subsequent recognition task (analogous to that provided by a cue in a free-recall task) and that the probability of an item being correctly recognized increases if an association to that item is achieved. Thus for the amnesic both yes/no and forced-choice recognition memory, if mediated by associative retrieval mechanisms, would be impaired. Irrelevant associations could be a source of interference in the absence of a cue or other means of constraint.

Encoding and Associative Learning Hypothesis

These hypotheses have much in common insofar as both stress the importance of classification and organization of new memories. Whereas the associative learning hypothesis, of which there are a number of variants (e.g. a failure of context cues, a failure of spatial mapping, a failure of time-tagging), has been advanced to explain memory deficits in the animal, only the encoding hypothesis has received serious consideration for the amnesic patient. There is very little positive evidence to indicate that impaired encoding mechanisms are the basis of the amnesic deficit. Cermak, Butters and Gerrein (1973) used Wickens' technique of release from proactive interference and found that amnesic Korsakoff patients were less sensitive to taxonomic shifts than their control group. The significance of this finding is perhaps blunted by the finding that this same group of amnesic patients demonstrated a normal or even enhanced release effect with an alphanumeric shift. Moreover, with both classes of material the build-up of proactive interference was somewhat greater in the amnesic patients, which is hardly to be predicted on the encoding hypothesis (Cermak and Butters, 1972). On the other hand, it has been shown that amnesic patients respond normally to semantic and acoustic clustering (Baddeley and Warrington, 1973) and to semantic organization (Warrington and Weiskrantz, 1971). Using a paired-associate learning paradigm, it has been shown that amnesic patients were normally sensitive to a shift from a phonetic to a semantic rule (Winocur and Weiskrantz, 1975, in preparation). Furthermore, as was indicated before, a taxonomic cue, provided it is effective in reducing response alternatives, is as effective as an acoustic cue for the amnesic patient. Of more interest is the one finding which suggests that semantic variables operate in cued recall as effectively as in recall. Retention tested by cued recall with the first three letters of concrete words was significantly better than for abstract words in amnesic and control subjects alike (Warrington and Weiskrantz, 1974).

However, a further complication has been raised by Baddeley (1975), who, following Paivio (1971b) and Bower (1972a), suggests that there are two components of semantic memory, one linguistic and the other based on imagery, and that it is the imagery component which is impaired in amnesic patients. Instructing subjects to use a mnemonic involving visual imagery was a powerful aid to retention in normal subjects but had no effect in the amnesic patients (Baddeley and Warrington, 1973). If one assumes that the imagery condition is mediated by associative recall mechanisms, then this result could be accommodated by the interfering hypothesis (as will be argued below in the case of recognition memory). More important evidence comes from two tasks in which it is also reasonable to suppose that there is an imagery component, the McGill anomalies test (Warrington and Weiskrantz, 1973) and jigsaw learning (Baddeley, 1975). Preliminary results from both these tests suggest that amnesics can learn and retain this class of information. It may not be unimportant that both these tasks impose constraints on performance, perhaps in a manner analogous to the cue in verbal-learning paradigms. It is in any case reasonable to assume that interference effects would be minimal in these two tasks both of which involve learning responses to 'new' pictorial material.

Recognition Memory Hypothesis

This hypothesis, put forward by Gaffan (discussed fully in Chapter 9), has the advantage of accounting very well for the evidence in human amnesic patients that the deficit in recognition memory may be greater than in recall, and it also offers a very plausible explanation of the cued-recall effects. Briefly, Gaffan has suggested that amnesic patients are impaired in discriminating degrees of familiarity of a stimulus item, associative memory being intact (Gaffan, 1974). Thus, the amnesics could generate responses adequately but, lacking a recognition memory, have no means of checking whether the gene-rated item is correct, i.e. they are unable to test the item for familiarity. Thus in cued recall the cue provides, to use Gaffan's terminology, 'replacement therapy' (Gaffan, 1972).

This formulation is based on the premise that recognition depends on familiarity discrimination and is a subprocess of recall. There is, however, evidence to suggest that recognition is itself mediated by associative retrieval mechanisms (Anderson and Bower, 1972; Warrington and Ackroyd, 1975). Furthermore, there is little evidence that the role of recognition in recall is of such overriding importance as is suggested by this theory. For example, in formal learning experiments in normal subjects the incidence of prior-list intrusions is low even when conditions would seem to be optimal (Craik, 1968). The converse would be expected if in recall one was selecting by familiarity from a number of generated responses.

Leaving theoretical speculation aside, there are several findings which are awkward for Gaffan's recognition hypothesis. Even when an amnesic is encouraged to respond, and not penalized for wrong responses, the number of correct responses is still very low. Indeed, unless one uses techniques which constrain interference effects it is very difficult to avoid a 'floor' effect on recall tasks. The prepotent effects of prior learning are difficult for the recogni-tion theory, but perhaps the only critical finding is the amnesics' performance on the generating task following the reversal-learning experiment discussed above. According to the recognition theory, the amnesic patient would generate both responses on the reversal trials but be unable to discriminate between them. If this were so one would predict that the amnesic would show either the normal pattern of response on the generating task or generate equally from the two lists, and this was clearly not the case.

Conclusions

The cued-recall phenomena and the breakdown of the normal relationship between recall and recognition are the two major qualitative differences between normal and amnesic memory. The significance of these findings for the interpretation of the amnesic syndrome were considered above. What then are the implications for the operation of normal memory? The data are so scanty that one can hint or speculate at best. The distinction between the operation of normal recall and normal recognition is upheld. That recall is more dependent on differential strength of items in memory and recognition more dependent on associative retrieval mechanisms than has been hitherto supposed is to some extent suggested by the amnesic data. Recall can be achieved by amnesic patients given that certain constraints are imposed, and in some conditions the response strength may possibly be abnormally high. On the other hand, on recognition tasks in which associative retrieval mechanisms are known to play a significant role amnesics are especially impaired. If one accepts the present interpretation of the amnesic syndrome in terms of interference by competing or irrelevant information, then the argument in its most extreme form would be as follows: associative retrieval mechanisms are not merely one of a number of important factors in recognition, but without such mechanisms operating recognition could not be achieved. For the future a detailed comparison of recall and cued recall might be as rewarding for understanding memory processes as the comparison of recall and recognition. The power of the cued-recall technique for amnesic patients suggests that, if used together with proactive and retroactive interference paradigms, the analysis of the components of interference in normal memory might be furthered.

9 *Recognition memory in animals*

DAVID GAFFAN

Introduction

The other chapters of this book amply exemplify the detailed theoretical and experimental treatment which the distinction between recognition and recall has received in experiments with normal human subjects. In relation to the psychological effects of brain damage, however, and in experiments with animals, it has been widely neglected. The first section of this chapter argues that animals, too, have a recognition memory. Rats and monkeys are able to distinguish familiar from unfamiliar stimuli, and the memory they display in their familiarity discrimination cannot be ascribed merely to habituation or to processes of reinforcement. The second section argues that lesions of the hippocampal system impair recognition memory but leave purely associative memory intact. There may be no such thing as a pure recognition memory test, in the sense of a task which can only be performed by familiarity discrimination and in which associative processes play no part. However, some tasks are recognition memory tests in the sense that discrimination of the familiarity of the presented test items is an aid to performance, while on the other hand there are some purely associative tasks in which familiarity discrimination, whether of the presented test items or of the items with which they are associated in memory, is of no use, and the animal must instead discriminate the strength of associations between items. Animals with damage to the hippocampal system are severely impaired in the first kind of task but perform normally in the second, even when the two types are tested at equal level of difficulty. On the basis of this dissociation and from consideration of certain aspects of hippocampal electrophysiology, the last section of the chapter attempts to explain how the hippocampus might function as a familiarity discriminator and how familiarity discrimination might interact with. purely associative memory in normal recall.

Normal Animals

The reinforcement hypotheses that dominated classical theories of animal learning do not readily accommodate the idea of recognition memory. However, many of those theories include as a subsidiary postulate *habituation*, a 'marginal case' of learning (Hilgard and Bower, 1966, p. 5) defined as reduced responsiveness to a repeated stimulus (Hilgard and Bower, 1966, p. 4). Where animals exhibit what looks like recognition memory, the phenomena can often be explained as nothing more than an instance of habituation. For instance, if a rat is allowed to explore just one of the arms of a T-maze, and then later is given a choice between the two arms, it tends under certain conditions to explore preferentially the relatively unfamiliar arm. Are we to say that the rat has a recognition memory, that is, the ability to distinguish familiar from unfamiliar inputs, or simply that the exploratory response to the first arm has habituated?

Some further findings demonstrate that the concept of habituation is inadequate to explain that kind of behaviour. Following Dember (1956), Gaffan (1972) observed that if rats were first allowed to inspect both arms of a T-maze, and then on a second trial two minutes later the colour of one of the arms was changed, the animals chose to enter the changed, unfamiliar arm; however, he also found that if the animals were frightened by loud white noise at the second trial, they chose to enter the unchanged, familiar arm. The behaviour in the white noise condition cannot be explained by a decrement of response to repeatedly presented stimuli, that is, by habituation. Given the results in both conditions, the most economical supposition is that the rat has some means of discriminating familiarity, independent of reinforcement, which can be used according to the motivation of the moment in responding either to the unfamiliar arm or to the familiar arm.

Another task which at first seems susceptible to analysis in the terms of classical learning theory, whether habituation or reinforcement, but which turns out to demand a hypothesis of recognition memory, is delayed matching to sample. Formally, tasks of this type are similar to recognition tests in human subjects. In Table 1, (a) shows the paradigm of a task given to monkeys by Gaffan (1974). The different lower-case letters represent different stimulus objects which were successively presented to the monkey on top of a food-well, which might or might not have a piece of food in it. The piece of food is represented by an asterisk. In acquisition, five objects were presented one at a time together with food. The monkey displaced each of them as it was presented, and took the food. In the retention test, which followed after all five objects in acquisition had been presented once, 10 objects were presented one at a time, each paired with a constant alternative response, represented by the capital R in the table. Five of the 10 were familiar, being those that had appeared in acquisition. The other five were new. To get the food at the retention test, the monkey had to displace the stimulus object if it was familiar, eschewing the alternative response, and to make the alternative response, eschewing the stimulus object, if the object was unfamiliar. The alternative response was provided by a brass disc, which on all test trials covered a second food-well. The brass disc was not a discriminative stimulus, being the same on all test trials; the animal's choice between the two responses therefore had to be based on familiarity discrimination of a single discriminative stimulus object

Table 1. (a) Yes–no recognition

Acquisition	Retention
a*	a*—R
	f —R*
b*	b*—R
	c*—R
c*	g —R*
	h —R*
d*	k —R*
	d*—R
e*	e*—R
	m —R*

(b) Reward association

Acquisition	Retention
a	b*—R
b*	a —R*
c*	d —R*
d	c*—R
e	g*—R
f	k*—R
g*	e —R*
h	f —R*
k*	m*—R
m*	h —R*

at each trial. Thus the monkey's choice was formally similar to the judgment 'old' or 'new' in a yes–no recognition test. In order to find out how well the monkeys could perform the task, they were trained in it for four weeks with a different set of stimulus objects for each day's training. The sets were drawn at random from a population of 300 so-called 'junk objects', such as a toothbrush, a battery and a toy lorry.

Are we to account for the monkeys' memory performance in that task by saying that the response tendency to positive objects at retention has been strengthened by their reinforcement with food in acquisition? Or by saying that the monkeys are using recognition memory to discriminate the familiarity of the objects at the retention test? As happened in the case of Dember's task with rats, comparison with another task suggests that the account in terms of recognition memory is the more useful alternative. In the present case, the purpose was to draw the contrast mentioned in the Introduction, by changing from a task where familiarity discrimination was useful to a task where the discriminative stimuli were of equal familiarity and performance had to be based solely on discrimination of strengths of association between items—in this case, associations between stimulus objects and food reward. That purpose was achieved by changing only the acquisition trials. The retention

232

test was unchanged, so that performance on the two tasks should be strictly comparable. In Table 1, (b) shows the paradigm of the comparison task. (Some of the monkeys performed task (a) for four weeks then task (b) for five weeks; others performed task (b) for five weeks then task (a) for four weeks.) Comparing the two tasks from the point of view of the reinforcement explanation, it seems that in task (b) not only are the response tendencies to the positive objects strengthened in acquisition by reward, but in addition those to the negative objects are weakened by non-reward. From that point of view, the animal receives less training in the acquisition trials of the yes–no recognition task than in those of the reward-association task, of which they are only a part. If therefore the animals are in both tasks responding to the different objects at the retention test simply according to the strength of the approach tendency to each object as determined by its history of reinforcement or non-reinforcement, then they should perform better (or at least as well) at reward association than at yes–no recognition. From the point of view of the hypothesis of recognition memory, however, the animal can use his discrimination of the familiar objects from the new objects at the retention test to aid his performance in the

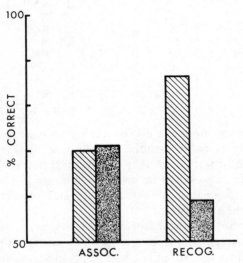

Figure 1. Average performance achieved after training by control monkeys (cross-hatched bars) and by monkeys with fornix transection (stippled bars) in the retention tests shown in Table 1 of two tasks described in the text, reward association (assoc.) and yes–no recognition (recog.).

From *Journal of Comparative and Physiological Psychology*, **86**, 1100–1109, 1974. Copyright 1974 by the American Psychological Association. Reprinted by permission.

yes–no recognition task, while in the reward-association task he must rely on his discrimination of the objects' association in memory with reward or non-reward, since all the objects are equally familiar to him. So if monkeys do have, like people, a recognition memory that is relatively powerful compared to other forms of memory, they might be expected to perform worse at the association task than at yes–no recognition, but the other way around if there is only reinforcement and non-reinforcement to consider. The results, shown in the cross-hatched bars of the histogram in Figure 1, support the former hypothesis. Normal monkeys performed significantly better at yes–no recognition than at reward association.

Effects of Brain Lesions

Figure 1 also shows, in the stippled bars, the performance of a separate group of monkeys, in which the fornix had been transected before training began. They performed very badly at yes–no recognition but were unimpaired at reward association. The two groups were also compared at forced-choice recognition, as follows. In acquisition, a list of objects was presented, one at a time, each with a piece of food under it to ensure that the animal responded

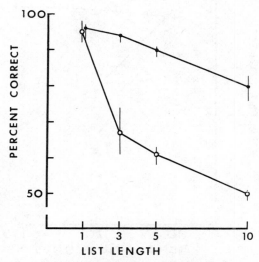

Figure 2. Average performance achieved by control monkeys (filled circles) and monkeys with fornix transection (open circles) in forced-choice recognition when the number of items in each acquisition list was varied, as described in the text.

From *Journal of Comparative and Physiological Psychology*, **86**, 1100–1109, 1974. Copyright 1974 by the American Psychological Association.

234

to it. At the retention test which followed after each object in the acquisition list had been presented once, two objects were presented together for the animal's choice. One of the two was a new object, which covered an empty food-well, and the other, which covered a food reward, was one of those that were familiar from acquisition. Thus the task was formally similar to forced-choice (as opposed to yes–no) recognition, in that not one but two discriminative stimuli were present at the test trial, of which one was a familiar object and the other a new distractor item at each test. As with the other two tasks, extensive training was given, with a new set of objects in each acquisition list, in order to find out how well the animals could perform the task. Figure 2 shows the results obtained when the number of objects given to the animal to remember in each acquisition trial was varied between sessions. Figure 3 shows the results obtained when the animals were given only one object to remember in each acquisition trial, but the delay between acquisition trial and retention test was varied randomly within sessions. These results strengthen the suggestion from task (a) and task (b) that the fornix-transected monkeys suffered from a specific impairment of recognition memory. For instance, it is possible to argue that some kind of attentional deficit could explain the

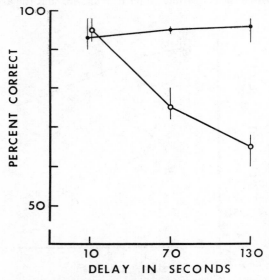

Figure 3. Average performance achieved by control monkeys (filled circles) and monkeys with fornix transection (open circles) in forced-choice recognition when the delay between acquisition and retention was varied, as described in the text.
From *Journal of Comparative and Physiological Psychology,* **86,** 1100–1109, 1974. Copyright 1974 by the American Psychological Association. Reprinted by permission.

results in Figure 1, if it was assumed that the fornix-transected monkeys were for some reason especially prone to lapses of attention when reward was certain, during acquisition in task (a), but had their attention sustained by the unpredictable reward during acquisition in task (b). (It should be noted that no such differences in attention were suggested by observation of the animals during training.) But reward was equally certain during acquisition in forced-choice recognition, where the objects were, as in task (a), always rewarded; and there the performance at 10-sec delay shows that the brain-damaged animals had indeed attended to the object at acquisition, though their memory at longer retention intervals was impaired.

Gaffan (1972) compared fornix-lesioned rats with normal (control-operated) rats in the two T-maze experiments that were described above. Both in the condition where the normal animals chose the unfamiliar arm and in that where they chose the familiar arm, fornix-lesioned animals chose at random. But in a further experiment reported in the same paper, fornix-lesioned rats learned as quickly as controls to go to a place in a runway where there was a food reward.

The results of the lesion experiments mentioned so far can be summarized quite simply. Whenever fornix-lesioned rats or monkeys performed a task where recognition memory was useful, they fared very badly. But in tasks where they had to learn associations between stimuli and rewards, and where discrimination of the familiarity of the stimuli was of no use, they were unimpaired.

This apparent simplicity must be judged, however, in the context of a long history of controversy over the function of the hippocampal system, of which the fornix is a part. In man, damage to the hippocampal system regularly produces the amnesic syndrome, that is, a severe memory impairment. Brion (1968) provides a general review of the anatomopathological evidence. For the fornix, two important papers are by Hassler and Riechert (1957) and by Brion, Pragier, Guérin and Teitgen (1969). On the nature of the clinical syndrome, which is further discussed below, see the review by Warrington (1971).) But those who have studied experimentally the effects of similar lesions in animals have concluded that they do not cause a memory impairment, for hippocampally damaged animals are not deficient in acquisition of many of the conventional instrumental-learning paradigms of animal pychology. (For a review and a statement of that conclusion, see Kimble, 1968.) As we have seen, those paradigms may not be an adequate model of memory in general, either human or animal. Hippocampal damage has been shown to cause behavioural changes, however, in some of these tasks. The biggest effects are in tasks like reversal and extinction, where the animal has to change or give up a learned response which is no longer rewarded. The brain-damaged animals take much longer to do so, and effects like these have led to the suggestion that the function of the hippocampus is the inhibition of prepotent responses (Douglas, 1967) or Pavlovian internal inhibition (Kimble, 1968). It is clear that these hypotheses do not immediately predict the pattern of results in the memory experiments described above, and an attempt to account for the deficits in familiarity discrimination in terms of an elaboration of Kimble's internal inhibition hypothesis has failed (Gaffan, 1973). However, there is a similar problem for the present hypothesis in accounting for the effects in extinction, reversal and other tasks which do not immediately appear to be tests of recognition memory. But it may be that the tendency to explore preferentially the relatively unfamiliar parts of an apparatus, as in the T-maze experiments discussed at the beginning of this chapter, is an important source of variability in the behaviour of normal animals in situations where they are required to give up a well-learned habit, and the fornix-lesioned animals' lack of that tendency might explain their greater persistence in such habits. For example, Gaffan (1972, experiments 3 and 4) showed that fornix-lesioned rats which had learned to run down a straight alley for food persisted very much longer than controls in doing so after the food was no longer provided, in an experiment where training was conducted in a large runway that offered to the control rats in extinction much opportunity for exploration of the relatively unfamiliar parts of the runway which they had sped past in performance before extinction began. But under similar conditions in a specially constructed small alley where there was little opportunity for exploration, extinction proceeded at the same rate in the fornix-lesioned and control rats. Thus the extinction deficit, when it does appear, is caused not so much by the normal animal's superior ability to inhibit the learned response as by his greater tendency to explore the relatively unfamiliar parts of an apparatus. In general, therefore, a defect of recognition memory should be expected to have profound and widespread effects on an animal's behaviour, especially in those situations where exploration is important; and for the rat, which has poor vision and is usually trained in an apparatus that is large relative to the size of the animal, that includes almost all experimental situations. There are indeed many reports of behavioural changes due to hippocampal lesions in rats which seem to be attributable to an inflexibility in the behaviour of the brain-damaged animals. The interested reader is referred to the review by Douglas (1967) of some of these reports, and to discussions of them from the present point of view in Gaffan (1972; 1973).

An Hypothesis

The evidence reviewed so far indicates that rats and monkeys discriminate familiarity in a way that cannot be explained by the principles of reinforcement or habituation; that a localized lesion of the hippocampal system impairs their recognition memory but leaves performance on a purely associative memory task intact; and that behavioural changes caused by hippocampal damage in some tasks which do not at first appear to be tests of recognition memory may be attributable to secondary effects of defective familiarity discrimination. To conclude that the function of the hippocampus is to facilitate recognition memory adds little, however, to our understanding of memory mechanisms. Rather, it is necessary to consider what hypothesis of the mechanism of recognition memory would be consistent both with its specific impairment by damage to the hippocampal system and also with what is known of the nervous activity of that system. Such a hypothesis is now proposed, and is then applied to the question of how familiarity discrimination and purely associative memory interact in recall by people.

Familiarity is nothing more than a universal association: the association of A with B is strengthened whenever A occurs with B, the association of A with C is strengthened whenever A occurs with C, and so on, but the familiarity of A is strengthened whenever A occurs, no matter with what. Thus any input item is linked to various other items in memory with various strengths of association; among these strengths, one is that of the universal association; and that dimension of memory, we suggest, is stored in the hippocampus.

There is some evidence of a possible physiological mechanism for such a store. In electrical recordings from the hippocampus of freely moving animals, a characteristic rhythmic slow activity (RSA) is observed all the time the animal is awake and attentive. It accompanies ambulation, sniffing, orienting head movements, and in general all active behaviour except certain automatic sequences, such as grooming (Vanderwolf, 1971). It occurs also when the animal is quite motionless but watching something (Kemp and Kaada, in press). Apart from these correlations between behaviour and RSA, there is also some evidence available of the effects on behaviour of manipulating RSA. Squire (1969) studied the effects of either physostigmine, which facilitates RSA, or scopolamine, which inhibits RSA, administered to rats either at the acquisition trial or at the retention test of a familiarity-discrimination task similar to those discussed at the beginning of this chapter. Administered at the retention test, neither drug had any effect on memory performance. That part of Squire's results rules out many of the less interesting interpretations of the other part, namely, that when administered at the acquisition trial, the drug that facilitates RSA improved retention above control levels, while the drug that inhibits RSA impaired retention. Thus it appears that input to recognition memory depends on RSA. That conclusion is consistent with the hypothesis that the hippocampus stores a record of the strength of association of each of its inputs with RSA, since those associations would be strengthened only during RSA. Moreover, a memory store of that kind would facilitate recognition memory, since the strength of association of an input with something that (like RSA) is happening all the time the animal is awake and attentive is nothing more than its familiarity. (This is the definition of familiarity, within the context of an associative memory, that was offered above.) The hypothesis which these physiological considerations suggest, then, is that while other parts of the brain discriminate all the various strengths of association of an input with various other items, the hippocampus discriminates the associative strength of the input with RSA. At any rate, it is an interesting possibility, that the remarkable power of recognition memory could derive simply from the devotion of a large amount of nervous tissue to storing associations with something that is happening all the time—in themselves theoretically no different from associations with food, other stimulus items, and so on.

It was noted above that in human patients damage to the hippocampal system produces the amnesic syndrome. Amnesics are impaired both in recognition and in recall, but the defect of recognition is greater than that of recall (Warrington and Weiskrantz, 1970). In recognition tests, they are impaired with all types of stimulus material (Warrington, 1974). In recall, their performance is as good as that of controls when a fragmented image of the item that has to be recalled is presented at the retention test (Warrington and Weiskrantz, 1970). It has been argued (Gaffan, 1972) that on the supposition that familiarity discrimination may be used as a subprocess in recall, these effects are consistent with the hypothesis that the basic impairment of amnesics is in familiarity discrimination. To assess this hypothesis, it is necessary to consider in more detail the interactions of familiarity discrimination and associative memory in recall and recognition tests.

Recognition tests may be defined as those in which the subject's memory performance is aided by discrimination of the familiarity of the presented test items. Thus, for example, in a yes–no recognition test with faces a list of faces is displayed in acquisition; in the retention test a face is presented and the subject is asked whether it is one of those that he has seen or a new one. Note that it is not claimed that discrimination of the presented test item's familiarity is the only memory mechanism which may aid the subject's performance in a recognition test. In the recognition tests with monkeys, the correct stimulus at the retention test was both more familiar than the wrong one (because it had just been presented) and also more strongly associated in memory with food (because food was one of the things that had been presented in conjunction with it). Thus the residual, though impaired, performance of the fornix transected monkeys in those tests may be attributable to the availability of an associative component in the tests, rather than to a residual though deficient ability to discriminate familiarity. The conclusion that the memory impairment of fornix-transected animals was specific to familiarity discrimination was based not on the premise that the memory tests in which they were impaired can only be performed by familiarity discrimination, but rather on the comparison of tests where the subject's familiarity discrimination is and is not an aid to performance.

Recall may be defined, conversely, as a test where familiarity discrimination of the presented test item does not aid memory performance, although familiarity discrimination of its associates in memory may or may not be of use. For example, the subject may be shown a list of faces and told the names of each person represented; in the retention test the item that is physically presented is a face which is avowed to be a member of the acquisition list, and the subject is asked what name went with it. Thus whether or not the presented item is familiar is not at issue. But if the test face evokes equally two names M and N, and yet the subject's familiarity discrimination tells, him, in the same way as it would in a recognition test of the names, that M was one of the names in the acquisition list and N was not, then the subject can reject N. Thus his familiarity discrimination of associates helps him to get the answer right. To put it more generally, the stimulus input at a retention test is linked to various items in memory with various degrees of strength, according to its correlation with them in the past. Among these, there is stored in the hippocampus the strength of the item's correlation with RSA, so that the hippocampal output carries the information not only that such and such an input has occurred, but also that it is familiar or unfamiliar, as the case may be.

The chains of association evoked in memory by a stimulus input include not only first-order associates of the input, but associates of associates, and so on in higher orders. A special case of this is that not only the stimulus input, but also the associates it evokes in memory, can pass through the level of association with RSA, that is, of having individually assigned to them values of familiarity. Thus in recall, the items that are evoked in memory pass through the stage of familiarity discrimination just as they would if they were presented in the retention test of a recognition task; and they can therefore be identified as stemming either from distant or from recent experience.

If, as we suggest, it is in the familiarity-discrimination stage of recall that amnesics are deficient, then in formal tests of recall, with relatively brief retention intervals, they should be expected to show many intrusion errors due to proactive interference from prior experience. Warrington (1971, pp. 245-6) has noted that this is the case; and furthermore, that when in a recall task the number of possible intrusion errors is severely limited by displaying at the retention test either a fragmented image of the item to be recalled or its initial letters, amnesics show no memory deficit compared with controls—even though that test is harder for the controls than a comparable recognition test, at which the amnesics are severely impaired (Warrington and Weiskrantz, 1970). She suggested that the abnormal susceptibility to intrusion errors which appears to be the cause of the recall deficit of amnesics might itself be due to a failure to inhibit or dissipate stored information. However, these effects are equally consistent with the present hypothesis, which suggests that at the retention test in recall the stimulus evokes as associates in memory those items that have occurred with it in the past, just as adequately in the amnesic's memory as in the normal subject's; but that the amnesic's memory cannot discriminate how recently each of the many items evoked was experienced. It follows that the amnesic's errors should consist of intrusions rather than failures of association.

Moreover, there is some evidence that in Warrington and Weiskrantz's task with recall cued by initial letters of a word, the crucial feature of the cue is that it renders familiarity discrimination otiose, for the amnesic defect reappears if familiarity discrimination is added to the task, although recall is still cued. In an experiment described by Warrington in Chapter 8, subjects were shown two lists of words in succession. For every word in the first list there was a word in the second that began with the same three letters; and no other English word than those two began with those letters. For example, one such pair is Enough–Enormous. At the retention test, the subjects were shown three letters (e.g. Eno—) and were asked for the word from list 2 that began with those letters. Amnesics performed badly, producing list 1 words instead of list 2 words. This result is to be expected, on the present hypothesis, because familiarity discrimination helps the normal subject to discriminate the more recently presented list 2 words from list 1 words. The contrast is between this first task and the second task that the subjects were given at the end of the experiment: to generate both of the words they had seen that began with the given three letters. Because the two that had been shown were the only English words that began with each group of three letters, there was no possibility of making an error by generating a word that fitted the three letters but was not one of the items that had been given to remember. Instead, errors could occur only by failure of generation. In that second task, there was no amnesic defect. Given the contrasting results in the first and second tasks, it appears that when the cue does cure amnesics, the aspect of it that is therapeutic is that it either obviates or severely curtails the possibility of making those errors which familiarity discrimination can help normal subjects to avoid; in other words, that it renders familiarity discrimination otiose.

When asked to generate both words, in the experiment just discussed, the normal subjects appeared to generate slightly more list 2 words and slightly fewer list 1 words than the amnesics did, although the total number generated by the two groups was the same. In Chapter 8, Warrington argues from this that the amnesics' failure in the first task to produce words specifically from list 2 cannot have been due to their lack of familiarity discrimination between list 2 and list 1 words, since even when given the opportunity to produce both words, they still produced fewer than the controls did from list 2. One weakness of this argument is that by the time the subjects were asked to produce both words, they had performed four retention tests in which they were asked to produce list 2 words. At those retention tests, the controls produced many more list 2 words than the amnesics, and the amnesics more list 1 words than the controls. If therefore the subjects' production of words during those retention tests added to the trace strength of the words produced, then by the item the subjects were asked to produce both words, the list 1 words would have been more available in the amnesics than in the controls, and the list 2 words vice versa, as observed.

In the recall test with monkeys described above, the reward-association task, not only was the familiarity of the stimulus objects irrelevant to discrimination, but also the familiarity of their associates, food and no food. The monkey had to discriminate simply which of the two relevant associates was more strongly evoked by each object at the retention test, for the relative familiarity of the two associated did not depend on whether or not they had accompanied any particular object, but on their recurrent appearances throughout the acquisition list. To test the hypothesis that the deficit of human amnesics in recall is due to their impairment in familiarity discrimination, it is clear that one critical experiment would be a human analogue of the monkey's reward-association task. However, apart from the difficulties of identifying patients with discrete damage to the hippocampal system, or of defining the 'pure' amnesic syndrome and finding instances of it, there are also difficulties in designing a human analogue of that task. These arise from the human subject's ability to elaborate verbal mediating associations between the items that the experimenter asks him to remember. Formally stated, the problem is that if the subject is required to remember that item A goes with item M, item B with item N, C with M, D with N, and so on, where M and N play the role of food and no food in the monkeys' task, then he elaborates a mediating association through A′ to carry him from A to M, a completely different mediator through C′ from C to M, and further unique mediators B′ and D′ each leading to N. Thus the task is changed by the subject into a recall task dependent on familiarity discrimination, because the recurring nominal associates are replaced by non-recurring associates. If at the retention test A evoked equally two associates, A′ leading to M and A″ leading to N, then the subject needs to remember which of them he went through in acquisition; but their familiarity is a reliable indication of that, since if he did not go through A″ in the case of A then he did not go through it at all, the mediators being each evoked by only one of the stimulus items. To state the problem informally, let us imagine a human subject performing the very same task as the monkeys performed. The first stimulus object is presented. Say it is a toothbrush. If it goes with food, the subject tells himself, as an aid to memory, that one cleans one's teeth after a meal. If it is one of the objects that has no food with it, the subject tells himself that toothpaste is inedible. At the retention test the more familiar of these two stories is the more likely to be recalled. The crucial point is that their relative familiarity depends only on which one the subject told himself in relation to the toothbrush, and it is therefore a reliable guide in answering the question whether the toothbrush was accompanied by food or by no food, because whichever of the two he did not tell himself in relation to the toothbrush, he is unlikely to have told himself that one in relation to the remaining objects in acquisition, say a battery, a toy lorry, and so on. Thus even if it is people whose basic memory mechanisms one is trying to elucidate, there are some advantages in using dumb animals as subjects; and some of the instrumental reward-learning paradigms in animals, which were citicized at the beginning of this chapter as being inadequate models of human memory in general, may be especially interesting precisely because they allow the study of a type of memory performance very rarely seen in people, that is, purely associative recall without a recognition component.

The difficulties of studying pure associative memory in people are similar to those of interpreting certain effects of hippocampal damage in animals, such as the extinction effects which were briefly discussed above. In both cases, familiarity discrimination intrudes into tasks which at first sight do not seem to require it. From the theoretical point of view, these considerations simply add to the difficulty of devising convincing tests of any general hypothesis of hippocampal function. But from the experimentalist's point of view, they

242

promise a wealth of future research that may sort out the fundamental impairment caused by a lesion from the secondary effects derived from it. And, most importantly, from the subject's point of view, they demonstrate how useful recognition memory is, in a wide variety of situations. If, as we have suggested, the brain has devoted the whole of one of its organs to familiarity discrimination, its extravagance seems to be justified.

References and Author Index

The pages in which each reference is cited are given in brackets

Abbot, E. E. (1909). On the analysis of the factor of recall in the learning process, *Psychological Monographs*, **11**, 159.   (134).

Abra, J. C. (1969). List-1 unlearning and recovery as a function of the point of interpolated learning, *Journal of Verbal Learning and Verbal Behaviour*, **8**, 494–500.   (158).

Ackroyd, C. See Warrington, E. K.

Adams, R. D. See Victor, M.

Allen, G. A., Mahler, W. A., and Estes, W. K. (1969). The effects of recall tests on the long-term retention of paired-associates, *Journal of Verbal Learning and Verbal Behavior*, **8**, 463–471.   (140).

Allen, L. R. See Garton, R. F.

Allen, L. R., and Garton, R. F. (1968). The influence of word-knowledge on the word frequency effect in recognition memory, *Psychonomic Science*, **10**, 401–402.   (206, 207, 212).

Anderson, J. R. (1971). FRAN. A simulation model of free recall. In G. H. Bower (Ed.), *The Psychology of Learning and Motivation*, Vol. 5, Academic Press, New York.   (4).

Anderson, J. R. See Reder, L. M.

Anderson, J. R., and Bower, G. H. (1972). Recognition and retrieval processes in free recall, *Psychological Review*, **79**, 3, 97–123.   (3, 5, 6, 41, 44, 45, 48, 50, 51, 56, 132, 177, 183, 201, 202, 225, 227).

Anderson, J. R., and Bower, G. H. (1973). *Human Associative Memory*, Winston, Washington DC.   (106, 112, 113, 211).

Anderson, J. R., and Bower, G. H. A propositional theory of recognition memory, *Memory and Cognition* (1974) **2**, no. 3, 406–412.   (44, 54, 60, 61, 71, 72, 73).

Anderson, R. C. See Watts, G. H.

Anderson, R. C., and Watts, G. H. (1971). Response competition in the forgetting of paired associates, *Journal of Verbal Learning and Verbal Behavior*, **10**, 29–34.   (164, 165, 168).

Anderson, R. E. See Murdock, B. B. Jr.

Anisfield, M., and Knapp, M. (1968). Association, synonymity and directionality in false recognition, *Journal of Experimental Psychology*, **77**, 171–179.   (210).

Antone, G. See Snodgrass, J. G.

Arbit, J. See Drachman, D. A.

Atkinson, R. C. See Juola, J. F.; Rundus, D.; Schnorr, J. A.; Shiffrin, R. M.

Atkinson, R. C., Herrmann, D. J., and Wescourt, K. T. (1974). Search processes in recognition memory. In R. L. Solso (Ed.), *Theories in Cognitive Psychology*, Winston, Washington, DC.   (70, 151).

Atkinson, R. C., and Juola, J. F. (1973). Factors influencing speed and accuracy of word recognition. In S. Kornblum (Ed.), *Attention and Performance IV*, Academic Press, New York, pp. 583–612.   (151, 153, 154, 155, 213).

Atkinson, R. C., and Juola, J. F. (1974). Search and decision processes in recognition memory. In D. H. Krantz, R. C. Atkinson and P. Suppes (Eds.), *Contemporary Developments in Mathematical Psychology*, W. H. Freeman, San Francisco.   (153, 154, 155).

Atkinson, R. C., and Shiffrin, R. M. (1968). Human memory: A proposed system and its control processes. In K. W. Spence and J. T. Spence (Eds.), *The Psychology of Learning and Motivation*, Vol. II, Academic Press, New York.   (173).

Atkinson, R. C., and Shiffrin, R. M. (1971). The control processes of short-term memory, *Scientific American*, **224**, 82–90.   (137).

Baddeley, A. D. (1975). Theories of ammesia. In R. A. Kennedy and A. L. Wilkes (Eds.), *Studies in Long-term Memory*, Wiley, London.   (223, 226).

Baddeley, A. D., and Ecob, J. R. (1970). Reaction time and short-term memory: a trace-strength alternative to the high-speed exhaustive-scanning hypothesis. University of California, San Diego, Center for Human Information Processing Report, No. 13, 1970.   (213).

Baddeley, A. D., and Scott, D. (1971). Word frequency and the unit sequence hypothesis in short-term memory, *Journal of Verbal Learning and Verbal Behavior*, **10**, 35–40.   (199).

Baddeley, A. D., and Warrington, E. K. (1970). Amnesia and the distinction between long and short-term memory, *Journal of Verbal Learning and Verbal Behavior*, **9**, 176–189.   (218, 224).

Baddeley, A. D., and Warrington, E. K. (1973). Memory coding and amnesia, *Neuropsychologia*, **11**, 159–165.   (224, 226).

Bahrick, H. P. (1969). Measurement of memory by prompted recall, *Journal of Experimental Psychology*, **79**, 213–219.   (44).

Bahrick, H. P. (1970). A two-phase model for prompted recall, *Psychological Review*, **77**, 215–222.   (41, 44, 48, 73).

Bahrick, H. P., and Bahrick, P. (1971). Independence of verbal and visual codes of the same stimuli, *Journal of Experimental Psychology*, **91**, 344–346.   (109).

Bahrick, H. P., and Boucher, B. (1968). Retention of visual and verbal codes of the same stimuli, *Journal of Experimental Psychology*, **78**, 417–422.   (48, 121).

Bahrick, P. See Bahrick, H. P.

Ballard, P. B. (1913). Oblivescence and reminiscence, *British Journal of Psychology Monographs*, **1**, No. 2.   (133, 134).

Banks, W. P. (1970). Signal detection theory and human memory, *Psychological Bulletin*, **74**, 81–99.   (24).

Barnes, J. M., and Underwood, B. J. (1959). 'Fate' of first-list associations in transfer theory, *Journal of Experimental Psychology*, **58**, 97–105.   (160, 170).

Bartlett, F. C. (1932). *Remembering: A Study in Experimental and Social Psychology*, Cambridge University Press, Cambridge, England.   (2, 136).

Bartlett, J. C., and Tulving, E. (1974). Effects of temporal and semantic encoding in immediate recall upon subsequent retrieval, *Journal of Verbal Learning and Verbal Behavior*, **13**, 297–309.   (95).

Bartz, W. H. See Jacoby, L. L.; Raser, G. A.

Barzeele, J. See Bertelson, P.

Bastian, J. See Dukes, W. F.

Begg, I. (1972). Recall of meaningful phrases, *Journal of Verbal Learning and Verbal Behavior*, **11**, 431–439.   (112, 129).

Begg, I. (1973). Imagery and integration in the recall of words, *Canadian Journal of Psychology*, **27**, 159–167.   (112).

Begg, I., and Robertson, R. (1973). Imagery and long term retention, *Journal of Verbal Learning and Verbal Behavior*, **12**, 689–700.   (112).

Beito, A. See Wallace, W. P.

Belbin, E. (1950). The effect of interpolated recall on recognition, *Quarterly Journal of Experimental Psychology*, **2**, 163–169.   (142).

Bell, B. See Groninger, L. D.

Bernbach, H. A. (1973). Processing strategies for recognition and recall, *Journal of Experimental Psychology*, **99**, 409–412.   (162).

Berry, C. (1971). Advanced frequency information and verbal response times, *Psychonomic Science*, **23**, 151–152.   (188).

Bertelson, P., and Barzeele, J. (1962). Interaction of time-uncertainty and relative signal frequency in determining choice reaction time, *Journal of Experimental Psychology*, **70**, 448–451.   (152).

Bertelson, P., and Tisseyre, F. (1966). Choice reaction time as a function of stimulus versus response relative frequency of occurrence, *Nature*, **212**, 1069–1070.   (152).

Bevan, W., and Steger, J. A. (1971). Free recall and abstractness of stimuli, *Science* **172**. 597–599.   (108).

Bever, T. G. See Savin, H. B.

Bindra, D. B., Williams, J. A., and Wise, J. S. (1965). Judgements of sameness and difference: Experiments on decision time, *Science*, **150**, 1625–1627.   (150).

Bieber, S. L. See Kroll, N. E. A.

Bird, C. P. See Weaver, G. E.

Birdsall, T. G. See Clarke, F. R.

Birnbaum, I. M. (1966). Unlearning in two directions, *Journal of Experimental Psychology*, **72**, 61–67.   (167).

Birnbaum, I. M. (1972). General and specific components of retroactive inhibition in the A–B, A–C paradigm, *Journal of Experimental Psychology*, **93**, 188–192.   (172).

Birnbaum, I. M. (1973). Retroactive inhibition in two paradigms of negative transfer, *Journal of Experimental Psychology*, **100**, 116–121.   (172).

Birnbaum, I. M., and Eichner, J. T. (1971). Study versus test trials and long-term retention in free recall learning, *Journal of Verbal Learning and Verbal Behavior*, **10**, 516–521. (136, 138).

Bjork, R. A. (1966). Learning and short-term retention of paired associates in relation to specific sequences of interpresentation intervals. Technical Report 106, Institute for Mathematical Studies in the Social Sciences, Stanford University, California.   (140).

Bjork, R. A. (1970). Positive forgetting: the non-interference of items intentionally forgotten, *Journal of Verbal Learning and Verbal Behavior*, **9**, 255–268.   (140).

Bjork, R. A. See Reder, L. M.

Bjork, R. A., and Whitten, W. B. (1972). Recency-sensitive retrieval processes in long-term free recall. Paper presented at meetings of the Psychonomic Society, St. Louis, Missouri.   (101).

Block, R. A. See Hintzman, D. L.

Bonge, D. See Keppel, G.

Borden, R. C. See Nelson, D. L.

Borkowski, J. G. (1967). Distributed practice in short-term memory, *Journal of Verbal Learning and Verbal Behavior*, **6**, 66–72.   (136).

Bostrom, A. See Bower, G. H.

Boucher, B. See Bahrick, H. P.

Bourne, L. E. See Jones, J. E.

Bousfield, W. A., and Cohen, B. H. (1955). The occurrence of clustering in the recall of randomly arranged words of different frequencies-of-usage, *Journal of General Psychology*, **52**, 83–95.   (191, 200).

Bousfield, W. A., Puff, C. R., and Cowan, T. M. (1964). The development of constancies in sequential organization during repeated free recall, *Journal of Verbal Learning and Verbal Behavior*, **3**, 449–459.   (138).

Bower, G. H. (1970). Imagery as a relational organizer in associative learning, *Journal of Verbal Learning and Verbal Behavior*, **9**, 529–533.   (110).

Bower, G. H. (1972a). Mental imagery and associative learning. In L. Gregg (Ed.), *Cognition in Learning and Memory*, Wiley, New York.   (104, 112, 226).

Bower, G. H. (1972b). Stimulus-sampling theory of encoding variability. In A. W. Melton and E. Martin (Eds.), *Coding Processes in Human Memory*, Winston, Washington, DC.   (207, 212, 215).

246

Bower, G. H. See Anderson, J. R.; Hilgard, E. R.; Tulving, E.

Bower, G. H., and Bostrom, A. (1968). Absence of within-list PI and RI in short-term recognition memory, *Psychonomic Science*, **10**, 211–212.   (169).

Bower, G. H., Clark, M. C., Lesgold, A. M., and Winzenz, D. (1969). Hierarchical retrieval schemes in recall of categorized word lists, *Journal of Verbal Learning and Verbal Behavior*, **8**, 323–343.   (91).

Bregman, A. S. (1968). Forgetting curves with semantic, phonetic, graphic and contiguity cues, *Journal of Experimental Psychology*, **78**, 539–546.   (87).

Bregman, A. S., and Wiener, J. R. (1970). Effects of test-trials in paired-associate and free-recall learning, *Journal of Verbal Learning and Verbal Behavior*, **9**, 689–698.   (140).

Brener, L. R. (1940). An experimental investigation of memory span, *Journal of Experimental Psychology*, **26**, 467–482.   (113).

Brewer, C. I. See Peterson, L. R.

Brion, S. (1968). Aspects anatomo-pathologiques des amnésies, *International Journal of Neurology*, **7**, 31–43.   (235).

Brion, S., Pragier, G., Guérin, R., and Mme Teitgen (1969). Syndrome de Korsakoff par ramollisement bilatéral du fornix, *Revue Neurologique*, **120**, 255–262.   (235).

Broadbent, D. E. (1958). *Perception and Communication*, Pergamon, London.   (137).

Broadbent, D. E. (1967). Word frequency effect and response bias, *Psychological Review*, **74**, 1–15.   (190).

Broadbent, D. E. (1973). *In Defence of Empirical Psychology*, Methuen, London.   (143).

Broder, P. M. See Underwood, B. J.

Brooks, D. H. See Nelson, D. L.

Brown, J. (1964). Two tests of all-or-none learning and retention, *Quarterly Journal of Experimental Psychology*, **16**, 2, 123–133.   (6).

Brown, J. (1965a). A comparison of recognition and recall by a multiple-response method, *Journal of Verbal Learning and Verbal Behavior*, **4**, 401–408.   (24, 25, 26, 28, 29, 35, 132).

Brown, J. (1965b). Multiple-response evaluation of discrimination, *British Journal of Mathematical and Statistical Psychology*, **18**, 125–137.   (22, 24, 26, 132, 142).

Brown, J. (1968). Reciprocal facilitation and impairment of free recall, *Psychonomic Science*, **10**, 2, 41–42.   (17, 135).

Brown, J. (1974). Recognition assessed by rating and ranking, *British Journal of Psychology*, **65**, 1, 13–22.   (25, 31, 35).

Brown, J., and Packham, D. W. (1967). Effect of prior recall on multiple response recognition, *Quarterly Journal of Experimental Psychology*, **19**, 356–361.   ʾ(34, 142).

Brown, J., and Routh, D. R. (1968). Recall, recognition and number of choices, *Journal of Verbal Learning and Verbal Behavior*, **7**, 1108–1111.   (11, 28, 132).

Brown, J., and Routh, D. R. (1970). Recognition assessed by d' and by a non-parametric alternative (The A-Index) as a function of the number of choices, *Quarterly Journal of Experimental Psychology*, **22**, 707–719.   (11, 24, 25).

Brown, R., and McNeill, D. (1966). The 'tip-of-the-tongue' phenomenon, *Journal of Verbal Learning and Verbal Behavior*, **5**, 325–337.   (4, 215).

Brown, W. (1923). To what extent is memory measured by a single recall?, *Journal of Experimental Psychology*, **6**, 377–382.   (134, 136).

Brown, W. P., and Ure, D. M. J. (1969). Five rated characteristics of 650 word association stimuli, *British Journal of Psychology*, **60**, 233–249.   (186, 187).

Bruce, D., and Fagan, R. L. (1970). More on the recognition and free recall of organized lists, *Journal of Experimental Psychology*, **85**, 153–154.   (45, 47).

Bruce, D., and Weaver, G. E. (1973). Retroactive facilitation in short-term retention of minimally learned paired associates, *Journal of Experimental Psychology*, **100**, 9–17 (172).

Bugelski, R. R. (1962). Presentation time, total time and mediation in paired associate learning, *Journal of Experimental Psychology*, **63**, 409–412.   (136, 140).

Burns, S. See Postman, L.
Butler, D. A., and Peterson, D. E. (1965). Learning during extinction with paired associates, *Journal of Verbal Learning and Verbal Behavior*, **4**, 103–106. (139).
Butters, N. See Cermak, L. S.
Buxton, C. E. (1943). The status of research in reminiscence, *Psychological Bulletin*, **40**, 313–337. (134).
Campbell, N. R. See Weaver, G. E.
Carey, S. T., and Lockhart, R. S. (1973). Encoding differences in recognition and recall, *Memory and Cognition*, **1**, 297–300. (62, 92, 162).
Carlson, J. B., and Duncan, C. P. (1955). A study of autonomous change in the memory trace by the method of recognition, *American Journal of Psychology*, **68**, 280–284. (11).
Carroll, J. B. (1971). Measurement properties of subjective magnitude estimates of word frequency, *Journal of Verbal Learning and Verbal Behavior*, **10**, 722–729. (185).
Carroll, J. B., and White, M. N. (1973). Word frequency and age of acquisition as determiners of picture-naming latency, *Quarterly Journal of Psychology*, **25**, 85–95. (121, 189).
Carter-Sobell, L. See Light, L. L.
Catlin, J. (1969). On the word-frequency effect, *Psychological Review*, **76**, 504–506. (190).
Catlin, P. A. See Holborn, S. W.
Ceraso, J., and Henderson, A. (1965). Unavailability and associative loss in RI and PI, *Journal of Experimental Psychology*, **70**, 300–303. (158, 178).
Ceraso, J., and Henderson, A. (1966). Unavailability and associative loss in RI and PI: second try, *Journal of Experimental Psychology*, **72**, 314–316. (158, 178).
Cermak, L. S., and Butters, N. (1972). The role of interference and encoding in the short-term memory deficits of Korsakoff patients, *Neuropsychologia*, **10**, 89–95. (226).
Cermak, L. S., and Butters, N. (1973). Information processing deficits of Alcoholic Korsakoff patients, *Quarterly Journal of Studies on Alcohol*, **34**, 1110–1132. (218).
Cermak, L. S., Butters, N., and Gerrein, J. (1973). The extent of verbal encoding ability of Korsakoff patients, *Neuropsychologia*, **11**, 85–94. (226).
Cermak, L. S., Butters, N., and Goodglass, H. (1971). The extent of memory loss in Korsakoff patients, *Neuropsychologia*, **9**, 309–315. (218).
Chang, J. J. See Shepard, R. N.
Chase, W. G., and Clark, H. H. (1972). Mental operations in the comparison of sentences and pictures. In L. Gregg (Ed.), *Cognition in Learning and Memory*, Wiley, New York. (106).
Clark, H. H. See Chase, W. G.
Clark, M. C. See Bower, G. H.
Clarke, F. R., Birdsall, T. G., and Tanner, W. P. (1959). Two types of ROC curve and definitions of parameters, *Journal of the Acoustical Society of America*, **31**, 629–630. (32).
Cofer, C. N. (1967). Does conceptual organization influence the amount retained in immediate free recall? In B. Kleinmuntz (Ed.), *Concepts and the Structure of Memory*, Wiley, New York, pp. 181–214. (50).
Cofer, C. N. See Sanders, A. F.
Cofer, C. N., and Shevitz, R. (1952). Word-association as a function of word-frequency, *Americal Journal of Psychology*, **65**, 75–79. (186).
Cohen, B. H. See Bousfield, W. A.
Coke, E. U. See Rothkoff, E. Z.
Collins, G. H. See Victor, M.
Conezio, J. See Standing, L.
Conn, C. P. See Winograd, E.
Cooper, A. J. R. (1974), The Differential Effects of Study and Test on Recognition and

248

Recall, Doctoral Thesis, University of Bristol, England.   (Chapter Five).

Cooper, E. H., and Pantle, A. J. (1967). The total time hypothesis in verbal learning, *Psychological Bulletin*, **68**, 221–234.   (136).

Corkin, S. See Milner, B.

Cowan, B. H. See Bousfield, W. A.

Craik, F. I. M. (1968). Types of error in free recall, *Psychonomic Science*, **10**, 353–354. (227).

Craik, F. I. M. (1970). The fate of primary memory items in free recall, *Journal of Verbal Learning and Verbal Behavior*, **9**, 143–148.   (93).

Craik, F. I. M. (1973). A 'Levels of Analysis' view of memory. In P. Pliner, L. Krames and T. M. Alloway (Eds.), *Communication and Effect: Language and Thought*, Academic Press, New York.   (86, 87, 88).

Craik, F. I. M., Gardiner, J. M., and Watkins, M. J. (1970). Further evidence for a negative recency effect in free recall, *Journal of Verbal Learning and Verbal Behavior*, **9**, 554–560. (137).

Craik, F. I. M., and Jacoby, L. L. (1975). A process view of short-term retention. In F. Restle (Ed.), *Cognitive Theory*, Volume One, Erlbaum Associates, Potomac, Maryland. (87, 88).

Craik, F. I. M., and Lockhart, R. S. (1972). Levels of processing: A framework for memory research, *Journal of Verbal Learning and Verbal Behavior*, **11**, 671–684.   (62, 77, 87, 93, 100, 107).

Craik, F. I. M., and Watkins, M. J. (1973). The role of rehearsal in short-term memory *Journal of Verbal Learning and Verbal Behavior*, **12**, 599–607.   (93, 137).

Crothers, E. J. See Estes, W. K.

Csapo, K. See Paivio, A.

Cushman, W. See Hall, J.

Cymer, W. See Groninger, L. D.

D'Agostino, P. R. (1969). The blocked-random effect in recall and recognition, *Journal of Verbal Learning and Verbal Behavior*, **8**, 815–820.   (90).

Dale, H. C. A. (1966). When recognition is no better than recall, *Nature*, **211**, 324.   (45).

Dale, H. C. A. (1967). Response availability and short-term memory, *Journal of Verbal Learning and Verbal Behavior*, **6**, 47–48.   (204).

D'Amato, M. R. (1973). Delayed matching and short-term memory in monkeys. In G. H. Bower (Ed.), *The Psychology of Learning and Motivation: Advances in Research and Theory*, Vol. 7, Academic Press, New York, pp. 227–269.   (42).

DaPolito, F. J. (1966). Proactive effects with independent retrieval of competing responses. Unpublished doctoral dissertation, Indiana University.   (172).

DaPolito, F. J. See Estes, W. K.; Greeno, J. G.

Darley, D. F., and Murdock, B. B. Jr. (1971). Effects of prior free recall testing on final recall and recognition, *Journal of Experimental Psychology*, **93**, 66–73.   (47, 136, 143).

Dashiell, J. F. (1928). *Fundamentals of Objective Psychology*, Houghton-Mifflin, New York.   (134).

Davies, G. M. (1969). Recognition memory for pictured and named objects, *Journal of Experimental Child Psychology*, **7**, 448–458.   (108, 118, 123).

Davies, G. M., Milne, J. E., and Glennie, B. J. (1973). On the significance of 'double encoding' for the superior recall of pictures to names, *Quarterly Journal of Experimental Psychology*, **25**, 413–423.   (109).

Davis, J. C., Lockhart, R. S., and Thomson, D. M. (1972). Repetition and context effects in recognition memory, *Journal of Experimental Psychology*, **92**, 96–102.   (91).

Davis, J. C., and Okada, R. (1971). Recognition and recall of positively forgotten items, *Journal of Experimental Psychology*, **89**, 181–186.   (137).

Davis, R., Sutherland, N. S., and Judd, B. R. (1961). Information content in recognition and recall, *Journal of Experimental Psychology*, **61**, 422–429.   (3, 22, 31, 183, 189).

249

Dean, P. J. See Mandler, G.

Decker, L. See Pollack, I.

Deese, J. (1960). Frequency of usage and number of words in free recall: The role of association, *Psychological Reports*, **7**, 337–344.   (193).

Del Castillo, D. M., and Gumenik, W. E. (1972). Sequential memory for familiar and unfamiliar forms, *Journal of Experimental Psychology*, **95**, 90–96.   (114).

Delprato, D. J. (1971). Specific-pair interference on recall and associative-matching retention tests, *American Journal of Psychology*, **84**, 185–193.   (161, 171).

Delprato, D. J. (1972). Pair-specific effects in retroactive inhibition, *Journal of Verbal Learning and Verbal Behavior*, **11**, 566–572.   (170, 172).

Dember, W. N. (1956). Response by the rat to environmental change, *Journal of Comparative and Physiological Psychology*, **49**, 93–95.   (230).

Deno, S. L. See Jenkins, J. R.

Dientsbier, R. A. See Silverstein, A.

Donaldson, W. A. (1971). Output effects in multi-trial free recall, *Journal of Verbal Learning and Verbal Behavior*, **10**, 5, 577–585.   (136, 137, 138).

Donaldson, W. See Tulving, E.

Donaldson, W., and Murdock, B. B. Jr. (1968). Criterion changes in continuous recognition memory, *Journal of Experimental Psychology*, **76**, 325–330.   (205, 208, 210).

Doré, L. R., and Hilgard, E. R. (1937). Spaced practice and the maturation hypothesis, *Journal of Psychology*, **4**, 245–259.   (134).

Douglas, R. J. (1967). The hippocampus and behaviour, *Psychological Bulletin*, **67**, 416–442.   (235, 236).

Drachman, D. A., and Arbit, J. (1966). Memory and hippocampal complex II, *Archives of Neurology*, **15**, 52–61.   (218, 221).

Duffy, P. O. See Murdock, B. B. Jr.

Dukes, W. F., and Bastian, J. (1966). Recall of abstract and concrete words equated for meaningfulness, *Journal of Verbal Learning and Verbal Behavior*, **5**, 455–458.   (194).

Duncan, C. P. (1970). Thinking of a word under different retrieval constraints, *Journal of Verbal Learning and Verbal Behavior*, **9**, 356–361.   (189).

Duncan, C. P. (1973). Storage and retrieval of low-frequency words, *Memory and Cognition*, **1**, 129–132.   (189, 204).

Duncan, C. P. See Carlson, J. B.

Duncan, E. M. See Weaver, G. E.

Earhard, M. (1967). Subjective organization and list organization as determinants of free recall and serial recall memorization, *Journal of Verbal Learning and Verbal Behavior*, **6**, 501–507.   (145).

Ecob, J. R. See Baddeley, A. D.

Egan, J. P. (1958). Recognition memory and the operating characteristic. Indiana University Hearing and Communication Laboratory, AFCRC-TN-58–51, AD. 152650.   (148).

Eichner, J. T. See Birnbaum, I. M.

Eimas, P. D., and Zeaman, D. (1963). Response speed changes in an Estes' paired associate miniature experiment, *Journal of Verbal Learning and Verbal Behavior*, **1**, 384–388.   (140).

Ekstrand, B. R. See Underwood, B. J.

Ekstrand, B. R., Wallace, W. P., and Underwood, B. J. (1966). A frequency theory of verbal discrimination learning, *Psychological Review*, **73**, 566–578.   (168, 180).

Ellis, H. C. (1972). Verbal processes in the encoding of visual pattern information: an approach to language, perception and memory. In M. E. Meyer (Ed.), *Third Western Symposium on Learning: Cognitive Learning*, Western Washington State College, Bellingham.   (105, 115).

Engen, T., and Ross, B. M. (1973). Long-term memory of odors with and without verbal descriptions, *Journal of Experimental Psychology*, **100**, 221–227.   (52).

250

Epstein, W., Rock, I., and Zuckerman, C. B. (1960). Meaning and familiarity in associative learning, *Psychological Monographs*, **74**, (4, Whole No. 491). (112).

Ernest, C. H., and Paivio, A (1969). Imagery ability in paired-associate and incidental learning, *Psychonomic Science*, **15**, 181–182. (111).

Ernest, C. H., and Paivio, A. (1971). Imagery and sex differences in incidental recall, *British Journal of Psychology*, **62**, 67–72. (108, 111).

Eschenbrenner, A. J. Jr. (1969). Retroactive and proactive inhibition in verbal discrimination learning, *Journal of Experimental Psychology*, **81**, 576–583. (180).

Eschenbrenner, A. J. Jr. See Kausler, D. H.

Estes, W. K. (1955). Statistical theory of distributional phenomena in learning, *Psychological Review*, **62**, 369–377. (140).

Estes, W. K. (1959). The statistical approach to a learning theory. In S. Koch (Ed.), *Psychology: a Study of a Science*, Vol. 2, McGraw-Hill, New York, pp. 380–491. (139).

Estes, W. K. (1960). Learning theory and the new mental chemistry, *Psychological Review*, **67**, 207–223. (139).

Estes, W. K. See Allen, G. A.

Estes, W. K., and DaPolito, F. (1967). Independent variation of information storage and retrieval processes in paired-associate learning, *Journal of Experimental Psychology*, **75**, 18–26. (3, 4, 46).

Estes, W. K., Hopkins, B. L., and Crothers, E. J. (1960). All-or-none and conservation effects in the learning and retention of paired associates, *Journal of Experimental Psychology*, **60**, 329–339. (140).

Evans, J. D., and Jacoby, L. L. (1973). Long-term storage: Rehearsal or encoding demands. Paper presented at the Forty-Fifth Annual Meeting of the Midwestern Psychological Association, Chicago. (92).

Fagan, R. L. See Bruce, D.

Field, W. H. See Lachman, R.

Finkelstein, M. See Snodgrass, J. G.

Fischler, I. See Juola, J. F.

Fitter, M. J. See Simpson, A. J.

Forbach, B. G. See Stanners, R. F.

Forrester, W. E. (1970). Retroactive inhibition and spontaneous recovery in the A–B, D–C Paradigm, *Journal of Verbal Learning and Verbal Behavior*, **9**, 525–528. (158).

Foth, D. See Paivio, A.

Francis, W. N. See Kucera, H.

Fraser, J. See Postman, L.

Frederiksen, J. R. (1971). Statistical decision model for auditory word recognition, *Psychological Review*, **78**, 409–419. (187, 190, 199).

Freedman, J. L. See Loftus, E. F.

Freedman, J. L., and Loftus, E. F. (1971). Retrieval of words from long-term memory, *Journal of Verbal Learning and Verbal Behavior*, **10**, 107–115. (188).

Freund, J. S. See Underwood, B. J.

Frincke, G. (1968). Word characteristics, associative-relatedness, and the free recall of nouns, *Journal of Verbal Learning and Verbal Behavior*, **7**, 366–372. (186, 195).

Frincke, G. See Gupton, T.

Frost, N. (1972). Encoding and retrieval in visual tasks, *Journal of Experimental Psychology*, **95**, 317–326. (92).

Fulkerson, F. E. See Kausler, D. H.

Gaffan, D. (1972). Loss of recognition memory in rats with lesions of the fornix, *Neuropsychologia*, **10**, 327–341. (227, 230, 235, 236, 238).

Gaffan, D. (1973). Inhibitory gradients and behavioural constrast in rats with lesions in the fornix, *Physiology and Behaviour*, **11**, 215–220. (236).

Gaffan, D. (1974). Recognition impaired and association intact in the memory of monkeys after transaction of the fornix, *Journal of Comparative and Physiological Psychology*, **86**, 1100–1109.   (227–230).

Galbraith, R. C., and Underwood, B. J. (1973). Perceived frequency of concrete and abstract words, *Memory and Cognition*, **1**, 56–60.   (185, 195, 198).

Gardiner, J. M. See Craik, F. I. M.

Garfield, L. See Rubenstein, H.

Garskof, B. E. (1968). Unlearning as a function of degree of interpolated learning and method of testing in the A–B, A–C and A–B, C–D paradigms, *Journal of Experimental Psychology*, **76**, 579–583.   (161).

Garskof, B. E. See Sandak, J. M.

Garskof, B. E., and Sandak, J. M. (1964). Unlearning in recognition memory, *Psychonomic Science*, **1**, 197–198.   (161).

Gartman, L. M., and Johnson, N. F. (1972). Massed versus distributed repetition of homographs: A test of the differential encoding hypothesis, *Journal of Verbal Learning and Verbal Behavior*, **11**, 801–808.   (99).

Garton, R. F. See Allen, L. R.

Garton, R. F., and Allen, L. R. (1968). Familiarity and word recognition, *Quarterly Journal of Experimental Psychology*, **20**, 385–389.   (206).

Gates, A. I. (1917). Recitation as a factor in memorizing, *Arch. Psychology*, No. 40.   (134).

Gerrein, J. See Cermak, L. S.

Gibson, E. J. (1940). A systematic application of the concepts of generalization and differentiation to verbal learning, *Psychological Review*, **47**, 196–229.   (157).

Glanzer, M., and Meinzer, A. (1967). The effects of intralist activity on free recall, *Journal of Verbal Learning and Verbal Behavior*, **6**, 928–935.   (137).

Glennie, B. J. See Davies, G. M.

Goldberg, L. B. See Snodgrass, J. G.

Golin, S. J. See Goss, A. E.

Goodglass, H. See Cermak, L. S.

Gordon, G. P. See Shapiro, S. I.

Gorman, A. M. (1961). Recognition memory for nouns as a function of abstractness and frequency, *Journal of Experimental Psychology*, **61**, 23–29.   (108, 116, 206, 207, 209, 212).

Goss, A. E., Morgan, C. H., and Golin, S. J. (1959). Paired-associate learning as a function of percentage occurrence of response members (reinforcement), *Journal of Experimental Psychology*, **57**, 96–104.   (139).

Goss, A. E., Nodine, C. F., Gregory, B. N., Taub, H. A., and Kennedy, K. E. (1962). Stimulus characteristics and percentage of occurrence of response members in paired associate learning, *Psychological Monographs*, **77**, 12 (Whole Number 531).   (139).

Götz, A., and Jacoby, L. L. (1974). Encoding and retrieval processes in long-term retention, *Journal of Experimental Psychology*, **102**, 291–297.   (92).

Green, D. M., and Swets, J. A. (1966). *Signal Detection Theory and Psychophysics*, Wiley, New York. (26).

Greenberg, S., and Wickens, D. D. (1972). Is matching performance an adequate test of 'extinction' effects on individual associations?, *Psychonomic Science*, **27**, 227–229. (161, 166).

Greeno, J. G., James, C. T., and DaPolito, F. J. (1971). A cognitive interpretation of negative transfer and forgetting of paired-associates, *Journal of Verbal Learning and Verbal Behavior*, **10**, 331–345.   (173, 176).

Gregg, V. H. (1970). Word frequency effects in human memory. Unpublished Ph.D. thesis, Birkbeck College, University of London.   (196, 200, 202, 206, 207, 208, 211, 213).

Gregory, B. N. See Goss, A. E.

Groninger, L. D. (1972). Storage and retrieval aspects of imagery instructions on indi-

252

vidual words. Unpublished manuscript, University of Maryland.   (108, 117).

Groninger, L. D. (1974). The role of images as a word feature in recognition memory. Unpublished manuscript, University of Maryland.   (126).

Groninger, L. D., Bell, B., Cymer, W., and Wess, B. Jr. (1972). Storage aspects of nouns presented under imagery and acoustic coding instructions, *Journal of Experimental Psychology*, **95**, 195–201.   (108).

Gropper, M. S. See Richardson, J.

Gross, K. L. See Holborn, S. W.

Guerin, R. See Brion, S.

Gumenik, W. E. See Del Castillo, D. M.

Gupton, T., and Frincke, G. (1970). Imagery, mediational instructions, and noun position in free recall of noun-verb pairs, *Journal of Experimental Psychology*, **86**, 461–462. (108).

Haber, R. N. See Standing, L.

Hall, J. F. (1954). Learning as a function of word-frequency, *American Journal of Psychology*, **67**, 138–140.   (194).

Hall, J. F. (1972). Associative strength and word frequency as related to stages of paired-associate learning, *Canadian Journal of Psychology*, **26**, 252–258.   (198).

Hall, J. F., Sekuler, R., and Cushman, W. (1969). Effects of IAR occurrence during learning on response-time during subsequent recognition, *Journal of Experimental Psychology*, **79**, 39–42.   (150).

Hall, J. F., and Ugelow, A. (1957). Free association time as a function of word frequency, *Canadian Journal of Psychology*, **11**, 29–32.   (186).

Hanawalt, N. G., and Tarr, A. G. (1961). The effect of recall upon recognition, *Journal of Experimental Psychology*, **62**, 4, 361–367.   (142).

Hardyck, C. D., and Petrinovich, L. F. (1970). Subvocal speech and comprehension level as a function of the difficulty level of reading material, *Journal of Verbal Learning and Verbal Behavior*, **9**, 647–652.   (78).

Hasher, L. See Postman, L.

Hassler, R., and Riechert, T. (1957). Über einen Fall von doppelseitiger Fornicotomie bei sogenannter temporaler Epilepsie, *Acta Neurochirurgica, Wien*, **5**, 330–340.   (235).

Hastie, R. See Tulving, E.

Heine, R. (1914). Über Wiedererkennen und rückwirkende Hemmung, *Zeitschrift für Psychologie*, **68**, 161–236.   (157).

Henderson, A. See Ceraso, J.

Hendrick, R. L. See Jacoby, L. L.

Henschel, D. See Postman, L.

Herrmann, D. J. See Atkinson, R. C.

Herrmann, D. J., and McLaughlin, J. P. (1973). Effects of experimental and pre-experimental organization on recognition: Evidence for two storage systems in long-term memory, *Journal of Experimental Psychology*, **99**, 2, 174–179.   (52, 70).

Hilgard, E. R. See Dore, L. R.

Hilgard, E. R., and Bower, G. H. (1966). *Theories of Learning* (3rd edn.), Appleton-Century-Crofts, New York.   (230).

Hintzman, D. L. (1972). On testing the independence of associations, *Psychological Review*, **79**, 261–264.   (174).

Hintzman, D. L., and Block, R. A. (1970). Memory judgments and the effects of spacing, *Journal of Verbal Learning and Verbal Behavior*, **9**, 561–566.   (70).

Hintzman, D. L., and Block, R. A. (1971). Repetition and memory: Evidence for a multiple-trace hypothesis, *Journal of Experimental Psychology*, **88**, 297–306.   (180).

Hintzman, D. L., Block, R. A., and Summers, J. J. (1973). Modality tags and memory for repetitions: Locus of the spacing effect, *Journal of Verbal Learning and Verbal Behavior*, **12**, 229–238.   (99).

Hogan, R. M., and Kintsch, W. (1971). Differential effects of study and test trials on long-term recognition and recall, *Journal of Verbal Learning and Verbal Behavior*, **10**, 562–567.   (136, 141, 143).

Hoggart, K. See Matthews, W. A.

Holborn, S. W., Gross, K. L., and Catlin, P. A. (1973). Effects of word frequency and acoustic similarity on free-recall and paired-associate-recognition learning, *Journal of Experimental Psychology*, **101**, 169–174.   (198).

Hollenberg, C. K. (1970). Functions of visual imagery in the learning and concept formation of children, *Child Development*, **4**, 1003–1016.   (111).

Hollingworth, H. L. (1913). Characteristic differences between recall and recognition, *American Journal of Psychology*, **24**, 532–544.   (42).

Hopkins, B. L. See Estes, W. K.

Horowitz, L. M., and Manelis, L. (1973). Recognition and cued recall of idioms and phrases, *Journal of Experimental Psychology*, **100**, 291–296.   (90, 91).

Houston, J. P. (1964). Verbal R–S strength following S–R extinction, *Psychonomic Science*, **1**, 173–174.   (167).

Houston, J. P. (1967). Proactive inhibition and competition at recall, *Journal of Experimental Psychology*, **75**, 118–121.   (178).

Hovland, C. I. (1940). Experimental studies in rote-learning theory vi. Comparison of retention following learning to the same criterion by massed and distributed practice, *Journal of Experimental Psychology*, **26**, 568–587.   (134).

Howell, W. C. (1973a). Effects of organization on discrimination of word frequency within and between categories, *Journal of Experimental Psychology*, **99**, 255–260. (212).

Howell, W. C. (1973b). Representation of frequency in memory, *Psychological Bulletin*, **80**, 44–53.   (184).

Howes, D. (1957). On the relation between the probability of a word as an association and in general linguistic usage, *Journal of Abnormal Social Psychology*, **54**, 75–85. (186).

Howes, D. H., and Solomon, R. C. (1951). Visual duration threshold as a function of word probability, *Journal of Experimental Psychology*, **41**, 401–410.   (190).

Huguenin, C. (1914). Reviviscence paradoxale, *Archives de Psychologie*, **14**, 379–383. (134).

Hull, C. L. (1943). *Principles of Behavior*, Appleton-Century-Crofts, New York.   (134, 177).

Humphreys, M. S. See Yuille, J. C.

Hyde, T. S., and Jenkins, J. J. (1969). The differential effects of incidental tasks on the organization of recall of a list of highly associated words, *Journal of Experimental Psychology*, **82**, 472–481.   (86, 87, 88, 225).

Hyde, T. S., and Jenkins, J. J. (1973). Recall for words as a function of semantic, graphic, and syntactic orienting tasks, *Journal of Verbal Learning and Verbal Behavior*, **12**, 471–480.   (107, 225).

Ingleby, J. D. (1969). Decision-making processes in human perception and memory, Ph.D. Thesis, University of Cambridge, Cambridge, England.   (25).

Ingleby, J. D. (1973). A test of current explanations of the effect of item availability on memory, *Quarterly Journal of Experimental Psychology*, **25**, 378–386.   (25, 189, 203, 204).

Irwin, J. M. See Melton, A. W.

Izawa, C. (1966a). Reinforcement-test sequences in paired-associate learning, *Psychological Reports*, **18**, 879–919.   (139).

Izawa, C. (1966b). Role of reinforcement and test in paired-associate learning. Proceedings of 74th Annual Convention, American Psychological Association, pp. 21–22. (139).

Izawa, C. (1967). Effect of consecutive test trials on the learning of verbal paired-associates, *Psychonomic Bulletin*, **1**, 11.   (140).

.awa, C. (1968a). Effects of reinforcement, neutral and test trials upon paired-associate acquisition and retention, *Psychological Reports*, **23**, 947–959. (139).

Izawa, C. (1968b). Effects of successive reinforcements, tests and neutral trials in paired associate learning. Proceedings of the 76th Annual Convention, American Psychological Association, **3**, 33–34. (139, 140).

Izawa, C. (1969). Long sequences of successive tests in paired-associate acquisition. Proceedings of the 77th Annual Convention, American Psychological Association, **4**, 57–58. (139).

Izawa, C. (1970a). Optimal potentiating effects and forgetting prevention effects in paired-associate learning, *Journal of Experimental Psychology*, **83**, 340–344. (140).

Izawa, C. (1970b). Reinforcement-test-blank acquisition programming under the unmixed list design in paired-associate learning, *Psychonomic Science*, **19**, 2, 75–77. (140).

Izawa, C. (1970c). List versus items in distributed practice in paired-associate learning. Proceedings of the 78th Annual Convention, American Psychological Association, **5**, 87–88. (139).

Jablonski, E. M. See Mueller, J. H.

Jacoby, L. L. (1972a). Effects of organization on recognition memory, *Journal of Experimental Psychology*, **92**, 325–331. (91).

Jacoby, L. L. (1972b). Context effects of frequency judgments of words and sentences, *Journal of Experimental Psychology*, **94**, 255–260. (99).

Jacoby, L. L. (1973a). Encoding processes, rehearsal and recall requirements, *Journal of Verbal Learning and Verbal Behavior*, **12**, 302–310. (137).

Jacoby, L. L. (1973b). Test appropriate strategies in retention of categorized lists, *Journal of Verbal Learning and Verbal Behavior*, **12**, 675–682. (92).

Jacoby, L. L. (1974). The role of mental contiguity in memory: Registration and retrieval effects, *Journal of Verbal Learning and Verbal Behavior*, **13**, 483–496. (87, 89, 100).

Jacoby, L. L. See Craik, F. I. M.; Evans, J. D.; Bartz, W. H.; Hendrick, R. L.

Jacoby, L. L., and Bartz, W. H. (1972). Encoding processes and the negative recency effect, *Journal of Verbal Learning and Verbal Behavior*, **11**, 561–565. (93).

Jacoby, L. L., and Hendricks, R. L. (1973). Recognition effects of study organization and test context, *Journal of Experimental Psychology*, **100**, 73–82. (91).

James, C. T. See Greeno, J. G.

James, W. (1890). *Principles of Psychology*, Holt, New York. (3, 183).

Jenkins, J. J. See Hyde, T. S.; Walsh, D. A.

Jenkins, J. R., Neale, D. C., and Deno, S. L. (1967). Differential memory for pictures and word stimuli, *Journal of Educational Psychology*, **58**, 303–307. (108, 118, 123).

Jenkins, W. O. See Postman, L.

Johnson, A. L. See Kroll, N. E. A.

Johnson, N. F. See Gartman, L. M.

Johnston, W. A. (1967). S–R, R–S independence and the interference potency of latent R–S associations, *Journal of Experimental Psychology*, **74**, 551–516. (167).

Jones, J. E. (1962). All-or-none versus incremental learning, *Psychological Review*, **69**, 2, 156–160. (139, 140).

Jones, J. E., and Bourne, L. E. (1964). Delay of information feedback in verbal learning, *Canadian Journal of Psychology*, **18**, 266–280. (140).

Judd, B. R. See Davis, R.

Juola, J. F. See Atkinson, R. C.

Kaada, B. R. See Kemp, I. R.

Kamman, R., and Melton, A. W. (1967). Absolute recovery of first-list responses from unlearning during 26 minutes filled with an easy or difficult information processing task. Proceedings 75th Annual Convention, Americal Psychological Association, **2**, 63–64. (158).

Kanungo, R. N., and Mohanty, G. S. (1970). Differential roles of frequency and meaningfulness in free recall, *Canadian Journal of Psychology*, **24**, 161–168. (195).

255

Karchmer, M. A. See Winograd, E.
Kausler, D. H., Fulkerson, F. E., and Eschenbrenner, A. J. Jr. (1967). Unlearning of list 1 right items in verbal discrimination transfer, *Journal of Experimental Psychology*, **75**, 379–385.   (180).
Kay, H., and Skemp, R. (1956). Different thresholds for recognition—further experiments on interpolated recall and recognition, *Quarterly Journal of Experimental Psychology*, **8**, 153–162.   (142).
Kemp, I. R. and Kaada, B. R., (1975). The relation of hippocampal theta activity to arousal, attentive behaviour, and somatomotor movements in unrestrained cats, *Brain Research*, **95**, 323–342.   (237).
Kennedy, K. E. See Goss, A. E.
Keppel, G. See Postman, L.; Underwood, B. J.
Keppel, G., Bonge, D., Strand, B. Z., and Parker, J. (1971). Direct and indirect interference in the recall of paired associates, *Journal of Experimental Psychology*, **88**, 414–422. (167).
Keppel, G., Postman, L., and Zavortink, B. (1968). Studies of learning to learn: VIII. The influence of massive amounts of training upon the learning and retention of paired-associate lists, *Journal of Verbal Learning and Verbal Behavior*, **7**, 790–796.   (180).
Kimble, D. P. (1968). Hippocampus and internal inhibition, *Psychological Bulletin*, **70**, 285–295.   (235).
Kintsch, W. (1968). Recognition and free recall of organized lists, *Journal of Experimental Psychology*, **78**, 3, 481–487.   (45, 48, 132, 183).
Kintsch, W. (1970a). *Learning, Memory and Conceptual Processes*, Wiley, New York. (3, 4, 113, 115, 183).
Kintsch, W. (1970b). Models for free recall and recognition. In D. A. Norman (Ed.), *Models of Human Memory*, Academic Press, New York.   (41, 43, 45, 51, 56, 75, 95, 96, 153).
Kintsch, W. (1972). Notes on the structure of semantic memory. In E. Tulving and W. Donaldson (Eds.), *Organization of Memory*, Academic Press, New York, pp. 247–308. (71).
Kintsch, W. (1974). *The Representation of Meaning in Memory*, Lawrence Erlbaum Associates, Potomac, Maryland.   (71, 72, 73).
Kintsch, W. See Hogan, R. M.
Kirkpatrick, E. A. (1894). An experimental study of memory, *Psychological Review*, **1**, 602–609.   (108, 117).
Knapp, M. See Anisfield, M.
Kohler, W. (1947). *Gestalt Psychology*, Liveright, New York.   (90).
Kolers, P. K. (1973), Remembering operations, *Memory and Cognition*, **1**, 347–355. (84).
Koopmans, H. S. See Mandler, G.
Koppenaal, R. J. (1963). Time changes in strengths of A–B, A–C lists; spontaneous recovery?, *Journal of Verbal Learning and Verbal Behavior*, **2**, 310–319.   (178).
Kressel, K. See Winnick, W. A.
Kroll, N. E. A., Parks, T. E., Parkinson, S. R., Bieber, S. L., and Johnson, A. L. (1970). Short-term memory while shadowing: Recall of visually and of aurally presented letters, *Journal of Experimental Psychology*, **85**, 220–224.   (87).
Kucera, H., and Francis, W. N. (1967). *A Computational Analysis of Present-day American English*, Brown University Press, Providence, R. I.   (147, 185).
Kuhn, A. (1914). Über Einpragung durch lesen und durch rezitieren, *Zeitschrift für Psychologie*, **68**, 396–481.   (134).
LaBerge, D., and Tweedy, J. R. (1964). Presentation probability and choice time, *Journal of Experimental Psychology*, **68**, 5, 477–481.   (152).
Lachman, R. (1973). Uncertainty effects on time to access the internal lexicon, *Journal of Experimental Psychology*, **99**, 199–208.   (187, 189).

...man, R., and Field, W. H. (1965). Recognition and recall of verbal material as a function of degree of training, *Psychonomic Science*, **2**, 225–226. (183).

Lachman, R., and Laughery, K. R. (1968). Is a test trial a training trial in free recall learning?, *Journal of Experimental Psychology*, **76**, 40–50. (136, 144).

Lachman, R., and Tuttle, A. V. (1965). Approximations to English (AE) and short-term memory: Construction or storage?, *Journal of Experimental Psychology*, **70**, 386–393. (56).

Landauer, T. K., and Streeter, L. A. (1973). Structural differences between common and uncommon words: Failure of equivalence assumptions for theories of word recognition, *Journal of Verbal Learning and Verbal Behavior*, **12**, 119–131. (190, 199).

Laughery, K. R. See Lachman, R.

Lecocq, P. See Tiberghien, G.

Lecocq, P., and Tiberghien, G. (1973). Rappel and reconnaissance, *Année Psychologique*, **73**, 635–680. (45).

Legge, D. See Thomas, E. A. C.

Lewis, S. S. See Rubenstein, H.

Light, L. L., and Carter-Sobell, L. (1970). Effects of changed semantic context on recognition memory, *Journal of Verbal Learning and Verbal Behavior*, **9**, 1–11. (9, 53, 71, 90, 184).

Light, L. L. and Schurr, S. C. (1973), Context effects in recognition memory: Item order and unitization, *Journal of Experimental Psychology*, **100**, 135–140. (91).

Lindig, K. See McNeill, D.

Lindsay, P. H. See Rumelhart, D. E.

Lockhart, R. S. (1969). Retrieval asymmetry in the recall of adjectives and nouns, *Journal of Experimental Psychology*, **79**, 12–17. (110).

Lockhart, R. S. (1973). The spacing effect in free recall. Paper presented at the meeting of the Psychonomic Society, St. Louis, November. (99).

Lockhart, R. S. See Carey, S. T.; Craik, F. I. M.; Davis, J. C.; Mazuryk, G. F.

Lockhart, R. S., and Murdock, B. B. Jr. (1970). Memory and the theory of signal detection, *Psychological Bulletin*, **74**, 100–109. (24).

Loftus, E. F. See Freedman, J. L.

Loftus, E. F., and Freedman, J. L. (1972). Effect of category-name frequency on the speed of naming an instance of the category, *Journal of Verbal Learning and Verbal Behavior*, **11**, 343–347. (188).

Loftus, G. R. (1972). Eye fixations and recognition memory for pictures, *Cognitive Psychology*, **3**, 525–551. (162).

Loftus, G. R. See Rundus, D.

Lorge, I. See Thorndike, E. L.

Lovelace, E. A. See Schulman, A. I.

Luce, R. D. (1959). *Individual Choice Behavior*, Wiley, New York. (25).

Luce, R. D. (1963). A threshold theory for simple detection experiments, *Psychological Review*, **70**, 61–79. (25).

Mackay, S. A. See Martin, E.

Madigan, S. A. (1969). Intraserial repetition and coding processes in free recall, *Journal of Verbal Learning and Verbal Behavior*, **8**, 828–835. (99, 136, 212).

Madigan, S. A. See Paivio, A.

Mahler, W. A. See Allen, G. A.

Meinzer, A. See Glanzer, M.

Manasse, K. See Matthews, W. A.

Mandelbrot, B. (1965). Information theory and psycholinguistics. In B. B. Wolman and E. Nagel (Eds.), *Scientific Psychology*, Basic Books, New York. (187).

Mandler, G. (1967). Organization and memory. In K. W. Spence and J. T. Spence (Eds.), *The Psychology of Learning and Motivation*, Academic Press, New York. (194).

Mandler, G. (1972). Organization and recognition. In E. Tulving and W. Donaldson

257

(Eds.), *Organization of Memory*, Academic Press, New York, pp. 139–166.   (11, 71, 76, 91, 142, 154, 162, 184, 206).

Mandler, G., and Dean, P. J. (1969). Seriation: Development of serial order in free-recall, *Journal of Experimental Psychology*, **81**, 2, 207–215.   (138).

Mandler, G., Pearlstone, Z., and Koopmans, H. S. (1969). Effects of organization and semantic similarity on recall and recognition, *Journal of Verbal Learning and Verbal Behavior*, **8**, 410–423.   (215, 225).

Mandler, G., and Worden, P. E. (1973). Semantic processing without storage, *Journal of Experimental Psychology*, **100**, 2, 277–283.   (137).

Manelis, L. See Horowitz, L. M.

Marcel, A. J., and Steel, R. G. (1973). Semantic cueing in recognition and recall, *Quarterly Journal of Experimental Psychology*, **25**, 368–377.   (53).

Marks, D. F. (1972). Individual differences in the vividness of visual imagery and their effect on function. In P. Sheehan (Ed.), *The Function and Nature of Imagery*, Academic Press, New York.   (104).

Martin, E. (1967a). Stimulus recognition in aural paired-associate learning, *Journal of Verbal Learning and Verbal Behavior*, **6**, 272–276.   (178).

Martin, E. (1967b). Relation between stimulus recognition and paired-associate learning, *Journal of Experimental Psychology*, **74**, 500–505.   (178).

Martin, E. (1968). Stimulus meaningfulness and paired-associate transfer: an encoding variability hypothesis, *Psychological Review*, **75**, 421–441.   (198).

Martin, E. (1971). Verbal learning theory and independent retrieval phenomena, *Psychological Review*, **78**, 314–332.   (173, 174, 175).

Martin, E. (1972). Stimulus encoding in learning and transfer. In A. W. Melton and E. Martin (Eds.), *Coding Processes in Human Memory*, Winston, Washington, DC.   (167, 168, 173, 175, 176, 177).

Martin, E. (1973). Memory codes and negative transfer, *Memory and Cognition*, **1**, 494–498.   (167, 173, 175, 177, 178).

Martin, E. (1975). Generation–recognition theory and the encoding specificity principle, *Psychological Review*, **82**, 150–153.   (54).

Martin, E. See Shulman, H. G.; Wichawut, C.

Martin, E. and Mackay, S. A. (1970). A test of the list-differentiation hypothesis, *American Journal of Psychology*, **83**, 311–321.   (158, 174).

Matthews, W. A. (1966). Continued word associations and free recall, *Quarterly Journal of Experimental Psychology*, **17**, 31–38.   (193, 197).

Matthews, W. A., and Hoggart, K. (1970). Associative group and free recall, *British Journal of Psychology*, **61**, 345–357.   (193, 194).

Matthews, W. A., and Manasse, K. (1970). Associative factors in free recall, *Quarterly Journal of Experimental Psychology*, **22**, 177–184.   (193, 194).

May, R. B., and Tryk, H. E. (1970). Word sequence, word frequency, and free recall, *Canadian Journal of Psychology*, **24**, 299–304.   (196).

Mayzner, M. S., and Tresselt, M. E. (1958). Anagram solution times: A function of letter order and word frequency, *Journal of Experimental Psychology*, **56**, 376–379.   (189).

Mazuryk, G. F., and Lockhart, R. S. (1974). Negative recency and levels of processing in free recall, *Canadian Journal of Psychology*, **28**, 114–123.   (93).

McCormack, P. D. (1972). Recognition memory: How complex a retrieval system? *Canadian Journal of Psychology*, **26**, 19–41.   (45, 56, 75, 115, 183).

McCormack, P. D., and Swenson, A. L. (1972). Recognition memory for common and rare words, *Journal of Experimental Psychology*, **95**, 72–77.   (206, 207, 209).

McCrystal, T. J. (1970). List differentiation as a function of time and test order, *Journal of Experimental Psychology*, **83**, 220–223.   (159).

McCullough, T. A. See Turnage, T. W.

McGee, S. H. See Peterson, M. J.

258

McGeoch, J. A. (1932). Forgetting and the law of disuse, *Psychological Review*, **39**, 352–370. (157).

McGeoch, J. A. (1942). *The Psychology of Human Learning*, Longman, Green, New York. (160).

McGill, W. J. (1963). Stochastic latency mechanisms. In R. D. Luce (Ed.), *Handbook of Mathematical Psychology*, Vol. 1, Wiley, New York. (150).

McGovern, J. G. (1964). Extinction of associations in four transfer paradigms, *Psychological Monographs*, **78**, No. 16. (160, 167, 170).

McLaughlin, J. P. See Herrmann, D. J.

McLelland, D. C. (1942). Studies in serial verbal discrimination learning. 1. Reminiscence with two speeds of pair presentation, *Journal of Experimental Psychology*, **31**, 44–56. (134).

McNeill, D. See Brown, R.

McNeill, D., and Lindig, K. (1973). The perceptual reality of phonemes, syllables, words and sentences, *Journal of Verbal Learning and Verbal Behavior*, **12**, 419–430. (80).

McNicol, D. (1972). *A Primer of Signal Detection Theory*, Allen and Unwin, Sydney, Australia. (150).

Melton, A. W. (1963). Implications of short-term memory for a general theory of memory, *Journal of Verbal Learning and Verbal Behavior*, **2**, 1–21. (41, 75).

Melton, A. W. (1967). Repetition and retrieval from memory, *Science*, **158**, 532. (136).

Melton, A. W. See Kamman, R.

Melton, A. W., and Irwin, J. M. (1940). The influence of degree of interpolated learning on retroactive inhibition and the overt transfer of specific responses, *American Journal of Psychology*, **53**, 173–203. (158).

Melton, A. W., Reicher, G. M., and Shulman, H. G. (1966). A distributed practice effect on probability of recall in free recall learning. Paper read at a meeting of the Psychonomic Society, St. Louis, October. (136).

Melton, A. W., and von Lackum, W. J. (1941). Retroactive and proactive inhibition in retention: evidence for a two-factory theory of retroactive inhibition, *American Journal of Psychology*, **54**, 157–173. (158).

Merryman, C. T. (1971). Retroactive inhibition in the A–B, A–D paradigm as measured by a multiple-choice test, *Journal of Experimental Psychology*, **91**, 212–214. (161, 166).

Meunier, J. See Meunier, G.

Meunier, G. F., Ritz, D., and Meunier, J. A. (1972). Rehearsal of individual items in short-term memory, *Journal of Experimental Psychology*, **95**, 465–467. (137).

Miller, G. A. (1963). Comments on Professor Postman's paper. In C. N. Cofer and B. S. Musgrave (Eds.), *Verbal Behavior and Learning: Problems and Processes*, McGraw-Hill, New York. (76).

Millikan, J. A. See Rubenstein, H.

Milne, J. E. See Davis, G. M.

Milner, B., Corkin, S., and Teuber, H. L. (1968). Further analysis of hippocampal amnesic syndrome: 14 year follow-up study of H. M., *Neuropsychologia*, **6**, 215–234. (221).

Mistler-Lachman, J. L. (1975). Queer sentences, ambiguity and levels of processing, *Memory and Cognition*, **3**, 395–400. (80).

Modigliani, V. See Saltz, E.

Modigliani, V., and Saltz, E. (1969). Evaluation of a model relating Thorndike–Lorge frequency and m to learning, *Journal of Experimental Psychology*, **82**, 584–586. (198).

Mohanty, G. S. See Kanungo, R. N.

Morgan, C. H. See Goss, A. E.

Morton, J. (1969). Interaction of information in word recognition, *Psychological Review*, **76**, 165–178. (190).

Morton, J. (1970). A functional model for memory. In D. A. Norman (Ed.), *Models of Human Memory*, Academic Press, New York. (187).

Mueller, J. H., and Jablonski, E. M. (1970). Instructions, noun imagery, and priority in free recall, *Psychological Reports*, **27**, 559–566. (108).

Müller, G. E. (1913). Zur Analyse der Gedächtnistatigkeit und des Vorstellungsverlaufe, III. Teil. *Zeitschriftfür Psychologie, Ergänzungsband 8*. (3, 43).

Müller, G. E., and Pilzecker, A. (1900). Experimentelle Beiträge zur Lehre vom Gedächtniss, *Zeitschrift für Psychologie, Erganzungsband 1*. (157).

Murdock, B. B. Jr. (1965). Signal detection theory and short-term memory, *Journal of Experimental Psychology*, **70**, 443–447. (132).

Murdock, B. B. Jr. (1966). The criterion problem in short-term memory, *Journal of Experimental Psychology*, **72**, 317–324. (32).

Murdock, B. B. Jr. (1968). Modality effects in short-term memory: storage or retrieval?, *Journal of Experimental Psychology*, **77**, 79–86. (57, 75).

Murdock, B. B. Jr. (1970). Short-term memory for associations. In D. A. Norman (Ed.), *Models of Human Memory*, Academic Press, New York, pp. 285–304. (42).

Murdock, B. B. Jr. (1974). *Human Memory: Theory and Data*, Lawrence Erlbaum Associates, Potomac, Maryland. (71).

Murdock, B. B. Jr. See Darley, D. F.; Donaldson, W.; Lockhart, R. S.

Murdock, B. B. Jr., and Anderson, R. E. (1975). Encoding, storage, and retrieval of item information. In R. S. Solso (Ed.), *Information Processing and Cognition*, The Loyola Symposium, Lawrence Erlbaum Associates, Potomac, Maryland. (52, 71).

Murdock, B. B. Jr., and Dufty, P. O. (1972). Strength theory and recognition memory, *Journal of Experimental Psychology*, **94**, 284–290. (93).

Murray, A. See Peterson, M. J.

Neale, D. C. See Jenkins, J. R.

Neisser, U. (1964). Visual search, *Scientific American*, **210**, 94–102. (86).

Nelson, D. L., and Brooks, D. H. (1973). Functional independence of pictures and their verbal memory codes, *Journal of Experimental Psychology*, **98**, 44–48. (109).

Nelson, D. L., Brooks, D. H., and Borden, R. C. (1973). Sequential memory for pictures and the role of the verbal system, *Journal of Experimental Psychology*, **101**, 242–245. (114).

Newton, J. M., and Wickens, D. D. (1956). Retroactive inhibition as a function of the temporal position of interpolated learning, *Journal of Experimental Psychology*, **51**, 149–154. (159, 170).

Noble, C. E. (1963). Meaningfulness and familiarity. In C. N. Cofer and B. S. Musgrave (Eds.), *Verbal Behavior and Learning*, McGraw-Hill, New York. (184, 186, 205).

Nodine, C. F. See Goss, A. E.

Norman, D. A. (1968). Toward a theory of memory and attention, *Psychological Review*, **75**, 522–536. (43, 78).

Norman, D. A. See Waugh, N. C.; Rumelhart, D. E.

Norman, D. A., and Wickelgren, W. A. (1969). Strength theory of decision rules and latency in retrieval from short-term memory, *Journal of Mathematical Psychology*, **6**, 192–208. (28, 213).

Norsworthy, N. (1912). Acquisition as related to attention, *Journal of Educational Psychology*, **3**, 216. (134).

Okada, R. (1971). Decision latencies in short-term recognition memory, *Journal of Experimental Psychology*, **90**, 27–32. (93).

Okada, R. See Davis, J. C.

Oldfield, R. C. (1966). Things, words and the brain, *Quarterly Journal of Experimental Psychology*, **18**, 340–353. (188).

Olver, M. A. (1965). Abstractness, imagery and meaningfulness in recognition and free recall. Unpublished Master's thesis, University of Western Ontario. (108, 115, 212).

O'Neill, B. J. See Paivio, A.; Yarmey, A. D.

Osgood, C. E. (1946). Meaningful similarity and interference in learning, *Journal of Experimental Psychology*, **36**, 277–301. (157).

260

Packham, D. W. (1968). Recognition of recalled and non-recalled items, *Psychonomic Science*, **11**, 8, 291–292.   (143).

Packham, D. W. See Brown, J.

Paivio, A. (1965). Abstractness, imagery, and meaningfulness in paired-associate learning, *Journal of Verbal Learning and Verbal Behavior*, **4**, 32–38.   (110).

Paivio, A. (1968). A factor-analytic study of word attributes and verbal learning, *Journal of Verbal Learning and Verbal Behavior*, **7**, 41–49.   (113, 185, 186, 187, 195).

Paivio, A. (1971a). *Imagery and Verbal Processes*, Holt, Rinehart and Winston, New York.   (103, 104, 106, 107, 108, 112, 113, 115, 116, 117, 195, 212).

Paivio, A. (1971b), Imagery and language. In S. J. Segal (Ed.), *Imagery: Current cognitive approaches*. Academic Press, New York.   (226).

Paivio, A. (1972a). A theoretical analysis of the significance of imagery in learning and memory. In P. Sheehan (Ed.), *The Function and Nature of Imagery*, Academic Press, New York.   (105, 107).

Paivio, A. (1972b). Symbolic and sensory modalities of memory. In M. E. Meyer (Ed.), *The Third Western Symposium on Learning: Cognitive Learning*, Western Washington State College, Bellingham.   (107).

Paivio, A. See Ernest, C. H.; Tulving, E.; Yuille, J. C.

Paivio, A., and Csapo, K. (1969). Concrete-image and verbal memory codes, *Journal of Experimental Psychology*, **80**, 279–285.   (108, 109, 113).

Paivio, A. and Csapo, K. (1971). Short-term sequential memory for pictures and words, *Psychonomic Science*, **24**, 50–51.   (113).

Paivio, A., and Csapo, K. (1973). Picture superiority in free recall: Imagery or dual coding?, *Cognitive Psychology*, **5**, 176–206.   (105, 108, 109, 116, 117, 120, 124, 127).

Paivio, A., and Foth, D. (1970). Imaginal and verbal mediators and noun concreteness in paired-associate learning: the elusive interaction, *Journal of Verbal Learning and Verbal Behavior*, **9**, 384–390.   (110, 113).

Paivio, A., and Madigan, S. A. (1970). Noun imagery and frequency in paired-associate and free recall learning, *Canadian Journal of Psychology*, **24**, 353–361.   (116, 194, 195, 198).

Paivio, A., and O'Neill, B. J. (1970). Visual recognition thresholds and dimensions of word meaning, *Perception and Psychophysics*, **8**, 273–275.   (106).

Paivio, A., Rogers, T. B., and Smythe, P. C. (1968). Why are pictures easier to recall than words?, *Psychonomic Science*, **11**, 137–138.   (108).

Paivio, A., and Rowe, E. J. (1970). Noun imagery, frequency and meaningfulness in verbal discrimination, *Journal of Experimental Psychology*, **85**, 264–269.   (205).

Paivio, A., and Rowe, E. J. (1971). Intrapair imagery effects in verbal discrimination and incidental associative learning, *Canadian Journal of Psychology*, **25**, 302–312.   (110).

Paivio, A., and Yarmey, A. D. (1966). Pictures versus words as stimuli and responses in paired-associate learning, *Psychonomic Science*, **5**, 235–236.   (110).

Paivio, A., Yuille, J. C., and Madigan, S. (1968). Concreteness, imagery and meaningfulness values for 925 nouns, *Journal of Experimental Psychology Monograph Supplement*, **76**, No. 1, Part 2, 1–25.   (103).

Pantle, A. J. See Cooper, E. H.

Parker, J. See Keppel, G.

Parkinson, S. R. See Kroll, N. E. A.

Parks, T. E. (1966). Signal-detectability theory of recognition-memory performance, *Psychological Review*, **73**, 44–58.   (10, 148, 152, 205, 210).

Parks, T. E. See Kroll, N. E. A.

Patkau, J. E. See Tulving, E.

Patterson, K. E. (1972). Some characteristics of retrieval limitation in long-term memory, *Journal of Verbal Learning and Verbal Behavior*, **11**, 685–691.   (137).

Pearlstone, A. See Tulving, E.

261

Pearlstone, Z. See Mandler, G.
Peterson, D. E. See Butler, D. A.
Peterson, L. R. (1967). Search and judgment in memory. In B. Kleinmuntz (Ed.), *Concepts and the Structure of Memory*, Wiley, New York.   (3).
Peterson, L. R., and Brewer, C. I. (1963). Confirmation, correction and contiguity, *Journal of Verbal Learning and Verbal Behavior*, **1**, 365–371.   (139).
Peterson, M. J., and McGee, S. H. (1974). The effects of imagery instructions, imagery ratings, and the number of dictionary meanings upon recognition and recall, *Journal of Experimental Psychology*, **102b**, 1107–1014.   (111, 113).
Peterson, M. J., and Murray, A. (1973). The enhancement of items and associations, *Journal of Experimental Psychology*, **101**, 82–89.   (110).
Petrich, J. A. (1970). S–R and R–S unlearning as a function of transfer paradigm, *Journal of Experimental Psychology*, **83**, 19–24.   (167).
Petrich, J. A. (1971). R–S unlearning as a function of degree of S–R unlearning, *Journal of Experimental Psychology*, **87**, 125–127.   (167).
Petrich, J. A. (1973). Organization of recall in the retroactive inhibition paradigm, *Journal of Verbal Learning and Verbal Behavior*, **12**, 294–301.   (174).
Petrinovich, L. F. See Hardyk, C. D.
Piéron, H. (1913). Recherche experimentale sur les phénomenes de mémoire, *Année Psychologie*, **19**, 91, 193.   (134).
Philipchalk, R., and Rowe, E. J. (1971). Sequential and nonsequential memory for verbal and nonverbal auditory stimuli, *Journal of Experimental Psychology*, **91**, 341–343. (113).
Phillips, L. W. See Postman, L.
Pilzecker, A. See Müller, G. E.
Pollack, I., and Hsieh, R. (1969). Sampling variability of the area under the ROC-curve and of of d′, *Psychological Bulletin*, **71**, No. 3.   (27).
Pollack, I., Rubenstein, H., and Decker, L. (1959). Intelligibility of known and unknown message sets, *Journal of the Acoustical Society of America*, **31**, 273–279.   (190).
Pollack, I., Rubenstein, H. and Decker, L. (1960). Analysis of incorrect responses to an unknown message set, *Journal of the Acoustical Society of America*, **32**, 454–457.   (190).
Posner, M. I., and Warren, R. E. (1972). Traces, concepts, and conscious constructions. In A. W. Melton and E. Martin (Eds.), *Coding Processes in Human Memory*, Winston, Washington, DC.   (79).
Postman, D. L. See Postman, L.
Postman, L. (1952). Retroactive inhibition in recall and recognition, *Journal of Experimental Psychology*, **44**, 165–169.   (165).
Postman, L. (1961). Extra-experimental interference and the retention of words, *Journal of Experimental Psychology*, **61**, 97–110.   (185, 200).
Postman, L. (1962). The effects of language habits on the acquisition and retention of verbal associations, *Journal of Experimental Psychology*, **64**, 7–19.   (197, 198, 200).
Postman, L. (1963). One trial learning. In C. N. Cofer and B. S. Musgrave (Eds.), *Verbal Behavior and Learning*, McGraw-Hill, New York, pp. 295–332.   (139).
Postman, L. (1966). Differences between unmixed and mixed transfer designs as a function of paradigm, *Journal of Verbal Learning and Verbal Behavior*, **5**, 240–248.   (172).
Postman, L. (1970). Effects of word frequency on acquisition and retention under conditions of free-recall learning, *Quarterly Journal of Experimental Psychology*, **22**, 185–195. (192, 200).
Postman, L. (1972). A pragmatic view of organization theory. In E. Tulving and W. A. Donaldson (Eds.), *Organization of Memory*, Academic Press, New York.   (138, 209).
Postman, L. See Keppel, G.; Underwood, B. J.
Postman, L., and Hasher, L. (1972). Conditions of proactive inhibition in free recall, *Journal of Experimental Psychology*, **92**, 276–284.   (178).
Postman, L., Jenkins, W. O., and Postman, D. L. (1948). An experimental comparison

262

of active recall and recognition, *American Journal of Psychology*, **61**, 511–519.   (142).

Postman, L., and Keppel, G. (1967). Retroactive inhibition in free recall, *Journal of Experimental Psychology*, **74**, 203–211.   (171).

Postman, L., and Phillips, L. W. (1961). Studies in incidental learning ix. A comparison of the methods of successive and single recalls, *Journal of Experimental Psychology*, **61**, 3, 236–241.   (136).

Postman, L., and Stark, K. (1962). Retroactive inhibition as a function of set during the interpolated task, *Journal of Verbal Learning and Verbal Behavior*, **1**, 304–311.   (173).

Postman, L., and Stark, K. (1969). The role of response availability in transfer and interference, *Journal of Experimental Psychology*, **79**, 168–177.   (163, 164, 168, 169).

Postman, L., and Stark, K. (1972). On the measurement of retroactive inhibition in the A–B, A–D paradigm by the multiple-choice method: Reply to Merryman, *Journal of Verbal Learning and Verbal Behavior*, **11**, 465–473.   (167).

Postman, L., Stark, K., and Burns, S. (1974). Sources of proactive inhibition on unpaced tests of retention, *American Journal of Psychology*, **87**, No. 1–2, 33–56.   (166).

Postman, L., Stark, K., and Fraser, J. (1968). Temporal changes in interference, *Journal of Verbal Learning and Verbal Behavior*, **7**, 672–694.   (158, 169, 178).

Postman, L., Stark, K., and Henschel, D. (1969). Conditions of recovery after unlearning, *Journal of Experimental Psychology*, **82**, 1, Part 2.   (158, 170).

Postman, L., Turnage, T. W., and Silverstein, A. (1964). The running memory span for words, *Quarterly Journal of Experimental Psychology*, **16**, 81–89.   (199).

Postman, L., and Underwood, B. J. (1973). Critical issues interference theory, *Memory and Cognition*, **1**, 19–40.   (97, 158, 167, 173, 176).

Postman, L., and Warren, L. (1972). Temporal changes in interference under different paradigms of transfer, *Journal of Verbal Learning and Verbal Behavior*, **11**, 120–128.   (171).

Potts, G. R. (1972). Distance from a massed double presentation or blank trial as a factor in paired associate list learning, *Journal of Verbal Learning and Verbal Behavior*, **11**, 357–386.   (140).

Pragier, C. See Brion, S.

Psotka, J. See Tulving, E.

Puff, C. R. See Bousfield, W. A.

Pylyshyn, Z. W. (1973). What the mind's eye tells the mind's brain: a critique of mental imagery, *Psychological Bulletin*, **80**, 1–24.   (106).

Quartermain, D., and Scott, T. H. (1960). Incidental learning in a simple task, *Canadian Journal of Psychology*, **14**, 175–182.   (97).

Raffel, G. (1934). The effect of recall on forgetting, *Journal of Experimental Psychology*, **17**, 828–838.   (134, 135, 136).

Raines, S. R. See Winograd, E.

Raser, G. A., and Bartz, W. H. (1968). Imagery and paired-associate recognition, *Psychonomic Science*, **12**, 385–386.   (110).

Reder, L. M., Anderson, J. R., and Bjork, R. A. (1974). A semantic interpretation of encoding specificity, *Journal of Experimental Psychology*, **102**, 648–656.   (54, 60, 61).

Reicher, G. M. See Melton, A. W.

Remington, R. J. (1969). Analysis of sequential effects in choice reaction times, *Journal of Experimental Psychology*, **82**, 250–257.   (99).

Remington, R. K. See Wallace, W. P.

Richardson, J. T. E. (1974). The effects of retention tests upon memory. Unpublished paper.   (141, 142).

Richardson, J., and Gropper, M. S. (1964). Learning during recall trials, *Psychological Reports*, **15**, 551–560.   (139, 140).

Riechert, T. See Hassler, R.

Robertson, R. See Begg, I.

Rock, I. See Epstein, W.

Roediger, H. L. (1973). Inhibition in recall from cueing with recall targets, *Journal of Verbal Learning and Verbal Behavior*, **12**, 644–657. (40).

Rogers, T. B. (1967). Coding instructions and item concreteness in free recall. Unpublished Master's thesis, University of Western Ontario. (108, 117).

Rogers, T. B. See Paivio, A.

Rohrer, J. H. (1949). Factors influencing the occurrence of reminiscence: attempted formal rehearsal during the interpolated period, *Journal of Experimental Psychology*, **39**, 484–491. (134, 136).

Rohwer, W. D. Jr. (1970). Images and pictures in children's learning: Research results and instructional implications. In H. W. Reese (Chm.), Imagery in children's learning: A symposium, *Psychological Bulletin*, **73**, 393–403. (104).

Rose, R. G. See Weaver, G. E.

Rosner, S. R. (1970). The effects of presentation and recall trials on organization in multi-trial free-recall, *Journal of Verbal Learning and Verbal Behavior*, **9**, 69–74. (4, 138).

Ross, B. M. See Engen, T.

Rothkopf, E. Z., and Coke, E. U. (1963). Repetition interval and rehearsal method in learning equivalences from written sequences, *Journal of Verbal Learning and Verbal Behavior*, **2**, 406–416. (136).

Rothkopf, E. Z., and Coke, E. U. (1966). The effect of some variations in procedure on response repetition following verbal outcomes, *Journal of Verbal Learning and Verbal Behavior*, **5**, 86–91. (136).

Routh, D. R. See Brown, J.

Rowe, E. J. See Paivio, A.; Philipchalk, R.

Rubenstein, H. See Pollack, I.

Rubenstein, M. See Rubenstein, H.

Rubenstein, H., Garfield, L., and Millikan, J. A. (1970). Homographic entries in the internal lexicon, *Journal of Verbal Learning and Verbal Behavior*, **9**, 487–492. (185, 188, 213).

Rubenstein, H., Lewis, S. S., and Rubenstein, M. A. (1971). Homographic entries in the internal lexicon: effects of systematicity and relative frequency meanings, *Journal of Verbal Learning and Verbal Behavior*, **10**, 57–62. (188).

Rumelhart, D. E., Lindsay, P. H., and Norman, D. A. (1972). A process model for long-term memory. In E. Tulving and W. Donaldson (Eds.), *Organization of Memory*, Academic Press, New York. (106).

Rundus, D. (1971). Analysis of rehearsal processes in free-recall, *Journal of Experimental Psychology*, **89**, 63–77. (137).

Rundus, D. (1973). Negative effects of using list items as recall cues, *Journal of Verbal Learning and Verbal Behavior*, **12**, 43–50. (40, 135).

Rundus, D., Loftus, G. R., and Atkinson, R. C, (1970). Immediate free-recall and three week delayed recognition, *Journal of Verbal Learning and Verbal Behavior*, **9**, 684–688. (137, 143).

Russell, I. S. See Winograd, E.

Saltz, E. (1967). Thorndike–Lorge frequency and *m* of stimuli as separate factors in paired-associate learning, *Journal of Experimental Psychology*, **73**, 473–478. (186, 198, 200, 213).

Saltz, E. See Modigliani, V.

Saltz, E., and Modigliani, V. (1967). Response meaningfulness in paired-associates: T–L frequency, *m*, and number of meanings (*dm*), *Journal of Experimental Psychology*, **75**, 313–320. (186, 198).

Saltz, E., and Modigliani, V. (1970). Meaningfulness and short-term memory: Test of a model, *Journal of Experimental Psychology*, **86**, 309–312. (198).

Sampson, J. R. (1970). Free recall of verbal and non-verbal stimuli, *Quarterly Journal of Experimental Psychology*, **22**, 215–221. (108).

Sandak, J. M. See Garskof, B. E.

264

Sandak, J. M., and Garskof, B. E. (1967). Associative unlearning as a function of degree of interpolated learning, *Psychonomic Science*, **7**, 215–216. (161).

Sanders, A. F. (1961). Rehearsal and recall in immediate memory, *Ergonomics*, **4**, 25–34. (137).

Sanders, A. F., Whitaker, L., and Cofer, C. N. (1974). Evidence for retroactive interference in recognition from reaction time, *Journal of Experimental Psychology*, **102**, 1126. (164, 165).

Sanders, H. I. See Warrington, E. K.

Savin, H. B., and Bever, T. G. (1970). The nonperceptual reality of the phoneme, *Journal of Verbal Learning and Verbal Behavior*, **9**, 295–302. (79).

Schlosberg, H. See Woodworth, R. S.

Schnorr, J. A., and Atkinson, R. C. (1969). Repetition versus imagery instructions in the short- and long-term retention of paired-associates, *Psychonomic Science*, **15**, 183–184. (110).

Schonfield, A., and Robertson, B. (1966). Memory storage and ageing, *Canadian Journal of Psychology*, **30**, 228–236. (219).

Schulman, A. I. (1967). Word length and rarity in recognition memory, *Psychonomic Science*, **9**, 211–212. (95, 206, 207).

Schulman, A. I. (1971). Recognition memory for targets from scanned word lists, *British Journal of Psychology*, **62**, 335–346. (87).

Schulman, A. I. (1973). Recognition memory and the recall of spatial location, *Memory and Cognition*, **1**, 256–260. (144).

Schulman, A. I., and Lovelace, E. A. (1970). Recognition memory for words presented at a slow or rapid rate, *Psychonomic Science*, **21**, 99–100. (206, 209).

Schulman, H. G. See Melton, A. W.

Schultz, W. See Tell, P. M.

Schulz, R. W. See Underwood, B. J.

Schwartz, H. A. (1963). Influence of instructional set and response frequency on retroactive interference, *Journal of Experimental Psychology*, **66**, 127–132. (173).

Scott, D. See Baddeley, A. D.

Scott, K. G. (1967). Clustering with perceptual and symbolic stimuli in free recall, *Journal of Verbal Learning and Verbal Behavior*, **6**, 864–866. (108).

Scott, T. H. See Quartermain, D.

Scoville, W. B., and Milner, B. (1957). Loss of immediate memory after bilateral hippocampal lesions, *Journal of Neurology, Neurosurgery and Psychiatry*, **20**, 11–21. (218).

Sekuler, R. W. (1965). Signal detection, choice response times and visual backward masking, *Canadian Journal of Psychology*, **19**, 2, 118–132. (150).

Sekuler, R. W. (1966). Choice times and detection with visual backward masking, *Canadian Journal of Psychology*, **20**, 1, 34–42. (150).

Sekuler, R. See Hall, J.

Semon, R. (1909). Die Mnemischen Empfindungen, Leipzig. (40).

Shallice, T., and Warrington, E. K. (1970). Independent functioning of verbal memory stores: a neuropsychological study, *Quarterly Journal of Experimental Psychology*, **22**, 261–273. (219).

Shapiro, B. J. (1969). The subjective estimation of relative word frequency, *Journal of Verbal Learning and Verbal Behavior*, **8**, 248–251. (185).

Shapiro, S. I., and Gordon, G. P. (1971). Contemporary norms of word and phonetic frequencies, *Journal of Verbal Learning and Verbal Behavior*, **10**, 92–94. (185).

Shaughnessy, J. J. See Underwood, B. J.; Zimmerman, J.

Sheehan, P. W. (1966). Accuracy and vividness of visual images, *Perceptual and Motor Skills*, **23**, 391–398. (104).

Shepard, R. N. (1961). Application of a trace model to the retention of information in a recognition task, *Psychometrika*, **26**, 185–203. (207).

Shepard, R. N. (1967). Recognition memory for words, sentences and pictures, *Journal of Verbal Learning and Verbal Behavior*, **6**, 156–163.   (108, 206, 207, 210).

Shepard, R. N., and Chang, J. J. (1963). Forced-choice tests of recognition memory under steady-state conditions, *Journal of Verbal Learning and Verbal Behavior*, **2**, 93–101.   (208).

Shepard, R. N., and Teghtsoonian, M. (1961). Retention of information under conditions approaching a steady state, *Journal of Experimental Psychology*, **62**, 3, 302–309.   (208, 209).

Shevitz, R. See Cofer, C. N.

Shiffrin, R. M. (1973). Information persistence in short-term memory, *Journal of Experimental Psychology*, **100**, 39–49.   (137).

Shiffrin, R. M., and Atkinson, R. C. (1969). Storage and retrieval processes in long-term memory, *Psychological Review*, **76**, 179–193.   (52, 71).

Shiffrin, R. M. See Atkinson, R. C.

Shuell, T. J. (1968). Retroactive inhibition in free-recall learning of categorized lists, *Journal of Verbal Learning and Verbal Behavior*, **7**, 797–805.   (171).

Shulman, H. G. (1970). Encoding and retention of semantic and phonemic information in short-term memory, *Journal of Verbal Learning and Verbal Behavior*, **9**, 499–508.   (87, 89, 100).

Shulman, H. G., and Martin, E. (1970). Effects of response-set similarity on unlearning and spontaneous recovery, *Journal of Experimental Psychology*, **86**, 230–235.   (158).

Silverstein, A. (1967). Unlearning, spontaneous recovery and the partial-reinforcement effect in paired-associate learning, *Journal of Experimental Psychology*, **73**, 15–21.   (158).

Silverstein, A. See Postman, L.

Silverstein, A., and Dienstbier, R. A. (1968). Rated pleasantness and association value of 101 English nouns, *Journal of Verbal Learning and Verbal Behavior*, **7**, 81–86.   (186).

Simpson, A. J., and Fitter, M. J. (1973). What is the best index of detectability?, *Psychological Bulletin*, **80**, 6, 481–488.   (150).

Simpson, H. M. (1972). Effects of instructional set, encoding time, and word type on recognition memory. Paper presented at meeting of the Canadian Psychological Association, Montreal.   (108, 126).

Skaggs, E. B. (1920). The relative value of grouped and interspersed recitation, *Journal of Experimental Psychology*, **3**, 424–446.   (134, 135).

Skemp, R. See Kay, H.

Slamecka, N. J. (1968). An examination of trace storage in free recall, *Journal of Experimental Psychology*, **76**, 504–513.   (40).

Smith, P. T. (1968). Cost, discriminability and response bias, *British Journal of Mathematical and Statistical Psychology*, **21**, 35–60.   (150, 151, 155).

Smith, P. See Standing, L.

Smythe, P. C. See Paivio, A.

Snodgrass, J. G., and Antone, G. (1974). Parallel vs. sequential processing of pictures and words, *Journal of Experimental Psychology*. **103**, 139–144.   (114).

Snodgrass, J. G., Wasser, B., Finkelstein, M., and Goldberg, L. B. (1974). On the fate of visual and verbal memory codes for pictures and words: evidence for a dual coding mechanism in recognition memory, *Journal of Verbal Learning and Verbal Behavior*, **13**, 27–37.   (118).

Sokolov, E. N. (1963). *Perception and the Conditioned Reflex*, Macmillan, New York.   (85).

Solomon, R. C. See Howes, D. H.

Squire, L. R. (1969). Effects of drugs on spontaneous alternation, *Journal of Comparative and Physiological Psychology*, **69**, 69–75.   (237).

Standing, L., Conezio, J., and Haber, R. N. (1970). Perception and memory for pictures: Single-trial learning of 2560 visual stimuli, *Psychonomic Science*, **19**, 73–74.   (108).

Standing, L., and Smith, P. (1974). Verbal–pictorial transformations in recognition memory, *Canadian Journal of Psychology*, (in press).   (104, 123).

Stanners, R. F. (1970). Language frequency correlates of rated pronunciability, *Journal of Verbal Learning and Verbal Behavior*, **9**, 373–378.   (187).

Stanners, R. F. and Forbach, G. B. (1973). Analysis of letter strings in word recognition, *Journal of Experimental Psychology*, **98**, 31–35.   (188).

Stark, K. See Postman, L.

Steel, R. G. See Marcel, A. J.

Steger, J. A. See Bevan, W.

Steinmetz, J. I. See Turnage, T. W.

Sternberg, S. (1969). Memory scanning: Mental processes revealed by reaction time experiments, *American Scientist*, **57**, 4, 421–457.   (150).

Stewart, J. C. (1965). An experimental investigation of imagery. Unpublished doctoral thesis, University of Toronto.   (108, 111).

Strand, B. Z. (1971). A further investigation of retroactive inhibition in categorized free recall, *Journal of Experimental Psychology*, **87**, 198–201.   (171).

Strand, B. Z. See Keppel, G.

Streeter, L. A. See Landauer, T. K.

Sumby, W. H. (1963). Word frequency and serial position effects, *Journal of Verbal Learning and Verbal Behavior*, **1**, 443–450.   (191).

Summers, J. J. See Hintzman, D. L.

Sutherland, N. S. (1972). Object recognition. In E. C. Carterette and M. P. Friedman (Eds.), *Handbook of Perception*, Academic Press, New York.   (78).

Sutherland, N. S. See Davis, R.

Swets, J. A. See Green, D. M.

Talland, G. A. (1965). *Deranged Memory*, Academic Press, New York.   (217, 221).

Tanner, W. A. See Clarke, F. R.

Tarr, A. G. See Hanawalt, N. G.

Taub, H. A. See Goss, A. E.

Taylor, D. W. See Wright, S. T. H.

Teitgen, Mme. See Brion, S.

Teghtsoonian, M. See Shepard, N. R.

Tell, P. M., and Schultz, W. (1972). Retroactive interference as a function of degree of interpolated learning and instructional set, *Journal of Experimental Psychology*, **94**, 337–339.   (173).

Teuber, H. L. See Milner, B.

Thomas, E. A. C., and Legge, D. (1970). Probability matching as a basis for detection and recognition decisions, *Psychological Review*, **77**, 65–72.   (10).

Thomson, D. M. (1972). Context effects in recognition memory, *Journal of Verbal Learning and Verbal Behavior*, **11**, 497–511.   (49, 53, 59, 71).

Thomson, D. M. See Davis, J. C.; Tulving, E.

Thomson, D. M. and Tulving, E. (1970). Associative encoding and retrieval: Weak and strong cues, *Journal of Experimental Psychology*, **86**, 2, 255–262.   (49, 60, 69, 138).

Thorndike, E. L., and Lorge, I. (1944). *The Teacher's Word Book of 30,000 Words*, Colombia University Press, New York.   (185).

Thornton, G. B. See Tulving, E.

Thune, L. E., and Underwood, B. J. (1943). Retroactive inhibition as a function of degree of interpolated learning, *Journal of Experimental Psychology*, **32**, 185–200.   (160).

Tiberghien, G., and Lecocq, P. (1973). Rappel et reconnaissance, *Année Psychologique*, **73**, 225–260.   (45).

Tiberghien, G. See Lecocq, P.

Tisseyre, F. See Bertelson, P.

Treisman, A. (1964). Monitoring and storage of irrelevant messages in selective attention, *Journal of Verbal Learning and Verbal Behavior*, **3**, 449–459.   (78).

Treisman, M. (1971). On the word frequency effect: comments on the papers by J. Catlin

267

and L. H. Nakatani, *Psychological Review*, **78**, 420–425.   (190).

Tresselt, M. E. See Mayzner, M. S.

Trow, W. C. (1928). Recall versus repetition in the learning of rote and meaningful material, *American Journal of Psychology*, **40**, 112–116.   (135, 136).

Tryk, E. H. (1968). Subjective scaling of word frequency, *American Journal of Psychology*, **81**, 170–177.   (185).

Tryk, H. E. See May, R. B.

Tulving, E. (1962). Subjective organization in free recall of 'unrelated' words, *Psychological Review*, **69**, 344–354.   (192).

Tulving, E. (1966). Subjective organization and effects of repetition in multi-trial free-recall learning, *Journal of Verbal Learning and Verbal Behavior*, **5**, 193–197.   (137).

Tulving, E. (1967). The effects of presentation and recall of material in free-recall learning, *Journal of Verbal Learning and Verbal Behavior*, **6**, 175–184.   (136, 137, 138).

Tulving, E. (1968a). Theoretical issues in free-recall. In T. R. Dixon and D. L. Horton (Eds.), *Verbal Learning and General Behavior Theory*, Prentice Hall, New Jersey, Englewood Cliffs.   (87).

Tulving, E. (1968b). When is recall higher than recognition?, *Psychonomic Science*, **10**, 53–54.   (55, 90, 183).

Tulving, E. (1972). Episodic and semantic memory. In E. Tulving and W. Donaldson (Eds.), *Organization of Memory*, Academic Press, New York. (41, 53, 62, 77, 81, 184).

Tulving, E. (1974). Recall and recognition of semantically encoded words, *Journal of Experimental Psychology*, **102**, 778–787.   (55, 69).

Tulving, E. See Bartlett, J. C.; Thomson, D. M.; Watkins, M. J.

Tulving, E., and Bower, G. H. (1974). The logic of memory representations. In G. H. Bower (Ed.), *The Psychology of Learning and Motivation: Advances in Research and Theory*, Vol. 8, Academic Press, New York.   (62, 69).

Tulving, E., and Donaldson, W. (1972) (Eds.). *Organization of Memory*, Academic Press, New York.   (132).

Tulving, E., and Hastie, R. (1972). Inhibition effects of intralist repetition in free recall, *Journal of Experimental Psychology*, **92**, 297–304.   (17).

Tulving, E., and Patkau, J. E. (1962). Concurrent effects, contextual constraint and word frequency on immediate recall and learning of verbal material, *Canadian Journal of Psychology*, **16**, 83–95.   (192).

Tulving, E., and Pearlstone, A. (1966). Availability versus accessibility of information in memory for words, *Journal of Verbal Learning and Verbal Behavior*, **5**, 381–391.   (76).

Tulving, E., and Psotka, J. (1971). Retroactive inhibition in free recall: Inaccessibility of information available in the memory store, *Journal of Experimental Psychology*, **87**, 1–8.   (171).

Tulving, E., and Thomson, D. M. (1971). Retrieval processes in recognition memory: Effects of associative context, *Journal of Experimental Psychology*, **87**, 1, 116–124. (8, 58, 60, 90, 101, 184).

Tulving, E., and Thomson, D. M. (1973). Encoding specificity and retrieval processes in episodic memory, *Psychological Review*, **80**, 5, 352–373.   (15, 55, 61, 62, 69, 71, 75, 96, 104, 112, 129, 183, 212).

Tulving, E., and Thornton, G. B. (1959). Interaction between proaction and retroaction in short-term retention, *Canadian Journal of Psychology*, **13**, 255–265.   (171).

Tulving, E., and Watkins, M. J. (1973). Continuity between recognition and recall, *American Journal of Psychology*, **86**, 739–748.   (65).

Turnage, T. W. (1967). Unit-sequence interference in short-term memory, *Journal of Verbal Learning and Verbal Behavior*, **6**, 61–65.   (200).

Turnage, T. W. (1970). Proactive inhibition of initial items in short-term recall, *Psychonomic Science*, **20**, 236–237.   (199).

Turnage, T. W. See Postman, L.

Turnage, T. W., and McCullough, T. A. (1968). Letter-sequence and unit-sequence

268

effects during learning and retention, *Journal of Experimental Psychology*, **76**, 141–146. (199).

Turnage, T. W., and Steinmetz, J. I. (1971). Unit-sequence inteference and short-term recall, *American Journal of Psychology*, **84**, 112–122.   (199).

Tuttle, A. V. See Lachman, R.

Tversky, B. (1973). Encoding processes in recognition and recall, *Cognitive Psychology*, **5**, 275–287.   (48, 62, 69, 92, 121, 125, 162).

Tversky, B. (1974). Eye fixations in prediction of recognition and recall, *Memory and Cognition*, **2**, 275–278.   (48, 57, 62, 69, 71).

Tweedy, J. R. See LaBerge, D.

Tzeng, O. J. L. (1973). Positive recency effect in a delayed free recall, *Journal of Verbal Learning and Verbal Behavior*, **12**, 436–439.   (101).

Ugelow, A. See Hall, J. F.

Underwood, B. J. (1945). The effect of successive interpolations on retroactive and pro-active inhibition, *Psychological Monographs*, **59**, No. 3.   (159).

Underwood, B. J. (1948a). Proactive and retroactive inhibition after five and forty-eight hours, *Journal of Experimental Psychology*, **38**, 29–38.   (158).

Underwood, B. J. (1948b). 'Spontaneous' recovery of verbal associations, *Journal of Experimental Psychology*, **38**, 429–439.   (158).

Underwood, B. J. (1957). Interference and forgetting, *Psychological Review*, **64**, 49–60. (157).

Underwood, B. J. (1964). Degree of learning and the measurement of forgetting, *Journal of Verbal Learning and Verbal Behavior*, **3**, 112–129.   (98).

Underwood, B. J. (1965). False recognition produced by implicit verbal responses, *Journal of Experimental Psychology*, **70**, 1, 122–129.   (210).

Underwood, B. J. (1969a). Attributes of memory, *Psychological Review*, **76**, 559–573. (16, 162, 181, 184).

Underwood, B. J. (1969b). Some correlates of item repetition in free-recall learning, *Journal of Verbal Learning and Verbal Behavior*, **8**, 83–94.   (136).

Underwood, B. J. (1970). A breakdown of the total-time law in free-recall learning, *Journal of Verbal Learning and Verbal Behavior*, **9**, 573–580.   (136).

Underwood, B. J. (1971). Recognition memory. In H. H. Kendler and J. T. Spence (Eds.), *Essays in Neobehaviorism*, Appleton-Century-Crofts, New York. (181).

Underwood, B. J. (1972). Are we overloading memory? In A. W. Melton and E. Martin (Eds.), *Coding Processes in Human Memory*, Winston, Washington, DC, pp. 1–23. (16, 56).

Underwood, B. J. See Barnes, J. M.; Ekstrand, B. R.; Galbraith, R. C.: Postman, L.; Thune, L. E.; Zimmerman, J.

Underwood, B. J., Broder, P. K., and Zimmerman, J. (1973). Retention of verbal discrimination lists as a function of number of prior lists, word frequency and type of list, *Journal of Experimental Psychology*, **100**, 101–105.   (180).

Underwood, B. J., and Ekstrand, B. R. (1966). An analysis of some shortcomings in the interference theory of forgetting, *Psychological Review*, **73**, 540–549.   (172).

Underwood, B. J., and Ekstrand, B. R. (1967). Studies of distributed practice: XXIV. Differentiation and proactive inhibition, *Journal of Experimental Psychology*, **74**, 574–580.   (172).

Underwood, B. J., and Freund, J. S. (1970a). Retention of a verbal discrimination, *Journal of Experimental Psychology*, **84**, 1–14.   (180).

Underwood, B. J., and Freund, J. S. (1970b). Word frequency and short-term recognition memory, *American Journal of Psychology*, **83**, 343–351.   (206, 208, 210).

Underwood, B. J., and Keppel, G. (1962). One-trial-learning, *Journal of Verbal Learning and Verbal Behavior*, **1**, 1–13.   (139).

Underwood, B. J., and Postman, L. (1960). Extra-experimental sources of interference in forgetting, *Psychological Review*, **67**, 73–95.   (199, 200).

269

Underwood, B. J., and Schulz, R. W. (1960). *Meaningfulness and Verbal Learning*, Lippincott, Philadelphia. (169, 183, 186, 197).

Underwood, B. J., Shaughnessy, J. J., and Zimmerman, J. (1972). List length and method of presentation in verbal discrimination learning with further evidence on retroaction, *Journal of Experimental Psychology*, **93**, 181–187. (180).

Underwood, B. J., Zimmerman, J., and Freund, J. S. (1971). Retention of frequency information with observations on recognition and recall, *Journal of Experimental Psychology*, **87**, 149–162. (205).

Ure, D. M. J. See Brown, W. P.

Ure, G. See Yarmey, A. D.

Vanderwolf, C. H. (1971). Limbic diencephalic mechanisms of voluntary movement, *Psychological Review*, **78**, 83–113. (237).

Victor, M., Adams, R. D., and Collins, G. H. (1971). *The Wernicke–Korsakoff Syndrome. A Clinical and Pathological Study of 245 Patients, 82 with Post Mortem Examination*, Blackwell Scientific Publications, Oxford. (218).

Von Frisch, K. (1953). *The Dancing Bees*, Harcourt Brace, New York. (88).

von Lackum, W. J. See Melton, A. W.

Wallace, W. P. See Ekstrand, B. R.

Wallace, W. P., Remington, R. K., and Beito, A. (1972). Retroactive inhibition as a function of transfer paradigm in verbal discrimination, *Journal of Experimental Psychology*, **96**, 463–465. (180).

Walsh, D. A., and Jenkins, J. J. (1973). Effects of orienting tasks on free recall in incidental learning: 'difficulty', 'effort', and 'process' explanations, *Journal of Verbal Learning and Verbal Behavior*, **12**, 481–488. (107).

Warr, P. B. (1964). The relative importance of proactive inhibition and degree of learning in retention of paired-associate items, *British Journal of Psychology*, **55**, 19–30. (98).

Warren, L. See Postman, L.

Warren, R. E. See Posner, M. I.

Warrington E. K., (1971). Neurological disorders of memory, *British Medical Bulletin*, **27**, 243–247. (235, 239).

Warrington, E. K. (1974). Deficient recognition in organic amnesia, *Cortex*, **10**, 289–291. (223, 238).

Warrington, E. K. See Baddeley, A. D.; Shallice, T.

Warrington, E. K., and Ackroyd, C. (1975). The effect of orienting tasks on recognition memory, *Memory and Cognition*, **3**, 140–142. (225, 227).

Warrington, E. K., and Baddeley, A. D. (1974). Amnesia and memory for visual location, *Neuropsychologia*, **12**, 257–263. (218).

Warrington, E. K., and Sanders, H. I. (1971). The fate of old memories, *Quarterly Journal of Experimental Psychology*, **23**, 432–442. (86, 219).

Warrington, E. K., and Silberstein, M. A. (1970). A questionnaire techinque for investigating very long-term memory, *Quarterly Journal of Experimental Psychology*, **22**, 508–512. (219).

Warrington, E. K., and Taylor, A. M. (1973). Immediate memory for faces: Long- or short-term memory, *Quarterly Journal of Experimental Psychology*, **25**, 316–322. (218).

Warrington, E. K., and Weiskrantz, L. (1968). A study of learning and retention in amnesic patients, *Neuropsychologia*, **6**, 283–291. (221, 224).

Warrington, E. K., and Weiskrantz, L. (1970). Amnesic syndrome: consolidation or retrieval, *Nature*, **228**, 628–630. (221, 223, 238, 239).

Warrington, E. K., and Weiskrantz, L. (1971). Organisational aspects of memory in amnesic patients, *Neuropsychologia*, **9**, 67–73. (226).

Warrington, E. K., and Weiskrantz, L. (1973). An analysis of short-term and long-term memory defects in man. In J. A. Deutsch (Ed.), *The Physiological Basis of Memory*, Academic Press, New York. (217, 226).

270

Warrington, E. K., and Weiskrantz, L. (1974). The effect of prior learning on subsequent retention in amnesic patients, *Neuropsychologia*, **12**, 419–428.   (221, 223, 226).

Wasser, B. See Snodgrass, J. G.

Watkins, M. J. (1974). When is recall spectacularly higher than recognition?, *Journal of Experimental Psychology*, **102**, 161–163.   (55).

Watkins, M. J. See Craik, F. I. M.; Tulving, E.

Watkins, M. J., and Tulving, E. (1975). Episodic memory: When recognition fails, *Journal of Experimental Psychology: General*, **104**, 5–29.   (55, 69).

Watts, G. H. See Anderson, R. C.

Watts, G. H., and Anderson, R. C. (1969). Retroactive inhibition in free recall as a function of first- and second-list organization, *Journal of Experimental Psychology*, **81**, 595–597. (171).

Waugh, N. C., and Norman, D. A. (1965). Primary memory, *Psychological Review*, **72**, 89–104.   (100).

Weaver, G. E. See Bruce, D.

Weaver, G. E., Duncan, E. M., and Bird, C. P. (1972). Cue-specific retroactive inhibition, *Journal of Verbal Learning and Verbal Behavior*, **11**, 362–366.   (172).

Weaver, G. E., Rose, R. G., and Campbell, N. R. (1971). Item-specific retroactive inhibition in mixed-list comparisons of the A–B, A–C and A–B, D–C paradigms, *Journal of Verbal Learning and Verbal Behavior*, **10**, 488–498.   (171).

Weaver, S. (1974). Unpublished work, Stanford University.   (151).

Weber, A. See Wollen, K. A.

Weiskrantz, L. See Warrington, E. K.

Weiskrantz, L., and Warrington, E. K. (1970a). Verbal learning and retention by amnesic patients using partial information, *Psychonomic Science*, **20**, 210–211.   (221).

Weiskrantz, L., and Warrington, E. K. (1970b). A study of forgetting in amnesic patients, *Neuropsychologia*, **8**, 281–288.   (221).

Wescourt, K. T. See Atkinson, R. C.

Wess, B. Jr. See Groninger, L. D.

Wheeler, R. H. (1929). *The Science of Psychology*, Cromwell, New York, pp. 299.   (134).

Whitaker, L. See Sanders, A. F.

White, M. N. See Carroll, J. B.

Whitely, P. L. (1927). The dependence of learning and recall upon prior intellectual activities, *Journal of Experimental Psychology*, **10**, 489–508.   (157).

Whitten, W. B. See Bjork, R. A.

Whitty, C. W. M., and Zangwill, O. L. (1966). *Amnesia*, Butterworths, London.   (221).

Wichawut, C., and Martin, E. (1971). Independence of A–B and A–C assocations in retroaction, *Journal of Verbal Learning and Verbal Behavior*, **10**, 316–321.   (171, 174).

Wickelgren, W. A. (1967). Exponential decay and independence from irrelevant associations in short-term recognition memory for serial order, *Journal of Experimental Psychology*, **73**, 165–171.   (169).

Wickelgren, W. A. (1968). Sparing of short-term memory in an amnesic patient: implications for strength theory of memory, *Neuropsychologia*, **6**, 235–244.   (218).

Wickelgren, W. A. (1972). Trace resistance and the decay of long-term memory, *Journal of Mathematical Psychology*, **9**, 418–455.   (169).

Wickelgren, W. A. (1973). The long and the short of memory, *Psychological Bulletin*, **80**, 425–438.   (164, 169).

Wickelgren, W. A. See Norman, D. A.

Wickens, D. D. (1970). Encoding categories of words: an empirical approach to meaning, *Psychological Review*, **77**, 1–15.   (79, 215).

Wickens, D. D. See Greenberg, S.; Newton, J. M.

Wiener, J. R. See Bregman, A. S.

Wilgosh, L. R. (1970). Interaction between pictures and their labels in the memory of four-year-old children. Unpublished doctoral dissertation, McMaster University. (115).

Williams, J. A. See Bindra, D. B.

Williams, O. A. (1926). A study of the phenomenon of reminiscence, *Journal of Experimental Psychology*, **9**, 368–387. (134).

Winnick, W. A., and Kressel, K. (1965). Tachistoscopic recognition thresholds, paired-associate learning and immediate recall as a function of abstractness–concreteness and word frequency, *Journal of Experimental Psychology*, **70**, 163–168. (186, 194).

Winograd, E. (1968). List differentiation as a function of frequency and retention interval, *Journal of Experimental Psychology*, **76**, 2, Part 2. (159).

Winograd, E., and Conn, C. P. (1971). Evidence from recognition memory for specific encoding of unmodified homographs, *Journal of Verbal Learning and Verbal Behavior*, **10**, 702–706. (213).

Winograd, E., Karchmer, M. A., and Russell, I. S. (1971). Role of encoding unitization in cued recognition memory, *Journal of Verbal Learning and Verbal Behavior*, **10**, 199–206. (57, 110).

Winograd, E., and Raines, S. R. (1972). Semantic and temporal variation in recognition memory, *Journal of Verbal Learning and Verbal Behavior*, **11**, 114–119. (71).

Winzenz, D. See Bower, G. H.

Wise, J. S. See Bindra, D. B.

Witasek, K. (1907). Uber lesen und retizieren in ihren Bezehungen zum Gedachtnis, *Zeitschrift fur Psychologie*, **44**, 161–185, 246–282. (134).

Wolford, G. (1971). Function of distinct associations for paired-associate performance, *Psychological Review*, **78**, 303–313. (167).

Wollen, K. A. (1962). One-trial versus incremental paired-associate learning, *Journal of Verbal Learning and Verbal Behavior*, **1**, 14–21. (139).

Wollen, K. A., Weber, A., and Lowry, D. H. (1972). Bizarreness versus interaction of mental images as determinants of learning, *Cognitive Psychology*, **3**, 518–523. (112).

Wood, G. T. See Juola, J. F.

Woodward, A. E. Jr., Bjork, R. A. and Jongeward, R. H. Jr. (1973). Recall and recognition as a function of primary rehearsal, *Journal of Verbal Learning and Verbal Behavior*, **12**, 608–617. (137).

Woodworth, R. S. (1938). *Experimental Psychology*, Holt, New York. (134).

Woodworth, R. S., and Schlosberg, H. (1954). *Experimental Psychology*, Holt, New York. (137).

Worden, P. E. See Mandler, G.

Wright, S. T. H., and Taylor, D. W. (1949). Distributed practice in verbal learning and the maturation hypothesis, *Journal of Experimental Psychology*, **39**, 527–531. (134).

Yarmey, A. D. See Paivio, A.

Yarmey, A. D., and O'Neill, B. J. (1969). S–R and R–S paired-associate learning as a function of concreteness, imagery, specificity, and association value, *Journal of Psychology*, **71**, 95–109. (110).

Yarmey, A. D., and Ure, G. (1971). Incidental learning, noun imagery-concreteness and direction of associations in paired-associate learning, *Canadian Journal of Psychology*, **25**, 91–102. (110).

Yuille, J. C. See Paivio, A.

Yuille, J. C., and Humphreys, M. S. (1970). Free recall and forward and backward recall of paired-associates as a function of noun concreteness. Paper presented at the meeting of the Canadian Psychological Association, Winnipeg, May, 1970. (110).

Yuille, J. C., and Paivio, A. (1968). Imagery and verbal mediation instructions, in paired-associate learning, *Journal of Experimental Psychology*, **78**, 436–441. (110).

Zacks, R. T. (1969). Invariance of total-learning time under different conditions of practice, *Journal of Experimental Psychology*, **82**, 441–447. (136).

272

Zangwill, O. L. (1937). An investigation of the relationship between the process of reproducing and recognizing simple figures with special reference to Koffka's trace theory, *British Journal of Psychology*, **27**, 250–276.   (136).

Zangwill, O. L. (1939). Some relations between reproducing and recognizing prose material, *British Journal of Psychology*, **29**, 370–382.   (136).

Zangwill, O. L. See Whitty, C. W. M.

Zavortink, B. See Keppel, G.

Zeaman, D. See Eimas, P. D.

Zimmerman, J. See Underwood, B. J.

Zimmerman, J., Shaughnessy, J. J., and Underwood, B. J. (1972). The role of associations in verbal-discrimination learning, *American Journal of Psychology*, **85**, 499–518.   (180).

Zipf, G. K. (1935). *The Psychology of Language*, Houghton-Mifflin, Boston.   (187).

Zipf, G. K. (1945). The meaning–frequency relationships of words, *Journal of General Psychology*, **33**, 251–256.   (186).

Zipf, G. K. (1949). *Human Behavior and the Principle of Least Effort*, Addison-Wesley, Cambridge, Massachusetts.   (187).

Zuckerman, C. B. See Epstein, W.

Subject Index

Abstract codes, 106, 125–126
Accessibility of codes, 14–18
Adopted chunks, 192
Affective attributes, 186–187
Age of acquisition, 121–122
Ammesia, 217–228
   anterograde, 220–222
   retrograde, 219–220
   theories, 222–227, 238–240
Area measure, 25
Associative attributes, 162
Attention, 96–97
Automaticity of encoding, 79

Bilingual coding, 127
Brain lesions, 217, 218, 233–236

Choice theory, 26, 203–204
Codes
   abstract, 106
   association, 14
   chunked, 13
   dual, 105–106
   image, 13–14, 104–105
   monoattribute, 13
   relational attribute, 13
   unit word, 12–13
   verbal, 105
Coding strategy, 117
Concreteness variable, 103, 105, 108–110, 112–116, 126, 186
Confidence, 18–22
Confidence ratings, 26–27, 31, 148, 150, 200–203
Confusion factors, 168
Consolidation, 136–141, 221, 223
Context
   code, 8–10
   elements, 6, 132, 144, 154, 202
   in recognition, 15, 53–54, 58–61, 91, 101
Contextual associations, 4, 160, 170
Control processes, 173
Copy cues, 37, 43
Criterion

recall, 204
recognition, 9–10, 55, 208, 210
Cued recall, 49, 53, 60, 65–66, 69, 221, 227, 240

d' measure, 24–25
Depth of processing, 75–96
Differential effects, assessment of, 32–34
Discriminability, 15–16, 32
Discriminative attributes, 16, 162, 184
Dishabituation, 85
Distractor interference, 10–11, 210
Distributional assumptions, 24–25
Distributed practice, see Spacing of repetitions
Drug effects, 237
Dual coding hypothesis, 105–106, 111, 115, 121–124, 128, 195

Ecphoric process, 40
Encoding specificity principle, 71, 104, 112, 119, 128–129, 138
Encoding variability, 78–79, 175–178, 207, 212, 215
Encoding variables, 57, 116–120
Episodic
   ecphory, 37, 61–73
   memory, 41, 77, 81–82
   traces, 61, 79, 85, 96

Familiarity
   feeling of, 84
   physiological basis, 236–239
   role in recognition, 3, 5, 183, 227
Feature sampling bias, 175–177
Focal element, 42
Forced recognition, 27–28
FRAN, 4
Frequency paradox, 16, 95, 183–184

Generalized competition, 159, 170
Generate-recognize models, 85
Generation-discrimination theory, 3–4
Generative grammar, 112